GEORGE MÜLLER OF BRISTOL

Portrait and Autograph of Mr. Müller

GEORGE MÜLLER

of

BRISTOL

by

ARTHUR T. PIERSON

Author of
"The Crisis of Missions," "The New Acts of the Apostles," etc.

Editor of
"The Missionary Review of the World," etc.

With an Introduction by

JAMES WRIGHT

Son-in-law and successor in the work of George Müller

ANNOTATED & ILLUSTRATED

SCRIPTURE TESTIMONY EDITION

WALKING TOGETHER PRESS
ESTES PARK · JENTA MANGORO

Published in 2023 by
Walking Together Press
Estes Park, Colorado USA
Jenta Mangoro, Jos, Plateau Nigeria
https://walkingtogether.press

ISBN 978-1-961568-00-6

George Müller of Bristol is in the public domain
Originally published in 1901 by James Nisbet & Co. Limited, London
Text and images from the 1901 edition

Cover design by D. Thaine Norris
Typeset in Adobe Garamond Pro by D. Thaine Norris

ABOUT THE SCRIPTURE TESTIMONY EDITION

GEORGE MÜLLER would be the first to say, that if he is anything, he is only one of many servants of the Lord Jesus Christ. This inspiring biography is one book—albiet one of the very best—among thousands that glorify God by telling stories of His faithfulness.

The *Scripture Testimony Index* is an extensive research project by Walking Together Press to use artificial intelligence and data science to develop a New-Testament-driven subject index across a large body of missionary biographies and personal narratives. In analyzing the database of these books programmatically; beautiful, bright threads emerge—threads of prayer, provision, deliverance, specific leading, healing, transformation, revival, and miraculous conversion. The end result is an index of short story excerpts organized by subject and Bible verse that empirically demonstrate the truth of the Scriptures, and which is freely available on our website at https://walkingtogether.life.

Walking Together Press has enhanced this classic title, *George Müller of Bristol,* by identifying and marking fifty-seven portions of the narrative that illustrate specific Biblical topics and verses. An extensive *Scripture Testimony Index* has also been added containing short summaries of how each Scriptural topic is illustrated, making locating specific stories easy. Furthermore, this title is one of many in the *Scripture Testimony Collection.*

INTRODUCTION

VERY SOON after the decease of my beloved father-in-law I began to receive letters pressing upon me the desirableness of issuing as soon as possible a memoir of him and his work.

The well-known autobiography, entitled "Narrative of the Lord's Dealings with George Müller," had been, and was still being, so greatly used by God in the edification of believers and the conversion of unbelievers that I hesitated to countenance any attempt to supersede or even supplement it. But as, with prayer, I reflected upon the subject, several considerations impressed me:

1st. The last volume of the Narrative ends with the year 1885, so that there is no record of the last thirteen years of Mr. Müller's life excepting what is contained in the yearly reports of "The Scriptural Knowledge Institution."

2d. The last three volumes of the Narrative, being mainly a condensation of the yearly reports during the period embraced in them, contain much unavoidable repetition.

3d. A book of, say, four hundred and fifty pages, containing the substance of the four volumes of the Narrative, and carrying on the history to the date of the decease of the founder of the institution, would meet the desire of a large class of readers.

4th. Several brief sketches of Mr. Müller's career had issued from the press within a few days after the funeral; and one (written by Mr. F. Warne and published by W. F. Mack & Co., Bristol), a very accurate and truly appreciative sketch, had had a large circulation; but I was convinced by the letters that reached me that a more comprehensive memoir was called for, and *would be* produced, so I was led especially to pray for guidance that such a book might be entrusted to the author fitted by God to undertake it.

While waiting for the answer to this definite petition, though greatly urged by publishers to proceed, I steadily declined to take any step until I had clearer light.

Moreover, I was, personally, occupied during May and June in preparing the Annual Report of "The Scriptural Knowledge Institution," and could not give proper attention to the other matter.

Just then I learned from Dr. Arthur T. Pierson, of Brooklyn, N. Y., that he had been led to undertake the production of a memoir of Mr. Müller for American readers, and requesting my aid by furnishing him with some materials needed for the work.

SCRIPTURE TESTIMONY
God using circumstances and timing to communicate Acts 11:11

Having complied with this request I was favoured by Dr. Pierson with a syllabus of the method and contents of his intended work.

The more I thought upon the subject the more satisfied I became that no one could be found more fitted to undertake the work which had been called for on this side of the Atlantic also than this my well-known and beloved friend.

He had had exceptional opportunities twenty years ago in the United States, and in later years when visiting Great Britain, for becoming intimately acquainted with Mr. Müller, with the principles on which the Orphanage and other branches of "The Scriptural Knowledge Institution" were carried on, and with many details of their working. I knew that Dr. Pierson most thoroughly sympathized with these principles as being according to the mind of God revealed in His word; and that he could, therefore, present not merely the history of the external facts and results of Mr. Müller's life and labours, but could and would, by God's help, unfold, with the ardour and force of *conviction,* the secret springs of that life and of those labours.

I therefore intimated to my dear friend that, provided he would allow me to read the manuscript and have thus the opportunity of making any suggestions that I felt necessary, I would, as my beloved father-in-law's executor and representative, gladly endorse his work as the authorized memoir for British as well as American readers.

To this Dr. Pierson readily assented; and now, after carefully going through the whole, I confidently recommend the book to esteemed readers on both sides of the Atlantic, with the earnest prayer that the result, in relation to the subject of this memoir, may be identical with that produced by the account of the Apostle Paul's "manner of life" upon the churches of Judea which were in Christ (Galatians 1:24), viz.,

"They glorified GOD" in him.

James Wright
13 Charlotte Street, Park Street,
Bristol, Eng., March, 1899

A PREFATORY WORD

DR. OLIVER W. HOLMES wittily said that an autobiography is what every biography *ought to be*. The four volumes of "The Narrative of the Lord's Dealings with George Müller," already issued from the press and written by his own hand, with a fifth volume covering his missionary tours, and prepared by his wife, supplemented by the Annual Reports since published, constitute essentially an autobiography—Mr. Müller's own life-story, stamped with his own peculiar individuality, and singularly and minutely complete. To those who wish the simple journal of his life with the details of his history, these printed documents make any other sketch of him from other hands so far unnecessary.

There are, however, two considerations which have mainly prompted the preparation of this brief memoir: first, that the facts of this remarkable life might be set forth not so much with reference to the chronological order of their occurrence, as events, as for the sake of the lessons in living which they furnish, illustrating and enforcing grand spiritual principles and precepts: and secondly, because no man so humble as he would ever write of himself what, after his departure, another might properly write of him that others might glorify God in him.

No one could have undertaken this work of writing Mr. Müller's life-story without being deeply impressed with the opportunity thus afforded for impressing the most vital truths that concern holy living and holy serving; nor could any one have completed such a work without feeling overawed by the argument which this narrative furnishes for a present, living, prayer-hearing God, and for a possible and practical daily walk with Him and work with Him. It has been a great help in the preparation of this book that the writer has had such frequent converse with Mr. James Wright, who was so long Mr. Müller's associate and knew him so intimately.

So prominent was the word of God as a power in Mr. Müller's life that, in an appendix, we have given peculiar emphasis to the great leading texts of Scripture which inspired and guided his faith and conduct, and, so far as possible, in the order in which such texts became practically influential in his life; and so many wise and invaluable counsels are to be found scattered throughout his journal that some of the most striking and helpful have been selected, which may also be found in the appendix.

This volume has, like the life it sketches, but one aim. It is simply and solely meant to extend, emphasize, and perpetuate George Müller's witness to a prayer-hearing God; to present, as plainly, forcibly, and briefly as is practicable, the outlines of a human history, and an experience of the Lord's leadings and dealings, which furnish a sufficient answer to the question:

WHERE IS THE LORD GOD OF ELIJAH?

CONTENTS

LIST OF ILLUSTRATIONS

GEORGE MÜLLER OF BRISTOL

CHAPTER I

From His Birth to His New Birth

A HUMAN LIFE, filled with the presence and power of God, is one of God's choicest gifts to His church and to the world.

Things which are unseen and eternal seem, to the carnal man, distant and indistinct, while what is seen and temporal is vivid and real. Practically, any object in nature that can be seen or felt is thus more real and actual to most men than the Living God. Every man who walks with God, and finds Him a present Help in every time of need; who puts His promises to the practical proof and verifies them in actual experience; every believer who with the key of faith unlocks God's mysteries, and with the key of prayer unlocks God's treasuries, thus furnishes to the race a demonstration and an illustration of the fact that "He is, and is a Rewarder of them that diligently seek Him."

George Müller was such an argument and example incarnated in human flesh. Here was a man of like passions as we are and tempted in all points like as we are, but who believed God and was established by believing; who prayed earnestly that he might live a life and do a work which should be a convincing proof that God hears prayer and that it is safe to trust Him at all times; and who has furnished just such a witness as he desired. Like Enoch, he truly walked with God, and had abundant testimony borne to him that he pleased God. And when, on the tenth day of March, 1898, it was told us of George Müller that "he was not," we knew that "God had taken him": it seemed more like a translation than like death.

To those who are familiar with his long life-story, and, most of all, to those who intimately knew him and felt the power of personal contact with him, he was one of God's ripest saints and himself a living proof that a life of faith is possible; that God may be known, communed with, found, and may become a conscious companion in the daily life. George Müller proved for himself and for all others who will receive his witness that, to those who are willing to take God at His word and to yield self to His will, He is "the same yesterday and to-day and forever": that the days of divine intervention and deliverance are past only to those with whom the days of faith and obedience are past—in a word, that believing prayer works still the wonders which our fathers told of in the days of old.

The life of this man may best be studied, perhaps, by dividing it into certain marked periods, into which it naturally falls, when we look at those leading events and experiences which are like punctuation-marks or paragraph divisions,—as, for example:

1. From his birth to his new birth or conversion: 1805-1825.
2. From his conversion to full entrance on his life-work: 1825-35.
3. From this point to the period of his mission tours: 1835-75.
4. From the beginning to the close of these tours: 1875-92.
5. From the close of his tours to his death: 1892-98.

Thus the first period would cover twenty years; the second, ten; the third, forty; the fourth, seventeen; and the last, six. However thus unequal in length, each forms a sort of epoch, marked by certain conspicuous and characteristic features which serve to distinguish it and make its lessons peculiarly important and memorable. For example, the first period is that of the lost days of sin, in which the great lesson taught is the bitterness and worthlessness of a disobedient life. In the second period may be traced the remarkable steps of preparation for the great work of his life. The third period embraces the actual working out of the divine mission committed to him. Then for seventeen or eighteen years we find him bearing in all parts of the earth his world-wide witness to God; and the last six years were used of God in mellowing and maturing his Christian character. During these years he was left in peculiar loneliness, yet this only made him lean more on the divine companionship, and it was noticeable with those who were brought into most intimate contact with him that he was more than ever before heavenly-minded, and the beauty of the Lord his God was upon him.

The first period may be passed rapidly by, for it covers only the wasted years of a sinful and profligate youth and early manhood. It is of interest mainly as illustrating the sovereignty of that Grace which abounds even to the chief of sinners. Who can read the story of that score of years and yet talk of piety as the product of evolution? In his case, instead of evolution, there was rather a *revolution,* as marked and complete as ever was found, perhaps, in the annals of salvation. If Lord George Lyttelton could account for the conversion of Saul of Tarsus only by supernatural power, what would he have thought of George Müller's transformation! Saul had in his favor a conscience, however misguided, and a morality, however pharisaic. George Müller was a flagrant sinner against common honesty and decency, and his whole early career was a revolt, not against God only, but against his own moral sense. If Saul was a hardened transgressor, how callous must have been George Müller!

He was a native of Prussia, born at Kroppenstaedt, near Halberstadt, September 27, 1805. Less than five years later his parents removed to Heimersleben, some four miles off, where his father was made collector of the excise, again removing about eleven years later to Schoenebeck, near Magdeburg, where he had obtained another appointment.

George Müller had no proper parental training. His father's favoritism toward him was harmful both to himself and to his brother, as in the family of Jacob, tending to jealousy and estrangement. Money was put too freely into the hands of these boys, hoping that they might learn how to use it and save it; but the result was, rather, careless and vicious waste, for it became the source of many childish sins of indulgence. Worse still, when called upon to render any account of their stewardship, sins of lying and deception were used to cloak wasteful spending. Young George systematically deceived his father, either by false entries of what he had received, or by false statements of what he had spent or had on hand. When his tricks were found out, the punishment which followed led to no reformation, the only effect being more ingenious devices of trickery and fraud. Like the Spartan lad, George Müller reckoned it no fault to steal, but only to have his theft found out.

His own brief account of his boyhood shows a very bad boy and he attempts no disguise. Before he was ten years old he was a habitual thief and an expert at cheating; even government funds, entrusted to his father, were not safe from his hands. Suspicion led to the laying of a snare into which he fell: a sum of money was carefully counted and put where he would find it and have a chance to steal it. He took it and hid it under his foot in his shoe, but, he being searched and the money being found, it became clear to whom the various sums previously missing might be traced.

His father wished him educated for a clergyman, and before he was eleven he was sent to the cathedral classical school at Halberstadt to be fitted for the university. That such a lad should be deliberately set apart for such a sacred office and calling, by a father who knew his moral obliquities and offences, seems incredible—but, where a state church exists, the ministry of the Gospel is apt to be treated as a human profession rather than as a divine vocation, and so the standards of fitness often sink to the low secular level, and the main object in view becomes the so-called "living," which is, alas, too frequently independent of *holy* living.

From this time the lad's studies were mixed up with novel-reading and various vicious indulgences. Card-playing and even strong drink got hold of him. The night when his mother lay dying, her boy of fourteen was reeling through the streets, drunk; and even her death failed to arrest his wicked course or to arouse his sleeping conscience. And—as must always be the case when such solemn reminders make one no better—he only grew worse.

When he came to the age for confirmation He had to attend the class for preparatory religious teaching; but this being to him a mere form, and met in a careless spirit, another false step was taken: sacred things were treated as common, and so conscience became the more callous. On the very eve of confirmation and of his first approach to the Lord's Table he was guilty of gross sins; and on the day previous, when he met the clergyman for the customary "confession of sin," he planned and practised another shameless fraud, withholding from him eleven-twelfths of the confirmation fee entrusted to him by his father!

In such frames of mind and with such habits of life George Müller, in the Easter season of 1820, was confirmed and became a communicant. Confirmed, indeed! but in sin, not only immoral and unregenerate, but so ignorant of the very rudiments of the Gospel of Christ that he could not have stated to an inquiring soul the simple terms of the plan of salvation. There was, it is true about such serious and sacred transactions, a vague solemnity which left a transient impression and led to shallow resolves to live a better life; but there was no real sense of sin or of repentance toward God, nor was there any dependence upon a higher strength: and, without these, efforts at self-amendment never prove of value or work lasting results.

The story of this wicked boyhood presents but little variety, except that of sin and crime. It is one long tale of evil-doing and of the sorrow which it brings. Once, when his money was all recklessly wasted, hunger drove him to steal a bit of coarse bread from a soldier who was a fellow lodger; and looking back, long afterward, to that hour of extremity, he exclaimed, "What a bitter thing is the service of Satan, even in this world!"

On his father's removal to Schoenebeck in 1821 he asked to be sent to the cathedral school at Magdeburg, inwardly hoping thus to break away from his sinful snares and vicious companions, and, amid new scenes, find help in self-reform. He was not, therefore, without at least occasional aspirations after moral improvement; but again he made the common and fatal mistake of overlooking the Source of all true betterment. "God was not in all his thoughts." He found that to leave one place for another was not to leave his sin behind, for he took himself along.

His father, with a strange fatuity, left him to superintend sundry alterations in his house at Heimersleben, arranging for him meanwhile to read classics with the resident clergyman, Rev. Dr. Nagel. Being thus for a time his own master, temptation opened wide doors before him. He was allowed to collect dues from his father's debtors, and again he resorted to fraud, spending large sums of this money and concealing the fact that it had been paid.

In November, 1821, he went to Magdeburg and to Brunswick, to which latter place he was drawn by his passion for a young Roman Catholic girl, whom he had met there soon after confirmation. In this absence from home he took one step after another in the path of wicked indulgence. First of all, by lying to his tutor he got his consent to his going; then came a week of sin at Magdeburg and a wasting of his father's means at a costly hotel in Brunswick. His money being gone, he went to the house of an uncle until he was sent away; then, at another expensive hotel, he ran up bills until, payment being demanded, he had to leave his best clothes as a security, barely escaping arrest. Then, at Wolfenbuttel, he tried the same bold scheme again, until, having nothing for deposit, he ran off, but this time was caught and sent to jail. This boy of sixteen was already a liar and thief, swindler and drunkard, accomplished only in crime, a companion of convicted felons and himself in a felon's cell. This cell, a few days later, a thief shared: and these two held converse as fellow thieves, relating their adventures to one another, and young Müller, that he might not be outdone, invented lying tales of villainy to make himself out the more famous fellow of the two!

Ten or twelve days passed in this wretched fellowship, until disagreement led to a sullen silence between them. And so passed away twenty-four dark days, from December 18, 1821, until the 12th of January ensuing, during all of which George Müller was shut up in prison and during part of which he sought as a favour the company of a thief.

His father learned of his disgrace and sent money to meet his hotel dues and other "costs" and pay for his return home. Yet such was his persistent wickedness that, going from a convict's cell to confront his outraged but indulgent parent, he chose as his companion in travel an avowedly wicked man.

He was severely chastised by his father and felt that he must make some effort to reinstate himself in his favour. He therefore studied hard and took pupils in arithmetic and German, French and Latin. This outward reform so pleased his father that he shortly forgot as well as forgave his evil-doing; but again it was only the outside of the cup and platter that was made clean: the secret heart was still desperately wicked and the whole life, as God saw it, was an abomination.

George Müller now began to forge what he afterward called "a whole chain of lies." When his father would no longer consent to his staying at home, he left, ostensibly for Halle, the university town, to be examined, but really for Nordhausen to seek entrance into the gymnasium. He avoided Halle because he dreaded its severe discipline, and foresaw that restraint would be doubly irksome when constantly meeting young fellows of his acquaintance who, as students in the university, would have much more freedom than himself. On returning home he tried to conceal this fraud from his father; but just before he was to leave again for Nordhausen the truth became known, which made needful new links in that chain of lies to account for his systematic disobedience and deception. His father, though angry, permitted him to go to Nordhausen, where he remained from October, 1822, till Easter, 1825.

During these two and a half years he studied classics, French, history, etc., living with the director of the gymnasium. His conduct so improved that he rose in favour and was pointed to as an example for the other lads, and permitted to accompany the master in his walks, to converse with him in Latin. At this time he was a hard student, rising at four A.M. the year through, and applying himself to his books till ten at night.

Nevertheless, by his own confession, behind all this formal propriety there lay secret sin and utter alienation from God. His vices induced an illness which for thirteen weeks kept him in his room. He was not without a religious bent, which led to the reading of such books as Klopstock's works, but he neither cared for God's word, nor had he any compunction for trampling upon God's law. In his library, now numbering about three hundred books, no Bible was found. Cicero and Horace, Moliere and Voltaire, he knew and valued, but of the Holy Scriptures he was grossly ignorant, and as indifferent to them as he was ignorant of them. Twice a year, according to prevailing custom, he went to the Lord's Supper, like others who had passed the age of confirmation, and he could not at such seasons quite avoid religious impressions. When the consecrated bread and wine touched his lips he would sometimes take an oath to reform, and for a few days refrain from some open sins; but there was no spiritual life to act as a force within, and his vows were forgotten almost as soon as made. The old Satan was too strong for the young Müller, and, when the mighty passions of his evil nature were roused, his resolves and endeavours were as powerless to hold him as were the new cords which bound Samson, to restrain him, when he awoke from his slumber.

It is hard to believe that this young man of twenty could lie without a blush and with the air of perfect candor. When dissipation dragged him into the mire of debt, and his allowance would not help him out, he resorted again to the most ingenious devices of falsehood. He pretended that the money wasted in riotous living had been stolen by violence, and, to carry out the deception he studied the part of an actor. Forcing the locks of his trunk and guitar-case, he ran into the director's room half dressed and feigning fright, declaring that he was the victim of a robbery, and excited such pity that friends made up a purse to cover his supposed losses. Suspicion was, however, awakened that he had been playing a false part, and he never regained the master's confidence; and though he had even then no sense of sin, shame at being detected in such meanness and hypocrisy made him shrink from ever again facing the director's wife, who, in his long sickness, had nursed him like a mother.

Such was the man who was not only admitted to honourable standing as a university student, but accepted as a candidate for holy orders, with permission to preach in the Lutheran establishment. This student of divinity knew nothing of God or salvation, and was ignorant even of the gospel plan of saving grace. He felt the need for a better life, but no godly motives swayed him. Reformation was a matter purely of expediency: to continue in profligacy would bring final exposure, and no parish would have him as a pastor. To get a valuable "cure" and a good "living" he must make attainments in divinity, pass a good examination, and have at least a decent reputation. Worldly policy urged him to apply himself on the one hand to his studies and on the other to self-reform.

Again he met defeat, for he had never yet found the one source and secret of all strength. Scarce had he entered Halle before his resolves proved frail as a spider's web, unable to restrain him from vicious indulgences. He refrained indeed from street brawls and duelling, because they would curtail his liberty, but he knew as yet no moral restraints. His money was soon spent, and he borrowed till he could find no one to lend, and then pawned his watch and clothes.

He could not but be wretched, for it was plain to what a goal of poverty and misery, dishonour and disgrace, such paths lead. Policy loudly urged him to abandon his evil-doing, but piety had as yet no voice in his life. He went so far, however, as to choose for a friend a young man and former schoolmate, named Beta, whose quiet seriousness might, as he hoped, steady his own course. But he was leaning on a broken reed, for Beta was himself a backslider. Again he was taken ill. God made him to "possess the iniquities of his youth." After some weeks he was better, and once more his conduct took on the semblance of improvement.

The true mainspring of all well-regulated lives was still lacking, and sin soon broke out in unholy indulgence. George Müller was an adept at the ingenuity of vice. What he had left he pawned to get money, and with Beta and two others went on a four days' pleasure-drive, and then planned a longer tour in the Alps. Barriers were in the way, for both money and passports were lacking; but fertility of invention swept all such barriers away. Forged letters, purporting to be from their parents, brought passports for the party, and books, put in pawn, secured money. Forty-three days were spent in travel, mostly afoot; and during this tour George Müller, holding, like Judas, the common purse, proved, like him, a thief, for he managed to make his companions pay one third of his own expenses.

The party were back in Halle before the end of September, and George Müller went home to spend the rest of his vacation. To account plausibly to his father for the use of his allowance a new chain of lies was readily devised. So soon and so sadly were all his good resolves again broken.

When once more in Halle, he little knew that the time had come when he was to become a new man in Christ Jesus. He was to find God, and that discovery was to turn into a new channel the whole current of his life. The sin and misery of these twenty years would not have been reluctantly chronicled but to make the more clear that his conversion was a supernatural work, inexplicable without God. There was certainly nothing in himself to 'evolve' such a result, nor was there anything in his 'environment.' In that university town there were no natural forces that could bring about a revolution in character and conduct such as he experienced. Twelve hundred and sixty students were there gathered, and nine hundred of them were divinity students, yet even of the latter number, though all were permitted to preach, not one hundredth part, he says, actually "feared the Lord." Formalism displaced pure and undefiled religion, and with many of them immorality and infidelity were cloaked behind a profession of piety. Surely such a man, with such surroundings, could undergo no radical change of character and life without the intervention of some mighty power from without and from above! What this force was, and how it wrought upon him and in him, we are now to see.

CHAPTER II

The New Birth and the New Life

THE LOST days of sin, now forever past, the days of heaven upon earth began to dawn, to grow brighter till the perfect day.

We enter the second period of this life we are reviewing. After a score of years of evil-doing George Müller was converted to God, and the radical nature of the change strikingly proves and displays the sovereignty of Almighty Grace. He had been kept amid scenes of outrageous and flagrant sin, and brought through many perils, as well as two serious illnesses, because divine purposes of mercy were to be fulfilled in him. No other explanation can adequately account for the facts.

Let those who would explain such a conversion without taking God into account remember that it was at a time when this young sinner was as careless as ever; when he had not for years read the Bible or had a copy of it in his possession; when he had seldom gone to a service of worship, and had never yet even heard one gospel sermon; when he had never been told by any believer what it is to believe on the Lord Jesus Christ and to live by God's help and according to His Word; when, in fact, he had no conception of the first principles of the doctrine of Christ, and knew not the real nature of a holy life, but thought all others to be as himself, except in the degree of depravity and iniquity. This young man had thus grown to manhood without having learned that rudimental truth that sinners and saints differ not in degree but in kind; that if any man be in Christ, he is a new creation; yet the hard heart of such a man, at such a time and in such conditions, was so wrought upon by the Holy Spirit that he suddenly found entrance into a new sphere of life, with new adaptations to its new atmosphere.

The divine Hand in this history is doubly plain when, as we now look back, we see that this was also the period of preparation for his life-work—a preparation the more mysterious because he had as yet no conception or forecast of that work.

During the next ten years we shall watch the divine Potter, to Whom George Müller was a chosen vessel for service, moulding and fitting the vessel for His use. Every step is one of preparation, but can be understood only in the light which that future casts backward over the unique ministry to the church and the world, to which this new convert was all unconsciously separated by God and was to become so peculiarly consecrated.

One Saturday afternoon about the middle of November, 1825, Beta said to Müller, as they were returning from a walk, that he was going that evening to a meeting at a believer's house, where he was wont to go on Saturdays, and where a few friends met to sing, to pray, and to read the word of God and a printed sermon. Such a programme held out nothing fitted to draw a man of the world who sought his daily gratifications at the card-table and in the wine-cup, the dance and the drama, and whose companionships were found in dissipated young fellows; and yet George Müller felt at once a wish to go to this meeting, though he could not have told why. There was no doubt a conscious void within him never yet filled, and some instinctive inner voice whispered that he might there find food for his soul-hunger—a satisfying something after which he had all his life been unconsciously and blindly groping. He expressed the desire to go, which his friend hesitated to encourage lest such a gay and reckless devotee of vicious pleasures might feel ill at ease in such an assembly. However, he called for young Müller and took him to the meeting.

During his wanderings as a backslider, Beta had both joined and aided George Müller in his evil courses, but, on coming back from the Swiss tour, his sense of sin had so revived as to constrain him to make a full confession to his father; and, through a Christian friend, one Dr. Richter, a former student at Halle, he had been made acquainted with the Mr. Wagner at whose dwelling the meetings were held. The two young men therefore went together, and the former backslider was used of God to "convert a sinner from the error of his way and save a soul from death and hide a multitude of sins."

That Saturday evening was the turning-point in George Müller's history and destiny. He found himself in strange company, amid novel surroundings, and breathing a new atmosphere. His awkwardness made him feel so uncertain of his welcome that he made some apology for being there. But he never forgot brother Wagner's gracious answer: "Come as often as you please! house and heart are open to you." He little knew then what he afterward learned from blessed experience, what joy fills and thrills the hearts of praying saints when an evil-doer turns his feet, however timidly, toward a place of prayer!

All present sat down and sang a hymn. Then a brother—who afterward went to Africa under the London Missionary Society—fell on his knees and prayed for God's blessing on the meeting. That *kneeling before God in prayer* made upon

House of J. V. Wagner, in Halle

Müller an impression never lost. He was in his twenty-first year, and yet he had *never before seen any one on his knees praying,* and of course had never himself knelt before God,—the Prussian habit being to stand in public prayer.

A chapter was read from the word of God, and—all meetings where the Scriptures were expounded, unless by an ordained clergyman, being under the ban as irregular—a printed sermon was read. When, after another hymn, the master of the house prayed, George Müller was inwardly saying: "I am much more learned than this illiterate man, but I could not pray as well as he." Strange to say, a new joy was already springing up in his soul for which he could have given as little explanation as for his unaccountable desire to go to that meeting. But so it was; and on the way home he could not forbear saying to Beta: "All we saw on our journey to Switzerland, and all our former pleasures, are as nothing compared to this evening."

Whether or not, on reaching his own room, he himself knelt to pray he could not recall, but he never forgot that a new and strange peace and rest somehow found him as he lay in bed that night. Was it God's wings that folded over him, after all his vain flight away from the true nest where the divine Eagle flutters over His young?

How sovereign are God's ways of working! In such a sinner as Müller, theologians would have demanded a great 'law work' as the necessary doorway to a new life. Yet there was at this time as little deep conviction of guilt and condemnation as there was deep knowledge of God and of divine things, and perhaps it was because there was so little of the latter that there was so little of the former.

Our rigid theories of conversion all fail in view of such facts. We have heard of a little child who so simply trusted Christ for salvation that she could give no account of any 'law work.' And as one of the old examiners, who thought there could be no genuine conversion without a period of deep conviction, asked her, "But, my dear, how about the Slough of Despond?" she dropped a courtesy and said, "*Please, sir, I didn't come that way!*"

George Müller's eyes were but half opened, as though he saw men as trees walking; but Christ had touched those eyes, He knew little of the great Healer, but somehow he had touched the hem of His garment of grace, and virtue came out of Him who wears that seamless robe, and who responds even to the faintest contact of the soul that is groping after salvation. And so we meet here another proof of the infinite variety of God's working which, like the fact of that working, is so wonderful. That Saturday evening in November, 1825, was to this young student of Halle *the parting of the ways.* He had tasted that the Lord is gracious, though he himself could not account for the new relish for divine things which made it seem too long to wait a week for another meal; so that thrice before the Saturday following he sought the house of brother Wagner, there, with the help of brethren, to search the Scriptures.

Portrait and Autograph of Mr. Wagner

We should lose one of the main lessons of this life-story by passing too hastily over such an event as this conversion and the exact manner of it, for here is to be found the first great step in God's preparation of the workman for his work.

Nothing is more wonderful in history than the unmistakable signs and proofs of *preadaptation.* Our life-occurrences are not *disjecta membra*—scattered, disconnected, and accidental fragments. In God's book all these events were written beforehand, when as yet there was nothing in existence but the plan in God's mind—to be fashioned in continuance in actual history—as is perhaps suggested in Psalm 139:16 (margin).

We see stones and timbers brought to a building site—the stones from different quarries and the timbers from various shops—and different workmen have been busy upon them at times and places which forbade all conscious contact or cooperation. The conditions oppose all preconcerted action, and yet, without chipping or cutting, stone fits stone, and timber fits timber—tenons and mortises, and proportions and dimensions, all corresponding so that when the building is complete it is as perfectly proportioned and as accurately fitted as though it had been all prepared in one workshop and put together in advance as a test. In such circumstances no sane man would doubt that *one presiding mind*—one architect and master builder—had planned that structure, however many were the quarries and workshops and labourers.

And so it is with this life-story we are writing. The materials to be built into one structure of service were from a thousand sources and moulded into form by many hands, but there was a mutual fitness and a common adaptation to the end in view which prove that He whose mind and plan span the ages had a supreme purpose to which all human agents were unconsciously tributary. The awe of this vision of God's workmanship will grow upon us as we look beneath and behind the mere human occurrences to see the divine Hand shaping and building together all these seemingly disconnected events and experiences into one life-work.

For example, what have we found to be the initial step and stage in George Müller's spiritual history? In a little gathering of believers, where for the first time he saw a child of God pray on his knees, he found his first approach to a pardoning God. Let us observe: this man was henceforth to be singularly and peculiarly identified with simple scriptural assemblies of believers after the most primitive and apostolic pattern—meetings for prayer and praise, reading and expounding of the Word, such as doubtless were held at the house of Mary the mother of John Mark—assemblies mainly and primarily for believers, held wherever a place could be found, with no stress laid on consecrated buildings and with absolutely no secular or aesthetic attractions. Such assemblies were to be so linked with the whole life, work, and witness of George Müller as to be inseparable from his name, and it was in such an assembly that the night before he died he gave out his last hymn and offered his last prayer.

Not only so, but *prayer, on the knees, both in secret and in such companionship of believers,* was henceforth to be the one great central secret of his holy living and holy serving. Upon this corner-stone of prayer all his life-work was to be built. Of Sir Henry Lawrence the native soldiers during the Lucknow mutiny were wont to say that, "when he looked twice up to heaven, once down to earth, and then stroked his beard, he knew what to do." And of George Müller it may well be said that he was to be, for more than seventy years, the man who conspicuously looked up to heaven to learn what he was to do. Prayer for direct divine guidance in every crisis, great or small, was to be the secret of his whole career. Is there any accident in the exact way in which he was first led to God, and in the precise character of the scenes which were thus stamped with such lasting interest and importance?

The thought of a divine plan which is thus emphasized at this point we are to see singularly illustrated as we mark how stone after stone and timber after timber are brought to the building site, and all so mutually fitted that no sound of any human tool is to be heard while the life-work is in building.

Of course a man that had been so profligate and prodigal must at least begin at conversion to live a changed life. Not that all at once the old sins were abandoned, for such total transformation demands deeper knowledge of the word and will of God than George Müller yet had. But within him a new separating and sanctifying Power was at work. There was a distaste for wicked joys and former companions; the frequenting of taverns entirely ceased, and a lying tongue felt new and strange bands about it. A watch was set at the door of the lips, and every word that went forth was liable to a challenge, so that old habits of untamed speech were arrested and corrected.

At this time he was translating into German for the press a French novel, hoping to use the proceeds of his work for a visit to Paris, etc. At first the plan for the pleasure-trip was abandoned, then the question arose whether the work itself should not be. Whether his convictions were not clear or his moral courage not sufficient, he went on with the novel. It was finished, but never published. Providential hindrances prevented or delayed the sale and publication of the manuscript until clearer spiritual vision showed him that the whole matter was not of faith and was therefore sin, so that he would neither sell nor print the novel, but burned it—another significant step, for it was his *first courageous act of self-denial in surrender to the voice of the Spirit*—and another stone or timber was thus ready for the coming building.

He now began in different directions a good fight against evil. Though as yet weak and often vanquished before temptation, he did not habitually 'continue in sin,' nor offend against God without godly sorrow. Open sins became less frequent and secret sins less ensnaring. He read the word of God, prayed often, loved fellow disciples, sought church assemblies from right motives, and boldly took his stand on the side of his new Master, at the cost of reproach and ridicule from his fellow students.

George Müller's next marked step in his new path was *the discovery of the preciousness of the word of God.*

At first he had a mere hint of the deep mines of wealth which he afterward explored. But his whole life-history so circles about certain great texts that whenever they come into this narrative they should appear in capitals to mark their prominence. And, of them all, that 'little gospel' in John 3:16 is the first, for by it he found a full salvation:

> "God so loved the world that He gave His only-
> begotten Son, that whosoever believeth in Him
> should not perish, but have everlasting life."

From these words he got his first glimpse of the philosophy of the plan of salvation—why and how the Lord Jesus Christ bore our sins in His own body on the tree as our vicarious Substitute and suffering Surety, and how His sufferings in Gethsemane and Golgotha made it forever needless that the penitent believing sinner should bear his own iniquity and die for it.

Truly to grasp this fact is the beginning of a true and saving faith—what the Spirit calls "laying hold." He who believes and knows that God so loved him first, finds himself loving God in return, and faith works by love to purify the heart, transform the life, and overcome the world.

It was so with George Müller. He found in the word of God *one great fact:* the love of God in Christ. Upon that fact faith, not feeling, laid hold; and then the feeling came naturally without being waited for or sought after. The love of God in Christ constrained him to a love—infinitely unworthy, indeed, of that to which it responded, yet supplying a new impulse unknown before. What all his father's injunctions, chastisements, entreaties, with all the urgent dictates of his own conscience, motives of expediency, and repeated resolves of amendment, utterly failed to effect, the love of God both impelled and enabled him to do—renounce a life of sinful self-indulgence. Thus early he learned that double truth, which he afterwards passionately loved to teach others, that in the blood of God's atoning Lamb is the Fountain of both forgiveness and cleansing. Whether we seek pardon for sin or power over sin, the sole source and secret are in Christ's work for us.

The new year 1826 was indeed a *new year* to this newborn soul. He now began to read *missionary* journals, which kindled a new flame in his heart. He felt a yearning—not very intelligent as yet—to be himself a messenger to the nations, and frequent praying deepened and confirmed the impression. As his knowledge of the world-field enlarged, new facts as to the destitution and the desolation of heathen peoples became as fuel to feed this flame of the mission spirit.

SCRIPTURE TESTIMONY

Disciples are devoted to Christ above anything or anyone

Matthew 4:20-22 · Matthew 16:24-25 · Mark 1:19-20 · Mark 10:28 · Luke 9:23-27 · Luke 9:57-62 · Luke 14:25-35

A carnal attachment, however, for a time almost quenched this fire of God within. He was drawn to a young woman of like age, a professed believer, whom he had met at the Saturday-evening meetings; but he had reason to think that her parents would not give her up to a missionary life, and he began, half-unconsciously, to weigh in the balance his yearning for service over against his passion for a fellow creature. Inclination, alas, outweighed duty. Prayer lost its power and for the time was almost discontinued, with corresponding decline in joy. His heart was turned from the foreign field, and in fact from all self-denying service. Six weeks passed in this state of spiritual declension, when God took a strange way to reclaim the backslider.

A young brother, Hermann Ball, wealthy, cultured, with every promising prospect for this world to attract him, made a great self-sacrifice. He chose Poland as a field, and work among the Jews as his mission, refusing to stay at home to rest in the soft nest of self-indulgent and luxurious ease. This choice made on young Müller a deep impression. He was compelled to contrast with it his own course. For the sake of a passionate love for a young woman he had given up the work to which he felt drawn of God, and had become both joyless and prayerless: another young man, with far more to draw him worldward, had, for the sake of a self-denying service among despised Polish Jews, resigned all the pleasures and treasures of the world. Hermann Ball was acting and choosing as Moses did in the crisis of his history, while he, George Müller, was acting and choosing more like that profane person Esau, when for one morsel of meat he bartered his birthright. The result was a new renunciation—he gave up the girl he loved, and forsook a connection which had been formed without faith and prayer and had proved a source of alienation from God.

Here we mark another new and significant step in preparation for his life-work—a decided step forward, which became a pattern for his after-life. For the second time a *decision for God had cost him marked self-denial.* Before, he had burned his novel; now, on the same altar, he gave up to the consuming fire a human passion which had over him an unhallowed influence. According to the measure of his light thus far, George Müller was *fully, unreservedly given up to God,* and therefore walking in the light. He did not have to wait long for the recompense of the reward, for the smile of God repaid him for the loss of a human love, and the peace of God was his because the God of peace was with him.

Every new spring of inward joy demands a channel for outflow, and so he felt impelled to bear witness. He wrote to his father and brother of his own happy experience, begging them to seek and find a like rest in God, thinking that they had but to know the path that leads to such joy to be equally eager to enter it. But an angry response was all the reply that his letter evoked.

SCRIPTURE TESTIMONY
God's work will not lack God's supply Philippians 4:19

About the same time the famous Dr. Tholuck took the chair of professor of divinity at Halle, and the advent of such a godly man to the faculty drew pious students from other schools of learning, and so enlarged George Müller's circle of fellow believers, who helped him much through grace. Of course the missionary spirit revived, and with such increased fervor, that he sought his father's permission to connect himself with some missionary institution in Germany. His father was not only much displeased, but greatly disappointed, and dealt in reproaches very hard to bear. He reminded George of all the money he had spent on his education in the expectation that he would repay him by getting such a 'living' as would insure to the parent a comfortable home and support for his old age; and in a fit of rage he exclaimed that he would no longer look on him as a son.

Then, seeing that son unmoved in his quiet steadfastness, he changed tone, and from threats turned to tears of entreaty that were much harder to resist than reproaches. The result of the interview was a *third* significant step in preparation for his son's life's mission. His resolve was unbroken to follow the Lord's leading at any cost, but he now clearly saw that he could be *independent of man only by being more entirely dependent on God, and that henceforth he should take no more money from his father.* To receive such support implied obedience to his wishes, for it seemed plainly wrong to look to him for the cost of his training when he had no prospect nor intention of meeting his known expectations. If he was to live on his father's money, he was under a tacit obligation to carry out his plans and seek a good living as a clergyman at home. Thus early in life George Müller learned the valuable lesson that one must preserve his independence if he would not endanger his integrity.

God was leading His servant in his youth to *cast himself upon Him for temporal supplies.* This step was not taken without cost, for the two years yet to be spent at the university would require more outlay than during any time previous. But thus early also did he find God a faithful Provider and Friend in need. Shortly after, certain American gentlemen, three of whom were college professors,[1] being in Halle and wishing instruction in German, were by Dr. Tholuck recommended to employ George Müller as tutor; and the pay was so ample for the lessons taught them and the lectures written out for them, that all wants were more than met. Thus also in his early life was written large in the chambers of his memory another golden text from the word of God:

1 One of them, the Rev. Charles Hodge, afterward so well known as professor at Princeton Theological Seminary, etc.

"O fear the Lord, ye His saints! For there is no want to them that fear Him." (Psalm 34:9)

CHAPTER III

Making Ready the Chosen Vessel

THE WORKMAN of God needs to wait on Him to know the work he is to do and the sphere where he is to serve Him.

Mature disciples at Halle advised George Müller for the time thus quietly to wait for divine guidance, and meanwhile to take no further steps toward the mission field. He felt unable, however, to dismiss the question, and was so impatient to settle it that he made the common blunder of attempting to come to a decision in a carnal way. *He resorted to the lot,* and not only so, but to the lot as cast in the lap of the *lottery!* In other words, he first drew a lot in private, and then bought a ticket in a royal lottery, expecting his steps to be guided in a matter so solemn as the choice of a field for the service of God, by the turn of the 'wheel of fortune!' Should his ticket draw a prize he would *go;* if not, *stay* at home. Having drawn a small sum, he accordingly accepted this as a 'sign,' and at once applied to the Berlin Missionary Society, but was not accepted because his application was not accompanied with his father's consent.

Thus a higher Hand had disposed while man proposed. God kept out of the mission field, at this juncture, one so utterly unfit for His work that he had not even learned that primary lesson that he who would work with God must first wait on Him and wait for Him, and that all undue haste in such a matter is worse than waste. He who kept Moses waiting forty years before He sent him to lead out captive Israel, who withdrew Saul of Tarsus three years into Arabia before he sent him as an apostle to the nations, and who left even His own Son thirty years in obscurity before His manifestation as Messiah—this God is in no hurry to put other servants at work. He says to all impatient souls: "My time is not yet full come, but your time is always ready."

Only twice after this did George Müller ever resort to the lot: once at a literal parting of the ways when he was led by it to take the wrong fork of the road, and afterward in a far more important matter, but with a like result: in both cases he found he had been misled, and henceforth abandoned all such chance methods of determining the mind of God. He learned two lessons, which new dealings of God more and more deeply impressed:

First, that the safe guide in every crisis is believing prayer in connection with the word of God.

Secondly, that continued uncertainty as to one's course is a reason for continued waiting.

These lessons should not be lightly passed over, for they are too valuable. The flesh is impatient of all delay, both in decision and action; hence all carnal choices are immature and premature, and all carnal courses are mistaken and unspiritual. God is often moved to delay that we may be led to pray, and even the answers to prayer are deferred that the natural and carnal spirit may be kept in check and self-will may bow before the will of God.

In a calm review of his course many years later George Müller saw that he "ran hastily to the lot" as a shorter way of settling a doubtful matter, and that, especially in the question of God's call to the mission field, this was shockingly improper. He saw also how unfit he had been at that time for the work he sought: he should rather have asked himself how one so ignorant and so needing to be taught could think of teaching others! Though a child of God, he could not as yet have given a clear statement or explanation of the most elementary gospel truths. The one thing needful was therefore to have sought through much prayer and Bible study to get first of all a deeper knowledge and a deeper experience of divine things. Impatience to settle a matter so important was itself seen to be a positive disqualification for true service, revealing unfitness to endure hardship as a good soldier of Jesus Christ. There is a constant strain and drain on patient waiting which is a necessary feature of missionary trial and particularly the trial of deferred harvests. One who, at the outset, could not brook delay in making his first decision, and wait for God to make known His will in His own way and time, would not on the field have had long patience as a husbandman, waiting for the precious fruit of his toil, or have met with quietness of spirit the thousand perplexing problems of work among the heathen!

Moreover the conviction grew that, could he have followed the lot, his choice would have been a life-mistake. His mind, at that time, was bent upon the East Indies as a field. Yet all subsequent events clearly showed that God's choice for him was totally different. His repeated offers met as repeated refusals, and though on subsequent occasions he acted most deliberately and solemnly, no open door was found, but he was in every case kept from following out his honest purpose. Nor could the lot be justified as an indication of his *ultimate* call to the mission field, for the purpose of it was definite, namely, to ascertain, not whether *at some period of his life* he was to go forth, but whether *at that time* he was to go or stay. The whole after-life of George Müller proved that God had for him an entirely different plan, which He was not ready yet to reveal, and which His servant was not yet prepared to see or follow. If any man's life ever was a plan of God, surely this life was; and the Lord's distinct, emphatic leading, when made known, was not in this direction. He had purposed for George Müller a larger field than the Indies, and a wider witness than even the gospel message to heathen peoples. He was 'not suffered' to go into 'Bithynia' because 'Macedonia' was waiting for his ministry.

With increasing frequency, earnestness, and minuteness, was George Müller led to put before God, in prayer, all matters that lay upon his mind. This man was to be peculiarly an example to believers as an *intercessor;* and so God gave him from the outset a very *simple, childlike disposition* toward Himself. In many things he was in knowledge and in strength to outgrow childhood and become a man, for it marks immaturity when we err through ignorance and are overcome through weakness. But in faith and in the filial spirit, he always continued to be a little child. Mr. J. Hudson Taylor well reminds us that while in nature the normal order of growth is from childhood to manhood and so to maturity, in *grace* the true development is perpetually backward toward the cradle: we must become and continue as little children, not losing, but rather gaining, childlikeness of spirit. The disciple's maturest manhood is only the perfection of his childhood. George Müller was never so really, truly, fully a little child in all his relations to his Father, as when in the ninety-third year of his age.

Being thus providentially kept from the Indies, he began definite work at home, though yet having little real knowledge of the divine art of coworking with God. He spoke to others of their soul's welfare, and wrote to former companions in sin, and circulated tracts and missionary papers. Nor were his labours without encouragement, though sometimes his methods were awkward or even grotesque, as when, speaking to a beggar in the fields about his need of salvation, he tried to overcome apathetic indifference by speaking louder and louder, as though, mere bawling in his ears would subdue the hardness of his heart!

In 1826 he first attempted to *preach.* An unconverted schoolmaster some six miles from Halle he was the means of turning to the Lord; and this schoolmaster asked him to come and help an aged, infirm clergyman in the parish. Being a student of divinity he was at liberty to preach, but conscious ignorance had hitherto restrained him. He thought, however, that by committing some other man's sermon to memory he might profit the hearers, and so he undertook it. It was slavish work to prepare, for it took most of a week to memorize the sermon, and it was joyless work to deliver it, for there was none of the living power that attends a man's God-given message and witness. His conscience was not yet enlightened enough to see that he was acting a false part in preaching another's sermon as his own; nor had he the spiritual insight to perceive that it is not God's way to set up a man to preach who knows not enough of either His word or the life of the Spirit within him, to prepare his own discourse. How few even among preachers feel preaching to be *a divine vocation and not a mere human profession;* that a ministry of the truth implies the witness of experience, and that to preach another man's sermon is, at the best, unnatural walking on stilts!

George Müller 'got through' his painful effort of August 27, 1826, reciting this memoriter sermon at eight A.M. in the chapel of ease, and three hours later in the parish church. Being asked to preach again in the afternoon, but having no second sermon committed to memory, he had to keep silent, or *depend on the Lord for help.* He thought he could at least read the fifth chapter of Matthew, and simply expound it. But he had no sooner begun the first beatitude than he felt himself greatly assisted. Not only were his lips opened, but the Scriptures were opened too, his own soul expanded, and a peace and power, wholly unknown to his tame, mechanical repetitions of the morning, accompanied the simpler expositions of the afternoon, with this added advantage, that he talked on a level with the people and not over their heads, his colloquial, earnest speech riveting their attention.

Going back to Halle, he said to himself, 'This is the *true way to preach,*' albeit he felt misgivings lest such a simple style of exposition might not suit so well a cultured refined city congregation. He had yet to learn how the enticing words of man's wisdom make the cross of Christ of none effect, and how the very simplicity that makes preaching intelligible to the illiterate makes sure that the most cultivated will also understand it, whereas the reverse is not true.

Here was another very important *step in his preparation* for subsequent service. He was to rank throughout life among the simplest and most scriptural of preachers. This first trial of pulpit-work led to frequent sermons, and in proportion as his speech was in the simplicity that is in Christ did he find joy in his work and a harvest from it. The committed sermon of some great preacher might draw forth human praise, but it was the simple witness of the Word, and of the believer to the Word, that had praise of God. His preaching was not then much owned of God in fruit. Doubtless the Lord saw that he was not ready for reaping, and scarcely for sowing: there was yet too little prayer in preparation and too little unction in delivery, and so his labours were comparatively barren of results.

About this same time he took another step—perhaps the most significant thus far in its bearing on the precise form of work so closely linked with his name. For some two months he availed himself of the free lodgings furnished for poor divinity students in the famous *Orphan Houses built by A. H. Francké.* This saintly man, a professor of divinity at Halle, who had died a hundred years before (1727), had been led to found an orphanage in entire dependence upon

Francké's Orphan Houses, Halle

God. Half unconsciously George Müller's whole life-work at Bristol found both its suggestion and pattern in Francké's orphanage at Halle. The very building where this young student lodged was to him an object lesson—a visible, veritable, tangible proof that the Living God hears prayer, and can, in answer to prayer alone, build a house for orphan children. That lesson was never lost, and George Müller fell into the apostolic succession of such holy labour! He often records how much his own faith-work was indebted to that example of simple trust in prayer exhibited by Francké. Seven years later he read his life, and was thereby still more prompted to follow him as he followed Christ.

George Müller's spiritual life in these early days was strangely chequered. For instance, he who, as a Lutheran divinity student, was essaying to preach, hung up in his room a framed crucifix, hoping thereby to keep in mind the sufferings of Christ and so less frequently fall into sin. Such helps, however, availed him little, for while he rested upon such artificial props, it seemed as though he sinned the oftener.

He was at this time overworking, writing sometimes fourteen hours a day, and this induced nervous depression, which exposed him to various temptations. He ventured into a confectioner's shop where wine and beer were sold, and then suffered reproaches of conscience for conduct so unbecoming a believer; and he found himself indulging ungracious and ungrateful thoughts of God, who, instead of visiting him with deserved chastisement, multiplied His tender mercies.

He wrote to a rich, liberal and titled lady, asking a loan, and received the exact sum asked for, with a letter, not from her, but from another into whose hands his letter had fallen by "a peculiar providence," and who signed it as "An adoring worshipper of the Saviour Jesus Christ." While led to send the money asked for, the writer added wise words of caution and counsel—words so fitted to George Müller's exact need that he saw plainly the higher Hand that had guided the anonymous writer. In that letter he was urged to "seek by watching and prayer to be delivered from all vanity and self-complacency," to make it his "chief aim to be more and more humble, faithful, and quiet," and not to be of those who "say 'Lord, Lord,' but have Him not deeply in their hearts." He was also reminded that "Christianity consists not in words but in power, and that there must be life in us."

He was deeply moved by this message from God through an unknown party, and the more as it had come, with its enclosure, at the time when he was not only guilty of conduct unbecoming a disciple, but indulging hard thoughts of his heavenly Father. He went out to walk alone, and was so deeply wrought on by God's goodness and his own ingratitude that he knelt behind a hedge, and, though in snow a foot deep, he forgot himself for a half-hour in praise, prayer, and self-surrender.

Yet so deceitful is the human heart that a few weeks later he was in such a backslidden state that, for a time, he was again both careless and prayerless, and one day sought to drown the voice of conscience in the wine-cup. The merciful Father gave not up his child to folly and sin. He who once could have gone to great lengths in dissipation now found a few glasses of wine more than enough; his relish for such pleasures was gone, and so was the power to silence the still small voice of conscience and of the Spirit of God.

Such vacillations in Christian experience were due in part to the lack of holy associations and devout companionships. Every disciple needs help in holy living, and this young believer yearned for that spiritual uplift afforded by sympathetic fellow believers. In vacation times he had found at Gnadau, the Moravian settlement some three miles from his father's residence, such soul refreshment, but Halle itself supplied little help. He went often to church, but seldom heard the Gospel, and in that town of over 30,000, with all its ministers, he found not one enlightened clergyman. When, therefore, he could hear such a preacher as Dr. Tholuck, he would walk ten or fifteen miles to enjoy such a privilege. The meetings continued at Mr. Wagner's house; and on the Lord's day evenings some six or more believing students were wont to gather, and both these assemblies were means of grace. From Easter, 1827, so long as he remained in Halle, this latter meeting was held in his own room, and must rank alongside those little gatherings of the "Holy Club" in Lincoln College, Oxford, which a hundred years before had shaped the Wesleys and Whitefield for their great careers. Before George Müller left Halle the attendance at this weekly meeting in his room had grown to twenty.

These assemblies were throughout very simple and primitive. In addition to prayer, singing, and reading of God's word, one or more brethren exhorted or read extracts from devout books. Here young Müller freely opened his heart to others, and through their counsels and prayers was delivered from many snares.

One lesson, yet to be learned, was that the one fountain of all wisdom and strength is the Holy Scriptures. Many disciples practically prefer religious books to the Book of God. He had indeed found much of the reading with which too many professed believers occupy their minds to be but worthless chaff—such as French and German novels; but as yet he had not formed the habit of reading the word of God daily and systematically as in later life, almost to the exclusion of other books. In his ninety-second year, he said to the writer, that for every page of any other reading he was sure he read ten of the Bible. But, up to that November day in 1825 when he first met a praying band of disciples, he had never to his recollection read one chapter in the Book of books; and for the first four years of his new life he gave to the works of uninspired men practical preference over the Living Oracles.

After a true relish for the Scriptures had been created, he could not understand how he could ever have treated God's Book with such neglect. It seemed obvious that *God's having condescended to become an Author*, inspiring holy men to write the Scriptures, He would in them impart the most vital truths; His message would cover all matters which concern man's welfare, and therefore, under the double impulse of duty and delight, we should instinctively and habitually turn to the Bible. Moreover, as he read and studied this Book of God, he felt himself admitted to more and more *intimate acquaintance with the Author.* During the last twenty years of his life he read it carefully through, four or five times annually, with a growing sense of his own rapid increase in the knowledge of God thereby.

Such motives for Bible study it is strange that any true believer should overlook. Ruskin, in writing "Of the King's Treasuries," refers to the universal ambition for 'advancement in life,' which means 'getting into good society.' How many obstacles one finds in securing an introduction to the great and good of this world, and even then in getting access to them, in securing an audience with the kings and queens of human society! Yet there is open to us a society of people of the very first rank who will meet us and converse with us so long as we like, whatever our ignorance, poverty, or low estate—namely, the society of authors; and the key that unlocks their private audience-chamber is their books.

So writes Ruskin, and all this is beautifully true; but how few, even among believers, appreciate the privilege of access to the great Author of the universe through His word! Poor and rich, high and low, ignorant and learned, young and old, all alike are welcomed to the audience-chamber of the King of kings. The most intimate knowledge of God is possible on one condition—that we search His Holy Scriptures, prayerfully and habitually, and translate what we there find, into obedience. Of him who thus meditates on God's law day and night, who looks and continues looking into this perfect law of liberty, the promise is unique, and found in both Testaments: "Whatsoever he doeth shall prosper"; "that man shall be blessed in his deed." (Compare Psalm 1:3; Joshua 1:8; James 1:25)

So soon as George Müller found this well-spring of delight and success, he drank habitually at this fountain of living waters. In later life he lamented that, owing to his early neglect of this source of divine wisdom and strength, he remained so long in spiritual infancy, with its ignorance and impotence. So long and so far as his growth in knowledge of God was thus arrested his growth in grace was likewise hindered. His close walk with God began at the point where he learned that such walk is always in the light of that inspired word which is divinely declared to be to the obedient soul "a lamp unto the feet and a light unto the path." He who would keep up intimate converse with the Lord must habitually find in the Scriptures the highway of such companionship. God's aristocracy, His nobility, the princes of His realm, are not the wise, mighty, and high-born of earth, but often the poor, weak, despised of men, who abide in His presence and devoutly commune with Him through His inspired word.

Blessed are they who have thus learned to use the key which gives free access, not only to the King's Treasuries, but to the King Himself!

CHAPTER IV

New Steps and Stages of Preparation

PASSION FOR souls is a divine fire, and in the heart of George Müller that fire now began to burn more brightly, and demanded vent.

In August, 1827, his mind was more definitely than before turned toward mission work. Hearing that the Continental Society of Britain sought a minister for Bucharest, he offered himself through Dr. Tholuck, who, in behalf of the Society, was on the lookout for a suitable candidate. To his great surprise his father gave consent, though Bucharest was more than a thousand miles distant and as truly missionary ground as any other field. After a short visit home he came back to Halle, his face steadfastly set toward his far-off field, and his heart seeking prayerful preparation for expected self-sacrifice and hardship. But God had other plans for His servant, and he never went to Bucharest.

In October following, Hermann Ball, passing through Halle, and being at the little weekly meeting in Müller's room, told him how failing health forbade his continuing his work among Polish Jews; and at once there sprang up in George Müller's mind a strong desire to take his place. Such work doubly attracted him, because it would bring him into close contact with God's chosen but erring people, Israel; and because it would afford opportunity to utilize those Hebrew studies which so engrossed him.

At this very time, calling upon Dr. Tholuck, he was asked, to his surprise, whether he had ever felt a desire to *labour among the Jews*—Dr. Tholuck then acting as agent for the London Missionary Society for promoting missions among them. This question naturally fanned the flame of his already kindled desire; but, shortly after, Bucharest being the seat of the war then raging between the Russians and Turks, the project of sending a minister there was for the time abandoned. But a door seemed to open before him just as another shut behind him.

The committee in London, learning that he was available as a missionary to the Jews, proposed his coming to that city for six months as a missionary student to prepare for the work. To enter thus on a sort of probation was trying to the flesh, but, as it seemed right that there should be opportunity for mutual acquaintance between committee and candidate, to insure harmonious cooperation, his mind was disposed to accede to the proposal.

There was, however, a formidable obstacle. Prussian male subjects must commonly serve three years in the army, and classical students who have passed the university examinations, at least one year. George Müller, who had not served out even this shorter term, could not, without royal exemption, even get a passport out of the country. Application was made for such exemption, but it failed. Meanwhile he was taken ill, and after ten weeks suffered a relapse. While at Leipzig with an American professor with whom he went to the opera, he unwisely partook of some refreshments between the acts, which again brought on illness. He had broken a blood-vessel in the stomach, and he returned to Halle, never again to enter a theatre. Subsequently being asked to go to Berlin for a few weeks to teach German, he went, hoping at the Prussian capital to find access to the court through persons of rank and secure the desired exemption. But here again he failed. There now seemed no way of escaping a soldier's term, and he submitted himself for examination, but was pronounced physically unfit for military duty. In God's providence he fell into kind hands, and, being a second time examined and found unfit, he was thenceforth *completely exempted for life from all service in the army.*

God's lines of purpose mysteriously converged. The time had come; the Master spake and it was done: all things moved in one direction—to set His servant free from the service of his country, that, under the Captain of his salvation, he might endure hardness as a good soldier of Christ, without entanglement in the affairs of this life. Aside from this, his stay at the capital had not been unprofitable, for he had preached five times a week in the poorhouse and conversed on the Lord's days with the convicts in the prison.

In February, 1829, he left for London, on the way visiting his father at Heimersleben, where he had returned after retirement from office; and he reached the English metropolis March 19th. His liberty was much curtailed as a student in this new seminary, but, as no rule conflicted with his conscience, he submitted. He studied about twelve hours daily, giving attention mainly to Hebrew and cognate branches closely connected with his expected field. Sensible of the risk of that deadness of soul which often results from undue absorption in mental studies, he committed to memory much of the Hebrew Old Testament and pursued his tasks in a prayerful spirit, seeking God's help in matters, however minute, connected with daily duty.

Tempted to the continual use of his native tongue by living with his German countrymen, he made little progress in English, which he afterward regretted; and he was wont, therefore, to counsel those who propose to work among a foreign people, not only to live among them in order to learn their language, but to keep aloof as far as may be from their own countrymen, so as to be compelled to use the tongue which is to give them access to those among whom they labour.

In connection with this removal to Britain a seemingly trivial occurrence left upon him a lasting impress—another proof that there are no little things in life. Upon a very small hinge a huge door may swing and turn. It is, in fact, often the apparently trifling events that mould our history, work, and destiny.

A student incidentally mentioned a dentist in Exeter—a Mr. Groves—who for the Lord's sake had resigned his calling with fifteen hundred pounds a year, and with wife and children offered himself as a missionary to Persia, *simply trusting the Lord for all temporal supplies.* This act of self-denying trust had a strange charm for Mr. Müller, and he could not dismiss it from his mind; indeed, he distinctly entered it in his journal and wrote about it to friends at home. It was *another lesson in faith,* and in the very line of that trust of which for more than sixty years he was to be so conspicuous an example and illustration.

In the middle of May, 1829, he was taken ill and felt himself to be past recovery. Sickness is often attended with strange *self-disclosure.* His conviction of sin and guilt at his conversion was too superficial and shallow to leave any after-remembrance. But, as is often true in the history of God's saints, the sense of guilt, which at first seemed to have no roots in conscience and scarce an existence, struck deeper into his being and grew stronger as he knew more of God and grew more like Him. This common experience of saved souls is susceptible of easy explanation. Our conceptions of things depend mainly upon two conditions: first, the clearness of our vision of truth and duty; and secondly, the standard of measurement and comparison. The more we live in God and unto God, the more do our eyes become enlightened to see the enormity and deformity of sin, so that we recognize the hatefulness of evil more distinctly: and the more clearly do we recognize the perfection of God's holiness and make it the pattern and model of our own holy living.

The amateur musician or artist has a false complacency in his own very imperfect work only so far as his ear or eye or taste is not yet trained to accurate discrimination; but, as he becomes more accomplished in a fine art, and more appreciative of it, he recognizes every defect or blemish of his previous work, until the musical performance seems a wretched failure and the painting a mere daub. The change, however, is wholly in the *workman* and not in the *work:* both the music and the painting are in themselves just what they were, but the man is capable of something so much better, that his standard of comparison is raised to a higher level, and his capacity for a true judgment is correspondingly enlarged.

Even so a child of God who, like Elijah, stands before Him as a waiting, willing, obedient servant, and has both likeness to God and power with God, may get under the juniper-tree of despondency, cast down with the sense of unworthiness and ill desert. As godliness increases the sense of ungodliness becomes more acute, and so feelings never accurately gauge real assimilation to God. We shall seem worst in our own eyes when in His we are best, and conversely.

A Mohammedan servant ventured publicly to challenge a preacher who, in an Indian bazaar, was asserting the universal depravity of the race, by affirming that he knew at least one woman who was immaculate, absolutely without fault, and that woman, his own Christian mistress. The preacher bethought himself to ask in reply whether he had any means of knowing whether that was her opinion of herself, which caused the Mohammedan to confess that there lay the mystery: she had been often overheard in prayer confessing herself the most unworthy of sinners.

To return from this digression, Mr. Müller, not only during this illness, but down to life's sudden close, had a growing sense of sin and guilt which would at times have been overwhelming, had he not known upon the testimony of the Word that "whoso covereth his sins shall not prosper, but he that confesseth and forsaketh them shall find mercy." From his own guilt he turned his eyes to the cross where it was atoned for, and to the mercy-seat where forgiveness meets the penitent sinner; and so sorrow for sin was turned into the joy of the justified.

This confidence of acceptance in the Beloved so stripped death of its terrors that during this illness he longed rather to depart and to be with Christ; but after a fortnight he was pronounced better, and, though still longing for the heavenly rest, he submitted to the will of God for a longer sojourn in the land of his pilgrimage, little foreseeing what joy he was to find in living for God, or how much he was to know of the days of heaven upon earth.

During this illness, also, he showed the growing tendency to bring before the Lord in prayer even the minutest matters which his later life so signally exhibited. He constantly besought God to guide his physician, and every new dose of medicine was accompanied by a new petition that God would use it for his good and enable him with patience to await His will. As he advanced toward recovery he sought rest at Teignmouth, where, shortly after his arrival, "Ebenezer" chapel was reopened. It was here also that Mr. Müller became acquainted with Mr. Henry Craik, who was for so many years not only his friend, but fellow labourer.

It was also about this time that, as he records, certain great truths began to be made clear to him and to stand out in much prominence. This period of personal preparation is so important in its bearing on his whole after-career that the reader should have access to his own witness.[2]

On returning to London, prospered in soul-health as also in bodily vigor, he proposed to fellow students a daily morning meeting, from 6 to 8, for prayer and Bible study, when each should give to the others such views of any passage

2 See Appendix B.

read as the Lord might give him. These spiritual exercises proved so helpful and so nourished the appetite for divine things that, after continuing in prayer late into the evening hours, he sometimes at midnight sought the fellowship of some like-minded brother, and thus prolonged the prayer season until one or two o'clock in the morning; and even then sleep was often further postponed by his overflowing joy in God. Thus, under his great Teacher, did this pupil, early in his spiritual history, learn that supreme lesson that to every child of God the word of God is the bread of life, and the prayer of faith the breath of life.

Mr. Müller had been back in London scarcely ten days before health again declined, and the conviction took strong hold upon him that he should not spend his little strength in confining study, but at once get about his work; and this conviction was confirmed by the remembrance of the added light which God had given him and the deeper passion he now felt to serve Him more freely and fully. Under the pressure of this persuasion that both his physical and spiritual welfare would be promoted by actual labours for souls, he sought of the Society a prompt appointment to his field of service; and that they might with the more confidence commission him, he asked that some experienced man might be sent out with him as a fellow counsellor and labourer.

After waiting in vain for six weeks for an answer to this application, he felt another strong conviction: that *to wait on his fellow men to be sent out to his field and work was unscriptural and therefore wrong.* Barnabas and Saul were called by name and sent forth by the Holy Spirit, before the church at Antioch had taken any action; and he felt himself so called of the Spirit to his work that he was prompted to begin at once, without waiting for human authority,—and why not among the Jews in London? Accustomed to act promptly upon conviction, he undertook to distribute among them tracts bearing his name and address, so that any who wished personal guidance could find him. He sought them at their gathering-places, read the Scriptures at stated times with some fifty Jewish lads, and taught in a Sunday-school. Thus, instead of lying like a vessel in dry-dock for repairs, he was launched into Christian work, though, like other labourers among the despised Jews, he found himself exposed to petty trials and persecutions, called to suffer reproach for the name of Christ.

Before the autumn of 1829 had passed, a further misgiving laid hold of him as to whether he could in good conscience remain longer connected in the usual way with this London Society, and on December 12th he concluded to dissolve all such ties except upon certain conditions. To do full justice both to Mr. Müller and the Society, his own words will again be found in the Appendix.[3]

Early in the following year it was made clear that he could labour in connection with such a society only as they would consent to his *serving without salary and*

---

3 See Appendix C.

labouring when and where the Lord might seem to direct. He so wrote, eliciting a firm but kind response to the effect that they felt it "inexpedient to employ those who were unwilling to submit to their guidance with respect to missionary operations," etc.

Thus this link with the Society was broken. He felt that he was acting up to the light God gave, and, while imputing to the Society no blame, he never afterward repented this step nor reversed this judgment. To those who review this long life, so full of the fruits of unusual service to God and man, it will be quite apparent that the Lord was gently but persistently thrusting George Müller out of the common path into one where he was to walk very closely with Himself; and the decisions which, even in lesser matters furthered God's purpose were wiser and weightier than could at the time be seen.

One is constantly reminded in reading Mr. Müller's journal that he was a man of like frailties as others. On Christmas morning of this year, after a season of peculiar joy, he awoke to find himself in the Slough of Despond, without any sense of enjoyment, prayer seeming as fruitless as the vain struggles of a man in the mire. At the usual morning meeting he was urged by a brother to continue in prayer, notwithstanding, until he was again melted before the Lord—a wise counsel for all disciples when the Lord's presence seems strangely withdrawn. Steadfast continuance in prayer must never be hindered by the want of sensible enjoyment; in fact, it is a safe maxim that the less joy, the more need. Cessation of communion with God, for whatever cause, only makes the more difficult its resumption and the recovery of the prayer habit and prayer spirit; whereas the persistent outpouring of supplication, together with continued activity in the service of God, soon brings back the lost joy. Whenever, therefore, one yields to spiritual depression so as to abandon, or even to suspend, closet communion or Christian work, the devil triumphs.

So rapid was Mr. Müller's recovery out of this Satanic snare, through continuance in prayer, that, on the evening of that same Christmas day whose dawn had been so overcast, he expounded the Word at family worship in the house where he dined by invitation, and with such help from God that two servants who were present were deeply convicted of sin and sought his counsel.

Here we reach another mile-stone in this life-journey. George Müller had now come to the end of the year 1829, and he had been led of the Lord in a truly remarkable path. It was but about four years since he first found the narrow way and began to walk in it, and he was as yet a young man, in his twenty-fifth year. Yet already he had been taught some of the grand secrets of a holy, happy, and useful life, which became the basis of the whole structure of his after-service.

Indeed, as we look back over these four years, they seem crowded with significant and eventful experiences, all of which forecast his future work, though he as yet saw not in them the Lord's sign. His conversion in a primitive assembly of believers where worship and the word of God were the only attractions, was the starting-point in a career every step of which seems a stride forward. Think of a young convert, with such an ensnaring past to reproach and retard him, within these few years learning such advanced lessons in *renunciation:* burning his manuscript novel, giving up the girl he loved, turning his back on the seductive prospect of ease and wealth, to accept self-denial for God, cutting loose from dependence on his father and then refusing all stated salary lest his liberty of witness be curtailed, and choosing a simple expository mode of preaching, instead of catering to popular taste! Then mark how he fed on the word of God; how he cultivated the habits of searching the Scriptures and praying in secret; how he threw himself on God, not only for temporal supplies, but for support in bearing all burdens, however great or small; and how thus early he offered himself for the mission field and was impatiently eager to enter it. Then look at the sovereign love of God, imparting to him in so eminent a degree the childlike spirit, teaching him to trust not his own variable moods of feeling, but the changeless word of His promise; teaching him to wait patiently on Him for orders, and not to look to human authority or direction; and so singularly releasing him from military service for life, and mysteriously withholding him from the far-off mission field, that He might train him for his unique mission to the race and the ages to come!

These are a few of the salient points of this narrative, thus far, which must, to any candid mind, demonstrate that a higher Hand was moulding this chosen vessel on His potter's wheel, and shaping it unmistakably for the singular service to which it was destined!

CHAPTER V

The Pulpit and the Pastorate

NO WORK for God surpasses in dignity and responsibility the Christian ministry. It is at once the consummate flower of the divine planting, the priceless dower of His church, and through it works the power of God for salvation.

Though George Müller had begun his 'candidacy for holy orders' as an unconverted man, seeking simply a human calling with a hope of a lucrative living, he had heard God's summons to a divine vocation, and he was from time to time preaching the Gospel, but not in any settled field.

SCRIPTURE TESTIMONY
God's work will not lack God's supply Philippians 4:19

While at Teignmouth, early in 1830, preaching by invitation, he was asked to take the place of the minister who was about to leave, but he replied that he felt at that time called of God, not to a stationary charge, but rather to a sort of itinerant evangelism. During this time he preached at Shaldon for Henry Craik, thus coming into closer contact with this brother, to whom his heart became knit in bonds of love and sympathy which grew stronger as the acquaintance became more intimate.

Certain hearers at Teignmouth, and among them some preachers, disliked his sermons, albeit they were owned of God; and this caused him to reflect upon the probable causes of this opposition, and whether it was any indication of his duty. He felt that they doubtless looked for outward graces of oratory in a preacher, and hence were not attracted to a foreigner whose speech had no rhetorical charms and who could not even use English with fluency. But he felt sure of a deeper cause for their dislike, especially as he was compelled to notice that, the summer previous, when he himself was less spiritually minded and had less insight into the truth, the same parties who now opposed him were pleased with him. His final conclusion was that the Lord meant to work through him at Teignmouth, but that Satan was acting, as usual, the part of a hinderer, and stirring up brethren themselves to oppose the truth. And as, notwithstanding the opposers, the wish that he should minister at the chapel was expressed so often and by so many, he determined to remain for a time until he was openly rejected as God's witness, or had some clear divine leading to another field of labour.

He announced this purpose, at the same time plainly stating that, should they withhold salary, it would not affect his decision, inasmuch as he did not preach as a hireling of man, but as the servant of God, and would willingly commit to Him the provision for his temporal needs. At the same time, however, he reminded them that it was alike their duty and privilege to minister in carnal things to those who served them in things spiritual, and that while he did not desire a gift, he did desire fruit that might abound to their account.

These experiences at Teignmouth were typical: "Some believed the things which were spoken, and some believed not;" some left the chapel, while others stayed; and some were led and fed, while others maintained a cold indifference, if they did not exhibit an open hostility. But the Lord stood by him and strengthened him, setting His seal upon his testimony; and Jehovah Jireh also moved two brethren, unasked, to supply all the daily wants of His servant. After a while the little church of eighteen members unanimously called the young preacher to the pastorate, and he consented to abide with them for a season, without abandoning his original intention of going from place to place as the Lord might lead. A stipend, of fifty-five pounds annually, was offered him, which somewhat increased as the church membership grew; and so the university student of Halle was settled in his first pulpit and pastorate.

While at Sidmouth, preaching, in April, 1830, three believing sisters held in his presence a conversation about '*believers' baptism,*' which proved the suggestion of another important step in his life, which has a wider bearing than at first is apparent.

They naturally asked his opinion on the subject about which they were talking, and he replied that, having been baptized as a child, he saw no need of being baptized again. Being further asked if he had ever yet prayerfully searched the word of God as to its testimony in this matter, he frankly confessed that he had not.

At once, with unmistakable plainness of speech and with rare fidelity, one of these sisters in Christ promptly said: *"I entreat you, then, never again to speak any more about it till you have done so."*

Such a reply George Müller was not the man either to resent or to resist. He was too honest and conscientious to dismiss without due reflection any challenge to search the oracles of God for their witness upon any given question. Moreover, if, at that very time, his preaching was emphatic in any direction, it was in the boldness with which he insisted that *all pulpit teaching and Christian practice must be subjected to one great test,* namely, *the touchstone of the word of God.* Already an Elijah in spirit, his great aim was to repair the broken-down altar of the Lord, to expose and rebuke all that hindered a thoroughly scriptural worship and service, and, if possible, to restore apostolic simplicity of doctrine and life.

As he thought and prayed about this matter, he was forced to admit to himself that he had never yet earnestly examined the Scriptures for their teaching as to the position and relation of baptism in the believer's life, nor had he even prayed for light upon it. He had nevertheless repeatedly spoken against believers' baptism, and so he saw it to be possible that he might himself have been opposing the teaching of the Word. He therefore determined to study the subject until he should reach a final, satisfactory, and scriptural conclusion; and thenceforth, whether led to defend infant baptism or believers' baptism, to do it only on scriptural grounds.

The mode of study which he followed was characteristically simple, thorough, and business-like, and was always pursued afterward. He first sought from God the Spirit's teaching that his eyes might be opened to the Word's witness, and his mind illumined; then he set about a systematic examination of the New Testament from beginning to end. So far as possible he sought absolutely to rid himself of all bias of previous opinion or practice, prepossession or prejudice; he prayed and endeavoured to be free from the influence of human tradition, popular custom, and churchly sanction, or that more subtle hindrance, *personal pride in his own consistency.* He was humble enough to be willing to retract any erroneous teaching and renounce any false position, and to espouse that wise maxim: "Don't be *consistent,* but simply be *true!*" Whatever may have been the case with others who claim to have examined the same question for themselves, the result in his case was that he came to the conclusion, and, as he believed, from the word of God and the Spirit of God, that none but believers are the proper subjects of baptism, and that only immersion is its proper mode. Two passages of Scripture were very marked in the prominence which they had in compelling him to these conclusions, namely: Acts 8:36-38, and Romans 6:3-5. The case of the Ethiopian eunuch strongly convinced him that baptism is proper, only as the act of a believer confessing Christ; and the passage in the Epistle to the Romans equally satisfied him that only immersion in water can express the typical burial with Christ and resurrection with Him, there and elsewhere made so prominent. He intended no assault upon brethren who hold other views, when he thus plainly stated in his journal the honest and unavoidable convictions to which he came; but he was too loyal both to the word of God and to his own conscience to withhold his views when so carefully and prayerfully arrived at through the searching of the Scriptures.

Conviction compelled action, for in him there was no spirit of compromise; and he was accordingly promptly baptized. Years after, in reviewing his course, he records the solemn conviction that "of all revealed truths, not one is more clearly revealed in the Scriptures—not even the doctrine of justification by faith—and that the subject has only become obscured by men not having been willing to take *the Scriptures alone* to decide the point."

He also bears witness incidentally that not one true friend in the Lord had ever turned his back upon him in consequence of his baptism, as he supposed some would have done; and that almost all such friends had, since then, been themselves baptized. It is true that in one way he suffered some pecuniary loss through this step taken in obedience to conviction, but the Lord did not suffer him to be ultimately the loser even in this respect, for He bountifully made up to him any such sacrifice, even in things that pertain to this life. He concludes this review of his course by adding that through his example many others were led both to examine the question of baptism anew and to submit themselves to the ordinance.

Such experiences as these suggest the honest question whether there is not imperative need of subjecting all current religious customs and practices to the one test of conformity to the scripture pattern. Our Lord sharply rebuked the Pharisees of His day for making "the commandment of God of none effect by their tradition," and, after giving one instance, He added, "and many other such like things do ye."[4] It is very easy for doctrines and practices to gain acceptance, which are the outgrowth of ecclesiasticism, and neither have sanction in the word of God, nor will bear the searching light of its testimony. Cyprian has forewarned us that even *antiquity* is not *authority,* but may be only *vetustas erroris*—the old age of error. What radical reforms would be made in modern worship, teaching and practice,—in the whole conduct of disciples and the administration of the church of God,—if the one final criterion of all judgment were: What do the Scriptures teach?' And what revolutions in our own lives as believers might take place, if we should first put every notion of truth and custom of life to this one test of scripture authority, and then with the courage of conviction dare to do according to that word—counting no cost, but studying to show ourselves approved of God! Is it possible that there are any modern disciples who "reject the commandment of God that they may keep their own tradition"?

This step, taken by Mr. Müller as to baptism, was only a precursor of many others, all of which, as he believed, were according to that Word which, as the lamp to the believer's feet, is to throw light upon his path.

During this same summer of 1830 the further study of the Word satisfied him that, though there is no direct *command* so to do, the scriptural and apostolic *practice* was to *break bread every Lord's day.* (Acts 20:7, etc.) Also, that the Spirit

4 Matthew 15:6. Mark 7:9-13.

of God should have unhindered liberty to work through any believer according to the gifts He had bestowed, seemed to him plainly taught in Romans 7; 1 Corinthians 7; Ephesians 4, etc. These conclusions likewise this servant of God sought to translate at once into conduct, and such conformity brought increasing spiritual prosperity.

Conscientious misgivings, about the same time, ripened into settled convictions that he could no longer, upon the same principle of obedience to the word of God, consent to *receive any stated salary* as a minister of Christ. For this latter position, which so influenced his life, he assigns the following grounds, which are here stated as showing the basis of his life-long attitude:

1. A stated salary implies a fixed sum, which cannot well be paid without a fixed income through pew-rentals or some like source of revenue. This seemed plainly at war with the teaching of the Spirit of God in James 2:1-6, since the poor brother cannot afford as good sittings as the rich, thus introducing into church assemblies invidious distinctions and respect of persons, and so encouraging the caste spirit.
2. A fixed pew-rental may at times become, even to the willing disciple, a burden. He who would gladly contribute to a pastor's support, if allowed to do so according to his ability and at his own convenience, might be oppressed by the demand to pay a stated sum at a stated time. Circumstances so change that one who has the same cheerful mind as before may be unable to give as formerly, and thus be subjected to painful embarrassment and humiliation if constrained to give a fixed sum.
3. The whole system tends to the bondage of the servant of Christ. One must be unusually faithful and intrepid if he feels no temptation to keep back or in some degree modify his message in order to please men, when he remembers that the very parties, most open to rebuke and most liable to offence, are perhaps the main contributors toward his salary.

Whatever others may think of such reasons as these, they were so satisfactory to his mind that he frankly and promptly announced them to his brethren; and thus, as early as the autumn of 1830, when just completing his twenty-fifth year, he took a position from which he never retreated, that he would thenceforth *receive no fixed salary for any service rendered to God's people.* While calmly assigning scriptural grounds for such a position he, on the same grounds, urged *voluntary offerings,* whether of money or other means of support, as the proper acknowledgment of service rendered by God's minister, and as a sacrifice acceptable, well-pleasing to God. A little later, seeing that, when such voluntary gifts came direct from the givers personally, there was a danger that some might feel self-complacent over the largeness of the amount given by them, and others equally humbled by the smallness of their offerings, with consequent damage to both classes, of givers, he took a step further: he had a *box put up in the chapel,* over which was written, that whoever had a desire to do something for his support might put such an offering therein as ability and disposition might direct. His intention was, that thus the act might be wholly as in God's sight, without the risk of a sinful pride or false humility.

He further felt that, to be entirely consistent, he should *ask no help from man,* even in bearing necessary costs of travel in the Lord's service, nor even state his needs beforehand in such a way as indirectly to appeal for aid. All of these methods he conceived to be forms of trusting in an arm of flesh, going to man for help instead of going at once, always and only, to the Lord. And he adds: *"To come to this conclusion before God required more grace than to give up my salary."*

These successive steps are here recorded explicitly and in their exact order because they lead up directly to the ultimate goal of his life-work and witness. Such decisions were vital links connecting this remarkable man and his "Father's business," upon which he was soon more fully to enter; and they were all necessary to the fulness of the world-wide witness which he was to bear to a prayer-hearing God and the absolute safety of trusting in Him and in Him alone.

On October 7, 1830, George Müller, in finding a wife, found a good thing and obtained new favour from the Lord. Miss Mary Groves, sister of the self-denying dentist whose surrender of all things for the mission field had so impressed him years before, was married to this man of God, and for forty blessed years proved an help meet for him. It was almost, if not quite, an ideal union, for which he continually thanked God; and, although her kingdom was one which came not with observation,' the sceptre of her influence was far wider in its sway than will ever be appreciated by those who were strangers to her personal and domestic life. She was a rare woman and her price was above rubies. The heart of her husband safely trusted, in her, and the great family of orphans who were to her as children rise up even to this day to call her blessed.

SCRIPTURE TESTIMONY
Exchange earthly possessions for heavenly treasure
Matthew 6:19-21 · Luke 12:33

Married life has often its period of estrangement, even when temporary alienation yields to a deeper love, as the parties become more truly wedded by the assimilation of their inmost being to one another. But to Mr. and Mrs. Müller there never came any such experience of even temporary alienation. From the first, love grew, and with it, mutual confidence and trust. One of the earliest ties which bound these two in one was the bond of a *common self-denial.* Yielding literal obedience to Luke 12:33, they sold what little they had and gave alms, henceforth laying up no treasures on earth (Matthew 6:19-34; 19:21) The step then taken—accepting, for Christ's sake, voluntary poverty—was never regretted, but rather increasingly rejoiced in; how faithfully it was followed in the same path of continued self-sacrifice will sufficiently appear when it is remembered that, nearly sixty-eight years afterward, George Müller passed suddenly into the life beyond, a poor man; his will, when admitted to probate, showing his entire personal property, under oath, to be but one hundred and sixty pounds! And even that would not have been in his possession had there been no daily need of requisite comforts for the body and of tools for his work. Part of this amount was in money, shortly before received and not yet laid out for his Master, but held at His disposal. Nothing, even to the clothes he wore, did he treat as his own. He was a consistent steward.

This final farewell to all earthly possessions, in 1830, left this newly married husband and wife to look only to the Lord. Thenceforth they were to put to ample daily test both their faith in the Great Provider and the faithfulness of the Great Promiser. It may not be improper here to anticipate, what is yet to be more fully recorded, that, from day to day and hour to hour, during more than threescore years, George Müller was enabled to set to his seal that God is true. If few men have ever been permitted so to trace in the smallest matters God's care over His children, it is partly because few have so completely abandoned themselves to that care. He dared to trust Him, with whom the hairs of our head are all numbered, and who touchingly reminds us that He cares for what has been quaintly called *"the odd sparrow."* Matthew records (10:29) how two sparrows are sold for a farthing, and Luke (12:6) how five are sold for two farthings; and so it would appear that, when two farthings were offered, an odd sparrow was thrown in, as of so little value that it could be given away with the other four. And yet even for that one sparrow, not worth taking into account in the bargain, *God cares.* Not one of them is forgotten before God, or falls to the ground without Him. With what force then comes the assurance: "Fear ye not therefore; ye are of more value than many sparrows!"

So George Müller found it to be. He was permitted henceforth to know as never before, and as few others have ever learned, how truly God may be approached as "Thou that hearest prayer." God can keep His trusting children not only from falling but from stumbling; for, during all those after-years that spanned the lifetime of two generations, there was no drawing back. Those precious promises, which in faith and hope were "laid hold" of in 1830, were "held fast" until the end. (Hebrews 6:18, 10:23) And the divine faithfulness proved a safe anchorage-ground in the most prolonged and violent tempests. The anchor of hope, sure and steadfast, and entering into that within the veil, was never dragged from its secure hold on God. In fifty thousand cases, Mr. Müller calculated that he could trace distinct answers to definite prayers; and in multitudes of instances in which God's care was not definitely traced, it was day by day like an encompassing passing but invisible presence or atmosphere of life and strength.

On August 9, 1831, Mrs. Müller gave birth to a stillborn babe, and for six weeks remained seriously ill. Her husband meanwhile laments that his heart was so cold and carnal, and his prayers often so hesitating and formal; and he detects, even behind his zeal for God, most unspiritual frames. He especially chides himself for not having more seriously thought of the peril of child-bearing, so as to pray more earnestly for his wife; and he saw clearly that the prospect of parenthood had not been rejoiced in as a blessing, but rather as implying a new burden and hindrance in the Lord's work.

SCRIPTURE TESTIMONY
Don't be anxious, for He cares for us
1 Peter 5:6-7 · Matthew 6:25-34

While this man of God lays bare his heart in his journal, the reader must feel that "as in water face answereth to face, so the heart of man to man." How many a servant of God has no more exalted idea of the divine privilege of a sanctified parenthood! A wife and a child are most precious gifts of God when received, in answer to prayer, from His hand. Not only are they not hindrances, but they are helps, most useful in fitting a servant of Christ for certain parts of his work for which no other preparation is so adequate. They serve to teach him many most valuable lessons, and to round out his character into a far more symmetrical beauty and serviceableness. And when it is remembered how a godly *association* in holiness and usefulness may thus be supplied, and above all a godly *succession* through many generations, it will be seen how wicked is the spirit that treats holy wedlock and its fruits in offspring,—with lightness and contempt. Nor let us forget that promise: "If two of you agree on earth as touching any thing that they shall ask, it shall be done for them of My Father which is in heaven." (Matthew 18:19) The Greek word for "agree" is *symphonize,* and suggests a musical harmony where chords are tuned to the same key and struck by a master hand. Consider what a blessed preparation for such habitual symphony in prayer is to be found in the union of a husband and wife in the Lord! May it not be that to this the Spirit refers when He bids husband and wife dwell in unity, as "heirs together of the grace of life," and adds, *"that your prayers be not hindered"?* (1 Peter 3:7)

God used this severe lesson for permanent blessing to George Müller. He showed him how open was his heart to the subtle power of selfishness and carnality, and how needful was this chastisement to teach him the sacredness of marital life and parental responsibility. Henceforth he judged himself, that he might not be "judged of the Lord." (1 Corinthians 11:31)

A crisis like his wife's critical illness created a demand for much extra expense, for which no provision had been made, not through carelessness and improvidence, but upon principle. Mr. Müller held that to lay by in store is inconsistent with full trust in God, who in such case would send us to our hoardings before answering prayer for more supplies. Experience in this emergency justified his faith; for not only were all unforeseen wants supplied, but even the delicacies and refreshments needful for the sick and weak; and the two medical attendants graciously declined all remuneration for services which extended through six weeks. Thus was there given of the Lord more than could have been laid up against this season of trial, even had the attempt been made.

The principle of committing future wants to the Lord's care, thus acted upon at this time, he and his wife consistently followed so long as they lived and worked together. Experience confirmed them in the conviction that a life of trust forbids laying up treasures against unforeseen foreseen needs, since with God *no emergency is unforeseen and no want unprovided for;* and He may be as implicitly trusted for extraordinary needs as for our common daily bread.

Yet another law, kindred to this and thoroughly inwrought into Mr. Müller's habit of life, was *never to contract debt,* whether for personal purposes or the Lord's work. This matter was settled on scriptural grounds once for all (Romans 13:8), and he and his wife determined if need be to suffer starvation rather than to buy anything without paying for it when bought. Thus they always knew how much they had to buy with, and what they had left to give to others or use for others' wants.

There was yet another law of life early framed into Mr. Müller's personal decalogue. He regarded any money which was in his hands *already designated for, or appropriated to, a specific use,* as *not his to use, even temporarily, for any other ends.* Thus, though he was often reduced to the lowest point of temporal supplies, he took no account of any such funds set apart for other outlays or due for other purposes. Thousands of times he was in straits where such diversion of funds for a time seemed the only and the easy way out, but where this would only have led him into new embarrassments. This principle, intelligently adopted, was firmly adhered to, that what properly belongs to a particular branch of work, or has been already put aside for a certain use, even though yet in hand, is not to be reckoned on as available for any other need, however pressing. Trust in God implies such knowledge on His part of the exact circumstances that He will not constrain us to any such misappropriation. Mistakes, most serious and fatal, have come from lack of conscience as well as of faith in such exigencies—drawing on one fund to meet the overdraught upon another, hoping afterward to replace what is thus withdrawn. A well-known college president had nearly involved the institution of which he was the head, in bankruptcy, and himself in worse moral ruin, all the result of one error—money given for endowing certain chairs had been used for current expenses until public confidence had been almost hopelessly impaired.

Thus a life of *faith* must be no less a life of *conscience.* Faith and trust in God, and truth and faithfulness toward man, walked side by side in this life-journey in unbroken agreement.

CHAPTER VI

"The Narrative of the Lord's Dealings"

THINGS WHICH are sacred forbid even a careless touch.

The record written by George Müller of the Lord's dealings reads, especially in parts, almost like an inspired writing, because it is simply the tracing of divine guidance in a human life—not this man's own working or planning, suffering or serving, but the *Lord's dealings* with him and workings through him.

It reminds us of that conspicuous passage in the Acts of the Apostles where, within the compass of twenty verses, God is fifteen times put boldly forward as the one Actor in all events. Paul and Barnabas rehearsed, in the ears of the church at Antioch, and afterward at Jerusalem, not what *they had done* for the Lord, but all that *He had done* with them, and how *He had opened* the door of faith unto the Gentiles; what miracles and wonders *God had wrought* among the Gentiles by them. And, in the same spirit, Peter before the council emphasizes how God had made choice of his mouth, as that whereby the Gentiles should hear the word of the Gospel and believe; how He had given them the Holy Ghost and put no difference between Jew and Gentile, purifying their hearts by faith; and how He who knew all hearts had thus borne them witness. Then James, in the same strain, refers to the way in which *God had visited* the Gentiles to *take out* of them a people for His name; and concludes by two quotations or adaptations from the Old Testament, which fitly sum up the whole matter:

> "The Lord *who doeth* all these things."
> "Known unto God are *all His works* from the beginning of the world." (Acts 14:27 to 15:18)

The meaning of such repeated phraseology cannot be mistaken. God is here presented as the one agent or actor, and even the most conspicuous apostles, like Paul and Peter, as only His instruments. No twenty verses in the word of God contain more emphatic and repeated lessons on man's insufficiency and nothingness, and God's all-sufficiency and almightiness. It was God that wrought upon man through man. It was He who chose Peter to be His mouthpiece, He whose key unlocked shut doors, He who visited the nations, who turned sinners into saints, who was even then taking out a people for His name, purifying hearts and bearing them witness; it was He and He alone who did all these wondrous things, and according to His knowledge and plan of what He would do, from the beginning. We are not reading so much the Acts of the Apostles as the acts of God through the apostles. Was it not this very passage in this inspired book that suggested, perhaps, the name of this journal: *"The Lord's dealings with George Müller?"*

At this narrative or journal, as a whole, we can only rapidly glance. In this shorter account, purposely condensed to secure a wider reading even from busy people, that narrative could not be more fully treated, for in its original form it covers about three thousand printed pages, and contains close to one million words. To such as can and will read that more minute account it is accessible at a low rate,[5] and is strongly recommended for careful and leisurely perusal. But for the present purpose the life-story, as found in these pages, takes both a briefer and a different form.

The journal is largely composed of, condensed from, and then supplemented by, annual reports of the work, and naturally and necessarily includes, not only thousands of little details, but much inevitable repetition year by year, because each new report was likely to fall into the hands of some who had never read reports of the previous years. The desire and design of this briefer memoir is to present the salient points of the narrative, to review the whole life-story as from the great summits or outlooks found in this remarkable journal; so that, like the observer who from some high mountain-peak looks toward the different points of the compass, and thus gets a rapid, impressive, comparative, and comprehensive view of the whole landscape, the reader may, as at a glance, take in those marked features of this godly man's character and career which incite to new and advance steps in faith and holy living. Some few characteristic entries in the journal will find here a place; others, only in substance; while of the bulk of them it will be sufficient to give a general survey, classifying the leading facts, and under each class giving a few representative examples and illustrations.

Looking at this narrative as a whole, certain prominent peculiarities must be carefully noted. We have here a record and revelation of seven conspicuous experiences:

5 Five volumes at 16s. Published by Jas. Nisbet & Co., London. With subsequent Annual Reports at 3d. each.

1. An experience of frequent and at times prolonged *financial straits.*

The money in hand for personal needs, and for the needs of hundreds and thousands of orphans, and for the various branches of the work of the Scriptural Knowledge Institution, was often reduced to a single *pound,* or even *penny,* and sometimes to *nothing.* There was therefore a necessity for constant waiting on God, looking to Him directly for all supplies. For months, if not years, together, and at several periods in the work, supplies were furnished only from month to month, week to week, day to day, *hour to hour!* Faith was thus kept in lively exercise and under perpetual training.

2. An experience of the *unchanging faithfulness of the Father-God.*

The straits were long and trying, but never was there one case of failure to receive help; never a meal-time without at least a frugal meal, never a want or a crisis unmet by divine supply and support. Mr. Müller said to the writer: "Not once, or five times, or five hundred times, but thousands of times in these threescore years, have we had in hand not enough *for one more meal,* either in food or in funds; but not once has God failed us; not once have we or the orphans gone hungry or lacked any good thing." From 1838 to 1844 was a period of peculiar and prolonged straits, yet when the time of need actually came the supply was always given, though often at the last moment.

3. An experience of the working of God upon the minds, hearts, and consciences of *contributors to the work.*

It will amply repay one to plod, step by step, over these thousands of pages, if only to trace the hand of God touching the springs of human action all over the world in ways of His own, and at times of great need, and adjusting the amount and the exact day and hour of the supply, to the existing want. Literally from the earth's ends, men, women, and children who had never seen Mr. Müller and could have known nothing of the pressure at the time, have been led at the exact crisis of affairs to send aid in the very sum or form most needful. In countless cases, while he was on his knees asking, the answer has come in such close correspondence with the request as to shut out chance as an explanation, and compel belief in a prayer-hearing God.

4. An experience of habitual *hanging upon the unseen God* and nothing else.

The reports, issued annually to acquaint the public with the history and progress of the work, and give an account of stewardship to the many donors who had a right to a report—these made *no direct appeal for aid.* At one time, and that of great need, Mr. Müller felt led to *withhold* the usual annual statement, lest some might construe the account of work already done as an appeal for aid in work yet to be done, and thus detract from the glory of the Great Provider.[6] The Living God alone was and is the Patron of these institutions; and not even the wisest and wealthiest, the noblest and the most influential of human beings, has ever been looked to as their dependence.

5. An experience of conscientious *care in accepting and using gifts.*

SCRIPTURE TESTIMONY
Not for the approval of men
Matthew 6:1-4

Here is a pattern for all who act as stewards for God. Whenever there was any ground of misgiving as to the propriety or expediency of receiving what was offered, it was declined, however pressing the need, unless or until all such objectionable features no more existed. If the party contributing was known to dishonour lawful debts, so that the money was righteously due to others; if the gift was encumbered and embarrassed by restrictions that hindered its free use for God; if it was designated for endowment purposes or as a provision for Mr. Müller's old age, or for the future of the institutions; or if there was any evidence or suspicion that the donation was given grudgingly, reluctantly, or for self-glory, it was promptly declined and returned. In some cases, even where large amounts were involved, parties were urged to wait until more prayer and deliberation made clear that they were acting under divine leading.

6. An experience of extreme caution lest there should be even a careless *betrayal of the fact of pressing need,* to the outside public.

---

6 For example, Vol II. 102, records that the report given is for 1846-1848, no report having been issued for 1847; and on page 113, under date of May 25th, occur these words: "not being nearly enough to meet the housekeeping expenses," etc.; and, May 28th and 30th, such other words as these: "now our poverty," "in this our great need," "in these days of straitness." Mr. Wright thinks that *on that very account* Mr. Müller did not publish the report for 1847.

The helpers in the institutions were allowed to come into such close fellowship and to have such knowledge of the exact state of the work as aids not only in common labours, but in common prayers and self-denials. Without such acquaintance they could not serve, pray, nor sacrifice intelligently. But these associates were most solemnly and repeatedly charged never to reveal to those without, not even in the most serious crises, any want whatsoever of the work. The one and only resort was ever to be the God who hears the cry of the needy; and the greater the exigency, the greater the caution lest there should even seem to be a looking away from divine to human help.

7. An experience of growing boldness of faith in *asking and trusting for great things.*

As faith was exercised it was energized, so that it became as easy and natural to ask confidently for a hundred, a thousand, or ten thousand pounds, as once it had been for a pound or a penny. After confidence in God had been strengthened through discipline, and God had been proven faithful, it required no more venture to cast himself on God for provision for two thousand children and an annual outlay of at least twenty-five thousand pounds for them than in the earlier periods of the work to look to Him to care for twenty homeless orphans at a cost of two hundred and fifty pounds a year. Only by *using* faith are we kept from practically *losing* it, and, on the contrary, to use faith is to lose the unbelief that hinders God's mighty acts.

This brief resume of the contents of thousands of entries is the result of a repeated and careful examination of page after page where have been patiently recorded with scrupulous and punctilious exactness the innumerable details of Mr. Müller's long experience as a coworker with God. He felt himself not only the steward of a celestial Master, but the trustee of human gifts, and hence he sought to "provide things honest in the sight of all men." He might never have published a report or spread these minute matters before the public eye, and yet have been an equally faithful steward toward *God;* but he would not in such case have been an equally faithful trustee toward man.

Frequently, in these days, men receive considerable sums of money from various sources for benevolent work, and yet give no account of such trusteeship. However honest such parties may be, they not only act unwisely, but, by their course, lend sanction to others with whom such irresponsible action is a cloak for systematic fraud. Mr. Müller's whole career is the more without fault because in this respect his administration of his great trust challenges the closest investigation.

The brief review of the lessons taught in his journal may well startle the incredulous and unbelieving spirit of our skeptical day. Those who doubt the power of prayer to bring down actual blessing, or who confound faith in God with credulity and superstition, may well wonder and perhaps stumble at such an array of facts. But, if any reader is still doubtful as to the facts, or thinks they are here arrayed in a deceptive garb or invested with an imaginative halo, he is hereby invited to examine for himself the singularly minute records which George Müller has been led of God to put before the world in a printed form which thus admits no change, and to accompany with a bold and repeated challenge to any one so inclined, to subject every statement to the severest scrutiny, and prove, if possible, one item to be in any respect false, exaggerated, or misleading. The absence of all enthusiasm in the calm and mathematical precision of the narrative compels the reader to feel that the writer was almost mechanically exact in the record, and inspires confidence that it contains the absolute, naked truth.

One caution should, like Habakkuk's gospel message—"The just shall live by his faith"—be written large and plain so that even a cursory glance may take it in. Let no one ascribe to George Müller such a *miraculous gift of faith* as lifted him above common believers and out of the reach of the temptations and infirmities to which all fallible souls are exposed. He was constantly liable to satanic assaults, and we find him making frequent confession of the same sins as others, and even of unbelief, and at times overwhelmed with genuine sorrow for his departures from God. In fact he felt himself rather more than usually wicked by nature, and utterly helpless even as a believer: was it not this poverty of spirit and mourning over sin, this consciousness of entire unworthiness and dependence, that so drove him to the throne of grace and the all-merciful and all-powerful Father? Because he was so weak, he leaned hard on the strong arm of Him whose strength is not only manifested, but can only be made perfect, in weakness.[7]

To those who think that no man can wield such power in prayer or live such a life of faith who is not an exception to common mortal frailties, it will be helpful to find in this very journal that is so lighted up with the records of God's goodness, the dark shadows of conscious sin and guilt. Even in the midst of abounding mercies and interpositions he suffered from temptations to distrust and disobedience, and sometimes had to mourn their power over him, as when once he found himself inwardly complaining of the cold leg of mutton which formed the staple of his Sunday dinner! We discover as we read that we are communing with a man who was not only of like passions with ourselves, but who felt himself rather more than most others subject to the sway

7 1 Corinthians 12:1-10

of evil, and needing therefore a special keeping power. Scarce had he started upon his new path of entire dependence on God, when he confessed himself "so sinful" as for some time to entertain the thought that "it would be of no use to trust in the Lord in this way," and fearing that he had perhaps gone already too far in this direction in having committed himself to such a course.[8] True, this temptation was speedily overcome and Satan confounded; but from time to time similar fiery darts were hurled at him which had to be quenched by the same shield of faith. Never, to the last hour of life, could he trust himself, or for one moment relax his hold on God, and neglect the word of God and prayer, without falling into sin. The 'old man,' of sin always continued too strong for George Müller alone, and the longer he lived a 'life of trust' the less was his trust placed upon himself.

Another fact that grows more conspicuous with the perusal of every new page in his journal is that in things common and small, as well as uncommon and great, he took no step without first asking counsel of the oracles of God and seeking guidance from Him in believing prayer. It was his life-motto to learn the will of God before undertaking anything, and to wait till it is clear, because only so can one either be blessed in his own soul or prospered in the work of his hands.[9] Many disciples who are comparatively bold to seek God's help in great crises, fail to come to Him with like boldness in matters that seem too trivial to occupy the thought of God or invite the interposition of Him who numbers the very hairs of our heads and suffers not one hair to perish. The writer of this journal escaped this great snare and carried even the smallest matter to the Lord.

Again, in his journal he constantly seeks to save from reproach the good name of Him whom he serves: he cannot have such a God accounted a hard Master. So early as July, 1831, a false rumour found circulation that he and his wife were half-starving and that certain bodily ailments were the result of a lack of the necessities of life; and he is constrained to put on record that, though often brought so low as not to have one penny left and to have the last bread on the table, they had never yet sat down to a meal unprovided with some nourishing food. This witness was repeated from time to time, and until just before his departure for the Father's house on high; and it may therefore be accepted as covering that whole life of faith which reached over nearly threescore years and ten.

A kindred word of testimony, first given at this same time and in like manner reiterated from point to point in his pilgrimage, concerns the Lord's faithfulness in accompanying His word with power, in accordance with that positive and unequivocal promise in Isaiah 55:11: "My word shall not return unto Me void; but it shall accomplish that which I please, and it shall prosper in the thing whereto I sent it." It is very noticeable that this is not said of *man's* word, however wise, important,

8 Vol. I. 73
9 Vol. I. 74.

or sincere, but of *God's* word. We are therefore justified in both expecting and claiming that, just so far as our message is not of human invention or authority, but is God's message through us, it shall never fail to accomplish His pleasure and its divine errand, whatever be its apparent failure at the time. Mr. Müller, referring to his own preaching, bears witness that in almost if not quite every place where he spoke God's word, whether in larger chapels or smaller rooms, the Lord gave the seal of His own testimony. He observed, however, that blessing did not so obviously or abundantly follow his open-air services: only in one instance had it come to his knowledge that there were marked results, and that was in the case of an army officer who came to make sport. Mr. Müller thought that it might please the Lord not to let him see the real fruit of his work in open-air meetings, or that there had not been concerning them enough believing prayer; but he concluded that such manner of preaching was not his present work, since God had not so conspicuously sealed it with blessing.

His journal makes very frequent reference to the physical weakness and disability from which he suffered.

The struggle against bodily infirmity was almost life-long, and adds a new lesson to his life-story. The strength of faith had to triumph over the weakness of the flesh. We often find him suffering from bodily ills, and sometimes so seriously as to be incapacitated for labour.

For example, early in 1832 he broke a blood-vessel in the stomach and lost much blood by the hemorrhage. The very day following was the Lord's day, and four outside preaching stations needed to be provided for, from which his disablement would withdraw one labourer to take his place at home. After an hour of prayer he felt that faith was given him to rise, dress, and go to the chapel; and, though very weak, so that the short walk wearied him, he was helped to preach as usual. After the service a medical friend remonstrated against his course as tending to permanent injury; but he replied that he should himself have regarded it presumptuous had not the Lord given him the faith. He preached both afternoon and evening, growing stronger rather than weaker with each effort, and suffering from no reaction afterward.

In reading Mr. Müller's biography and the record of such experiences, it is not probable that all will agree as to the wisdom of his course in every case. Some will commend, while others will, perhaps, condemn. He himself qualifies this entry in his journal with a wholesome caution that no reader should in such a matter follow his example, who *has not faith given him;* but assuring him that if God does give faith so to undertake for Him, such trust will prove like good coin and be honoured when presented. He himself did not always pursue a like course, because he had not always a like faith, and this leads him in his journal to draw a valuable distinction between the *gift of faith* and the *grace of faith,* which deserves careful consideration.

He observed that repeatedly he prayed with the sick till they were restored, he *asking unconditionally for the blessing of bodily health,* a thing which, he says, later on, he could not have done. Almost always in such cases the petition was granted, yet in some instances not. Once, in his own case, as early as 1829, he had been healed of a bodily infirmity of long standing, and which never returned. Yet this same man of God subsequently suffered from disease which was not in like manner healed, and in more than one case submitted to a costly operation at the hands of a skilful surgeon.

Some will doubtless say that even this man of faith lacked the faith necessary for the healing of his own body; but we must let him speak for himself, and especially as he gives his own view of the gift and the grace of faith. He says that the *gift* of faith is exercised, whenever we "do or believe a thing where the not doing or not believing would *not* be sin"; but the *grace* of faith, "where we do or believe what not to do or believe *would* be sin"; in one case we have no unequivocal command or promise to guide us, and in the other we have. The gift of faith is not always in exercise, but the grace must be, since it has the definite word of God to rest on, and the absence or even weakness of faith in such circumstances implies sin. There were instances, he adds, in which it pleased the Lord at times to bestow upon him something like the gift of faith so that he could ask unconditionally and expect confidently.

This journal we may now dismiss as a whole, having thus looked at the general features which characterize its many pages. But let it be repeated that to any reader who will for himself carefully examine its contents its perusal will prove a means of grace. To read a little at a time, and follow it with reflection and self-examination, will be found most stimulating to faith, though often most humiliating by reason of the conscious contrast suggested by the reader's unbelief and unfaithfulness. This man lived peculiarly with God and in God, and his senses were exercised to discern good and evil. His conscience became increasingly sensitive and his judgment singularly discriminating, so that he detected fallacies where they escape the common eye, and foresaw dangers which, like hidden rocks ahead, risk damage and, perhaps, destruction to service if not to character. And, therefore, so far is the writer of this memoir from desiring to displace that journal, that he rather seeks to incite many who have not read it to examine it for themselves. It will to such be found to mark a path of close daily walk with God, where, step by step, with circumspect vigilance, conduct and even motive are watched and weighed in God's own balances.

To sum up very briefly the impression made by the close perusal of this whole narrative with the supplementary annual reports, it is simply this: CONFIDENCE IN GOD.

In a little sketch of Beate Paulus, the Frau Pastorin pleads with God in a great crisis not to forsake her, quaintly adding that she was "willing to be the second whom He might forsake," but she was "determined not to be the *first.*"[10] George Müller believed that, in all ages, there had never yet been one true and trusting believer to whom God had proven false or faithless, and he was perfectly sure that He could be safely trusted who, "if we believe not, yet abideth faithful: He cannot deny Himself."[11] God has not only *spoken,* but *sworn;* His word is confirmed by His oath: because He could swear by no greater He sware by Himself. And all this that we might have a strong consolation; that we might have boldness in venturing upon Him, laying hold and holding fast His promise. Unbelief makes God a *liar* and, worse still, a *perjurer,* for it accounts Him as not only false to His word, but to His oath. George Müller believed, and because he believed, prayed; and praying, expected; and expecting, received. Blessed is he that believes, for there shall be a performance of those things which are spoken of the Lord.

10 Faith's Miracles, p. 48.
11 2 Timothy 2:13

CHAPTER VII

Led of God into a New Sphere

IF MUCH hangs and turns upon the choice of the *work* we are to do and the *field* where we are to do it, it must not be forgotten how much also depends on the *time* when it is undertaken, the *way* in which it is performed, and the *associates* in the labour. In all these matters the true workman will wait for the Master's beck, glance, or signal, before a step is taken.

We have come now to a new fork in the road where the path ahead begins to be more plain. The future and permanent centre of his life-work is at this point clearly indicated to God's servant by divine leading.

In March, 1832, his friend Mr. Henry Craik left Shaldon for four weeks of labour *in Bristol*, where Mr. Müller's strong impression was that the Lord had for Mr. Craik some more lasting sphere of work, though as yet it had not dawned upon his mind that he himself was to be a co-worker in that sphere, and to find in that very city the place of his permanent abode and the centre of his life's activities. God again led the blind by a way he knew not. The conviction, however, had grown upon him that the Lord was loosing him from Teignmouth, and, without having in view any other definite field, he felt that his ministry there was drawing to a close; and he inclined to go about again from place to place, seeking especially to bring believers to a fuller trust in God and a deeper sense of His faithfulness, and to a more thorough search into His word. His inclination to such itinerant work was strengthened by the fact that outside of Teignmouth his preaching both gave him much more enjoyment and sense of power, and drew more hearers.

On April 13th a letter from Mr. Craik, inviting Mr. Müller to join in his work at Bristol, made such an impression on his mind that he began prayerfully to consider whether it was not God's call, and whether a field more suited to his gifts was not opening to him. The following Lord's day, preaching on the Lord's coming, he referred to the effect of this blessed hope in impelling God's messenger to bear witness more widely and from place to place, and reminded the brethren that he had refused to bind himself to abide with them that he might at any moment be free to follow the divine leading elsewhere.

SCRIPTURE TESTIMONY
Like Jesus, the believer needs time alone with God Mark 1:35 · Luke 5:15-16

On April 20th Mr. Müller left for Bristol. On the journey he was dumb, having no liberty in speaking for Christ or even in giving away tracts, and this led him to reflect. He saw that the so-called 'work of the Lord' had tempted him to substitute *action for meditation and communion.* He had neglected that still hour' with God which supplies to spiritual life alike its breath and its bread. No lesson is more important for us to learn, yet how slow are we to learn it: that for the lack of habitual seasons set apart for devout meditation upon the word of God and for prayer, nothing else will compensate.

We are prone to think, for example, that converse with Christian brethren, and the general round of Christian activity, especially when we are much busied with preaching the Word and visits to inquiring or needy souls, make up for the loss of aloneness with God in the secret place. We hurry to a public service with but a few minutes of private prayer, allowing precious time to be absorbed in social pleasures, restrained from withdrawing from others by a false delicacy, when to excuse ourselves for needful communion with God and his word would have been perhaps the best witness possible to those whose company was holding us unduly! How often we rush from one public engagement to another without any proper interval for renewing our strength in waiting on the Lord, as though God cared more for the quantity than the quality of our service!

Here Mr. Müller had the grace to detect one of the foremost perils of a busy man in this day of insane hurry. He saw that if we are to feed others we must be fed; and that even public and united exercises of praise and prayer can never supply that food which is dealt out to the believer only in the closet—the shut-in place with its closed door and open window, where he meets God alone. In a previous chapter reference has been made to the fact that three times in the word of God we find a divine prescription for a true prosperity. God says to Joshua, "This book of the law shall not depart out of thy mouth; but thou shalt meditate therein day and night, that thou mayest observe to do according to all that is written therein: *for then thou shalt make thy way prosperous, and then thou shalt have good success"* (Joshua 1:8) Five hundred years later the inspired author of the first Psalm repeats the promise in unmistakable terms. The Spirit there says of him whose delight is in the law of the Lord and who in His law doth meditate day and night, that "he shall be like a tree planted by the rivers of water, that bringeth forth his fruit in his season; his leaf also shall not wither; and *whatsoever he doeth shall prosper."*

Here the devout meditative student of the blessed book of God is likened to an evergreen tree planted beside unfailing supplies of moisture; his fruit is perennial, and so is his verdure—and *whatsoever he doeth* prospers! More than a thousand years pass away, and, before the New Testament is sealed up as complete, once more the Spirit bears essentially the same blessed witness. "Whoso looketh into the perfect law of liberty and *continueth*" (i.e. continueth *looking*—meditating on what he there beholds, lest he forget the impression received through the mirror of the Word), *"this man shall be blessed in his deed"* (James 1:25)

Here then we have a threefold witness to the secret of true prosperity and unmingled blessing: devout meditation and reflection upon the Scriptures, which are at once a book of law, a river of life, and a mirror of self—fitted to convey the will of God, the life of God, and the transforming power of God. That believer makes a fatal mistake who *for any cause* neglects the prayerful study of the word of God. To read God's holy book, by it search one's self, and turn it into prayer and so into holy living, is the one great secret of growth in grace and godliness. The worker *for* God must first be a worker *with* God: he must have power with God and must prevail with Him in prayer, if he is to have power with men and prevail with men in preaching or in any form of witnessing and serving. At all costs let us make sure of that highest preparation for our work—the preparation of our own souls; and for this we must *take time* to be alone with His word and His Spirit, that we may truly meet God, and understand His will and the revelation of Himself.

If we seek the secrets of the life George Müller lived and the work he did, this is the very key to the whole mystery, and with that key any believer can unlock the doors to a prosperous growth in grace and power in service. God's word is His WORD—the expression of His thought, the revealing of His mind and heart. The supreme end of life is to know God and make Him known; and how is this possible so long as we neglect the very means He has chosen for conveying to us that knowledge! Even Christ, the Living Word, is to be found enshrined in the written word. Our knowledge of Christ is dependent upon our acquaintance with the Holy Scriptures, which are the reflection of His character and glory—the firmament across the expanse of which He moves as the Sun of righteousness.

On April 22, 1832, George Müller first stood in the pulpit of Gideon Chapel. The fact and the date are to be carefully marked as the new turning-point in a career of great usefulness. Henceforth, for almost exactly sixty-six years, Bristol is to be inseparably associated with his name. Could he have foreseen, on that Lord's day, what a work the Lord would do through him in that city; how from it as a centre his influence would radiate to the earth's ends, and how, even after his departure, he should continue to bear witness by the works which should follow him, how his heart would have swelled and burst with holy gratitude and praise,—while in humility he shrank back in awe and wonder from a responsibility and an opportunity so vast and overwhelming!

In the afternoon of this first Sabbath he preached at Pithay Chapel a sermon conspicuously owned of God. Among others converted by it was a young man, a notorious drunkard. And, before the sun had set, Mr. Müller, who in the evening heard Mr. Craik preach, was fully persuaded that the Lord had brought him to Bristol for a purpose, and that for a while, at least, there he was to labour. Both he and his brother Craik felt, however, that Bristol was not the place to reach a clear decision, for the judgment was liable to be unduly biassed when subject to the pressure of personal urgency, and so they determined to return to their respective fields of previous labour, there to wait quietly upon the Lord for the promised wisdom from above. They left for Devonshire on the first of May; but already a brother had been led to assume the responsibility for the rent of Bethesda Chapel as a place for their joint labours, thus securing a second commodious building for public worship.

Such blessing had rested on these nine days of united testimony in Bristol that they both gathered that the Lord had assuredly called them thither. The seal of His sanction had been on all they had undertaken, and the last service at Gideon Chapel on April 29th had been so thronged that many went away for lack of room.

SCRIPTURE TESTIMONY
God will exalt the humble Matthew 23:12 · James 4:10 · 1 Peter 5:5-6 *Love and honor one another in brotherly affection* Romans 12:10

Mr. Müller found opportunity for the exercise of humility, for he saw that by many his brother's gifts were much preferred to his own; yet, as Mr. Craik would come to Bristol only with him as a yokefellow, God's grace enabled him to accept the humiliation of being the less popular, and comforted him with the thought that two are better than one, and that each might possibly fill up some lack in the other, and thus both together prove a greater benefit and blessing alike to sinners and to saints—as the result showed. That same grace of God helped Mr. Müller to rise higher—nay, let us rather say, to sink lower and, "in honor preferring one another," to rejoice rather than to be envious; and, like John the Baptist, to say within himself: "A man can receive nothing except it be given him from above." Such a humble spirit has even in this life oftentimes its recompense of reward. Marked as was the impress of Mr. Craik upon Bristol, Mr. Müller's influence was even deeper and wider. As Henry Craik died in 1866, his own work reached through a much longer period; and as he was permitted to make such extensive mission tours throughout the world, his witness was far more outreaching. The lowly-minded man who bowed down to take the lower place, consenting to be the more obscure, was by God exalted to the higher seat and greater throne of influence.

Within a few weeks the Lord's will, as to their new sphere, became so plain to both these brethren that on May 23d Mr. Müller left Teignmouth for Bristol, to be followed next day by Mr. Craik. At the believers' meeting at Gideon Chapel they stated their terms, which were acceded to: that they were to be regarded as accepting no fixed relationship to the congregation, preaching in such manner and for such a season as should seem to them according to the Lord's will; that they should not be under bondage to any rules among them; that *pew-rents should be done away with;* and that they should, as in Devonshire, *look to the Lord to supply all temporal wants through the voluntary offerings of those to whom they ministered.*

Within a month Bethesda Chapel had been so engaged for a year as to risk no debt, and on July 6th services began there as at Gideon. From the very first, the Spirit set His seal on the joint work of these two brethren. Ten days after the opening service at Bethesda, an evening being set for inquirers, the throng of those seeking counsel was so great that more than four hours were consumed in ministering to individual souls, and so from time to time similar meetings were held with like encouragement.

August 13, 1832, was a memorable day. On that evening at Bethesda Chapel Mr. Müller, Mr. Craik, one other brother, and four sisters—*only seven in all*—sat down together, uniting in church fellowship *"without any rules,—desiring to act only as the Lord should be pleased to give light through His word."*

This is a very short and simple entry in Mr. Müller's journal, but it has most solemn significance. It records what was to him separation to the hallowed work of building up a simple apostolic church, with no manual of guidance but the New Testament; and in fact it introduces us to the THIRD PERIOD of his life, when he entered fully upon the work to which God had set him apart. The further steps now followed in rapid succession. God having prepared the workman and gathered the material, the structure went on quietly and rapidly until the life-work was complete.

Cholera was at this time raging in Bristol. This terrible 'scourge of God' first appeared about the middle of July and continued for three months, prayer-meetings being held often, and for a time daily, to plead for the removal of this visitation. Death stalked abroad, the knell of funeral-bells almost constantly sounding, and much solemnity hanging like a dark pall over the community. Of course many visits to the sick, dying, and afflicted became necessary, but it is remarkable that, among all the children of God among whom Mr. Müller and Mr. Craik laboured, but one died of this disease.

In the midst of all this gloom and sorrow of a fatal epidemic, a little daughter was born to Mr. and Mrs. Müller September 17, 1832. About her name, Lydia, sweet fragrance lingers, for she became one of God's purest saints and the beloved wife of James Wright. How little do we forecast at the time the future of a new-born babe who, like Samuel, may in God's decree be established to be a prophet of the Lord, or be set apart to some peculiar sphere of service, as in the case of another Lydia, whose heart the Lord opened and whom He called to be the nucleus of the first Christian church in Europe.

SCRIPTURE TESTIMONY
A workman of God handles the Word correctly 2 Timothy 2:15

Mr. Müller's unfeigned humility, and the docility that always accompanies that unconscious grace, found new exercise when the meetings with inquirers revealed the fact that his colleague's preaching was much more used of God than his own, in conviction and conversion. This discovery led to much self-searching, and he concluded that three reasons lay back of this fact: first, Mr. Craik was more spiritually minded than himself; second, he was more earnest in prayer for converting power; and third, he oftener spoke directly to the unsaved, in his public ministrations. Such disclosures of his own comparative lack did not exhaust themselves in vain self-reproaches, but led at once to more importunate prayer, more diligent preparation for addressing the unconverted, and more frequent appeals to this class. From this time on, Mr. Müller's preaching had the seal of God upon it equally with his brother's. What a wholesome lesson to learn, that for every defect in our service there is a cause, and that the one all-sufficient remedy is the throne of grace, where in every time of need we may boldly come to find grace and help! It has been already noted that Mr. Müller did not satisfy himself with more prayer, but gave new diligence and study to the preparation of discourses adapted to awaken careless souls. In the supernatural as well as the natural sphere, there is a law of cause and effect. Even the Spirit of God works not without order and method; He has His chosen channels through which He pours blessing. There is no accident in the spiritual world. "The Spirit bloweth where He listeth," but even the wind has its circuits. There is a kind of preaching, fitted to bring conviction and conversion, and there is another kind which is not so fitted. Even in the faithful use of truth there is room for discrimination and selection. In the armory of the word of God are many weapons, and all have their various uses and adaptations. Blessed is the workman or warrior who seeks to know what particular implement or instrument God appoints for each particular work or conflict. We are to study to keep in such communion with His word and Spirit as that we shall be true workmen that need "not to be ashamed, rightly dividing the word of truth." (2 Timothy 2:15)

This expression, found in Paul's second letter to Timothy, is a very peculiar one (*ορθοτομοΰντα τον λόγον τής αληθειας*). It seems to be nearly equivalent to the Latin phrase *recte viam secare—to cut a straight road*—and to hint that the true workman of God is like the civil engineer to whom it is given to construct a direct road to a certain point. The hearer's heart and conscience is the objective point, and the aim of the preacher should be, so to use God's truth as to reach most directly and effectively the needs of the hearer. He is to avoid all circuitous routes, all evasions, all deceptive apologies and by-ways of argument, and seek by God's help to find the shortest, straightest, quickest road to the convictions and resolutions of those to whom he speaks. And if the road-builder, before he takes any other step, first carefully *surveys his territory and lays out his route,* how much more should the preacher first study the needs of his hearers and the best ways of successfully dealing with them, and then with even more carefulness and prayerfulness study the adaptation of the word of God and the gospel message to meet those wants.

SCRIPTURE TESTIMONY
God communicating during prayer   Acts 11:5 · Acts 13:2-3

Early in the year 1833, letters from missionaries in Baghdad urged Messrs. Müller and Craik to join them in labours in that distant field, accompanying the invitation with drafts for two hundred pounds for costs of travel. Two weeks of prayerful inquiry as to the mind of the Lord, however, led them to a clear decision *not* to go—a choice never regretted, and which is here recorded only as part of a complete biography, and as illustrating the manner in which each new call for service was weighed and decided.

We now reach another stage of Mr. Müller's entrance upon his complete life-work. In February, 1832, he had begun to read the biography of A. H. Francké, the founder of the Orphan Houses of Halle. As that life and work were undoubtedly used of God to make him a like instrument in a kindred service, and to mould even the methods of his philanthropy, a brief sketch of Francké's career may be helpful.

August H. Francké was Müller's fellow countryman. About 1696, at Halle in Prussia, he had commenced the largest enterprise for poor children then existing in the world. He trusted in God, and He whom he trusted did not fail him, but helped him throughout abundantly.

The institutions, which resembled rather a large street than a building, were erected, and in them about two thousand orphan children were housed, fed, clad, and taught. For about thirty years all went on under Francké's own eyes, until 1727, when it pleased the Master to call the servant up higher; and after his departure his like-minded son-in-law became the director. Two hundred years have passed, and these Orphan Houses are still in existence, serving their noble purpose.

It is needful only to look at these facts and compare with Francké's work in Halle George Müller's monuments to a prayer-hearing God on Ashley Down, to see that in the main the latter work so far resembles the former as to be in not a few respects its counterpart. Mr. Müller began his orphan work a little more than one hundred years after Francké's death; ultimately housed, fed, clothed, and taught over two thousand orphans year by year; personally supervised the work for over sixty years—twice as long a period as that of Francké's personal management—and at his decease likewise left his like minded son-in-law to be his successor as the sole director of the work. It need not be added that, beginning his enterprise like Francké in dependence on God alone, the founder of the Bristol Orphan Houses trusted from first to last only in Him.

Memorial Statue of A. H. Francké, Halle

It is very noticeable how, when God is preparing a workman for a certain definite service, He often leads him out of the beaten track into a path peculiarly His own by means of some striking biography, or by contact with some other living servant who is doing some such work, and exhibiting the spirit which must guide if there is to be a true success. Meditation on Francké's life and work naturally led this man who was hungering for a wider usefulness to think more of the poor homeless waifs about him, and to ask whether he also could not plan under God some way to provide for them; and as he was musing the fire burned.

As early as June 12, 1833, when not yet twenty-eight years old, the inward flame began to find vent in a scheme which proved the first forward step toward his orphan work. It occurred to him to gather out of the streets, at about eight o'clock each morning, the poor children, give them a bit of bread for breakfast, and then, for about an hour and a half, teach them to read or read to them the Holy Scriptures; and later on to do a like service to the adult and aged poor. He began at once to feed from thirty to forty such persons, confident that, as the number increased, the Lord's provision would increase also. Unburdening his heart to Mr. Craik, he was guided to a place which could hold one hundred and fifty children and which could be rented for ten shillings yearly; as also to an aged brother who would gladly undertake the teaching.

Unexpected obstacles, however, prevented the carrying out of this plan. The work already pressing upon Mr. Müller and Mr. Craik, the rapid increase of applicants for food, and the annoyance to neighbours of having crowds of idlers congregating in the streets and lying about in troops—these were some of the reasons why this method was abandoned. But the *central thought and aim* were never lost sight of: God had planted a seed in the soil of Mr. Müller's heart, presently to spring up in the orphan work, and in the Scriptural Knowledge Institution with its many branches and far-reaching fruits.

From time to time a backward glance over the Lord's dealings encouraged his heart, as he looked forward to unknown paths and untried scenes. He records at this time—the close of the year 1833—that during the four years since he first began to trust in the Lord alone for temporal supplies he had suffered no want. He had received during the first year one hundred and thirty pounds, during the second one hundred and fifty-one, during the third one hundred and ninety-five, and during the last two hundred and sixty-seven—all in free-will offerings and without ever asking any human being for a penny. He had looked alone to the Lord, yet he had not only received a supply, but an increasing supply, year by year. Yet he also noticed that at each year's close he had very little, if anything, left, and that much had come through strange channels, from distances very remote, and from parties whom he had never seen. He observed also that in every case, according as the need was greater or less, the supply corresponded. He carefully records for the benefit of others that, when the calls for help were many, the Great

Provider showed Himself able and willing to send help accordingly.[12] The ways of divine dealing which he had thus found true of the early years of his life of trust were marked and magnified in all his after-experience, and the lessons learned in these first four years prepared him for others taught in the same school of God and under the same Teacher.

Thus God had brought His servant by a way which he knew not to the very place and sphere of his life's widest and most enduring work. He had moulded and shaped His chosen vessel, and we are now to see to what purposes of world-wide usefulness that earthen vessel was to be put, and how conspicuously the excellency of the power was to be of God and not of man.

12 Vol. I 105.

CHAPTER VIII

A Tree of God's Own Planting

THE TIME was now fully come when the divine Husbandman was to glorify Himself by a product of His own husbandry in the soil of Bristol.

On February 20, 1834, George Müller was led of God to sow the seed of what ultimately developed into a great means of good, known as "The Scriptural Knowledge Institution, for Home and Abroad." As in all other steps of his life, this was the result of much prayer, meditation on the Word, searching of his own heart, and patient waiting to know the mind of God.

A brief statement of the reasons for founding such an institution, and the principles on which it was based, will be helpful at this point. Motives of conscience controlled Mr. Müller and Mr. Craik in starting a new work rather than in uniting with existing societies already established for missionary purposes, Bible and tract distribution, and for the promotion of Christian schools. As they had sought to conform personal life and church conduct wholly to the scriptural pattern, they felt that all work for God should be carefully carried on in exact accordance with His known will, in order to have His fullest blessing. Many features of the existing societies seemed to them extra-scriptural, if not decidedly anti-scriptural, and these they felt constrained to avoid.

For example, they felt that the *end proposed* by such organizations, namely, *the conversion of the world* in this dispensation, was not justified by the Word, which everywhere represents this as the age of the *outgathering of the church* from the world, and not the *ingathering of the world* into the church. To set such an end before themselves as the world's conversion would therefore not only be unwarranted by Scripture, but delusive and disappointing, disheartening God's servants by the failure to realize the result, and dishonoring to God Himself by making Him to appear unfaithful.

Again, these existing societies seemed to Mr. Müller and Mr. Craik to sustain a *wrong relation to the world*—mixed up with it, instead of separate from it. Any one by paying a certain fixed sum of money might become a member or even a director, having a voice or vote in the conduct of affairs and becoming eligible to office. Unscriptural means were commonly used to *raise money*, such as appealing for aid to unconverted persons, asking for donations simply for money's sake and without regard to the character of the donors or the manner in which the money was obtained. The custom of *seeking patronage* from men of the world and asking such to preside at public meetings, and the habit of *contracting debts*,—these and some other methods of management seemed so unscriptural and unspiritual that the founders of this new institution could not with a good conscience give them sanction. Hence they hoped that by basing their work upon thoroughly biblical principles they might secure many blessed results.

First of all, they confidently believed that the work of the Lord could be best and most successfully carried on within the landmarks and limits set up in His word; that the fact of thus carrying it on would give boldness in prayer and confidence in labour. But they also desired the work itself to be a witness to the living God, and a testimony to believers, by calling attention to the objectionable methods already in use and encouraging all God's true servants in adhering to the principles and practices which He has sanctioned.

On March 5th at a public meeting a formal announcement of the intention to found such an institution was accompanied by a full statement of its purposes and principles,[13] in substance as follows:

1. Every believer's duty and privilege is to help on the cause and work of Christ.
2. The patronage of the world is not to be sought after, depended upon, or countenanced.
3. Pecuniary aid, or help in managing or carrying on its affairs, is not to be asked for or sought from those who are not believers.
4. Debts are not to be contracted or allowed for any cause in the work of the Lord.
5. The standard of success is not to be a numerical or financial standard.
6. All compromise of the truth or any measures that impair testimony to God are to be avoided.

Thus the word of God was accepted as counsellor, and all dependence was on God's blessing in answer to prayer.

The *objects* of the institution were likewise announced as follows:

---

13 Appendix D. Journal I. 107-118.

1. To establish or aid day-schools, Sunday-schools, and adult-schools, taught and conducted only by believers and on thoroughly scriptural principles.
2. To circulate the Holy Scriptures, wholly or in portions, over the widest possible territory.
3. To aid missionary efforts and assist labourers, in the Lord's vineyard anywhere, who are working upon a biblical basis and looking only to the Lord for support.

To project such a work, on such a scale, and at such a time, was doubly an act of faith; for not only was the work already in hand enough to tax all available time and strength, but at this very time this record appears in Mr. Müller's journal: *"We have only one shilling left."* Surely no advance step would have been taken, had not the eyes been turned, not on the empty purse, but on the full and exhaustless treasury of a rich and bountiful Lord!

It was plainly God's purpose that, out of such abundance of poverty, the riches of His liberality should be manifested. It pleased Him, from whom and by whom are all things, that the work should be begun when His servants were poorest and weakest, that its growth to such giant proportions might the more prove it to be a plant of His own right hand's planting, and that His word might be fulfilled in its whole history:

> "I the Lord do keep it:
> I will water it every moment:
> Lest any hurt it, I will keep it night and day:" (Isaiah 27:3)

Whatever may be thought as to the need of such a new organization, or as to such scruples as moved its founders to insist even in minor matters upon the closest adherence to scripture teaching, this at least is plain, that for more than half a century it has stood upon its original foundation, and its increase and usefulness have surpassed the most enthusiastic dreams of its founders; nor have the principles first avowed ever been abandoned. With the Living God as its sole patron, and prayer as its only appeal, it has attained vast proportions, and its world-wide work has been signally owned and blessed.

On March 19th Mrs. Müller gave birth to a son, to the great joy of his parents; and, after much prayer, they gave him the name Elijah—"My God is Jah"—the name itself being one of George Müller's life-mottoes. Up to this time the families of Mr. Müller and Mr. Craik had dwelt under one roof, but henceforth it was thought wise that they should have separate lodgings.

When, at the close of 1834, the usual backward glance was cast over the Lord's leadings and dealings, Mr. Müller gratefully recognized the divine goodness which had thus helped him to start upon its career the work with its several departments. Looking to the Lord alone for light and help, he had laid the corner-stone of this "little institution"; and in October, after only seven months' existence, it had already begun to be established. In the Sunday-school there were one hundred and twenty children; in the adult classes, forty; in the four day-schools, two hundred and nine boys and girls; four hundred and eighty-two Bibles and five hundred and twenty Testaments had been put into circulation, and fifty-seven pounds had been spent in aid of missionary operations. During these seven months the Lord had sent, in answer to prayer, over one hundred and sixty-seven pounds in money, and much blessing upon the work itself. The brothers and sisters who were in charge had likewise been given by the same prayer-hearing God, in direct response to the cry of need and the supplication of faith.

Meanwhile another *object* was coming into greater prominence before the mind and heart of Mr. Müller: it was the thought of *making some permanent provision for fatherless and motherless children.*

An orphan boy who had been in the school had been taken to the poorhouse, no longer able to attend on account of extreme poverty; and this little incident set Mr. Müller thinking and praying about orphans. Could not something be done to meet the temporal and spiritual wants of this class of very poor children? Unconsciously to himself, God had set a seed in his soul, and was watching and watering it. The idea of a definite orphan work had taken root within him, and, like any other living germ, it was springing up and growing, he knew not how. As yet it was only in the blade, but in time there would come the ear and the full-grown corn in the ear, the new seed of a larger harvest.

Meanwhile the church was growing. In these two and a half years over two hundred had been added, making the total membership two hundred and fifty-seven; but the enlargement of the work generally neither caused the church life to be neglected nor any one department of duty to suffer declension—a very noticeable fact in this history.

The point to which we have now come is one of double interest and importance, as at once a point of arrival and of departure. The work of God's chosen servant may be considered as fairly if not fully inaugurated *in all its main forms of service.* He himself is in his thirtieth year, the age when his divine Master began to be fully manifest to the world and to go about doing good. Through the preparatory steps and stages leading up to his complete mission and ministry to the church and the world, Christ's humble disciple has likewise been brought, and his fuller career of usefulness now begins, with the various agencies in operation whereby for more than threescore years he was to show both proof and example of what God can do through one man who is willing to be simply the instrument for Him to work with. Nothing is more marked in George Müller, to the very day of his death, than this, that he so looked to God and leaned on

God that he felt himself to be nothing, and God everything. He sought to be always and in all things surrendered as a passive tool to the will and hand of the Master Workman.

This point of arrival and of departure is also a point of *prospect.* Here, halting and looking backward, we may take in at a glance the various successive steps and stages of preparation whereby the Lord had made His servant ready for the sphere of service to which He called, and for which He fitted him. One has only, from this height, to look over the ten years that were past, to see beyond dispute or doubt the divine design that lay back of George Müller's life, and to feel an awe of the God who thus chooses and shapes, and then uses, His vessels of service.

It will be well, even if it involves some repetition, to pass in review the more important steps in the process by which the divine Potter had shaped His vessel for His purpose, educating and preparing George Müller for His work.

1. First of all, his *conversion.* In the most unforeseen manner and at the most unexpected time God led him to turn from the error of his way, and brought him to a saving knowledge of Jesus Christ.
2. Next, his *missionary spirit.* That consuming flame was kindled within him which, when it is fanned by the Spirit and fed by the fuel of facts, inclines to unselfish service and makes one willing to go wherever, and to do whatever, the Lord will.
3. Next, his *renunciation of self.* In more than one instance he was enabled to give up for Christ's sake an earthly attachment that was idolatrous, because it was a hindrance to his full obedience and single-eyed loyalty to his heavenly Master.
4. Then his *taking counsel of God.* Early in his Christian life he formed the habit, in things great and small, of ascertaining the will of the Lord before taking action, asking guidance in every matter, through the Word and the Spirit.
5. His humble and *childlike temper.* The Father drew His child to Himself, imparting to him the simple mind that asks believingly and trusts confidently, and the filial spirit that submits to fatherly counsel and guidance.
6. His *method of preaching.* Under this same divine tuition he early learned how to preach the Word, in simple dependence on the Spirit of God, studying the Scriptures in the original and expounding them without wisdom of words.
7. His *cutting loose from man.* Step by step, all dependence on man or appeals to man for pecuniary support were abandoned, together with all borrowing, running into debt, stated salary, etc. His eyes were turned to God alone as the Provider.

8. His *satisfaction in the Word.* As knowledge of the Scriptures grew, love for the divine oracles increased, until all other books, even of a religious sort, lost their charms in comparison with God's own text-book, as explained and illumined by the divine Interpreter.
9. His *thorough Bible study.* Few young men have ever been led to such a systematic search into the treasures of God's truth. He read the Book of God through and through, fixing its teachings on his mind by meditation and translating them into practice.
10. His *freedom from human control.* He felt the need of independence of man in order to complete dependence on God, and boldly broke all fetters that hindered his liberty in preaching, in teaching, or in following the heavenly Guide and serving the heavenly Master.
11. His *use of opportunity.* He felt the value of souls, and he formed habits of approaching others as to matters of salvation, even in public conveyances. By a word of witness, a tract, a humble example, he sought constantly to lead some one to Christ.
12. His *release from civil obligations.* This was purely providential. In a strange way God set him free from all liability to military service, and left him free to pursue his heavenly calling as His soldier, without entanglement in the affairs of this life.
13. His *companions in service.* Two most efficient coworkers were divinely provided: first his brother Craik so like-minded with himself, and secondly, his wife, so peculiarly God's gift, both of them proving great aids in working and in bearing burdens of responsibility.
14. His *view of the Lord's coming.* He thanked God for unveiling to him that great truth, considered by him as second to no other in its influence upon his piety and usefulness; and in the light of it he saw clearly the purpose of this gospel age, to be not to convert the world but to call out from it a believing church as Christ's bride.
15. His *waiting on God for a message.* For every new occasion he asked of Him a word in season; then a mode of treatment, and unction in delivery; and, in godly simplicity and sincerity, with the demonstration of the Spirit, he aimed to reach the hearers.
16. His submission to the *authority of the Word.* In the light of the holy oracles he reviewed all customs, however ancient, and all traditions of men, however popular, submitted all opinions and practices to the test of Scripture, and then, regardless of consequences, walked according to any new light God gave him.
17. His *pattern of church life.* From his first entrance upon pastoral work, he sought to lead others only by himself following the Shepherd and Bishop of Souls. He urged the assembly of believers to conform in all

things to New Testament models so far as they could be clearly found in the Word, and thus reform all existing abuses.

18. His *stress upon voluntary offerings.* While he courageously gave up all fixed salary for himself, he taught that all the work of God should be maintained by the freewill gifts of believers, and that pew-rents promote invidious distinctions among saints.
19. His *surrender of all earthly possessions.* Both himself and his wife literally sold all they had and gave alms, henceforth to live by the day, hoarding no money even against a time of future need, sickness, old age, or any other possible crisis of want.
20. His habit of *secret prayer.* He learned so to prize closet communion with God that he came to regard it as his highest duty and privilege. To him nothing could compensate for the lack or loss of that fellowship with God and meditation on His word which are the support of all spiritual life.
21. His *jealousy of his testimony.* In taking oversight of a congregation he took care to guard himself from all possible interference with fulness and freedom of utterance and of service. He could not brook any restraints upon his speech or action that might compromise his allegiance to the Lord or his fidelity to man.
22. His *organizing of work.* God led him to project a plan embracing several departments of holy activity, such as the spreading of the knowledge of the word of God everywhere, and the encouraging of world-wide evangelization and the Christian education of the young; and to guard the new Institution from all dependence on worldly patronage, methods, or appeals.
23. His *sympathy with orphans.* His loving heart had been drawn out toward poverty and misery everywhere, but especially in the case of destitute children bereft of both parents; and familiarity with Francké's work at Halle suggested similar work at Bristol.
24. Beside all these steps of preparation, he had been guided by the Lord from his birthplace in Prussia to London, Teignmouth, and Bristol in Britain, and thus the chosen vessel, shaped for its great use, had by the same divine Hand been borne to the very place where it was to be of such signal service in testimony to the Living God.

Surely no candid observer can survey this course of divine discipline and preparation, and remember how brief was the period of time it covers, being less than ten years, and mark the many distinct steps by which this education for a life of service was made singularly complete, without a feeling of wonder and awe. Every prominent feature, afterward to appear conspicuous in the career of this servant of God, was anticipated in the training whereby he was fitted for his work and introduced to it. We have had a vivid vision of the divine Potter sitting at His wheel, taking the clay in His hands, softening its hardness, subduing it to His own will; then gradually and skilfully shaping from it the earthen vessel; then baking it in His oven of discipline till it attained the requisite solidity and firmness, then filling it with the rich treasures of His word and Spirit, and finally setting it down where He would have it serve His special uses in conveying to others the excellency of His power!

To lose sight of this sovereign shaping Hand is to miss one of the main lessons God means to teach us by George Müller's whole career. He himself saw and felt that he was only an earthen vessel; that God had both chosen and filled him for the work he was to do; and, while this conviction made him happy in his work, it made him humble, and the older he grew the humbler he became. He felt more and more his own utter insufficiency. It grieved him that human eyes should ever turn away from the Master to the servant, and he perpetually sought to avert their gaze from himself to God alone. "For of Him, and through Him, and to Him are all things—to Whom be glory for ever and ever. Amen."

There are several important episodes in Mr. Müller's history which may be lightly passed by, because not so characteristic of him as that they might not have been common to many others, and therefore not constituting features so distinguishing this life from others as to make it a special lesson to believers.

For example, early in 1835 he made a visit to Germany upon a particular errand. He went to aid Mr. Groves, who had come from the East Indies to get missionary recruits, and who asked help of him, as of one knowing the language of the country, in setting the claims of India before German brethren, and pleading for its unsaved millions.

When Mr. Müller went to the alien office in London to get a passport, he found that, through ignorance, he had broken the law which required every alien semi-annually to renew his certificate of residence, under penalty of fifty pounds fine or imprisonment. He confessed to the officer his non-compliance, excusing himself only on the ground of ignorance, and trusted all consequences with God, who graciously inclined the officer to pass over his non-compliance with the law. Another hindrance which still interfered with obtaining his passport, was also removed in answer to prayer; so that at the outset he was much impressed with the Lord's sanction of his undertaking.

His sojourn abroad continued for nearly two months, during which time he was at Paris, Strasburg, Basle, Tubingen, Wurtemberg, Sehaffhausen, Stuttgart, Halle, Sandersleben, Aschersleben, Heimersleben, Halberstadt, and Hamburg. At Halle, calling on Dr. Tholuck after seven years of separation, he was warmly welcomed and constrained to lodge at his house. From Dr. Tholuck he heard many delightful incidents as to former fellow students who had been turned to the Lord from impious paths, or had been strengthened in their Christian faith

Bethesda Chapel, Bristol

Bethesda Chapel, Interior

and devotion. He also visited Francké's orphan houses, spending an evening in the very room where God's work of grace had begun in his heart, and meeting again several of the same little company of believers that in those days had prayed together.

He likewise gave everywhere faithful witness to the Lord. While at his father's house the way was opened for him to bear testimony indirectly to his father and brother. He had found that a direct approach to his father upon the subject of his soul's salvation only aroused his anger, and he therefore judged that it was wiser to refrain from a course which would only repel one whom he desired to win. An unconverted friend of his father was visiting him at this time, before whom he put the truth very frankly and fully, in the presence of both his father and brother, and thus quite as effectively gave witness to them also. But he was especially moved to pray that he might by his whole life bear witness at his home, manifesting his love for his kindred and his own joy in God, his satisfaction in Christ, and his utter indifference to all former fascinations of a worldly and sinful life, through the supreme attraction he found in Him; for this, he felt sure, would have far more influence than any mere words: our walk counts for more than our talk, always.

The effect was most happy. God so helped the son to live before the father that, just before his leaving for England, he said to him: "My son, may God help me to follow your example, and to act according to what you have said to me!"

On June 22, 1835, Mr. Müller's father-in-law, Mr. Groves, died; and both of his own children were very ill, and four days later little Elijah was taken. Both parents had been singularly prepared for these bereavements, and were divinely upheld. They had felt no liberty in prayer for the child's recovery, dear as he was; and grandfather and grandson were laid in one grave. Henceforth Mr. and Mrs. Müller were to have no son, and Lydia was to remain their one and only child.

About the middle of the following month, Mr. Müller was quite disabled from work by weakness of the chest, which made necessary rest and change. The Lord tenderly provided for his need through those whose hearts He touched, leading them to offer him and his wife hospitalities in the Isle of Wight, while at the same time money was sent him which was designated for 'a change of air.' On his thirtieth birthday, in connection with specially refreshing communion with God, and for the first time since his illness, there was given him a spirit of believing prayer for his own recovery; and his strength so rapidly grew that by the middle of October he was back in Bristol.

It was just before this, on the ninth of the same month, that *the reading of John Newton's Life stirred him up to bear a similar witness to the Lord's dealings with himself.* Truly there are no little things in our life, since what seems to be trivial may be the means of bringing about results of great consequence. This is the second time that a chance reading of a book had proved a turning-point with George Müller. Francké's life stirred his heart to begin an orphan work, and Newton's life suggested the narrative of the Lord's dealings. To what is called an accident are owing, under God, those pages of his life-journal which read like new chapters in the Acts of the Apostles, and will yet be so widely read, and so largely used of God.

CHAPTER IX

The Growth of God's Own Plant

THE LAST great step of full entrance upon Mr. Müller's life-service was the *founding of the orphan work,* a step so important and so prominent that even the lesser particulars leading to it have a strange significance and fascination.

In the year 1835, on November 20th, in taking tea at the house of a Christian sister, he again saw a copy of Francké's life. For no little time he had thought of like labours, though on no such scale, nor in mere imitation of Francké, but under a sense of similar divine leading. This impression had grown into a conviction, and the conviction had blossomed into a resolution which now rapidly ripened into corresponding action. He was emboldened to take this forward step in sole reliance on God, by the fact that at that very time, in answer to prayer, ten pounds more had been sent him than he had asked for other existing work, as though God gave him a token of both willingness and readiness to supply all needs.

Nothing is more worthy of imitation, perhaps, than the uniformly deliberate, self-searching, and prayerful way in which he set about any work which he felt led to undertake. It was preeminently so in attempting this new form of service, the future growth of which was not then even in his thought. In daily prayer he sought as in his Master's presence to sift from the pure grain of a godly purpose to glorify Him, all the chaff of selfish and carnal motives, to get rid of every taint of worldly self-seeking or lust of applause, and to bring every thought into captivity to the Lord. He constantly probed his own heart to discover the secret and subtle impulses which are unworthy of a true servant of God; and, believing that a spiritually minded brother often helps one to an insight into his own heart, he spoke often to his brother Craik about his plans, praying God to use him as a means of exposing any unworthy motive, or of suggesting any scriptural objections to his project. His honest aim being to please God, he yearned to know his own heart, and welcomed any light which revealed his real self and prevented a mistake.

Mr. Craik so decidedly encouraged him, and further prayer so confirmed previous impressions of God's guidance, that on December 2, 1835, the *first formal step was taken* in ordering printed bills announcing a public meeting for the week following, when the proposal to open an orphan house was to be laid before brethren, and further light to be sought unitedly as to the mind of the Lord.

Three days later, in reading the Psalms, he was struck with these nine words:

> "Open thy mouth wide, and I will fill it." (Psalm 81:10)

From that moment this text formed one of his great life-mottoes, and this promise became a power in moulding all his work. Hitherto he had not prayed for the supply of money or of helpers, but he was now led to apply this scripture confidently to this new plan, and at once boldly to ask *for premises, and for one thousand pounds in money, and for suitable helpers to take charge of the children.* Two days after, he received, in furtherance of his work, the *first gift of money—one shilling*—and within two days more the *first donation in furniture*—a large wardrobe.

The day came for the memorable public meeting—December 9th. During the interval Satan had been busy hurling at Mr. Müller his fiery darts, and he was very low in spirit. He was taking a step not to be retraced without both much humiliation to himself and reproach to his Master: and what if it were a *misstep* and he were moving without real guidance from above! But as soon as he began to speak, help was given him. He was borne up on the Everlasting Arms, and had the assurance that the work was of the Lord. He cautiously avoided all appeals to the transient feelings of his hearers, and took no collection, desiring all these first steps to be calmly taken, and every matter carefully and prayerfully weighed before a decision. Excitement of emotion or kindlings of enthusiasm might obscure the vision and hinder clear apprehension of the mind of God. After the meeting there was a voluntary gift of ten shillings, and one sister offered herself for the work. The next morning a statement concerning the new orphan work was put in print, and on January 16, 1836, a supplementary statement appeared.[14]

At every critical point Mr. Müller is entitled to explain his own views and actions; and the work he was now undertaking is so vitally linked with his whole after-life that it should here have full mention. As to his proposed orphan house he gives three chief reasons for its establishment:

1. That God may be glorified in so furnishing the means as to show that it is not a vain thing to trust in Him.

14 Appendix E. Narrative 1: 143-146, 148-152, 154, 155.

2. That the spiritual welfare of fatherless and motherless children may be promoted.
3. That their temporal good may be secured.

He had frequent reminders in his pastoral labours that the *faith of God's children greatly needed strengthening;* and he longed to have some visible proof to point to, that the heavenly Father is the same faithful Promiser and Provider as ever, and as willing to PROVE Himself the LIVING GOD to *all who put their trust in Him,* and that even in their old age He does not forsake those who rely only upon Him. Remembering the great blessing that had come to himself through the work of faith of Francké, he judged that he was bound to serve the Church of Christ *in being able to take God at His word and rely upon it.*

If he, a poor man, *without asking any one but God,* could get means to carry on an orphan house, it would be seen that God is FAITHFUL STILL and STILL HEARS PRAYER. While the orphan work was to be a branch of the Scriptural Knowledge Institution, only those funds were to be applied thereto which should be expressly given for that purpose; and it would be carried on only so far and so fast as the Lord should provide both money and helpers.

It was proposed to receive only such children as had been bereft of both parents, and to take in such from their seventh to their twelfth year, though later on younger orphans were admitted; and to bring up the boys for a trade, and the girls for service, and to give them all a plain education likely to fit them for their life-work.

So soon as the enterprise was fairly launched, the Lord's power and will to provide began at once and increasingly to appear; and, from this point on, the journal is one long record of man's faith and supplication and of God's faithfulness and interposition. It only remains to note the new steps in advance which mark the growth of the work, and the new straits which arise and how they are met, together with such questions and perplexing crises as from time to time demand and receive a new divine solution.

SCRIPTURE TESTIMONY
God's work will not lack God's supply Philippians 4:19

A foremost need was that of able and suitable helpers, which only God could supply. In order fully to carry out his plans, Mr. Müller felt that he must have men and women like-minded, who would naturally care for the state of the orphans and of the work. If one Achan could disturb the whole camp of Israel, and one Ananias or Saphira, the whole church of Christ, one faithless, prayerless, self-seeking assistant would prove not a helper but a hinderer both to the work itself and to all fellow-workers. No step was therefore hastily taken. He had patiently waited on God hitherto, and he now waited to receive at His hands His own chosen servants to join in this service and give to it unity of plan and spirit.

Before he called, the Lord answered. As early as December 10th a brother and sister had willingly offered themselves, and the spirit that moved them will appear in the language of their letter:

> "We propose ourselves for the service of the intended orphan house, if you think us qualified for it; also to give up all the furniture, etc., which the Lord has given us, for its use; and to do this without receiving any salary whatever; believing that, if it be the will of the Lord to employ us, He will supply all our need."

Other similar self-giving followed, proving that God's people are willing in the day of His power. He who wrought in His servant to will and to work, sent helpers to share his burdens, and to this day has met all similar needs out of His riches in glory. There has never yet been any lack of competent, cheerful, and devoted helpers, although the work so rapidly expanded and extended.

The gifts whereby the work was supported need a separate review that many lessons of interest may find a record. But it should here be noted that, among the first givers, was a poor needlewoman who brought the surprising sum of one hundred pounds, the singular self-denial and whole-hearted giving exhibited making this a peculiarly sacred offering and a token of God's favour. There was a felt significance in His choice of a poor sickly seamstress as His instrument for laying the foundations for this great work. He who worketh all things after the counsel of His own will, passing by the rich, mighty, and noble somethings of this world, chose again the poor, weak, base, despised nothings, that no flesh should glory in His presence.

For work among orphans a house was needful, and for this definite prayer was offered; and April 1, 1836, was fixed as the date for opening such house for female orphans, as the most helplessly destitute. The building, No. 6 Wilson Street, where Mr. Müller had himself lived up to March 25th, having been rented for one year, was formally opened April 21st, the day being set apart for prayer and praise. The public generally were informed that the way was open to receive needy applicants, and the intimation was further made on May 18th that it was intended shortly to open a second house for infant children—both boys and girls.

We now retrace our steps a little to take special notice of a fact in Mr. Müller's experience which, in point of time, belongs earlier.

Though he had brought before the Lord even the most minute details about his plans for the proposed orphan work and house and helpers, asking in faith for building and furnishing, money for rent and other expenses, etc., he confesses that he had never once asked the Lord to send the orphans! This seems an unaccountable omission; but the fact is he had assumed that there would be applications in abundance. His surprise and chagrin cannot easily be imagined, when the appointed time came for receiving applications, February 3rd, and *not one*

The First Orphan Houses (Rented), Bristol

application was made! Everything was ready *except the orphans.* This led to the deepest humiliation before God. All the evening of that day he literally lay on his face, probing his own heart to read his own motives, and praying God to search him and show him His mind. He was thus brought so low that from his heart he could say that, if God would thereby be more glorified, he would rejoice in the fact that his whole scheme should come to nothing. The very *next day* the first application was made for admission; on April 11th orphans began to be admitted; and by May 18th there were in the house twenty-six, and more daily expected. Several applications being made for children *under seven,* the conclusion was reached that, while vacancies were left, the limit of years at first fixed should not be adhered to; but every new step was taken with care and prayer, that it should not be in the energy of the flesh, or in the wisdom of man, but in the power and wisdom of the Spirit. How often we forget that solemn warning of the Holy Ghost, that even when our whole work is not imperilled by a false beginning, but is well laid upon a true foundation, we may carelessly build into it wood, hay, and stubble, which will be burned up in the fiery ordeal that is to try every man's work of what sort it is!

The first house had scarcely been opened for girls when the way for the second was made plain, suitable premises being obtained at No. 1 in the same street, and a well-fitted matron being given in answer to prayer. On November 28th, some seven months after the opening of the first, this second house was opened. Some of the older and abler girls from the first house were used for the domestic work of the second, partly to save hired help, and partly to accustom them to working for others and thus give a proper dignity to what is sometimes despised as a degrading and menial form of service. By April 8, 1837, there were in each house thirty orphan children.

SCRIPTURE TESTIMONY
Whatever you ask in prayer, in faith, abiding, you will receive Matthew 21:22 · Mark 11:24 · John 15:7 · 1 John 5:14-15

The founder of this orphan work, who had at the first asked for one thousand pounds of God, tells us that, in his own mind, the thing was *as good as done,* so that he often gave thanks for this large sum as though already in hand. (Mark 11:24; 1 John 5:13, 14) This habit of counting a promise as fulfilled had much to do with the triumphs of his faith and the success of his labour. Now that the first part of his Narrative of the Lord's Dealings was about to issue from the press, he felt that it would much honour the Master whom he served *if the entire amount should be actually in hand before the Narrative should appear, and without any one having been asked to contribute.* He therefore gave himself anew to prayer; and on June 15th the whole sum was complete, no appeal having been made but to the Living God, before whom, as he records with his usual mathematical precision, he had daily brought his petition for *eighteen months and ten days.*

In closing this portion of his narrative he hints at a proposed further enlargement of the work in a third house for orphan boys above seven years, with accommodations for about forty. Difficulties interposed, but as usual disappeared before the power of prayer. Meanwhile the whole work of the Scriptural Knowledge Institution prospered, four day-schools having been established, with over one thousand pupils, and more than four thousand copies of the word of God having been distributed.

George Müller was careful always to consult and then to obey conviction. Hence his moral sense, by healthy exercise, more and more clearly discerned good and evil. This conscientiousness was seen in the issue of the first edition of his Narrative. When the first five hundred copies came from the publishers, he was so weighed down by misgivings that he hesitated to distribute them. Notwithstanding the spirit of prayer with which he had begun, continued, and ended the writing of it and had made every correction in the proof; notwithstanding the motive, consciously cherished throughout, that God's glory might be promoted in this record of His faithfulness, he reopened with himself the whole question whether this published Narrative might not turn the eyes of men from the great Master Workman to His human instrument. As he opened the box containing the reports, he felt strongly tempted to withhold from circulation the pamphlets it held; but from the moment when he gave out the first copy, and the step could not be retraced, his scruples were silenced.

He afterward saw his doubts and misgivings to have been a temptation of Satan, and never thenceforth questioned that in writing, printing, and distributing this and the subsequent parts of the Narrative he had done the will of God. So broad and clear was the divine seal set upon it in the large blessing it brought to many and widely scattered persons that no room was left for doubt. It may be questioned whether any like journal has been as widely read and as remarkably used, both in converting sinners and in quickening saints. Proofs of this will hereafter abundantly appear.

It was in the year 1837 that Mr. Müller, then in his thirty-second year, felt with increasingly deep conviction that to his own growth in grace, godliness, and power for service *two things* were quite indispensable: first, more *retirement for secret communion with God,* even at the apparent expense of his public work; and second, ampler provision for the *spiritual oversight of the flock of God,* the total number of communicants now being near to four hundred.

The former of these convictions has an emphasis which touches every believer's life at its vital centre. George Müller was conscious of being too busy to pray as he ought. His outward action was too constant for inward reflection, and he saw that there was risk of losing peace and power, and that activity even in the most sacred sphere must not be so absorbing as to prevent holy meditation on the Word and fervent supplication. The Lord said first to Elijah, "GO, HIDE

THYSELF"; then, "GO, SHOW THYSELF." He who does not first hide himself in the secret place to be alone with God, is unfit to show himself in the public place to move among men. Mr. Müller afterward used to say to brethren who had "too much to do" to spend proper time with God, that four hours of work for which one hour of prayer prepares, is better than five hours of work with the praying left out; that our service to our Master is more acceptable and our mission to man more profitable, when saturated with the moisture of God's blessing—the dew of the Spirit. Whatever is gained in quantity is lost in quality whenever one engagement follows another without leaving proper intervals for refreshment and renewal of strength by waiting on God. No man, perhaps, since John Wesley has accomplished so much even in a long life as George Müller; yet few have ever withdrawn so often or so long into the pavilion of prayer. In fact, from one point of view his life seems more given to supplication and intercession than to mere action or occupation among men.

At the same time he felt that the curacy of souls must not be neglected by reason of his absorption in either work or prayer. Both believers and inquirers needed pastoral oversight; neither himself nor his brother Craik had time enough for visiting so large a flock, many of whom were scattered over the city; and about fifty new members were added every year who had special need of teaching and care. Again, as there were two separate congregations, the number of meetings was almost doubled; and the interruptions of visitors from near and far, the burdens of correspondence, and the oversight of the Lord's work generally, consumed so much time that even with two pastors the needs of the church could not be met. At a meeting of both congregations in October, these matters were frankly brought before the believers, and it was made plain that other helpers should be provided, and the two churches so united as to lessen the number of separate meetings.

SCRIPTURE TESTIMONY
If possible, live at peace with all Romans 12:18

In October, 1837, a building was secured for a third orphan house, for boys; but as the neighbours strongly opposed its use as a charitable institution, Mr Müller, with meekness of spirit, at once relinquished all claim upon the premises, being mindful of the maxim of Scripture: "As much as lieth in you, live peaceably with all men." (Romans 12:18) He felt sure that the Lord would provide, and his faith was rewarded in the speedy supply of a building in the same street where the other two houses were.

Infirmity of the flesh again tried the faith and patience of Mr. Müller. For eight weeks he was kept out of the pulpit. The strange weakness in the head, from which he had suffered before and which at times seemed to threaten his reason, forced him to rest; and in November he went to Bath and Weston-super-Mare, leaving to higher Hands the work to which he was unequal.

One thing he noticed and recorded: that, even during this head trouble, prayer and Bible-reading could be borne better than anything else. He concluded that whenever undue carefulness is expended on the body, it is very hard to avoid undue carelessness as to the soul; and that it is therefore much safer comparatively to disregard the body, that one may give himself wholly to the culture of his spiritual health and the care of the Lord's work. Though some may think that in this he ran to a fanatical extreme, there is no doubt that such became more and more a law of his life. He sought to dismiss all anxiety, as a duty; and, among other anxious cares, that most subtle and seductive form of solicitude which watches every change of symptoms and rushes after some new medical man or medical remedy for all ailments real or fancied.

Mr. Müller was never actually reckless of his bodily health. His habits were temperate and wholesome, but no man could be so completely wrapped up in his Master's will and work without being correspondingly forgetful of his physical frame. There are not a few, even among God's saints, whose bodily weaknesses and distresses so engross them that their sole business seems to be to nurse the body, keep it alive and promote its comfort. As Dr. Watts would have said, this is living "at a poor dying rate."

When the year 1838 opened, the weakness and distress in the head still afflicted Mr. Müller. The symptoms were as bad as ever, and it particularly tried him that they were attended by a tendency to irritability of temper, and even by a sort of satanic feeling wholly foreign to him at other times. He was often reminded that he was by nature a child of wrath even as others, and that, as a child of God, he could stand against the wiles of the devil only by putting on the whole armour of God. The pavilion of God is the saint's place of rest; the panoply of God is his coat of mail. Grace does not at once remove or overcome all tendencies to evil, but, if not *eradicated,* they are *counteracted* by the Spirit's wondrous working. Peter found that so long as his eye was on His Master he could walk on the water. There is always a tendency to sink, and a holy walk with God, that defies the tendency downward, is a divine art that can neither be learned nor practised except so long as we keep 'looking unto Jesus': that look of faith counteracts the natural tendency to sink, so long as it holds the soul closely to Him. This man of God felt his risk, and, sore as this trial was to him, he prayed not so much for its removal as that he might be kept from any open dishonour to the name of the Lord, beseeching God that he might rather die than ever bring on Him reproach.

Mr. Müller's journal is not only a record of his outer life of consecrated labour and its expansion, but it is a mirror of his inner life and its growth. It is an encouragement to all other saints to find that this growth was, like their own, in spite of many and formidable hindrances, over which only grace could triumph. Side by side with glimpses of habitual conscientiousness and joy in God, we have revelations of times of coldness and despondency. It is a wholesome lesson in holy living that we find this man setting himself to the deliberate task of *cultivating obedience and gratitude;* by the culture of obedience growing in knowledge and strength, and by the culture of gratitude growing in thankfulness and love. Weakness and coldness are not hopeless states: they have their divine remedies which strengthen and warm the whole being.

SCRIPTURE TESTIMONY
By degrees, believers are being transformed in Christ's image   2 Corinthians 3:18

Three entries, found side by side in his journal, furnish pertinent illustration and most wholesome instruction on this point. One entry records his deep thankfulness to God for the privilege of being permitted to be His instrument in providing for homeless orphans, as he watches the little girls, clad in clean warm garments, pass his window on their way to the chapel on the Lord's day morning. A second entry records his determination, with God's help, to send no more letters in parcels because he sees it to be a violation of the postal laws of the land, and because he desires, as a disciple of the Lord Jesus, to submit himself to all human laws so far as such submission does not conflict with loyalty to God. A third entry immediately follows which reveals this same man struggling against those innate tendencies to evil which compel a continual resort to the throne of grace with its sympathizing High Priest. "This morning," he writes, "I greatly dishonoured the Lord by irritability manifested towards my dear wife; and that, almost immediately after I had been on my knees before God, praising Him for having given me such a wife."

These three entries, put together, convey a lesson which is not learned from either of them alone. Here is gratitude for divine mercy, conscientious resolve at once to stop a doubtful practice, and a confession of inconsistency in his home life. All of these are typical experiences and suggest to us means of gracious growth. He who lets no mercy of God escape thankful recognition, who never hesitates at once to abandon an evil or questionable practice, and who, instead of extenuating a sin because it is comparatively small, promptly confesses and forsakes it,—such a man will surely grow in Christlikeness.

We must exercise our spiritual senses if we are to discern things spiritual. There is a clear vision for God's goodness, and there is a dull eye that sees little to be thankful for; there is a tender conscience, and there is a moral sense that grows less and less sensitive to evil; there is an obedience to the Spirit's rebuke which leads to immediate confession and increases strength for every new conflict. Mr. Müller cultivated habits of life which made his whole nature more and more open to divine impression, and so his sense of God became more and more keen and constant.

One great result of this spiritual culture was a growing absorption in God and jealousy for His glory. As he saw divine things more clearly and felt their supreme importance, he became engrossed in the magnifying of them before men; and this is glorifying God. We cannot make God essentially any more glorious, for He is infinitely perfect; but we can help men to see what a glorious God He is, and thus come into that holy partnership with the Spirit of God whose office it is to take of the things of Christ and show them unto men, and so glorify Christ. Such fellowship in glorifying God Mr. Müller set before him: and in the light of such sanctified aspiration we may read that humble entry in which, reviewing the year 1837 with all its weight of increasing responsibility, he lifts his heart to his divine Lord and Master in these simple words:

"Lord, Thy servant is a poor man; but he has trusted in Thee and made his boast in Thee before the sons of men; therefore let him not be confounded! Let it not be said, 'All this is enthusiasm, and therefore it is come to naught.'"

One is reminded of Moses in his intercession for Israel, of Elijah in his exceeding jealousy for the Lord of hosts, and of that prayer of Jeremiah that so amazes us by its boldness:

> "Do not abhor us for Thy name's sake!
> *Do not disgrace the throne of Thy glory!*"[15]

Looking back over the growth of the work at the end of the year 1837, he puts on record the following facts and figures:

Three orphan houses were now open with eighty-one children, and nine helpers in charge of them. In the Sunday-schools there were three hundred and twenty, and in the day-schools three hundred and fifty; and the Lord had furnished over three hundred and seven pounds for temporal supplies.

From this same point of view it may be well to glance back over the five years of labour in Bristol up to July, 1837. Between himself and his brother Craik uninterrupted harmony had existed from the beginning. They had been perfectly at one in their views of the truth, in their witness to the truth, and in their judgment as to all matters affecting the believers over whom the Holy Ghost had made them overseers. The children of God had been kept from heresy and schism under their joint pastoral care; and all these blessings Mr. Müller and his true yoke-fellow humbly traced to the mercy and grace of the great Shepherd and Bishop of souls. Thus far over one hundred and seventy had been converted and admitted to fellowship, making the total number of communicants three hundred and seventy, nearly equally divided between Bethesda and Gideon. The whole history of these years is lit up with the sunlight of God's smile and blessing.

15 Compare Numbers 14:13-19. 1 Kings 19:10; Jeremiah 14:21

CHAPTER X

The Word of God and Prayer

HABIT BOTH *shows* and *makes* the man, for it is at once historic and prophetic, the mirror of the man as he is and the mould of the man as he is to be. At this point, therefore, special attention may properly be given to the two marked habits which had principally to do with the man we are studying.

Early in the year 1838, he began reading that third biography which, with those of Francké and John Newton, had such a singular influence on his own life—Philip's Life of George Whitefield. The life-story of the orphan's friend had given the primary impulse to his work; the life-story of the converted blasphemer had suggested his narrative of the Lord's dealings; and now the life-story of the great evangelist was blessed of God to shape his general character and give new power to his preaching and his wider ministry to souls. These three biographies together probably affected the whole inward and outward life of George Müller more than any other volumes but the Book of God, and they were wisely fitted of God to co-work toward such a blessed result. The example of Francké incited to faith in prayer and to a work whose sole dependence was on God. Newton's witness to grace led to a testimony to the same sovereign love and mercy as seen in his own case. Whitefield's experience inspired to greater fidelity and earnestness in preaching the Word, and to greater confidence in the power of the anointing Spirit.

Particularly was this impression deeply made on Mr. Müller's mind and heart: that Whitefield's unparalleled success in evangelistic labours was plainly traceable to two causes and could not be separated from them as direct effects; namely, his *unusual prayerfulness, and his habit of reading the Bible on his knees.*

The great evangelist of the last century had learned that first lesson in service, his own utter nothingness and helplessness: that he was nothing, and could do nothing, without God. He could neither understand the Word for himself, nor translate it into his own life, nor apply it to others with power, unless the Holy Spirit became to him both *insight* and *unction.* Hence his success; he was filled with the Spirit: and this alone accounts both for the quality and the quantity of his labours. He died in 1770, in the fifty-sixth year of his age, having preached his first sermon in Gloucester in 1736. During this thirty-four years his labours had been both unceasing and untiring. While on his journeyings in America, he preached one hundred and seventy-five times in seventy-five days, besides travelling, in the slow vehicles of those days, upwards of eight hundred miles. When health declined, and he was put on 'short allowance,' even that was *one sermon each week-day and three on Sunday.* There was about his preaching, moreover, a nameless charm which held thirty thousand hearers half-breathless on Boston Common and made tears pour down the sooty faces of the colliers at Kingswood.

The passion of George Müller's soul was to know fully the secrets of prevailing with God and with man. George Whitefield's life drove home the truth that God alone could create in him a holy earnestness to win souls and qualify him for such divine work by imparting a compassion for the lost that should become an absorbing passion for their salvation. And—let this be carefully marked as another secret of this life of service—*he now began himself to read the word of God upon his knees,* and often found for hours great blessing in such meditation and prayer over a single psalm or chapter.

Here we stop and ask what profit there can be in thus prayerfully reading and searching the Scriptures in the very attitude of prayer. Having tried it for ourselves, we may add our humble witness to its value.

First of all, this habit is a constant reminder and recognition of the need of spiritual teaching in order to the understanding of the holy Oracles. No reader of God's word can thus bow before God and His open book, without a feeling of new reverence for the Scriptures, and dependence on their Author for insight into their mysteries. The attitude of worship naturally suggests sober-mindedness and deep seriousness, and banishes frivolity. To treat that Book with lightness or irreverence would be doubly profane when one is in the posture of prayer.

Again, such a habit naturally leads to self-searching and comparison of the actual life with the example and pattern shown in the Word. The precept compels the practice to be seen in the light of its teaching; the command challenges the conduct to appear for examination. The prayer, whether spoken or unspoken, will inevitably be:

> "Search me, O God, and know my heart,
> Try me, and know my thoughts;
> And see if there be any wicked way in me,
> And lead me in the way everlasting!" (Psalm 139:23, 24)

The words thus reverently read will be translated into the life and mould the character into the image of God. "Beholding as in a glass the glory of the Lord, we are changed into the same image from glory to glory, even as by the Lord the Spirit."[16]

But perhaps the greatest advantage will be that the Holy Scriptures will thus suggest the very words which become the dialect of prayer. "We know not what we should pray for as we ought"—neither what nor how to pray. But here is the Spirit's own inspired utterance, and, if the praying be moulded on the model of His teaching, how can we go astray? Here is our God-given liturgy and litany—a divine prayer-book. We have here God's promises, precepts, warnings, and counsels, not to speak of all the Spirit-inspired literal prayers therein contained; and, as we reflect upon these, our prayers take their cast in this matrix. We turn precept and promise, warning and counsel into supplication, with the assurance that we *cannot be asking anything that is not according to His will,*[17] for are we not turning His own word into prayer?

So Mr. Müller found it to be. In meditating over Hebrews 13:8: "Jesus Christ the same yesterday and to-day and for ever," translating it into prayer, he besought God, with the confidence that the prayer was already granted, that, as Jesus had already in His love and power supplied all that was needful, in the same unchangeable love and power He would so continue to provide. And so a promise was not only turned into a prayer, but into a prophecy—an assurance of blessing—and a river of joy at once poured into and flowed through his soul.

The prayer habit, on the knees, with the Word open before the disciple, has thus an advantage which it is difficult to put into words: *It provides a sacred channel of approach to God.* The inspired Scriptures form the vehicle of the Spirit in communicating to us the knowledge of the will of God. If we think of God on the one side and man on the other, the word of God is the mode of conveyance from God to man, of His own mind and heart. It therefore becomes a channel of God's approach to us, a channel prepared by the Spirit for the purpose, and unspeakably sacred as such. When therefore the believer uses the word of God as the guide to determine both the spirit and the dialect of his prayer, he is inverting the process of divine revelation and using the channel of God's approach to him as the channel of his approach to God. How can such use of God's word fail to help and strengthen spiritual life? What medium or channel of approach could so insure in the praying soul both an acceptable frame and language taught of the Holy Spirit? If the first thing is not to pray but to hearken, this surely is hearkening for God to speak to us that we may know how to speak to Him.

16 2 Corinthians 3:18
17 1 John 5:13

It was habits of life such as these, and not impulsive feelings and transient frames, that made this man of God what he was and strengthened him to lift up his hands in God's name, and follow hard after Him and in Him rejoice.[18] Even his sore affliction, seen in the light of such prayer—prayer itself illuminated by the word of God—became radiant; and his soul was brought into that state where he so delighted in the will of God as to be able from his heart to say that he would not have his disease removed until through it God had wrought the blessing it was meant to convey. And when his acquiescence in the will of God had become thus complete he instinctively felt that he would speedily be restored to health.

Subsequently, in reading Proverbs 3:5-12, he was struck with the words, "Neither be *weary* of His correction." He felt that, though he had not been permitted to "despise the chastening of the Lord," he had at times been somewhat "weary of His correction," and he lifted up the prayer that he might so patiently bear it as neither to faint nor be weary under it, till its full purpose was wrought.

Frequent were the instances of the habit of translating promises into prayers, immediately applying the truth thus unveiled to him. For example, after prolonged meditation over the first verse of Psalm 65, *"O Thou that hearest prayer,"* he at once asked and recorded certain definite petitions. This writing down specific requests for permanent reference has a blessed influence upon the prayer habit. It assures practical and exact form for our supplications, impresses the mind and memory with what is thus asked of God, and leads naturally to the record of the answers when given, so that we accumulate evidences in our own experience that God is to us personally a prayer-hearing God, whereby unbelief is rebuked and importunity encouraged.

On this occasion eight specific requests are put on record, together with the solemn conviction that, having asked in conformity with the word and will of God, and in the name of Jesus, he has confidence in Him that He heareth and that he has the petitions thus asked of Him.[19] He writes:

> "I believe *He has heard me.* I believe He will make it *manifest* in His own good time *that He has heard me;* and I have recorded these my petitions this fourteenth day of January, 1838, that when God has answered them He may get, through this, glory to His name."

The thoughtful reader must see in all this a man of weak faith, feeding and nourishing his trust in God that his faith may grow strong. He uses the promise of a prayer-hearing God as a staff to stay his conscious feebleness, that he may lean hard upon the strong Word which cannot fail. He records the day when he thus takes this staff in hand, and the very petitions which are the burdens which

18 Psalm 63:4, 8, 11
19 1 John 5:13

he seeks to lay on God, so that his act of committal may be the more complete and final. Could God ever dishonour such trust?

It was in this devout reading on his knees that his whole soul was first deeply moved by that phrase,

> "A father of the fatherless." (Psalm 68:5)

He saw this to be one of those "names" of Jehovah which He reveals to His people to lead them to trust in Him, as it is written in Psalm 9:10:

> "They that know Thy name
> Will put their trust in Thee."

These five words from the sixty-eighth psalm became another of his life-texts, one of the foundation stones of all his work for the fatherless. These are his own words:

> "By the help of God, this shall be my argument before Him, respecting the orphans, in the hour of need. He is their Father, and therefore has pledged Himself, as it were, to provide for them; and I have only to remind Him of the need of these poor children in order to have it supplied."

This is translating the promises of God's word, not only into praying, but into living, doing, serving. Blessed was the hour when Mr. Müller learned that one of God's chosen names is "the Father of the fatherless"!

To sustain such burdens would have been quite impossible but for faith in such a God. In reply to oft-repeated remarks of visitors and observers who could not understand the secret of his peace, or how any man who had so many children to clothe and feed could carry such prostrating loads of care, he had one uniform reply: "By the grace of God, this is no cause of anxiety to me. These children I have years ago cast upon the Lord. The whole work is His, and it becomes me to be without carefulness. In whatever points I am lacking, in this point I am able by the grace of God to roll the burden upon my heavenly Father."[20]

In tens of thousands of cases this peculiar title of God, chosen by Himself and by Himself declared, became to Mr. Müller a peculiar revelation of God, suited to his special need. The natural inferences drawn from such a title became powerful arguments in prayer, and rebukes to all unbelief. Thus, at the outset of his work for the orphans, the word of God put beneath his feet a rock basis of

---

20 Journal 1: 285

confidence that he could trust the almighty Father to support the work. And, as the solicitudes of the work came more and more heavily upon him, he cast the loads he could not carry upon Him who, before George Müller was born, was the Father of the fatherless.

About this time we meet other signs of the conflict going on in Mr. Müller's own soul. He could not shut his eyes to the lack of earnestness in prayer and fervency of spirit which at times seemed to rob him of both peace and power. And we notice his experience, in common with so many saints, of the *paradox* of spiritual life. He saw that "such fervency of spirit is altogether the gift of God," and yet he adds, "I have to ascribe to myself the loss of it." He did not run divine sovereignty into blank fatalism as so many do. He saw that God must be sovereign in His gifts, and yet man must be free in his reception and rejection of them. He admitted the mystery without attempting to reconcile the apparent contradiction. He confesses also that the same book, Philip's Life of Whitefield, which had been used of God to kindle such new fires on the altar of his heart, had been also used of Satan to tempt him to neglect for its sake the systematic study of the greatest of books.

Thus, at every step, George Müller's life is full of both encouragement and admonition to fellow disciples. While away from Bristol he wrote in February, 1838, a tender letter to the saints there, which is another revelation of the man's heart. He makes grateful mention of the mercies of God, to him, particularly His gentleness, long-suffering, and faithfulness and the lessons taught him through affliction. The letter makes plain that much sweetness is mixed in the cup of suffering, and that our privileges are not properly prized until for a time we are deprived of them. He particularly mentions how *secret prayer,* even when reading, conversation, or prayer with others was a burden, *always brought relief to his head.* Converse with the Father was an indispensable source of refreshment and blessing at all times. As J. Hudson Taylor says "Satan, the Hinderer, may build a barrier about us, but he can never *roof us in,* so that we cannot *look up.*" Mr. Müller also gives a valuable hint that has already been of value to many afflicted saints, that he found he could help by prayer to fight the battles of the Lord even when he could not by preaching. After a short visit to Germany, partly in quest of health and partly for missionary objects, and after more than twenty-two weeks of retirement from ordinary public duties, his head was much better, but his mental health allowed only about three hours of daily work. While in Germany he had again seen his father and elder brother, and spoken with them about their salvation. To his father his words brought apparent blessing, for he seemed at least to feel his lack of the one thing needful. The separation from him was the more painful as there was so little hope that they should meet again on earth.

In May he once more took part in public services in Bristol, a period of six months having elapsed since he had previously done so. His head was still weak, but there seemed no loss of mental power.

About three months after he had been in Germany part of the fruits of his visit were gathered, for twelve brothers and three sisters sailed for the East Indies.

On June 13, 1838, Mrs. Müller gave birth to a stillborn babe,—another parental disappointment,—and for more than a fortnight her life hung in the balance. But once more prayer prevailed for her and her days were prolonged.

One month later another trial of faith confronted them in the orphan work. A twelvemonth previous there were in hand seven hundred and eighty pounds; now that sum was reduced to one thirty-ninth of the amount—twenty pounds. Mr. and Mrs. Müller, with Mr. Craik and one other brother, connected with the Boys' Orphan House, were the only four persons who were permitted to know of the low state of funds; and they gave themselves to united prayer. And let it be carefully observed that Mr. Müller testifies that his own faith was kept even stronger than when the larger sum was on hand a year before; and this faith was no mere fancy, for, although the supply was so low and shortly thirty pounds would be needed, notice was given for seven more children to enter, and it was further proposed to announce readiness to receive five others!

The trial-hour had come, but was not past. Less than two months later the money-supply ran so low that it was needful that the Lord should give *by the day and almost by the hour* if the needs were to be met. In answer to prayer for help God seemed to say, "Mine hour is not yet come." Many pounds would shortly be required, toward which there was not one penny in hand. When, one day, over four pounds came in, the thought occurred to Mr. Müller, "Why not lay aside three pounds against the coming need?" But immediately he remembered that it is written: "SUFFICIENT UNTO THE DAY IS THE EVIL THEREOF."[21] He unhesitatingly cast himself upon God, and paid out the whole amount for salaries then due, leaving himself again penniless.

At this time Mr. Craik was led to read a sermon on Abraham, from Genesis 12, making prominent two facts: first, that so long as he acted in faith and walked in the will of God, all went on well; but that, secondly, so far as he distrusted the Lord and disobeyed Him, all ended in failure. Mr. Müller heard this sermon and conscientiously applied it to himself. He drew two most practical conclusions which he had abundant opportunity to put into practice:

First, that he must go into no byways or paths of his own for deliverance out of a crisis;

And, secondly, that in proportion as he had been permitted to honour God and bring some glory to His name by trusting Him, he was in danger of dishonouring Him.

Having taught him these blessed truths, the Lord tested him as to how far he would venture upon them. While in such sore need of money for the orphan work, he had in the bank some two hundred and twenty pounds, intrusted to

21 Matthew 6:34

him for other purposes. He might *use this money for the time at least,* and so relieve the present distress. The temptation was the stronger so to do, because he knew the donors and knew them to be liberal supporters of the orphans; and he had only to explain to them the straits he was in and they would gladly consent to any appropriation of their gift that he might see best! Most men would have cut that Gordian knot of perplexity without hesitation.

Not so George Müller. He saw at once that this would be *finding a way of his own out of difficulty, instead of waiting on the Lord for deliverance.* Moreover, he also saw that it would be *forming a habit of trusting to such expedients of his own, which in other trials would lead to a similar course and so hinder the growth of faith.* We use italics here because here is revealed one of the *tests* by which this man of faith, was proven; and we see how he kept consistently and persistently to the one great purpose of his life—to demonstrate to all men that to *rest solely on the promise of a faithful God* is the only way to know for one's self and prove to others, His faithfulness.

At this time of need—the type of many others—this man who had determined to risk everything upon God's word of promise, turned from doubtful devices and questionable methods of relief to *pleading with God.* And it may be well to mark his *manner* of pleading. He used *argument* in prayer, and at this time he piles up *eleven reasons* why God should and would send help.

This method of *holy argument*—ordering our cause before God, as an advocate would plead before a judge—is not only almost a lost art, but to many it actually seems almost puerile. And yet it is abundantly taught and exemplified in Scripture. Abraham in his plea for Sodom is the first great example of it. Moses excelled in this art, in many crises interceding in behalf of the people with consummate skill, marshalling arguments as a general-in-chief marshals battalions. Elijah on Carmel is a striking example of power in this special pleading. What holy zeal and jealousy for God! It is probable that if we had fuller records we should find that all pleaders with God, like Noah, Job, Samuel, David, Daniel, Jeremiah, Paul, and James, have used the same method.

Of course God does not *need to be convinced:* no arguments can make any plainer to Him the claims of trusting souls to His intervention, claims based upon His own word, confirmed by His oath. And yet He will be inquired of and argued with. That is His way of blessing. He loves to have us set before Him our cause and His own promises: He delights in the well-ordered plea, where argument is piled upon argument. See how the Lord Jesus Christ commended the persistent argument of the woman of Canaan, who with the *wit of importunity* actually turned his own *objection* into a *reason.* He said, "It is not meet to take the children's bread and cast it to the little dogs."[22] "Truth, Lord," she answered,

---

22 Cf. Matthew 7:6, 15:26, 27. Not κυνίς, but κυναρίοις, the diminutive for little pet dogs.

"yet the little dogs under the master's tables eat of the crumbs which fall from the children's mouths!" What a triumph of argument! Catching the Master Himself in His words, as He meant she should, and turning His apparent reason for not granting into a reason for granting her request! "O woman," said He, "great is thy faith! Be it unto thee even as thou wilt"—thus, as Luther said, "flinging the reins on her neck."

This case stands unique in the word of God, and it is this use of argument in prayer that makes it thus solitary in grandeur. But one other case is at all parallel,—that of the centurion of Capernaum,[23] who, when our Lord promised to go and heal his servant, argued that such coming was not needful, since He had only to speak the healing word. And notice the basis of his argument: if he, a commander exercising authority and yielding himself to higher authority, both obeyed the word of his superior and exacted obedience of his subordinate, how much more could the Great Healer, in his absence, by a word of command, wield the healing Power that in His presence was obedient to His will! Of him likewise our Lord said: "I have not found so great faith, no, not in Israel!"

We are to argue our case with God, not indeed to convince *Him,* but to convince *ourselves.* In proving to Him that, by His own word and oath and character, He has bound Himself to interpose, we demonstrate *to our own faith* that He has given us the right to ask and claim, and that He will answer our plea because He cannot deny Himself.

There are two singularly beautiful touches of the Holy Spirit in which the right thus to order argument before God is set forth to the reflective reader. In Micah 7:20 we read:

> "Thou wilt perform the *truth* to Jacob,
> The *mercy* to Abraham,
> Which thou hast sworn unto our fathers,
> From the days of old."

Mark the progress of the thought. What was mercy to Abraham was truth to Jacob. God was under no obligation to extend covenant blessings; hence it was to Abraham a simple act of pure *mercy;* but, having so put Himself under voluntary bonds, Jacob could claim as *truth* what to Abraham had been mercy. So in 1 John 1:9:

> "If we confess our sins
> He is *faithful and just* to forgive us our sins,
> And to cleanse us from all unrighteousness."

---

23 Matthew 8:8

Plainly, forgiveness and cleansing are not originally matters of faithfulness and justice, but of mercy and grace. But, after God had pledged Himself thus to forgive and cleanse the penitent sinner who confesses and forsakes his sins,[24] what was originally grace and mercy becomes faithfulness and justice; for God owes it to Himself and to His creature to stand by His own pledge, and fulfil the lawful expectation which His own gracious assurance has created.

Thus we have not only examples of argument in prayer, but concessions of the living God Himself, that when we have His word to plead we may claim the fulfillment of His promise, on the ground not of His mercy only, but of His truth, faithfulness, and justice. Hence the 'holy boldness with which we are bidden to present our plea at the throne of grace. God owes to His faithfulness to do what He has promised, and to His justice not to exact from the sinner a penalty already borne in his behalf by His own Son.

No man of his generation, perhaps, has been more wont to plead thus with God, after the manner of holy argument, than he whose memoir we are now writing. He was one of the elect few to whom it has been given to revive and restore this lost art of pleading with God. And if all disciples could learn the blessed lesson, what a period of *renaissance* of faith would come to the church of God!

George Müller stored up reasons for God's intervention, As he came upon promises, authorized declarations of God concerning Himself, names and titles He had chosen to express and reveal His true nature and will, injunctions and invitations which gave to the believer a right to pray and boldness in supplication—as he saw all these, fortified and exemplified by the instances of prevailing prayer, he laid these arguments up in memory, and then on occasions of great need brought them out and spread them before a prayer-hearing God. It is pathetically beautiful to follow this humble man of God into the secret place, and there hear him pouring out his soul in these argumentative pleadings, as though he would so order his cause before God as to convince Him that He must interpose to save His own name and word from dishonour!

These were *His* orphans, for had He not declared Himself the Father of the fatherless? This was *His* work, for had He not called His servant to do His bidding, and what was that servant but an instrument that could neither fit itself nor use itself? Can the rod lift itself, or the saw move itself, or the hammer deal its own blow, or the sword make its own thrust? And if this were God's work, was He not bound to care for His own work? And was not all this deliberately planned and carried on for His own glory? And would He suffer His own glory to be dimmed? Had not His own word been given and confirmed by His oath, and could God allow His promise, thus sworn to, to be dishonoured even in the least particular? Were not the half-believing church and the unbelieving world looking on, to see

24 Proverbs 28:13

how the Living God would stand by His own unchanging assurance, and would He supply an argument for the skeptic and the scoffer? Would He not, must He not, rather put new proofs of His faithfulness in the mouth of His saints, and furnish increasing arguments wherewith to silence the cavilling tongue and put to shame the hesitating disciple?[25]

In some such fashion as this did this lowly-minded saint in Bristol plead with God for more than threescore years, *and prevail*—as every true believer may who with a like boldness comes to the throne of grace to obtain mercy and find grace to help in every time of need. How few of us can sincerely sing:

> I believe God answers prayer,
> Answers always, everywhere;
> I may cast my anxious care,
> Burdens I could never bear,
> On the God who heareth prayer.
> Never need my soul despair
> Since He bids me boldly dare
> To the secret place repair,
> There to prove He answers prayer.

25 Mr. Müller himself tells how he argued his case before the Lord at this time. (Appendix F. Narrative, vol. 1, 243, 244.)

CHAPTER XI

Trials of Faith, and Helpers to Faith

God has His own mathematics: witness that miracle of the loaves and fishes. Our Lord said to His disciples: "Give ye them to eat," and as they divided, He multiplied the scanty provision; as they subtracted from it He added to it; as they decreased it by distributing, He increased it for distributing. And it has been beautifully said of all holy partnerships, that griefs shared are divided, and joys shared are multiplied.

We have already seen how the prayer circle had been enlarged. The founder of the orphan work, at the first, had only God for his partner, telling Him alone his own wants or the needs of his work. Later on, a very few, including his own wife, Mr. Craik, and one or two helpers, were permitted to know the condition of the funds and supplies. Later still, in the autumn of 1838, he began to feel that he ought more fully to open the doors of his confidence to his associates in the Lord's business. Those who shared in the toils should also share in the prayers, and therefore in the knowledge of the needs which prayer was to supply; else how could they fully be partakers of the faith, the work, and the reward? Or, again, how could they feel the full proof of the presence and power of God in the answers to prayer, know the joy of the Lord which such answers inspire, or praise Him for the deliverance which such answers exhibit? It seemed plain that, to the highest glory of God, they must know the depths of need, the extremities of want out of which God had lifted them, and then ascribe all honour and praise to His name.

Accordingly Mr. Müller called together all the beloved brothers and sisters linked with him in the conduct of the work, and fully stated the case, keeping nothing back. He showed them the distress they were in, while he bade them be of good courage, assuring them of his own confidence that help was nigh at hand, and then united them with himself and the smaller praying circle which had previously existed, in supplication to Jehovah Jireh.

The step thus taken was of no small importance to all concerned. A considerable number of praying believers were henceforth added to the band of intercessors that gave God no rest day nor night. While Mr. Müller withheld no facts as to the straits to which the work was reduced, he laid down certain principles which from time to time were reiterated as unchanging laws for the conduct of the Lord's business. For example, nothing must be bought, whatever the extremity, for which there was not money in hand to pay: and yet it must be equally a settled principle that the children must not be left to lack anything needful; for better that the work cease, and the orphans be sent away, than that they be kept in a nominal home where they were really left to suffer from hunger or nakedness.

Again, nothing was ever to be revealed to outsiders of existing need, lest it should be construed into an appeal for help; but the only resort must be to the living God. The helpers were often reminded that the supreme object of the institutions, founded in Bristol, was to prove God's faithfulness and the perfect safety of trusting solely to His promises; jealousy for Him must therefore restrain all tendency to look to man for help. Moreover, they were earnestly besought to live in such daily and hourly fellowship with God as that their own unbelief and disobedience might not risk either their own power in prayer, or the agreement, needful among them, in order to common supplication. One discordant note may prevent the harmonious symphony of united prayer, and so far hinder the acceptableness of such prayer with God.

Thus informed and instructed, these devoted coworkers, with the beloved founder of the orphan work, met the crisis intelligently. If, when there were *no funds,* there must be *no leaning upon man, no debt* incurred, and yet *no lack* allowed, clearly the only resort or resource must be waiting upon the unseen God; and so, in these straits and in every succeeding crisis, they went to Him alone. The orphans themselves were never told of any existing need; in every case their wants were met, though they knew not how. The barrel of meal might be empty, yet there was always a handful when needed, and the cruse of oil was never so exhausted that a few drops were not left to moisten the handful of meal. Famine and drought never reached the Bristol orphanage: the supplies might come slowly and only for one day at a time, but somehow, when the need was urgent and could no longer wait, there was enough—though it might be barely enough to meet the want.

It should be added here, as completing this part of the Narrative, that, in August, 1840, this circle of prayer was still further enlarged by admitting to its intimacies of fellowship and supplication the brethren and sisters who laboured in the day-schools, the same solemn injunctions being repeated in their case against any betrayal to outsiders of the crises that might arise.

To impart the knowledge of affairs to so much larger a band of helpers brought in every way a greater blessing, and especially so to the helpers themselves. Their earnest, believing, importunate prayers were thus called forth, and God only knows how much the consequent progress of the work was due to their faith, supplication, and self-denial. The practical knowledge of the exigencies of their common experience begat an unselfishness of spirit which prompted countless acts of heroic sacrifice that have no human record or written history, and can be known only when the pages of the Lord's own journal are read by an assembled universe in the day when the secret things are brought to light. It has, since Mr. Müller's departure, transpired how large a share of the donations received are to be traced to him; but there is no means of ascertaining as to the aggregate amount of the secret gifts of his coworkers in this sacred circle of prayer.

We do know, however, that Mr. Müller was not the only self-denying giver, though he may lead the host. His true yoke-fellows often *turned the crisis* by their own offerings, which though small were costly! Instrumentally they were used of God to relieve existing want by their gifts, for out of the abundance of their deep poverty abounded the riches of their liberality. The money they gave was sometimes like the widow's two mites—all their living; and not only the last penny, but ornaments, jewels, heirlooms, long-kept and cherished treasures, like the alabaster flask of ointment which was broken upon the feet of Jesus, were laid down on God's altar as a willing sacrifice. They gave all they could spare and often what they could ill spare, so that there might be meat in God's house and no lack of bread or other needed supplies for His little ones. In a sublime sense this work was not Mr. Müller's only, but *theirs* also, who with him took part in prayers and tears, in cares and toils, in self-denials and self-offerings, whereby God chose to carry forward His plans for these homeless waifs! It was in thus *giving* that all these helpers found also new power, assurance, and blessing in praying; for, as one of them said, he felt that it would scarcely be *"upright to pray, except he were to give what he had."*[26]

The helpers, thus admitted into Mr. Müller's confidence, came into more active sympathy with him and the work, and partook increasingly of the same spirit. Of this some few instances and examples have found their way into his journal.

A gentleman and some ladies visiting the orphan houses saw the large number of little ones to be cared for. One of the ladies said to the matron of the Boys' House: "Of course you cannot carry on these institutions without a good stock of funds"; and the gentleman added, "Have you a good stock?" The quiet answer was, "Our funds are deposited in a bank which cannot break." The reply drew tears from the eyes of the lady, and a gift of five pounds from the pocket of the gentleman—a donation most opportune, as there was *not one penny then in hand.*

26 Narrative, 1: 246.

Fellow labourers such as these, who asked nothing for themselves, but cheerfully looked to the Lord for their own supplies, and willingly parted with their own money or goods in the hour of need, filled Mr. Müller's heart with praise to God, and held up his hands, as Aaron and Hur sustained those of Moses, till the sun of his life went down. During all the years of his superintendence these were the main human support of his faith and courage. They met with him in daily prayer, faithfully kept among themselves the secrets of the Lord's work in the great trials of faith; and, when the hour of triumph came, they felt it to be both duty and privilege in the annual report to publish their deliverance, to make their boast in God, that all men might know His love and faithfulness and ascribe unto Him glory.

From time to time, in connection with the administration of the work, various questions arose which have a wider bearing on all departments of Christian service, for their solution enters into what may be called the ethics and economics of the Lord's work. At a few of these we may glance.

As the Lord was dealing with them by the day, it seemed clear that they were to *live by the day.* No dues should be allowed to accumulate, even such as would naturally accrue from ordinary weekly supplies of bread, milk, etc. From the middle of September, 1838, it was therefore determined that every article bought was to be paid for at the time.

Again, rent became due in stated amounts and at stated times. This want was therefore not unforeseen, and, looked at in one aspect, rent was due daily or weekly, though collected at longer intervals. The principle having been laid down that no debt should be incurred, it was considered as implying that the amount due for rent should be put aside daily, or at least weekly, even though not then payable. This rule was henceforth adopted, with this understanding, that money thus laid aside was sacred to that end, and not to be drawn upon, even temporarily, for any other.

Notwithstanding such conscientiousness and consistency the trial of faith and patience continued. Money came in only in small sums, and barely enough with rigid economy to meet each day's wants. The outlook was often most dark and the prospect most threatening; but *no real need ever failed to be supplied:* and so praise was continually mingled with prayer, the incense of thanksgiving making fragrant the flame of supplication. God's interposing power and love could not be doubted, and in fact made the more impression as unquestionable facts, because help came so frequently at the hour of extremity, and in the exact form or amount needed. Before the provision was entirely exhausted, there came new supplies or the money wherewith to buy, so that these many mouths were always fed and these many bodies always clad.

To live up to such principles as had been laid down was not possible without faith, kept in constant and lively exercise. For example, in the closing months of

1838 God seemed purposely putting them to a severe test, whether or not they *did trust Him alone.* The orphan work was in continual straits: at times not one half-penny was in the hands of the matrons in the three houses. But not only was no knowledge of such facts ever allowed to leak out, or any hint of the extreme need ever given to outsiders, *but even those who inquired, with intent to aid, were not informed.*

One evening a brother ventured to ask how the balance would stand when the next accounts were made up, and whether it would be as great in favour of the orphans as when the previous balance-sheet had been prepared. Mr. Mutter's calm but evasive answer was: *"It will be as great as the Lord pleases."* This was no intentional rudeness. To have said more would have been turning from the one Helper to make at least an indirect appeal to man for help; and every such snare was carefully avoided lest the one great aim should be lost sight of: to prove to all men that it is safe to trust only in the Living God.

While admitting the severity of the straits to which the whole work of the Scriptural Knowledge Institution was often brought, Mr. Müller takes pains to assure his readers that these straits were never a surprise to him, and that his expectations in the matter of funds were not disappointed, but rather the reverse. He had looked for great emergencies as essential to his full witness to a prayer-hearing God. The almighty Hand can never be clearly seen while any human help is sought for or is in sight. We must turn absolutely away from all else if we are to turn fully unto the living God. The deliverance is signal, only in proportion as the danger is serious, and is most significant when, without God, we face absolute despair. Hence the exact end for which the whole work was mainly begun could be attained only through such conditions of extremity and such experiences of interposition in extremity.

Some who have known but little of the interior history of the orphan work have very naturally accounted for the regularity of supplies by supposing that the public statements, made about it by word of mouth, and especially by the pen in the printed annual reports, have constituted *appeals for aid.* Unbelief would interpret all God's working however wonderful, by 'natural laws,' and the carnal mind, refusing to see in any of the manifestations of God's power any supernatural force at work, persists in thus explaining away all the 'miracles of prayer.'

No doubt humane and sympathetic hearts have been strongly moved by the remarkable ways in which God has day by day provided for all these orphans, as well as the other branches of work of the Scriptural Knowledge Institution; and believing souls have been drawn into loving and hearty sympathy with work so conducted, and have been led to become its helpers. It is a well-known fact that God has used these annual reports to accomplish just such results. Yet it remains true that these reports were never intended or issued as appeals for aid, and no dependence has been placed upon them for securing timely help. It is also undeniable that, however frequent their issue, wide their circulation, or great their influence, the regularity and abundance of the supplies of all needs must in some other way be accounted for.

Only a few days after public meetings were held or printed reports issued, funds often fell to their lowest ebb. Mr. Müller and his helpers were singularly kept from all undue leaning upon any such indirect appeals, and frequently and definitely asked God that they might never be left to look for any inflow of means through such channels. For many reasons the Lord's dealings with them were made known, the main object of such publicity always being a *testimony to the faithfulness of God.* This great object Mr. Müller always kept foremost, hoping and praying that, by such records and revelations of God's fidelity to His promises, and of the manner in which He met each new need, his servant might awaken, quicken, and stimulate faith in Him as the Living God. One has only to read these reports to see the conspicuous absence of any appeal for human aid, or of any attempt to excite pity, sympathy and compassion toward the orphans. The burden of every report is to induce the reader to venture wholly upon God, to taste and see that the Lord is good, and find for himself how blessed are all they that put their trust in Him. Only in the light of this supreme purpose can these records of a life of faith be read intelligently and intelligibly.

Weakness of body again, in the autumn of 1839, compelled, for a time, rest from active labour, and Mr. Müller went to Trowbridge and Exeter, Teignmouth and Plymouth. God had precious lessons for him which He could best teach in the school of affliction.

While at Plymouth Mr. Müller felt anew the impulse to early rising for purposes of devotional communion. At Halle he had been an early riser, influenced by zeal for excellence in study. Afterwards, when his weak head and feeble nerves made more sleep seem needful, he judged that, even when he rose late, the day would be long enough to exhaust his little fund of strength; and so often he lay in bed till six or even seven o'clock, instead of rising at four; and after dinner took a nap for a quarter-hour. It now grew upon him, however, that he was losing in spiritual vigour, and that his soul's health was declining under this new regimen. The work now so pressed upon him as to prevent proper reading of the Word and rob him of leisure for secret prayer.

A 'chance remark'—there is no *chance* in a believer's life!—made by the brother at whose house he was abiding at Plymouth, much impressed him. Referring to the sacrifices in Leviticus, he said that, as the refuse of the animals was never offered up on the altar, but only the best parts and the fat, so the choicest of our time and strength, the best parts of our day, should be especially given to the Lord in worship and communion. George Müller meditated much on this; and determined, even at the risk of damage to bodily health, that he would no longer spend his best hours in bed. Henceforth he allowed himself but *seven hours' sleep* and gave up his after-dinner rest. This resumption of early rising secured long seasons of uninterrupted interviews 'with God, in prayer and meditation on the Scriptures, before breakfast and the various inevitable interruptions that followed. He found himself not worse but better, physically, and became convinced that to have lain longer in bed as before would have kept his nerves weak; and, as to spiritual life, such new vitality and vigour accrued from thus waiting upon God while others slept, that it continued to be the habit of his after-life.

In November, 1839, when the needs were again great and the supplies very small, he was kept in peace: "I was not," he says, "looking at the *little in hand, 'but at the fulness of God.*"

It was his rule to empty himself of all that he had, in order to greater boldness in appealing for help from above. All needless articles were sold if a market could be found. But what was useful in the Lord's work he did not reckon as needless, nor regard it right to sell, since the Father knew the need. One of his fellow labourers had put forward his valuable watch as a security for the return of money laid by for rent, but drawn upon for the time; yet even this plan was not felt to be scriptural, as the watch might be reckoned among articles needful and useful in the Lord's service, and, if such, expedients were quite abandoned, the deliverance would be more manifest as of the Lord. And so, one by one, all resorts were laid aside that might imperil full trust and sole dependence upon the one and only Helper.

When the poverty of their resources seemed most pinching, Mr. Müller still comforted himself with the daily proof that God had not forgotten, and would day by day feed them with 'the bread of their convenience.' Often he said to himself, If it is even a proverb of the world that "Man's necessity is God's opportunity," how much more may God's own dear children in their great need look to Him to make their extremity the fit moment to display His love and power!

In February, 1840, another attack of ill health combined with a mission to Germany to lead Mr. Müller for five weeks to the Continent. At Heimersleben, where he found his father weakened by a serious cough, the two rooms in which he spent most time in prayer and reading of the Word, and confession of the Lord, were the same in which, nearly twenty years before, he had passed most time as an unreconciled sinner against God and man. Later on, at Wolfenbuttel, he saw the inn whence in 1821 he ran away in debt. In taking leave once more of his father he was pierced by a keen anguish, fearing it was his last farewell, and an unusual tenderness and affection were now exhibited by his father, whom he yearned more and more to know as safe in the Lord Jesus, and depending no longer on outward and formal religiousness, or substituting the reading of prayers and of Scripture for an inward conformity to Christ. This proved the last interview, for the father died on March 30th of the same year.

The main purpose of this journey to Germany was to send forth more missionaries to the East. At Sandersleben Mr. Müller met his friend, Mr. Stahlschmidt, and found a little band of disciples meeting in secret to evade the police. Those who have always breathed the atmosphere of religious liberty know little of such intolerance as, in that nominally Christian land, stifled all freedom of Worship. Eleven years before, when Mr. Stahlschmidt's servant had come to this place, he had found scarce one true disciple beside his master. The first meetings had been literally of but two or three, and, when they had grown a little larger, Mr. Kroll was summoned before the magistrates and, like the apostles in the first days of the church, forbidden to speak in His name. But again, like those same primitive disciples, believing that they were to obey God rather than men, the believing band had continued to meet, notwithstanding police raids which were so disturbing, and government fines which were so exacting. So secret, however, were their assemblies, as to have neither stated place nor regular time.

George Müller found these persecuted believers, meeting in the room of a humble weaver where there was but one chair. The twenty-five or thirty who were present found such places to sit or stand as they might, in and about the loom, which itself filled half the space.

In Halberstadt Mr. Müller found seven large Protestant churches without one clergyman who gave evidence of true conversion, and the few genuine disciples there were likewise forbidden to meet together.

A few days after returning to Bristol from his few weeks in Germany, and at a time of great financial distress in the work, a letter reached him from a brother who had often before given money, as follows:

SCRIPTURE TESTIMONY
Don't be anxious, for He cares for us
Matthew 6:25-34 · 1 Peter 5:6-7

"Have you any *present* need for the Institution under your care? I know you do not *ask,* except indeed of Him whose work you are doing; but to *answer when asked* seems another thing, and a right thing. I have a reason for desiring to know the present state of your means towards the objects you are labouring to serve: viz., should you *not have* need, other departments of the Lord's work, or other people of the Lord, *may have* need. Kindly then inform me, and to what amount, i.e. what amount you at this present time need or can profitably lay out."

To most men, even those who carry on a work of faith and prayer, such a letter would have been at least a temptation. But Mr. Müller did not waver. To announce even to an inquirer the exact needs of the work would, in his opinion, involve two serious risks:

1. It would turn his own eyes away from God to man;
2. It would turn the minds of saints away from dependence solely upon Him.

This man of God had staked everything upon one great experiment—he had set himself to prove that the prayer which *resorts to God only* will bring help in every crisis, even when the crisis is unknown to His people whom He uses as the means of relief and help.

At this time there remained in hand but twenty-seven pence ha'penny, in all, to meet the needs of hundreds of orphans. Nevertheless this was the reply to the letter:

"Whilst I thank you for your love, and whilst I agree with you that, in general, there is a difference between *asking for money* and *answering when asked,* nevertheless, in our case, I feel not at liberty to speak about the state of our funds, as the primary object of the work in my hands is to lead those who are weak in faith to see that there is *reality* in dealing with God *alone.*"

Consistently with his position, however, no sooner was the answer posted than the appeal went up to the Living God: "Lord, thou knowest that, for Thy sake, I did not tell this brother about our need. Now, Lord, show afresh that there is reality in speaking to Thee only, about our need, and speak therefore to this brother so that he may help us." In answer, God moved this inquiring brother to send one hundred pounds, which came when *not one penny was in hand.*

The confidence of faith, long tried, had its increasing reward and was strengthened by experience. In July, 1845, Mr. Müller gave this testimony reviewing these very years of trial:

"Though for about seven years, our funds have been so exhausted that it has been comparatively a rare case that there have been means in hand to meet the necessities of the orphans *for three days* together, yet I have been only once tried in spirit, and that was on September 18, 1838, when for the first time the Lord seemed not to regard our prayer. But when He did send help at that time, and I saw that it was only for the trial of our faith, and not because He had forsaken the work, that we were brought so low, my soul was so strengthened and encouraged that I have not only not been allowed to distrust the Lord since that time, but I have not even been cast down when in the deepest poverty."

CHAPTER XII

New Lessons in God's School of Prayer

THE TEACHER must also be a learner, and therefore only he who continues to learn is competent to continue to teach. Nothing but new lessons, daily mastered, can keep our testimony fresh and vitalizing and enable us to give advance lessons. Instead of being always engaged in a sort of review, our teaching and testimony will thus be drawn each day from a new and higher level.

George Müller's experiences of prevailing prayer went on constantly accumulating, and so qualified him to speak to others, not as on a matter of speculation, theory, or doctrinal belief, but of long, varied, and successful personal experiment. Patiently, carefully and frequently, he seeks to impress on others the conditions of effective supplication. From time to time he met those to whom his courageous, childlike trust in God was a mystery; and occasionally unbelief's secret misgivings found a voice in the question, *what he would do if God did not send help!* what, if a meal-time actually came with no food, and no money to procure it; or if clothing were worn out, and nothing to replace it?

To all such questions there was always ready this one answer: that *such a failure on God's part is inconceivable,* and must therefore be put among the impossibilities. There are, however, conditions necessary on man's part: *the suppliant soul must come to God in the right spirit and attitude.* For the sake of such readers as might need further guidance as to the proper and acceptable manner of approach to God, he was wont to make very plain the scripture teaching upon this point.

Five grand conditions of prevailing prayer were ever before his mind:

1. Entire dependence upon the merits and mediation of the Lord Jesus Christ, as the only ground of any claim for blessing. (See John 14:13, 14; 15:16, etc.)

2. Separation from all known sin. If we regard iniquity in our hearts, the Lord will not hear us, for it would be sanctioning sin. (Psalm 66:18)
3. Faith in God's word of promise as confirmed by His oath. Not to believe Him is to make Him both a liar and a perjurer. (Hebrews 11:6; 6:13-20)
4. Asking in accordance with His will. Our motives must be godly: we must not seek any gift of God to consume it upon our own lusts. (1 John 5:14; James 4:3)
5. Importunity in supplication. There must be waiting on God and waiting for God, as the husbandman has long patience to wait for the harvest. (James 5:7; Luke 18:1-10)

The importance of firmly fixing in mind principles such as these cannot be overstated. The first lays the basis of all prayer, in our oneness with the great High Priest. The second states a condition of prayer, found in abandonment of sin. The third reminds us of the need of honouring God by faith that He is, and is the Rewarder of the diligent seeker. The fourth reveals the sympathy with God that helps us to ask what is for our good and His glory. The last teaches us that, having laid hold of God in prayer, we are to keep hold until His arm is outstretched in blessing.

Where these conditions do not exist, for God to answer prayer would be both a dishonour to Himself and a damage to the suppliant. To encourage those who come to Him in their own name, or in a self-righteous, self-seeking, and disobedient spirit, would be to set a premium upon continuance in sin. To answer the requests of the unbelieving would be to disregard the double insult put upon His word of promise and His oath of confirmation, by persistent doubt of His truthfulness and distrust of His faithfulness. Indeed not one condition of prevailing prayer exists which is not such in the very nature of things. These are not arbitrary limitations affixed to prayer by a despotic will; they are necessary alike to God's character and man's good.

All the lessons learned in God's school of prayer made Mr. Müller's feelings and convictions about this matter more profound and subduing. He saw the vital relation of prayer to holiness, and perpetually sought to impress it upon both his hearers and readers; and, remembering that for the purpose of persuasion the most effective figure of speech is *repetition,* he hesitated at no frequency of restatement by which such truths might find root in the minds and hearts of others.

There has never been a saint, from Abel's day to our own, who has not been taught the same essential lessons. All prayer which has ever brought down blessing has prevailed by the same law of success—*the inward impulse of God's Holy Spirit.* If, therefore, that Spirit's teachings be disregarded or disobeyed, or His inward movings be hindered, in just such measure will prayer become formal or be altogether abandoned. Sin, consciously indulged, or duty, knowingly neglected, makes supplication an offence to God.

Again, all prayer prevails only in the measure of our real, even if not conscious, unity with the Lord Jesus Christ as the ground of our approach, and in the degree of our dependence on Him as the medium of our access to God.

Yet again, all prayer prevails only as it is offered in faith; and the *answer* to such prayer can be recognized and received only *on the plane of faith;* that is, we must maintain the believing frame, expecting the blessing, and being ready to receive it in God's way and time and form, and not our own.

SCRIPTURE TESTIMONY
Our Father in heaven gives good things
Matthew 7:9-11

The faith that thus *expects* cannot be surprised at answers to prayer. When, in November, 1840, a sister gave ten pounds for the orphans, and at a time specially opportune, Mr. Müller records his triumphant joy in God as exceeding and defying all expression. Yet he was *free from excitement and not in the least surprised,* because by grace he had been trustfully waiting on God for deliverance. Help had been so long delayed that in one of the houses there was no bread, and in none of them any milk or any money to buy either. It was only a few minutes before the milkman's cart was due, that this money came.

However faithful and trustful in prayer, it behooves us to be none the less careful and diligent in the use of all proper means. Here again Mr. Müller's whole life is a lesson to other believers. For example, when travelling in other lands, or helping other brethren on their way, he besought the Lord's constant guardianship over the conveyances used, and even over the luggage so liable to go astray. But he himself looked carefully to the seaworthiness of the vessel he was to sail in, and to every other condition of safe and speedy transportation for himself and others. In one case where certain German brethren and sisters were departing for foreign shores, he noticed the manner in which the cabman stored away the small luggage in the fly; and observed that several carpetbags were hastily thrust into a hind boot. He also carefully counted the pieces of luggage and took note of the fact that there were seventeen in all. On arriving at the wharf, where there is generally much hurry and flurry, the dishonest cabman would have driven off with a large part of the property belonging to the party, but for this man of God who not only *prayed* but *watched.* He who trusted God implicitly, no less faithfully looked to the cabman's fidelity, who, after he pretended to have delivered all the luggage to the porters, was compelled to open that hind boot and, greatly to his own confusion, deliver up the five or six bags hidden away there. Mr. Müller adds in his Narrative that "such a circumstance should teach one to make the very smallest affairs a subject of prayer, as, for instance, that all the luggage might be safely taken out of a fly."

May we not add that such a circumstance teaches us that companion lesson, quite as important in its way, that we are to be watchful as well as prayerful, and see that a dishonest cab-driver does not run off with another's goods!

This praying saint, who watched man, most of all watched God. Even in the lesser details of his work, his eye was ever looking for God's unfailing supplies, and taking notice of the divine leadings and dealings; and, afterward, there always followed the fruit of the lips, giving thanks to His name. Here is another secret revealed: prayerfulness and thankfulness—those two handmaidens of God—always go together, each helping the other. "Pray without ceasing: in everything give thanks." (1 Thessalonians 5:17, 18) These two precepts stand side by side where they belong, and he who neglects one will find himself disobeying the other. This man who prayed so much and so well, offered the sacrifice of praise to God continually.

For example, on September 21, 1840, a specific entry was made in the Narrative, so simple, childlike, and in every way characteristic, that every word of it is precious.

> "The Lord, to show His continued care over us, raises up new helpers. They that trust in the Lord shall never be confounded. Some who helped for a while may fall asleep in Jesus; others grow cold in the service of the Lord; others be as desirous as ever to help, but no longer able; or, having means, feel it to be His will to lay them out in another way. But in leaning upon God, the Living God alone, we are BEYOND DISAPPOINTMENT and BEYOND *being forsaken because of death, or want of means, or want of love, or because of the claims of other work.* How precious to have learned, in any measure, to be content to stand with God alone in the world, and to know that surely no good thing shall be withheld from us, whilst we walk uprightly!"

Among the gifts received during this long life of stewardship for God some deserve individual mention.

SCRIPTURE TESTIMONY
Exchange earthly possessions for heavenly treasure
Matthew 6:19-21 · Luke 12:33
God will provide for our daily needs
Matthew 6:11

To an offering received in March, 1839, a peculiar history attaches. The circumstances attending its reception made upon him a deep impression. He had given a copy of the Annual Report to a believing brother who had been greatly stirred up to prayer by reading it; and knowing his own sister, who was also a disciple, to possess sundry costly ornaments and jewels, such as a heavy gold chain, a pair of gold bracelets, and a superb ring set with fine brilliants, this brother besought the Lord so to show her the uselessness of such trinkets that she should be led to lay them all upon His altar as an offering for the orphan work. This prayer was literally answered. Her sacrifice of jewels proved of service to the work at a time of such pressing need that Mr. Müller's heart specially rejoiced in God. By the proceeds of the sale of these ornaments he was helped to meet the expenses of a whole week, and besides to *pay the salaries* due to the helpers. But, before disposing of the diamond ring, he wrote with it upon the window-pane of his own room that precious name and title of the Lord—"JEHOVAH JIREH"—and henceforth whenever, in deep poverty, he cast his eyes upon those two words, imperishably written with the point of a diamond upon that pane, he thankfully remembered that "THE LORD WILL PROVIDE."

How many of his fellow believers might find unfailing refreshment and inspiration in dwelling upon the divine promises! Ancient believers were bidden to write God's words on the palms of their hands, the doorposts of their houses, and on their gates, so that the employments of their hands, their goings out and comings in, their personal and home life, might be constant reminders of Jehovah's everlasting faithfulness. He who inscribed this chosen name of God upon the window-pane of his dwelling, found that every ray of sunlight that shone into his room lit up his Lord's promise.

He thus sums up the experiences of the year 1840:

1. Notwithstanding multiplied trials of faith, the orphans have lacked nothing.
2. Instead of being disappointed in his expectations or work, the reverse had been true, such trials being seen to be needful to demonstrate that the Lord was their Helper in times of need.
3. Such a way of living brings the Lord very near, as one who daily inspects the need that He may send the more timely aid.
4. Such constant, instant reliance upon divine help does not so absorb the mind in temporal things as to unfit for spiritual employments and enjoyments; but rather prompts to habitual communion with the Lord and His Word.
5. Other children of God may not be called to a similar work, but are called to a like faith, and may experience similar interposition if they live according to His will and seek His help.
6. The incurring of debt, being unscriptural, is a sin needing confession and abandonment if we desire unhindered fellowship with God, and experience of His interposition.

It was in this year 1840, also, that a further object was embraced in the work of the Scripture Knowledge Institution, namely, the circulation of Christian books and tracts. But, as the continuance and enlargement of these benevolent activities made the needs greater, so, in answer to prayer, the Hand of the great Provider bestowed larger supplies.

Divine interposition will never be doubted by one who, like George Müller, gives himself to prayer, for the coincidences will prove too exact and frequent between demand and supply, times and seasons of asking and answering, to allow of doubt that God has helped.

The 'ethics of language' embody many lessons. For example, the term 'poetic retribution' describes a visitation of judgment where the penalty peculiarly befits the crime. As poetic lines harmonize, rhyme and rhythm showing the work of a designing hand, so there is often harmony between an offense and its retribution, as when Adonibezek, who had afflicted a like injury upon threescore and five captive kings, had his own thumbs and great toes cut off, or as when Haman was himself hung on the gallows that he built for Mordecai. We read in Psalm 9:16:

> "The Lord is known by the judgment which He executeth:
> The wicked is snared in the work of his own hands."

The inspired thought is that the punishment of evil-doers is in such exact correspondence with the character of their evil doings as to show that it is the Lord executing vengeance—the penalty shows a designing hand. He who watches the peculiar retributive judgments of God, how He causes those who set snares and pitfalls for others to fall into them themselves, will not doubt that behind such 'poetic retribution' there is an intelligent Judge.

Somewhat so the poetic harmony between prayer and its answer silences all question as to a discriminating Hearer of the suppliant soul. A single case of such answered prayer might be accounted accidental; but, ever since men began to call upon the name of the Lord, there have been such repeated, striking, and marvelous correspondences between the requests of man and the replies of God, that the inference is perfectly safe, the induction has too broad a basis and too large a body of particulars to allow mistake. The coincidences are both too many and too exact to admit the doctrine of *chance*. We are compelled, not to say justified, to conclude that the only sufficient and reasonable explanation must be found in a God who hears and answers prayer.

Mr. Müller was not the only party to these transactions, nor the only person thus convinced that God was in the whole matter of the work and its support. The *donors* as well as the receiver were conscious of divine leading.

Frequent were the instances also when those who gave most timely help conveyed to Mr. Müller the knowledge of the experiences that accompanied or preceded their offerings; as, for example, when, without any intimation being given them from man that there was special need, the heart was impressed in prayer to God that there was an emergency requiring prompt assistance.

For example, in June, 1841, fifty pounds were received with these words: *"I am not concerned at my having been prevented for so many days from sending this money; I am confident it has not been needed."*

"This last sentence is remarkable," says Mr. Müller. "It is now nearly three years since our funds were for the first time exhausted, and only at this period, since then, could it have been said in truth, so far as I remember, that a donation of fifty pounds was *not* needed. From the beginning in July, 1838, till now, there never had been a period when we so abounded as when this donation came; for there were then, in the orphan fund and the other funds, between two and three hundred pounds! The words of our brother are so much the more remarkable as, on four former occasions, when he likewise gave considerable donations, we were always in need, yea, great need, which he afterwards knew from the printed accounts."

Prevailing prayer is largely conditioned on constant obedience. "Whatsoever we ask we receive of Him, because we keep His commandments, and do those things which are well pleasing in His sight." (1 John 3:22) There is no way of keeping in close touch with God unless a *new step* is taken in advance whenever *new light* is given. Here is another of the life-secrets of George Müller. Without unduly counting the cost, he followed every leading of God.

In July, 1841, both Mr. Craik and Mr. Müller were impressed that the existing mode of receiving free-will offerings from those among whom they laboured was inexpedient. These contributions were deposited in boxes, over which their names were placed with an explanation of the purpose to which such offerings were applied. But it was felt that this might have the appearance of unduly elevating them above others, as though they were assuming official importance, or excluding others from full and equal recognition as labourers in word and doctrine. They therefore decided to discontinue this mode of receiving such offerings.

Such an act of obedience may seem to some, over-scrupulous, but it cost some inward struggles, for it threatened a possible and probable decrease in supplies for their own needs, and the question naturally arose how such lack should be supplied. Happily Mr. Müller had long ago settled the question that *to follow a clear sense of duty is always safe.* He could say, in every such crisis, "O God, my heart is fixed, my heart is fixed, trusting in Thee." (Psalm 112:7) Once for all having made such a decision, such apparent risks did not for a moment disturb his peace. Somehow or other the Lord would provide, and all he had to do was to serve and trust Him and leave the rest to His Fatherhood.

In the autumn of 1841 it pleased God that, beyond any previous period, there should be a severe test of faith. For some months the supplies had been comparatively abundant, but now, from day to day and from meal to meal, the eye of faith had to be turned to the Lord, and, notwithstanding continuance in prayer, *help seemed at times to fail,* so much so

SCRIPTURE TESTIMONY

Giving all one has to live on, and trusting God for provision

Mark 12:41-44 · Luke 21:1-4

God provides exactly what is needed

2 Corinthians 8:15

that it was a special sign of God's grace that, during this long trial of delay, the confidence of Mr. Müller and his helpers did not altogether give way. But he and they were held up, and he unwaveringly rested on the fatherly pity of God.

On one occasion a poor woman gave two pence, adding, "It is but a trifle, but I must give it to you." Yet so opportune was the gift of these 'two mites' that *one of these two pence* was just what was at that time needed to make up the sum required to buy bread for immediate use. At another time eight pence more being necessary to provide for the next meal, but *seven* pence were in hand; but on opening one of the boxes, *one penny* only was found deposited, and thus a single penny was traced to the Father's care.

It was in December of this same year, 1841, that, in order to show how solely dependence was placed on a heavenly Provider, it was determined to *delay for a while* both the holding of any public meeting and the printing of the Annual Report. Mr. Müller was confident that, though no word should be either spoken or printed about the work and its needs, the means would still be supplied. As a matter of fact the report of 1841-2 was thus postponed for five months; and so, *in the midst of deep poverty* and *partly because of the very pressure of such need,* another bold step was taken, which, like the cutting away of the ropes that held the life-boat, in that Mediterranean shipwreck, threw Mr. Müller, and all that were with him in the work, more completely on the promise and the providence of God.

It might be inferred that, where such a decision was made, the Lord would make haste to reward at once such courageous confidence. And yet, so mysterious are His ways, that never, up to that time, had Mr. Müller's faith been tried so sharply as between December 12, 1841, and April 12, 1842. During these four months, again, it was as though God were saying, "I will now see whether indeed you truly lean on Me and look to Me." At any time during this trial, Mr. Müller might have changed his course, holding the public meeting and publishing the report, for, outside the few who were in his councils, *no one knew of the determination,* and in fact many children of God, looking for the usual year's journal of 'The Lord's Dealings,' were surprised at the delay. But the conclusion conscientiously reached was, for the glory of the Lord, as steadfastly pursued, and again Jehovah Jireh revealed His faithfulness.

During this four months, on March 9, 1842, the need was so extreme that, had no help come, the work could not have gone on. But, *on that day,* from a brother living near Dublin, ten pounds came: and the hand of the Lord clearly appeared in this gift, for when the post had already come and no letter had come with it, there was a strong confidence suggested to Mr. Müller's mind that deliverance was at hand; and so it proved, for presently the letter was brought to him, having been delivered at one of the other houses. During this same month, it was necessary once to *delay dinner for about a half-hour,* because of a lack of supplies. Such a postponement had scarcely ever been known before, and very rarely was it repeated in the entire after-history of the work, though thousands of mouths had to be daily fed.

In the spring of 1843, Mr. Müller felt led to open a *fourth orphan house,* the third having been opened nearly six years before. This step was taken with his uniform conscientiousness, deliberation, and prayerfulness. He had seen many reasons for such enlargement of the work, but he had said nothing about the matter even to his beloved wife. Day by day he waited on God in prayer, preferring to take counsel only of Him, lest he might do something in haste, move in advance of clear leading, or be biassed unduly by human judgment.

Unexpected obstacles interfered with his securing the premises which had already been offered and found suitable; but he was in no way 'discomforted.' The burden of his prayer was, "Lord, if *Thou* hast no need of another orphan house, *I* have none"; and he rightly judged that the calm deliberation with which he had set about the whole matter, and the unbroken peace with which he met new hindrances, were proofs that he was following the guidance of God and not the motions of self-will.

As the public meeting and the publication of the Annual Report had been purposely postponed to show that no undue dependence was placed even on indirect appeals to man, much special prayer went up to God, that, *before July 15,* 1844, when the public meeting was to be held, He would so richly supply all need that it might clearly appear that, notwithstanding these lawful means of informing His servants concerning the work had for a time not been used, the prayer of faith had drawn down help from above. As the financial year had closed in May, it would be more than *two years* since the previous report had been made to the public.

George Müller was jealous for the Lord God of hosts, He desired that "even the shadow of ground might be cut off for persons to say, 'They cannot get any more money; and therefore they now publish another report.'" Hence, while, during the whole progress of the work, he desired to stand with his Master, without heeding either the favourable or unfavourable judgments of men, he felt strongly that God would be much honoured and glorified as the prayer-hearing God if, before the public had been at all apprised of the situation, an ample supply might be given. In such case, instead of appearing to ask aid of men, he and his associates would be able to witness to the church and the world, God's faithfulness, and offer Him the praise of joyful and thankful hearts. As he had asked, so was it done unto him. Money and other supplies came in, and, on the day before the accounts were closed, such liberal gifts, that there was a *surplus of over twenty pounds* for the whole work.

CHAPTER XIII

Following the Pillar of Cloud and Fire

"THE STEPS of a good man are ordered by the Lord." (Psalm 37: 23) Some one quaintly adds, "Yes, and the *stops, too!*" The pillar of cloud and fire is a symbol of that divine leadership which guides both as to forward steps and intervals of rest. Mr Müller found it blessed to follow, one step at a time, as God ordered his way, and to stand still and wait when He seemed to call for a halt.

At the end of May, 1843, a crisis was reached, which was a new example of the experiences to which faith is liable in the walk with God; and a new illustration of the duty and delight of depending upon Him in everything and for everything, habitually waiting upon Him, and trusting in Him to remove all hindrances in the way of service.

Some eighteen months previously, a German lady from Wurtemberg had called to consult him as to her own plans, and, finding her a comparative stranger to God, he spoke to her about her spiritual state, and gave her the first two parts of his Narrative. The perusal of these pages was so blest to her that she was converted to God, and felt moved to translate the Narrative into her own tongue as a channel of similar blessing to other hearts.

This work of translation she partially accomplished, though somewhat imperfectly; and the whole occurrence impressed Mr. Müller as an indication that God was once more leading him in the direction of Germany, for another season of labour in his native land. Much prayer deepened his persuasion that he had not misread God's signal, and that His time had now fully come. He records some of the motives which led to this conclusion.

1. First, he yearned to encourage believing brethren who for conscience' sake had felt constrained to separate themselves from the state churches,

and meet for worship in such conditions as would more accord with New Testament principles, and secure greater edification.

2. Being a German himself, and therefore familiar with their language, customs, and habits of thought, he saw that he was fitted to wield a larger influence among his fellow countrymen than otherwise.
3. He was minded to publish his Narrative in his own tongue wherein he was born, not so much in the form of a mere translation, as of an independent record of his life's experiences such as would be specially suited to its new mission.
4. An effectual door was opened before him, and more widely than ever, especially at Stuttgart; and although there were many adversaries, they only made his help the more needful to those whose spiritual welfare was in peril.
5. A distinct burden was laid on his heart, as from the Lord, which prayer, instead of relieving, increased—a burden which he *felt* without being able to explain—so that the determination to visit his native land gave him a certain peace which he did not have when he thought of remaining at home.

To avoid mistake, with equal care he records the counter-arguments.

1. The new orphan house, No. 4, was about to be opened, and his presence was desirable if not needful.
2. A few hundred pounds were needed, to be left with his helpers, for current expenses in his absence.
3. Money was also required for travelling expenses of himself and his wife, whose health called for a change.
4. Funds would be needful to publish four thousand copies of his Narrative and avoid too high a market-price.
5. A matron for the new orphan house was not yet found, suitable for the position.

In this careful *weighing of matters* many sincere disciples fail, prone to be impatient of delay in making decisions. Impulse too often sways, and self-willed plans betray into false and even disastrous mistakes. Life is too precious to risk one such failure. There is given us a promise of deep meaning:

> "The meek will He guide in judgment;
> And the meek will He teach His way." (Psalm 25:9)

Here is a double emphasis upon *meekness* as a condition of such guidance and teaching. *Meekness is a real preference for God's will.* Where this holy habit of mind exists, the whole being becomes so open to impression that, without any *outward* sign or token, there is an *inward* recognition and choice of the will of God. God guides, not by a visible sign, but by *swaying the judgment.* To wait before Him, weighing candidly in the scales every consideration for or against a proposed course, and in readiness to see which way the preponderance lies, is a frame of mind and heart in which one is fitted to be guided; and God touches the scales and makes the balance to sway as He will. *But our hands must be off the scales,* otherwise we need expect no interposition of His, in our favour. To return to the figure with which this chapter starts, the meek soul simply and humbly waits, and *watches the moving of the Pillar.*

SCRIPTURE TESTIMONY
The weary are invited to receive rest from Jesus Matthew 11:28-29

One sure sign of this spirit of meekness is the entire *restfulness* with which apparent obstacles to any proposed plan or course are regarded. When waiting and wishing only to know and do God's will, hindrances will give no anxiety, but a sort of pleasure, as affording a new opportunity for divine interposition. If it is the Pillar of God we are following, the Red Sea will not dismay us, for it will furnish but another scene for the display of the power of Him who can make the waters to stand up as an heap, and to become a wall about us as we go through the sea on dry ground.

Mr. Müller had learned this rare lesson, and in this case he says: *"I had a secret satisfaction in the greatness of the difficulties which were in the way.* So far from being cast down on account of them, they delighted my soul; for I only desired to do the will of the Lord in this matter."

Here is revealed another secret of holy serving. To him who sets the Lord always before him, and to whom the will of God is his delight, there pertains a habit of soul which, in advance settles a thousand difficult and perplexing questions.

The case in hand is an illustration of the blessing found in such meek preference for God's pleasure. If it were the will of the Lord that this Continental tour should be undertaken at that time, difficulties need not cast him down; for the *difficulties could not be of God;* and, if not of God, they should give him no unrest, for, in answer to prayer, they would all be removed. If, on the other hand, this proposed visit to the Continent were *not* God's plan at all, but only the fruit of self-will; if some secret, selfish, and perhaps subtle motive were controlling, then indeed hindrances might well be interferences of God, designed to stay his steps. In the latter case, Mr. Müller rightly judged that difficulties in the way would naturally vex and annoy him; that he would not like to look at them, and would seek to remove them by his own efforts. Instead of giving him an inward satisfaction as affording God an opportunity to intervene in his behalf, they would arouse impatience and vexation, as preventing self-will from carrying out its own purposes.

Such discriminations have only to be stated to any spiritual mind, to have their wisdom at once apparent. Any believing child of God may safely gauge the measure of his surrender to the will of God, in any matter, by the measure of impatience he feels at the obstacles in the way; for in proportion as self-will sways him, whatever seems to oppose or hinder his plans will disturb or annoy; and, instead of quietly leaving all such hindrances and obstacles to the Lord, to deal with them as He pleases, in His own way and time, the wilful disciple will, impatiently and in the energy of the flesh, set himself to remove them by his own scheming and struggling, and he will brook no delay.

Whenever Satan acts as a hinderer (1 Thessalonians 2:18) the obstacles which he puts in our way need not dismay us; God permits them to delay or deter us for the time, only as a test of our patience and faith, and the satanic hinderer will be met by a divine Helper who will sweep away all his obstacles, as with the breath of His mouth.

Mr. Müller felt this, and he waited on God for light and help. But, after forty days' waiting, the hindrances, instead of decreasing, seemed rather to increase. Much more money was spent than was sent in; instead of finding another suitable matron, a sister, already at work, was probably about to withdraw, so that two vacancies would need to be filled instead of one. Yet his rest and peace of mind were unbroken. Being persuaded that he was yielded up to the will of God, faith not only held him to his purpose, but saw the obstacles already surmounted, so that he gave thanks in advance. Because Caleb "followed the Lord fully," even the giant sons of Anak with their walled cities and chariots of iron had for him no terrors. Their defence was departed from them, but the Lord was with His believing follower, and made him strong to drive them out and take possession of their very stronghold as his own inheritance.

During this period of patient waiting, Mr. Müller remarked to a believing sister: "Well, my soul is at peace. The Lord's time is not yet come; but, when it is come, He will blow away all these obstacles, as chaff is blown away before the wind." *A quarter of an hour later,* a gift of seven hundred pounds became available for the ends in view, so that three of the five hindrances to this Continental tour were at once removed. All travelling expenses for himself and wife, all necessary funds for the home work for two months in advance, and all costs of publishing the Narrative in German, were now provided. This was on July 12th; and so soon afterward were the remaining impediments out of the way that, by August 9th, Mr. and Mrs. Müller were off for Germany.

The trip covered but seven months: and on March 6, 1844, they were once more in Bristol. During this sojourn abroad no journal was kept, but Mr. Müller's letters serve the purpose of a record. Rotterdam, Weinheim, Cologne, Mayence, Stuttgart, Heidelberg, etc., were visited, and Mr. Müller distributed tracts and conversed with individuals by the way; but his main work was to expound the

Word in little assemblies of believers, who had separated themselves from the state church on account of what they deemed errors in teaching, practice, modes of worship, etc.

The first hour of his stay at Stuttgart brought to him one of the sharpest trials of faith he had ever thus far experienced. The nature of it he does not reveal in his journal, but it now transpires that it was due to the recalling of the seven hundred pounds, the gift of which had led to his going to Germany. This fact could not at the time be recorded because the party would feel it a reproach. Nor was this the only test of faith during his sojourn abroad; in fact so many, so great, so varied, and so prolonged were some of these trials, as to call into full exercise all the wisdom and grace which he had received from God, and whatever lessons he had previously learned in the school of experience became now of use. Yet not only was his peace undisturbed, but he bears witness that the conviction so rooted itself in his inmost being that in all this God's goodness was being shown, that he would have had nothing different. The greatest trials bore fruit in the fullest blessings and sometimes in clusters of blessings. It particularly moved him to adoring wonder and praise to see God's wisdom in having delayed his visit until the very time when it occurred. Had he gone any earlier he would have gone too soon, lacking the full experience necessary to confront the perplexities of his work. When darkness seemed to obscure his way, faith kept him expectant of light, or at least of guidance in the darkness; and he found that promise to be literally fulfilled:

> "As thou goest, step by step, the way shall open up before thee." (See the Hebrew, of Proverbs 4:12)

SCRIPTURE TESTIMONY
A workman of God handles the Word correctly 2 Timothy 2:15

At Stuttgart he found and felt, like Jude, that it was "needful earnestly to contend for the faith once delivered to the saints." Even among believers, errors had found far too deep root. Especially was undue stress laid upon *baptism,* which was made to occupy a prominence and importance out of all due proportion of faith. One brother had been teaching that without it there is no new birth, and that, consequently, no one could, before baptism, claim the forgiveness of sins; that the apostles were not born from above until the day of Pentecost, and that our Lord Himself had not been new-born until His own baptism, and had thence, for the rest of His mortal life, ceased to be under the law! Many other fanciful notions were found to prevail, such as that baptism is the actual death of the old man by drowning, and that it is a covenant with the believer into which God enters; that it is a sin to break bread with unbaptized believers or with members of the state church; and that the bread and the cup used in the Lord's Supper not only mean but are the very body and blood of the Lord, etc.

A more serious and dangerous doctrine which it was needful to confront and confute was what Mr. Müller calls that "awful error," spread almost universally among believers in that land, that at last "all will be saved," not-sinful men only, but "even the devils themselves."

Calmly and courteously, but firmly and courageously, these and kindred errors were met with the plain witness of the Word. Refutation of false teaching aroused a spirit of bitterness in opposers of the truth, and, as is too often the case, faithful testimony was the occasion of acrimony; but the Lord stood by His servant and so strengthened him that he was kept both faithful and peaceful.

One grave practical lack which Mr. Müller sought to remedy was ignorance of those deeper truths of the Word, which relate to the power and presence of the Holy Spirit of God in the church, and to the ministry of saints, one to another, as fellow members in the body of Christ, and as those to whom that same Spirit divides severally, as He will, spiritual gifts for service. As a natural result of being untaught in these important practical matters, believers' meetings had proved rather opportunities for unprofitable talk than godly edifying which is in faith. The only hope of meeting such errors and supplying such lack lay in faithful scripture teaching, and he undertook for a time to act as the sole teacher in these gatherings, that the word of God might have free course and be glorified. Afterward, when there seemed to be among the brethren some proper apprehension of vital spiritual truths, with his usual consistency and humility he resumed his place as simply a brother among fellow believers, all of whom had liberty to teach as the Spirit might lead and guide. There was, however, no shrinking from any duty or responsibility laid upon him by larger, clearer acquaintance with truth, or more complete experience of its power. When called by the voice of his brethren to expound the Word in public assemblies, he gladly embraced all opportunities for further instruction out of Holy Scripture and of witness to God. With strong emphasis he dwelt upon the presiding presence of the Blessed Spirit in all assemblies of saints, and upon the duty and privilege of leaving the whole conduct of such assemblies to His divine ordering; and in perfect accord, with such teaching he showed that the Holy Spirit, if left free to administer all things, would lead such brethren to speak, at such times and on such themes as He mighty please; and that, whenever their desires and preferences were spiritual and not carnal, such choice of the Spirit would always be in harmony with their own.

These views of the Spirit's administration in the assemblies of believers, and of His manifestation in all believers for common profit, fully accord with scripture teaching. (1 Corinthians 12, Romans 12, Ephesians 4, etc.) Were such views practically held in the church of this day, a radical revolution would be wrought and a revival of apostolic faith and primitive church life would inevitably follow.

No one subject is perhaps more misunderstood, or less understood, even among professed believers, than the person, offices, and functions of the Spirit of God. John Owen, long since, suggested that the practical test of soundness in the faith, during the present gospel age, is *the attitude of the church toward the Holy Spirit.* If so, the great apostasy cannot be far off, if indeed it is not already upon us, for there is a shameful ignorance and indifference prevalent, as to the whole matter of His claim to holy reverence and obedience.

In connection with this visit to Germany, a curious misapprehension existed, to which a religious periodical had given currency, that Mr. Müller was deputed by the English Baptists to labour among German Baptists to bring them back to the state church. This rumour was of course utterly unfounded, but he had no chance to correct it until just before his return to Britain, as he had not until then heard of it. The Lord had allowed this false report to spread and had used it to serve His own ends, for it was due in part to this wrong impression of Mr. Müller's mission that he was not molested or interfered with by the officers of the government. Though for months openly and undisguisedly teaching vital gospel truths among believers who had separated from the established church, he had suffered no restraint, for, so long as it was thought that his mission in Germany was to reclaim to the fold of the state church those who had wandered away, he would of course be liable to no interference from state officials.

The Lord went before His servant also in preparing the way for the publishing of his Narrative, guiding him to a bookseller who undertook its sale on commission, enabling the author to retain two thousand copies to give away, while the rest were left to be sold.

Mr. Müller, about this time, makes special mention of his joy and comfort in the spiritual blessing attending his work, and the present and visible good, wrought through the publication of his Narrative. Many believers had been led to put more faith in the promises of the great Provider, and unbelievers had been converted by their perusal of the simple story of the Lord's dealings; and these tidings came from every quarter where the Narrative had as yet found its way.

The name of Henry Craik, hitherto affixed to every report together with George Müller's, appears for the last time in the Report of 1844. This withdrawal of his name resulted, not from any division of feeling or diminution of sympathy, but solely from Mr. Craik's conviction that the honour of being used of God as His instrument in forwarding the great work of the Scriptural Knowledge Institution belonged solely to George Müller.

The trials of faith ceased not although the occasions of praise were so multiplied. On September 4, 1844, day-dawn, but one farthing was left on hand, and hundred and forty mouths were to be fed at breakfast!'

The lack of money and such supplies was, however, only one form of these tests of faith and incentives to prayer. Indeed he accounted these the lightest of his burdens, for there were other cares and anxieties that called for greater exercise of faith resolutely to cast them on Him who, in exchange for solicitude, gives His own perfect peace. What these trials were, any thoughtful mind must at once see who remembers how these many orphans were needing, not only daily supplies of food and clothing, but education, in mind and in morals; preparation for, and location in, suitable homes; careful guards about their health and every possible precaution and provision to prevent disease; also the character of all helpers must be carefully investigated before they were admitted, and their conduct carefully watched afterward lest any unworthy or unqualified party should find a place, or be retained, in the conduct of the work.

These and other matters, too many to be individually mentioned, had to be borne daily to the great Helper, without whose Everlasting Arms they could not have been carried. And Mr. Müller seeks constantly to impress on all who read his pages or heard his voice, the perfect trustworthiness of God. For any and all needs of the work help was always given, and *it never once came too late.* However poor, and however long the suppliant believer waits on God, he never fails to get help, if he trusts the promises and is in the path of duty. Even the delay in answered prayer serves a purpose. God permits us to call on Him while He answers not a word, both to test our faith and importunity, and to encourage others who hear of His dealings with us.

And so it was that, whether there were on hand much or little, by God's grace the founder of these institutions remained untroubled, confident that deliverance would surely come in the best way and time, not only with reference to temporal wants, but in all things needful.

During the history of the Institution thus far, enlargement had been its law. Mr. Müller's heart grew in capacity for larger service, and his faith in capacity for firmer confidence, so that while he was led to attempt greater things for God, he was led also to expect greater things from God. Those suggestive words of Christ to Nathanael have often prompted like larger expectations: "Believest thou? thou shalt see greater things than these." (John 1:50)

In the year 1846, *the wants of the mission field* took far deeper hold of him than ever before. He had already been giving aid to brethren abroad, in British Guiana and elsewhere, as well as in fields nearer at home. But he felt a strong yearning to be used of God more largely in sending to their fields and supporting in their labours, the chosen servants of the Lord who were working on a scriptural basis and were in need of help. He had observed that whenever God had put into his heart to devise liberal things, He had put into his hand the means to carry out such liberal purposes; and from this time forth he determined, as far as God should enable him, to aid brethren of good report, labouring in word and doctrine, throughout the United Kingdom, who were faithful witnesses to God and were receiving no regular salary. The special object he had in view was to give a helping hand to such as for the sake of conscience and of Christ had relinquished former stipends or worldly emoluments.

Whatever enlargement took place in the work, however, it was no sign of *surplus funds.* Every department of service or new call of duty had separate and prayerful consideration. Advance steps were taken only when and where and so fast as the Pillar moved, and fresh work was often undertaken at a time when there was a lack rather than an abundance of money.

Some who heard of Mr. Müller's absence in Germany inferred plenty of funds on hand—a conclusion that was neither true nor legitimate. At times when poverty was most pressing, additional expenditure was not avoided nor new responsibility evaded if, after much prayer, the Lord seemed plainly leading in that direction. And it was beautiful to see how He did not permit any existing work to be embarrassed because at His bidding new work was Undertaken.

One great law for all who would be truly led by God's Pillar of cloud and fire, is to take no step at the bidding of self-will or without the clear moving of the heavenly Guide. Though the direction be new and the way seem beset with difficulty, there is never any risk, provided we are only led of God. Each new advance needs separate and special authority from Him, and yesterday's guidance is not sufficient for to-day.

It is important also to observe that, if one branch of the work is in straits, it is not necessarily a reason for abandoning another form of service. The work of God depends on Him alone. If the whole tree is His planting, we need not cut off one limb to save another. The whole body is His, and, if one member is weak, it is not necessary to cut off another to make it strong, for the strength of the whole body is the dependence of every part. In our many-branching service each must get vitality and vigour from the same source in God. Nevertheless let us not forget that the *stops,* as well as the *steps,* of a good man are ordered of the Lord. If the work is His work, let Him control it, and, whether we expand or contract, let it be at His bidding, and a matter of equal satisfaction to His servant.

CHAPTER XIV

God's Building: The New Orphan Houses

HOW COMPLEX are the movements of God's providence! Some events are themselves eventful. Like the wheels in Ezekiel's vision—a wheel in the middle of a wheel,—they involve other issues within their mysterious mechanism, and constitute epochs of history. Such an epochal event was the building of the first of the New Orphan Houses on Ashley Down.

After October, 1845, it became clear to Mr. Müller that the Lord was leading in this direction. Residents on Wilson Street had raised objections to the noise made by the children, especially in play hours; the playgrounds were no longer large enough for so many orphans; the drainage was not adequate, nor was the situation of the rented houses favourable, for proper sanitary conditions; it was also desirable to secure ground for cultivation, and thus supply outdoor work for the boys, etc. Such were some of the reasons which seemed to demand the building of a new orphan house; and the conviction steadily gained ground that the highest well-being of all concerned would be largely promoted if a suitable site could be found on which to erect a building adapted to the purpose.

There were objections to building which were carefully weighed: money in large sums would be needed; planning and constructing would severely tax time and strength; wisdom and oversight would be in demand at every stage of the work; and the question arose whether such permanent structures befit God's pilgrim people, who have here no continuing city and believe that the end of all things is at hand.

Continuance in prayer, however, brought a sense of quiet and restful conviction that all objections were overbalanced by other and favourable considerations. One argument seemed particularly weighty: Should God provide large amounts of money for this purpose, it would still further illustrate the power of prayer, offered in faith, to command help from on high. A lot of ground, spacious enough, would, at the outset, cost thousands of pounds; but why should this daunt a true child of God whose Father was infinitely rich? Mr. Müller and his helpers sought day by day to be guided of God, and, as faith fed on this daily bread of contact with Him, the assurance grew strong that help would come. Shortly Mr. Müller was as sure of this as though the building already stood before his eyes, though for five weeks not one penny had been sent in for this purpose. Meanwhile there went on that searching scrutiny of his own heart by which he sought to know whether any hidden motive of a selfish sort was swaying his will; but as strict self-examination brought to light no conscious purpose but to glorify God, in promoting the good of the orphans, and provoking to larger trust in God all who witnessed the work, it was judged to be God's will that he should go forward.

> SCRIPTURE TESTIMONY
>
> *God will provide for our daily needs*
>
> Matthew 6:11

In November of this year, he was much encouraged by a visit from a believing brother[27] who bade him go on in the work, but wisely impressed on him the need of asking for wisdom from above, at every step, seeking God's help in showing him the plan for the building, that all details might accord with the divine mind. On the thirty-sixth day after specific prayer had first been offered about this new house, on December 10, 1845, Mr. Müller received *one thousand pounds* for this purpose, the largest sum yet received *in one donation* since the work had begun, March 5, 1834. Yet he was as calm and composed as though the gift had been only a shilling; having full faith in God, as both guiding and providing, he records that he would not have been surprised had the amount been five or ten times greater.

Three days later, a Christian architect in London voluntarily offered not only to draught the plans, but gratuitously to superintend the building! This offer had been brought about in a manner so strange as to be naturally regarded as a new sign and proof of God's approval and a fresh pledge of His sure help. Mr. Müller's sister-in-law, visiting the metropolis, had met this architect; and, finding him much interested to know more of the work of which he had read in the narrative, she had told him of the purpose to build; whereupon, without either solicitation or expectation on her part, this cheerful offer was made. Not only was this architect not urged by her, but he pressed his proposal, himself, urged on by his deep interest in the orphan work. Thus, within forty days, the first thousand pounds had been given in answer to prayer, and a pious man, as yet unseen and unknown by Mr. Müller, had been led to offer his services in providing plans for the new building and superintending its erection. Surely God was moving before His servant.

---

27 Robert C. Chapman, of Barnstaple, yet living—and whom Mr. Müller cherished as his "oldest friend."

New Orphan Houses, No. 3 and No. 5

For a man, personally penniless, to attempt to erect such a house, on such a scale, without appeal to man and in sole dependence on God was no small venture of faith.

The full risk involved in such an undertaking, and the full force of the testimony which it has since afforded to a prayer-hearing God, can be felt only as the full weight of the responsibility is appreciated and all the circumstances are duly considered.

First of all, ground must be bought, and it must comprise six or seven acres, and the site must be in or near Bristol; for Mr. Müller's general sphere of work was in the city, the orphans and their helpers should be within reasonable reach of their customary meeting-place, and on many other accounts such nearness to the city was desirable. But such a site would cost from two thousand to three thousand pounds.

Next the building must be constructed, fitted up, and furnished, with accommodations for three hundred orphans and their overseers, teachers, and various helpers. However plain the building and its furnishings, the total cost would reach from three to four times the price of the site.

Then, the annual cost of keeping such house open and of maintaining such a large body of inmates would be four or five thousand pounds more.

Here, then, was a prospective outlay of somewhere between ten thousand and fifteen thousand pounds, for site and building, with a further expense of one third as much more every year. No man so poor as George Müller, if at the same time sane, would ever have *thought* of such a gigantic scheme, much less have undertaken to work it out, if his faith and hope were not fixed on God. Mr. Müller himself confesses that here lay his whole secret. He was not driven onward by any self-seeking, but drawn onward by a conviction that he was doing the will of God. When Constantine was laying out on a vast scale the new capital on the Bosphorus, he met the misgivings of those about him who wondered at his audacity, by simply saying, "I am following One who is leading me." George Müller's scheme was not self-originated. He followed One who was leading him; and, because confident and conscious of such guidance, he had only to follow, trust, and wait.

In proportion as the undertaking was great, he desired God's hand to be very clearly seen. Hence he forbore even to seem prominent: he issued no circular, announcing his purpose, and spoke of it only to the few who were in his councils, and even then only as conversation led in that direction. He remembered the promise, "I will guide thee with Mine eye," and looking up to God, he took no step unless the divine glance or beck made duty "clear as daylight." As he saw the matter, his whole business was to wait on God in prayer with faith and patience.

The assurance became doubly sure that *God would build for Himself* a large orphan house near Bristol, to show to all, near and far, what a blessed privilege it is to trust in Him. He desired God Himself so manifestly to act as that he should be seen by all men to be nothing but His instrument, passive in His hands. Meanwhile he went on with his daily search into the Word, where he found instruction so rich, and encouragement so timely, that the Scriptures seemed written for his special use—to convey messages to him from above. For example, in the opening of the Book of Ezra, he saw how God, when His time had fully come for the return of His exiled people to their own land and for the rebuilding of His Temple, used Cyrus, an idolatrous king, to issue an edict, and to provide means for carrying out His own unknown purpose. He saw also how God stirred up the people to help the returning exiles in their work; and he said to himself, this same God can and will, in His own way, supply the money and all the needed help of man, stirring up the hearts of His own children to aid as He may please.

The first donations toward the work themselves embody a suggestive lesson. On December 10th, one thousand pounds had been given in one sum; twenty days later, fifty pounds more; and the next day, three and sixpence, followed, the same evening, by a second gift of a thousand pounds. Shortly after, a little bag, made of foreign seeds, and a flower wrought of shells, were sent to be sold for the fund; and, in connection with these last gifts, of very little inherent value, a promise was quoted, which had been prominently before the giver's mind, and which brought more encouragement to Mr. Müller than any mere sum of money:

> "Who art thou, O great mountain?
> Before Zerubbabel, thou shalt become a plain!" (Zechariah 4:7)

Gifts, however large, were never estimated by intrinsic worth, but as tokens of God's working in the minds of His people, and of His gracious working with and through His servant; and, for this reason, a thousand pounds caused no more sincere praise to God and no more excitement of mind than the fourpence given subsequently by a poor orphan.

Specially asking the Lord to go before him, Mr. Müller now began to seek a suitable *site.* About four weeks passed in seemingly fruitless search, when he was strongly impressed that very soon the Lord would give the ground, and he so told his helpers on the evening of Saturday, January 31, 1846. Within two days, his mind was drawn to *Ashley Down,* where he found lots singularly suited for his needs. Shortly after, he called twice on the owner, once at his house and again at his office; but on both occasions failing to find him, he only left a message. He judged that God's hand was to be seen *even in his not finding the man he sought,* and that, having twice failed the same day, he was not to push the matter as though self-willed, but patiently wait till the morrow. When he did find the owner, his patience was unexpectedly rewarded. He confessed that he had spent two wakeful hours in bed, thinking about his land, and about what reply he should make to Mr. Müller's inquiry as to its sale for an orphan house; and that he had determined, if it were applied for, to ask but one hundred and twenty pounds an acre, instead of two hundred, his previous price.

The bargain was promptly completed; and thus the Lord's servant, by not being in a hurry, saved, in the purchase of the site of seven acres, five hundred and sixty pounds! Mr. Müller had asked the Lord to go before him, and He had done so in a sense he had not thought of, first speaking about the matter to the owner, holding his eyes waking till He had made clear to him, as His servant and steward, what He would have him do in the sale of that property.[28]

Six days after, came the formal offer from the London architect of his services in surveying, in draughting plans, elevations, sections, and specifications, and in overseeing the work of construction; and a week later he came to Bristol, saw the site, and pronounced it in all respects well fitted for its purpose.

Up to June 4, 1846, the total sum in hand for the building was a little more than twenty-seven hundred pounds, a small part only of the sum needful; but Mr. Müller felt no doubt that in God's own time all that was required would be given. Two hundred and twelve days he had been waiting on God for the way to be opened for building, and he resolved to wait still further until the *whole sum* was in hand, using for the purpose only such gifts as were specified or left free for that end. He also wisely decided that others must henceforth share the burden, and that he would look out ten brethren of honest report, full of the Holy Ghost and of wisdom, to act as trustees to hold and administer this property in God's name. He felt that, as this work was now so enlarging, and the foundations of a permanent Institution were to be laid, the Christian public, who would aid in its erection and support, would be entitled to a representation in its conduct. At such a point as this many others have made a serious mistake, forfeiting confidence by administering public benefactions in a private manner and an autocratic spirit—their own head being the office, and their own pocket the treasury, of a public and benevolent institution.

Satan again acted as a hinderer. After the ground for the new orphan house had been found, bought and paid for, unforeseen obstacles prevented prompt possession; but Mr. Müller's peace was not disturbed, knowing even hindrances to be under God's control. If the Lord should allow one piece of land to be taken from him, it would only be because He was about to give him one still better; and so the delay only proved his faith and perfected his patience.

On July 6th, two thousand pounds were given—twice as large a gift as had yet come in one donation; and, on January 25, 1847, another like offering, so that, on July 5th following, the work of building began. Six months later, after four

28 Appendix G.

hundred days of waiting upon God for this new orphan house, nine thousand pounds had been given in answer to believing prayer.

As the new building approached completion, with its three hundred large windows, and requiring full preparation for the accommodation of about three hundred and thirty inmates, although above eleven thousand pounds had been provided, several thousand more were necessary. But Mr. Müller was not only helped, but far beyond his largest expectations. Up to May 26, 1848, these latter needs existed, and, had but *one* serious difficulty remained unremoved, the result must have been failure. But all the necessary money was obtained, and even more, and all the helpers were provided for the oversight of the orphans. On June 18, 1849, more than twelve years after the beginning of the work, the orphans began to be transferred from the four rented houses on Wilson Street to the new orphan house on Ashley Down. Five weeks passed before fresh applicants were received, that everything about the new institution might first be brought into complete order by some experience in its conduct. By May 26, 1850, however, there were in the house two hundred and seventy-five children, and the whole number of inmates was three hundred and eight.

The name—"The New Orphan *House*" rather than *"Asylum"*—was chosen to distinguish it from another institution, near by; and particularly was it requested that it might never be known as *"Mr. Müller's* Orphan House," lest undue prominence be given to one who had been merely God's instrument in its erection. He esteemed it a sin to appropriate even indirectly, or allow others to attribute to him, any part of the glory which belonged solely to Him who had led in the work, given faith and means for it, and helped in it from first to last. The property was placed in the hands of eleven trustees, chosen by Mr. Müller, and the deeds were enrolled in chancery. Arrangements were made that the house should be open to visitors only on Wednesday afternoons, as about one hour and a half were necessary to see the whole building.

Scarcely were the orphans thus housed on Ashley Down, before Mr. Müller's heart felt enlarged desire that one thousand, instead of three hundred, might enjoy such privileges of temporal provision and spiritual instruction; and, before the new year, 1851, had dawned, this yearning had matured into a purpose. With his uniform carefulness and prayerfulness, he sought to be assured that he was not following self-will, but the will of God; and again in the scales of a pious judgment the reasons for and against were conscientiously weighed. Would he be going 'beyond his measure,' spiritually, or naturally? Was not the work, with its vast correspondence and responsibility, already sufficiently great? Would not a new orphan house for three hundred orphans cost another fifteen thousand pounds, or, if built for seven hundred, with the necessary ground, thirty-five thousand? And, even when built and fitted and filled, would there not be the providing for daily wants, which is a perpetual care, and cannot be paid for at once like a site and a building? It would demand eight thousand pounds annual outlay to provide for another seven hundred little ones. To all objections the one all-sufficient answer was the all-sufficient God; and, because Mr. Müller's eye was on His power, wisdom, and riches, his own weakness, folly, and poverty were forgotten. Another objection was suggested: What if he should succeed in thus housing and feeding a thousand poor waifs, what would become of the institution *after his death?* The reply is memorable: "My business is, with all my might, to *serve my own generation by the will of God:* in so doing I shall best serve the next generation, should the Lord Jesus tarry." Were such objection valid, it were as valid against beginning any work likely to outlive the worker. And Mr. Müller remembered how Francké at Halle had to meet the same objection when, now over two hundred years ago, he founded the largest charitable establishment which, up to 1851, existed in the world. But when, after about thirty years of personal superintendence, Francké was taken away, his son-in-law, as we have seen, became the director. That fellow countryman who had spoken to Mr. Müller's soul in 1826, thus twenty-five years later encouraged him to go forward, to do his own duty and leave the future to the Eternal God.

Several reasons are recorded by Mr. Müller as specially influencing still further advance: the many applications that could not, for want of room, be accepted; the low moral state of the poorhouses to which these children of poverty were liable to be sent; the large number of distressing cases of orphanhood, known to be deserving of help; the previous experiences of the Lord's gracious leading and of the work itself; his calmness in view of the proposed expansion; and the spiritual blessing possible to a larger number of homeless children. But one reason overtopped all others: an enlarged service to man, attempted and achieved solely in dependence upon God, would afford a correspondingly weightier witness to the Hearer of prayer. These reasons, here recorded, will need no repetition in connection with subsequent expansions of the work, for, at every new stage of advance, they were what influenced this servant of God.

On January 4, 1851, another offering was received, of three thousand pounds—the largest single donation up to that date—which, being left entirely to his own disposal, encouraged him to go forward.

Again, he kept his own counsel. Up to January 25th, he had not mentioned, even to his own wife, his thought of a further forward movement, feeling that, to avoid all mistakes, he must first of all get clear light from God, and not darken it by misleading human counsel. Not until the Twelfth Report of the Scriptural Knowledge Institution was issued, was the public apprised of his purpose, with God's help to provide for seven hundred more needy orphans.

Up to October 2, 1851, only about eleven hundred pounds had been given directly toward the second proposed orphan house, and, up to May 26th following, a total of some thirty-five hundred pounds. But George Müller remembered one who, "after he had patiently endured, obtained the promise." He had waited over two years before all means needful for the first house had been supplied, and could wait still longer, if so God willed it, for the answers to present prayers for means to build a second.

After waiting upwards of nineteen months for the building fund for the second house, and receiving, almost daily, something in answer to prayer, on January 4, 1853, he had intimation that there were about to be paid him, as *the joint donation of several Christians, eighty-one hundred pounds,* of which he appropriated six thousand for the building fund. Again he was not surprised nor excited, though exceeding joyful and triumphant in God. Just two years previous, when recording the largest donation yet received,—three thousand pounds,—he had recorded also his expectation of still greater things; and now a donation between two and three times as large was about to come into his hands. It was not the amount of money, however, that gave him his overflowing delight, but the fact that not in vain had he made his boast in God.

As now some four hundred and eighty-three orphans were waiting for admission, he was moved to pray that soon the way might be opened for the new building to be begun. James 1:4 was deeply impressed upon him as the injunction now to be kept before him: "But let patience have her perfect work, that ye may be perfect, and entire, wanting nothing."

On May 26, 1853, the total sum available for the new building was about twelve thousand five hundred pounds, and over five hundred orphans had applied. Twice this sum would be needed, however, before the new house could be begun without risk of debt.

On January 8, 1855, several Christian friends united in the promise that fifty-seven hundred pounds should be paid to him for the work of God, and of this, thirty-four hundred was by him set apart for the building fund. As there were now between seven hundred and eight hundred applicants, it seemed of God that, at least, a site should be secured for another new orphan house; and a few weeks later Mr. Müller applied for the purchase of two fields adjoining the site of the first house. As they could not, however, be sold at that time, the only resource was to believe that the Lord had other purposes, or would give better ground than that on which His servant had set his mind.

Further thought and prayer suggested to him that two houses could be built instead of one, and located on each side of the existing building, upon the ground already owned. Accordingly it was determined to begin, on the south side, the erection of a house to accommodate four hundred orphans, there being money in the bank, or soon to be available, sufficient to build, fit up, and furnish it.

On May 26, 1856, nearly thirty thousand pounds were in hand for the new Orphan House No. 2; and on November 12, 1857, this house was opened for four hundred additional orphans, and there was a balance of nearly twenty-three hundred pounds. The God who provided the building furnished the helpers, without either difficulty or advertising.

With the beginning of the new year, Mr. Müller began to lay aside six hundred pounds as the first of the appropriations for the *third* orphan house, and the steps which led to the accomplishment of this work, also, were identical with those taken hitherto. A purchase was made of additional ground, adjoining the two buildings; and, as there were so many applicants and the cost of providing for a larger number would be but little more, it was determined to build so as to receive four hundred and fifty instead of three hundred, rejoicing that, in every enlargement of the work, it would be more apparent how much one poor man, simply trusting in God, can bring about by prayer; and that thus other children of God might be led to carry on the work of God in dependence solely on Him, and generally to trust Him more in all circumstances and positions.

Orphan House No. 3 was opened March 12, 1862, and with over ten thousand pounds in hand for current expenses. All the helpers needed had not then been supplied, but this delay was only a new incentive to believing prayer: and, instead of *once, thrice,* a day, God was besought to provide suitable persons. One after another was thus added, and in no case too late, so that the reception of children was not hindered nor was the work embarrassed.

Still further enlargement seemed needful, for the same reasons as previously. There was an increasing demand for accommodation of new applicants, and past experience of God's wondrous dealings urged him both to attempt and to expect greater things. Orphan Houses Nos. 4 and 5 began to loom up above his horizon of faith. By May 26, 1862, he had over sixty-six hundred pounds to apply on their erection. In November, 1864, a large donation of five thousand pounds was received from a donor who would let neither his name nor residence be known, and by this time about twenty-seven thousand pounds had thus accumulated toward the fifty thousand required. As more than half the requisite sum was thus in hand, the purchase of a site might safely be made and the foundations for the buildings be laid. Mr. Müller eyes had, for years, been upon land adjoining the three houses already built, separated from them only by the turnpike road. He called to see the agent, and found that the property was subject to a lease that had yet two years to run. This obstacle only incited to new prayer, but difficulties seemed to increase: the price asked was too high, and the Bristol Waterworks Company was negotiating for this same piece of land for reservoir purposes. Nevertheless God successively removed all hindrances, so that the ground was bought and conveyed to the trustees in March, 1865; and, after the purchase-money was paid, about twenty-five thousand pounds yet remained for the structures. Both the cost and the inconvenience of building would be greatly lessened by erecting both houses at the same time; and God was therefore asked for ample means speedily to complete the whole work.

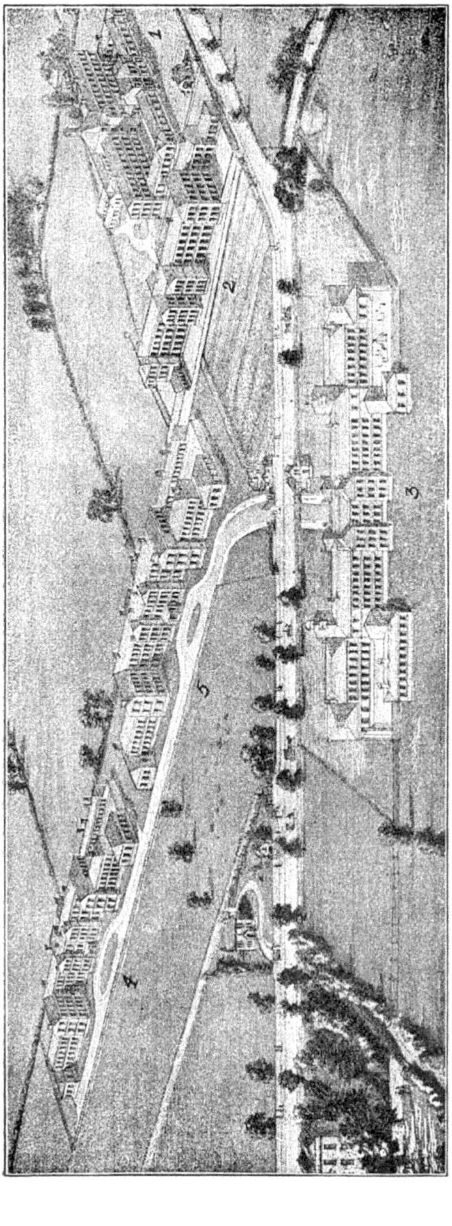

The Five New Orphan Houses, Ashley Down, Bristol

In May, 1866, over thirty-four thousand pounds being at Mr. Müller's disposal, No. 4 was commenced; and in January following, No. 5 also. Up to the end of March, 1867, over fifty thousand pounds had been supplied, leaving but six thousand more needful to fit and furnish the two buildings for occupancy. By the opening of February, 1868. fifty-eight thousand pounds in all had been donated; so that, on November 5, 1868, new Orphan House No. 4, and on January 6, 1870, No. 5, were thrown open, a balance of several thousand pounds remaining for general purposes. Thus, early in 1870, the orphan work had reached its complete outfit, in five large buildings on Ashley Down with accommodations for two thousand orphans and for all needed teachers and assistants.

Thus have been gathered, into one chapter, the facts about the erection of this great monument to a prayer-hearing God on Ashley Down, though the work of building covered so many years. Between the first decision to build, in 1845, and the opening of the third house, in 1862, nearly seventeen years had elapsed, and before No. 5 was opened, in 1870, twenty-five years. The work was one in its plan and purpose. At each new stage it supplies only a wider application and illustration of the same laws of life and principles of conduct, as, from the outset of the work in Bristol, had with growing power controlled George Müller. His one supreme aim was the glory of God; his one sole resort, believing prayer; his one trusted oracle, the inspired Word; and his one divine Teacher, the Holy Spirit. One step taken in faith and prayer had prepared for another; one act of trust had made him bolder to venture upon another, implying a greater apparent risk and therefore demanding more implicit trust. But answered prayer was rewarded faith, and every new risk only showed that there was no risk in confidently leaning upon the truth and faithfulness of God.

One cannot but be impressed, in visiting the orphan houses, with several prominent features, and first of all their magnitude. They are very spacious, with about seventeen hundred large windows, and accommodations for over two thousand inmates. They are also very substantial, being built of stone and made to last. They are scrupulously plain; utility rather than beauty seems conspicuously stamped upon them, within and without. Economy has been manifestly a ruling law in their construction; the furniture is equally unpretentious and unostentatious; and, as to garniture, there is absolutely none. To some few, they are almost too destitute of embellishment, and Mr. Müller has been blamed for not introducing some aesthetic features which might relieve this bald utilitarianism and serve to educate the taste of these orphans.

To all such criticisms, there are two or three adequate answers. First, Mr. Müller subordinated everything to his one great purpose, the demonstration of the fact that the Living God is the Hearer of prayer. Second, he felt himself to be the steward of God's property, and he hesitated to spend one penny on what was not necessary to the frugal carrying on of the work of God. He felt that all that could be spared without injury to health, a proper mental training, and a thorough scriptural and spiritual education, should be reserved for the relief of the necessities of the poor and destitute elsewhere. And again, he felt that, as these orphans were likely to be put at service in plain homes, and compelled to live frugally, any surroundings which would accustom them to indulge refined tastes, might by contrast make them discontented with their future lot. And so he studied to promote simply their health and comfort, and to school them to contentment when the necessities of life were supplied.

But, more than this, a moment's serious thought will show that, had he surrounded them with those elegancies which elaborate architecture and the other fine arts furnish, he might have been even more severely criticised. He would have been spending the gifts of the poor who often sorely denied themselves for the sake of these orphans, to purchase embellishments or secure decorations which, if they had adorned the humble homes of thousands of donors, would have made their gifts impossible. When we remember how many offerings, numbering tens of thousands, were, like the widow's mites, very small in themselves, yet, relatively to ability, very large, it will be seen how incongruous it would have been to use the gifts, saved only by limiting even the wants of the givers, to buy for the orphans what the donors could not and would not afford for themselves.

Cleanness, neatness, method, and order, however, everywhere reign, and honest labour has always had, at the orphan houses, a certain dignity. The tracts of land, adjoining the buildings, are set apart as vegetable-gardens, where wholesome exercise is provided for the orphan boys, and, at the same time, work that helps to provide daily food, and thus train them in part to self-support.

Throughout these houses studious care is exhibited, as to methodical arrangement. Each child has a square and numbered compartment for clothes, six orphans being told off, at a time, in each section, to take charge. The boys have each three suits, and the girls, five dresses each, the girls being taught to make and mend their own garments. In the nursery, the infant children have books and playthings to occupy and amuse them, and are the objects of tender maternal care. Several children are often admitted to the orphanage from one family, in order to avoid needless breaking of household ties by separation. The average term of residence is about ten years, though some orphans have been there for seventeen.

The daily life is laid out with regularity and goes on like clockwork in punctuality. The children rise at six and are expected to be ready at seven, the girls for knitting and the boys for reading, until eight o'clock, when breakfast is served. Half an hour later there is a brief morning service, and the school begins at ten. Half an hour of recreation on the playground prepares for the one-o'clock dinner, and school is resumed, until four; then comes an hour and a half of play or outdoor exercise, a half-hour service preceding the six-o'clock meal. Then the girls ply the needle, and the boys are in school, until bedtime, the younger children going to rest at eight, and the older, at nine. The food is simple, ample, and nutritious, consisting of bread, oatmeal, milk, soups, meat, rice, and vegetables. Everything is adjusted to one ultimate end; to use Mr. Müller's own words: "We aim at this: that, if any of them do not turn out well, temporally or spiritually, and do not become useful members of society, it shall not at least be *our* fault." The most thorough and careful examination of the whole methods of the institution will only satisfy the visitor that it will not be the fault of those who superintend this work, if the orphans are not well fitted, body and soul, for the work of life, and are not prepared for a blessed immortality.

CHAPTER XV

The Manifold Grace of God

Some one has quaintly said, in commenting upon the Twenty-third Psalm, that "the coach in which the Lord's saints ride has not only a driver, but two footmen"—*"goodness and mercy shall follow me."*

Surely these two footmen of the Lord, in their celestial livery of grace, followed George Müller all the days of his life. Wonderful as is the story of the building of those five orphan houses on Ashley Down, many other events and experiences no less showed the goodness and mercy of God, and must not be unrecorded in these pages, if we are to trace, however imperfectly, His gracious dealings; and having, by one comprehensive view, taken in the story of the orphan homes, we may retrace our steps to the year when the first of these houses was planned, and, following another path, look at Mr. Müller's personal and domestic life.

He himself loved to trace the Lord's goodness and mercy, and he saw abundant proofs that they had followed him. A few instances may be given, from different departments of experience, as representative examples.

The Lord's tender care was manifest as to his beloved daughter Lydia. It became clear in the year 1843, that, both for the relief of the mother and the profit of the daughter, it would be better that Lydia should be taught elsewhere than at home; and in answer to prayer, her father was divinely directed to a Christian sister, whose special gifts in the way of instructing and training children were manifestly from the Spirit, who divides unto all believers severally as He will. She seemed to be marked of God, as the woman to whom was to be intrusted the responsible task of superintending the education of Lydia. Mr. Müller both expected and desired to pay for such training, and asked for the account, which in the first instance he paid, but the exact sum was returned to him anonymously; and, for the six remaining years of his daughter's stay, he could get no further bills for her schooling. Thus God provided for the board and education of this only child, not only without cost to her parents, but to their intense satisfaction as being under the true "nurture and admonition of the Lord;" for while at this school, in April, 1846, Lydia found peace in believing, and began that beautiful life in the Lord Jesus Christ, that, for forty-four years afterward, so singularly exhibited His image.

Many Christian parents have made the fatal mistake of intrusting their children's education to those whose gifts were wholly intellectual and not spiritual, and who have misled the young pupils entrusted to their care, into an irreligious or infidel life, or, at best, a career of mere intellectualism and worldly ambition. In not a few instances, all the influences of a pious home have been counteracted by the atmosphere of a school which, if not godless, has been without that fragrance of spiritual devoutness and consecration which is indispensable to the true training of impressible children during the plastic years when character is forming for eternity!

Goodness and mercy followed Mr. and Mrs. Müller conspicuously in their sojourn in Germany in 1845, which covered about three months, from July 19th to October 11th.

God plainly led to Stuttgart, where brethren had fallen into grievous errors and needed again a helping hand. When the strong impression laid hold of Mr. Müller, more than two months before his departure for the Continent, that he was to return there for a season, he began definitely to pray for means to go with, on May 3rd, and, within a *quarter hour* after, five hundred pounds were received, the donor specifying that the money was given for all expenses needful, "preparatory to, and attendant upon" this proposed journey. The same goodness and mercy followed all his steps while abroad. Provision was made, in God's own strange way, for suitable lodgings in Stuttgart, at a time when the city was exceptionally crowded, a wealthy retired surgeon, who had never before rented apartments, being led to offer them. All Mr. Müller's labours were attended with blessing: during part of the time he held as many as eight meetings a week; and he was enabled to publish eleven tracts in German, and judiciously to scatter over two hundred and twenty thousand of them, as well as nearly four thousand of his Narrative, and yet evade interference from the police.

SCRIPTURE TESTIMONY
Become all things to all people 1 Corinthians 9:19-23

One experience of this sojourn abroad should have special mention for the lesson it suggests, both in charity for others' views and loving adaptation to circumstances. A providential opening occurred to address meetings of about one hundred and fifty members of the state church. In his view the character of such assemblies was not wholly conformed to the Scripture pattern, and hence did not altogether meet his approval; but such opportunity was afforded to bear testimony for the truth's sake, and to exhibit Christian unity upon essentials, for love's sake, that he judged it of the Lord that he should enter this open door. Those who knew Mr. Müller but little, but knew his positive convictions and uncompromising loyalty to them, might suspect that he would have little forbearance with even minor errors, and would not bend himself from his stern attitude of inflexibility to accommodate himself to those who were ensnared by them. But those who knew him better, saw that he held fast the form of sound words with faith and love which are in Christ Jesus. Like Paul, ever ready to be made all things to all men that by all means he might save some, in his whole character and conduct nothing shone more radiantly beautiful, than Love. He felt that he who would lift up others must bow himself to lay hold on them; that to help brethren we must bear with them, not insisting upon matters of minor importance as though they were essential and fundamental. Hence his course, instead of being needlessly repellant, was tenderly conciliatory; and it was a conspicuous sign of grace that, while holding his own views of truth and duty so positively and tenaciously, the intolerance of bigotry was so displaced by the forbearance of charity that, when the Lord so led and circumstances so required, he could conform for a time to customs whose propriety he doubted, without abating either the earnestness of his conviction or the integrity of his testimony.

God's goodness and mercy were seen in the fact that, whenever more liberal things were devised for Him, He responded in providing liberally means to carry out such desires. This was abundantly illustrated not only in the orphan work, but in the history of the Scriptural Knowledge Institution; when, for years together, the various branches of this work grew so rapidly, until the point of full development was reached. The time indeed came when, in some departments, it pleased God that contraction should succeed expansion, but even here goodness ruled, for it was afterward seen that it was because *other brethren* had been led to take up such branches of the Lord's work, in all of which developments Mr. Müller as truly rejoiced as though it had been his work alone that was honoured of God.

The aiding of brethren in the mission fields grew more and more dear to his heart, and the means to indulge his unselfish desires were so multiplied that, in 1846, he found, on reviewing the history of the Lord's dealings, that he had been enabled to expend about *seven times* as much of late years as previously. It may here be added, again by way of anticipation, that when, nineteen years later, in 1865, he sat down to apportion to such labourers in the Lord as he was wont to assist, the sums he felt it desirable to send to each, he found before him the names of *one hundred and twenty-two* such! Goodness and mercy indeed! Here was but one branch of his work, and yet to what proportions and fruitfulness it had grown! He needed four hundred and sixty-six pounds to send them to fill out his appropriations, and he lacked ninety-two of this amount. He carried the lack to the Lord, and *that evening* received five pounds, and the *next morning* a hundred more, and a further "birthday memorial" of fifty, so that he had in all thirty-seven more than he had asked.

What goodness and mercy followed him in the strength he ever had to bear the heavy loads of care incident to his work! The Lord's coach bore him and his burdens together. Day by day his gracious Master preserved his peace unbroken, though disease found its way into this large family, though fit homes and work must be found for outgoing orphans, and fit care and training for incoming orphans; though crises were constantly arising and new needs constantly recurring, grave matters daily demanded prayer and watching, and perpetual diligence and vigilance were needful; for the Lord was his Helper, and carried all his loads.

During the winter of 1846-7 there was a peculiar season of dearth. Would God's goodness and mercy fail? There were those who looked on, more than half incredulous, saying to themselves if not to others, "I wonder how it is now with Mr. Müller and his orphans! If he is able to provide for them now as he has been, we will say nothing." But all through this time of widespread want his witness was, "We lack nothing: God helps us." Faith led when the way was too dark for sight; in fact the darker the road the more was the Hand felt that leads the blind by a way they know not. *They went through that winter as easily as through any other from the beginning of the work!*

Was it no sign that God's 'footmen' followed George Müller that the work never ceased to be both a work of faith and of prayer? that no difficulties or discouragements, no successes or triumphs, ever caused for an hour a departure from the sublime essential principles on which the work was based, or a diversion from the purpose for which it had been built up?

We have heard it said of a brother, much honoured of God in beginning a work of faith, that, when it had grown to greater proportions, he seemed to change its base to that of a business scheme. How it glorifies God that the holy enterprise, planted in Bristol in 1834, has known no such alteration in its essential features during all these years! Though the work grew, and its needs with it, until the expenses were twofold, threefold, fourfold, and, at last, seventyfold what they were when that first Orphan House was opened in Wilson Street, there has been no *change of base,* never any looking to man for patronage or support, never any dependence upon a regular income or fixed endowment. God has been, all through these years, as at first, the sole Patron and Dependence. The Scriptural Knowledge Institution has not been wrecked on the rocks of financial failure, nor has it even drifted away from its original moorings in the safe anchorage-ground of the Promises of Jehovah.

Was it not goodness and mercy that kept George Müller ever grateful as well as faithful! He did not more constantly feel his need of faith and prayer than his duty and privilege of abounding joy and praise. Some might think that, after such experiences of answered prayer, one would be less and less moved by them, as the novelty was lost in the uniformity of such interpositions. But no. When, in June, 1853, at a time of sore need, the Lord sent, in one sum, three hundred pounds, he could scarcely contain his triumphant joy in God. He walked up and down his room for a long time, his heart overflowing and his eyes too, his mouth filled with laughter and his voice with song, while he gave himself afresh to the faithful Master he served. God's blessings were to him always new and fresh. Answered prayers never lost the charm of novelty; like flowers plucked fresh every hour from the gardens of God, they never got stale, losing none of their beauty or celestial fragrance.

And what goodness and mercy was it that never suffered prayerfulness and patience to relax their hold, either when answers seemed to come fast and thick like snow-flakes, or when the heavens seemed locked up and faith had to wait patiently and long! Every day brought new demands for continuance in prayer. In fact, as Mr. Müller testifies, the only difference between latter and former days was that the difficulties were greater in proportion as the work was larger. But he adds that this was to be expected, for the Lord gives faith for the very purpose of trying it for the glory of His own name and the good of him who has the faith, and it is by these very trials that trust learns the secret of its triumphs.

Goodness and mercy not only guided but also *guarded* this servant of God. God's footmen bore a protecting shield which was always over him. Amid thousands of unseen perils, occasionally some danger was known, though generally after it was passed. While at Keswick labouring in 1847, for example, a man, taken deranged while lodging in the same house, shot himself. It afterward transpired that he had an impression that Mr. Müller had designs on his life, and had he met Mr. Müller during this insane attack he would probably have shot him with the loaded pistol he carried about on his person.

The pathway of this man of God sometimes led through deep waters of affliction, but goodness and mercy still followed, and held him up. In the autumn of 1852, his beloved brother-in-law, Mr. A. N. Groves, came back from the East Indies, very ill; and in May of the next year, after blessed witness for God, he fell asleep at Mr. Müller's house. To him Mr. Müller owed much through grace at the outset of his labours in 1829. By his example his faith had been stimulated and helped when, with no visible support or connection with any missionary society, Mr. Groves had gone to Baghdad with wife and children, for the sake of mission work in this far-off field, resigning a lucrative practice of about fifteen hundred pounds a year. The tie between these men was very close and tender and the loss of this brother-in-law gave keen sorrow.

In July following, Mr. and Mrs. Müller went through a yet severer trial. Lydia, the beloved daughter and only child,—born in 1832 and new-born in 1846, and at this time twenty years old and a treasure without price,—was taken ill in the latter part of June, and the ailment developed into a malignant typhoid which, two weeks later, brought her to the gates of death. These parents had to face the prospect of being left childless. But faith triumphed and prayer prevailed. Their darling Lydia was spared to be, for many years to come, a blessing beyond words, not only to them and to her future husband, but to many others in a wider circle of influence. Mr. Müller found, in this trial, a special proof of God's goodness and mercy, which he gratefully records, in the growth in grace, evidenced in his entire and joyful acquiescence in the Father's will, when, with such a loss apparently before him, his confidence was undisturbed that all things would work together for good. He could not but contrast with this experience of serenity, that broken peace and complaining spirit with which he had met a like trial in August, 1831, twenty-one years before. How, like a magnet among steel filings, the thankful heart finds the mercies and picks them out of the black dust of sorrow and suffering!

The second volume of Mr. Müller's Narrative closes with a paragraph in which he formally disclaims as impudent presumption and pretension all high rank as a miracle-worker, and records his regret that any work, based on scriptural promises and built on the simple lines of faith and prayer, should be accounted either phenomenal or fanatical.

The common ways of accounting for its success would be absurdly ridiculous and amusing were they not so sadly unbelieving. Those who knew little or nothing, either of the exercise of faith or the experience of God's faithfulness, resorted to the most God-dishonouring explanations of the work. Some said: "Mr. Müller is a foreigner; his methods are so novel as to attract attention." Others thought that the "Annual Reports brought in the money," or suggested that he had "a *secret treasure.*" His quiet reply was, that his being a foreigner would be more likely to repel than to attract confidence; that the novelty would scarcely avail him after more than a score of years; that other institutions which issued reports did not always escape want and debt; but, as to the secret treasure to which he was supposed to have access, he felt constrained to confess that there was *more in that supposition than the objectors were aware of.* He had indeed a Treasury, inexhaustible—in the promises of a God unchangeably faithful—from which he admits that he had already in 1856 drawn for twenty-two years, and in all over one hundred and thirteen thousand pounds. As to the Reports, it may be worth while to notice that he never but once in his life advertised the public of any need, and that was the *need of more orphans*—more to care for in the name of the Lord—a single and singular ease of advertising, by which he sought not to increase his *income,* but his *expenditure*—not asking the public to aid him in supporting the needy, but to increase the occasion of his outlay!

So far was he from depending upon any such sources of supply as the unbelieving world might think, that it was in the drying up of all such channels that he found the opportunity of his faith and of God's power. The visible treasure was often so small that it was reduced to nothing, but the invisible Treasure was

God's riches in glory, and could be drawn from without limit. This it was to which he looked alone, and in which he felt that he had a river of supply that can never run dry.[29]

SCRIPTURE TESTIMONY
The righteous innately have God's heart toward those in need
Matthew 25:31-46

The orphan work had, to Mr. Müller, many charms which grew on him as he entered more fully into it. While his main hope was to be the means of spiritual health to these children, he had the joy of seeing how God used these homes for the promotion of their physical welfare also, and, in cases not a few, for the entire renovation of their weak and diseased bodies. It must be remembered that most of them owed their orphan condition to that great destroyer, Consumption. Children were often brought to the orphan houses thoroughly permeated by the poison of bad blood, with diseased tendencies, and sometimes emaciated and half-starved, having had neither proper food nor medical care.

For example, in the spring of 1855, four children from five to nine years old, and of one family, were admitted to the orphanage, all in a deplorable state from lack of both nursing and nutrition. It was a serious question whether they should be admitted at all, as such cases tended to turn the institution into a hospital, and absorb undue care and time. But to dismiss them seemed almost inhuman, certainly *inhumane.* So, trusting in God, they were taken in and cared for with parental love. A few weeks later these children were physically unrecognizable, so rapid had been the improvement in health, and probably there were with God's blessing four graves less to be dug.

The trials incident to the moral and spiritual condition of the orphans were even greater, however, than those caused by ill health and weakness. When children proved incorrigibly bad, they were expelled, lest they should corrupt others, for the institution was not a *reformatory,* as it was not a *hospital.* In 1849, a boy, of less than eight years, had to be sent away as a confirmed liar and thief, having twice run off with the belongings of other children and gloried in his juvenile crimes. Yet the forbearance exercised even in his case was marvelously godlike, for, during over five years, he had been the subject of private admonitions and prayers and all other methods of reclamation; and, when expulsion became the last resort, he was solemnly and with prayer, before all the others, sent away from the orphan house, that if possible such a course might prove a double blessing, a remedy to him and a warning to others; and even then this young practised sinner was followed, in his expulsion, by loving supplication.

Towards the end of November, 1857, it was found that a serious leak in the boiler of the heating apparatus of house No. 1 would make repairs at once necessary,

29 Appendix H.

and as the boilers were encased in bricks and a new boiler might be required, such repairs must consume time. Meanwhile how could three hundred children, some of them very young and tender, be kept warm? Even if gas-stoves could be temporarily set up, chimneys would be needful to carry off the impure air; and no way of heating was available during repairs, even if a hundred pounds were expended to prevent risk of cold. Again Mr. Müller turned to the Living God, and, trusting in Him, decided to have the repairs begun. A day or so before the fires had to be put out, a bleak north wind set in. The work could no longer be delayed; yet weather, prematurely cold for the season, threatened these hundreds of children with hurtful exposure. The Lord was boldly appealed to. "Lord, these are *Thy* orphans: be pleased to change this north wind into a south wind, and give the workmen a mind to work that the job may be speedily done."

SCRIPTURE TESTIMONY
God answers prayer
Luke 18:7 · John 15:7 · Acts 12:5 · James 5:15

The evening before the repairs actually began, the cold blast was still blowing; but *on that day a south wind blew, and the weather was so mild that no fire was needful!* Not only so, but, as Mr. Müller went into the cellar with the overseer of the work, to see whether the repairs could in no way be expedited, he heard him say, in the hearing of the men, "they will work late this evening, and come very early again to-morrow." *"We would rather, sir,"* was the reply, *"work all night."* And so, within about thirty hours, the fire was again burning to heat the water in the boiler; and, until the apparatus was again in order, that merciful soft south wind had continued to blow. Goodness and mercy were following the Lord's humble servant, made the more conspicuous by the crises of special trial and trouble.

Every new exigency provoked new prayer and evoked new faith. When, in 1862, several boys were ready to be apprenticed, and there were no applications such as were desired, prayer was the one resort, as advertising would tend to bring applications from masters who sought apprentices for the sake of the premium. But every one of the eighteen boys was properly bound over to a Christian master, whose business was suitable and who would receive the lad into his own family.

About the same time one of the drains was obstructed which runs about eleven feet underground. When three holes had been dug and as many places in the drain tapped in vain, prayer was offered that in the fourth case the workmen might be guided to the very spot where the stoppage existed—and the request was literally answered.

SCRIPTURE TESTIMONY
Ask me anything in My name
John 14:13-14 · Matthew 18:19 · John 16:23-24

Three instances of marked deliverance, in answer to prayer, are specially recorded for the year between May 26, 1864, and the same date in 1865, which should not be passed by without at least a mention.

First, in the great drought of the summer of 1864, when the fifteen large cisterns in the three orphan houses were empty, and the nine deep wells, and even the good spring which had never before failed, were almost all dry. Two or three thousand gallons of water were daily required, and daily prayer was made to the God of the rain. See how God provided, while pleased to withhold the supply from above! A farmer, near by, supplied, from his larger wells, about half the water needful, the rest being furnished by the half-exhausted wells on Ashley Down; and, when he could no longer spare water, without a day's interval, another farmer offered a supply from a brook which ran through his fields, and thus there was abundance until the rains replenished cisterns and wells.[30]

Second, when, for three years, scarlet and typhus fevers and smallpox, being prevalent in Bristol and the vicinity threatened the orphans, prayer was again made to Him who is the God of health as well as of rain. There was no case of scarlet or typhus fever during the whole time, though smallpox was permitted to find an entrance into the smallest of the orphan houses. Prayer was still the one resort. The disease spread to the other houses, until at one time fifteen were ill with it. The cases, however, were mercifully light, and the Lord was besought to allow the epidemic to spread *no further.* Not another child was taken; and when, after nine months, the disease altogether disappeared, not one child had died of it, and only one teacher or adult had had an attack, and that was very mild. What ravages the disease might have made among the twelve hundred inmates of these orphan houses, had it then prevailed as later, in 1872!

Third, tremendous gales visited Bristol and neighbourhood in January, 1865. The roofs of the orphan houses were so injured as to be laid open in at least twenty places, and large panes of glass were broken. The day was Saturday, and no glazier and slater could be had before Monday. So the Lord of wind and weather was besought to protect the exposed property during the interval. The wind calmed down, and the rain was restrained until midday of Wednesday, when the repairs were about finished, but heavy rainfalls drove the slaters from the roof. One exposed opening remained and much damage threatened; but, in answer to prayer, the rain was stayed, and the work resumed. No damage had been done while the last opening was unrepaired for it had exposed the building from the *south,* while the rain came from the *north.*

Mr. Müller records these circumstances with his usual particularity, as part of his witness to the Living God, and to the goodness and mercy that closely and continually followed him.

During the next year, 1865-6, scarlet fever broke out in the orphanage. In all thirty-nine children were ill, but all recovered. Whooping-cough also made its appearance; but though, during that season, it was not only very prevalent but

30 About twenty years later the Bristol Water Works Co. introduced pipes and thus a permanent and unfailing supply.

very malignant in Bristol, in all the three houses there were but seventeen cases, and the only fatal one was that of a little girl with constitutionally weak lungs.

SCRIPTURE TESTIMONY
Large groups of people converted at the same time
Acts 2:41 · Acts 4:4

During this same year, however, the Spirit of God wrought mightily among the girls, as in the previous year among the boys, so that over one hundred became deeply earnest seekers after salvation; and so, even in tribulation, consolation abounded in Christ. Mr. Müller and his wife and helpers now implored God to deepen and broaden this work of His Spirit. Towards the end of the year closing in May, 1866, Emma Bunn, an orphan girl of seventeen, was struck with consumption. Though, for fourteen years, she had been under Mr. Müller's care, she was, in this dangerous illness, still careless and indifferent; and, as she drew near to death, her case continued as hopeless as ever. Prayer was unceasing for her; and it pleased God suddenly to reveal Christ to her as her Saviour. Great self-loathing now at once took the place of former indifference; confession of sin, of previous callousness of conscience; and unspeakable joy in the Lord, of former apathy and coldness. It was a spiritual miracle—this girl's sudden transformation into a witness for God, manifesting deepest conviction for past sin and earnest concern for others. Her thoughtless and heedless state had been so well known that her conversion and dying messages were now the Lord's means of the *most extensive and God-glorifying work ever wrought up to that time among the orphans.* In one house alone three hundred and fifty were led to seek peace in believing.

What lessons lie hidden—nay, lie on the very surface—to be read of every willing observer of these events! Prayer can break even a hard heart; a memory, stored with biblical truth and pious teaching, will prove, when once God's grace softens the heart and unlooses the tongue, a source of both personal growth in grace and of capacity for wide service to others. We are all practically too careless of the training of children, and too distrustful of young converts. Mr. Müller was more and more impressed by the triumphs of the grace of God as seen in children converted at the tender age of nine or ten and holding the beginning of their confidence steadfast unto the end.

These facts and experiences, gleaned, like handfuls of grain, from a wide field, show the character both of the seed sown and the harvest reaped, from the sowing.

Again, when, in 1866, cholera developed in England, in answer to special prayer *not one* case of this disease was known in the orphan houses; and when, in the same autumn, whooping-cough and measles broke out, though eight children had the former and two hundred and sixty-two, the latter, not one child died, or was afterward debilitated by the attack. From May, 1866, to May, 1867, out of over thirteen hundred children under care, only eleven died, considerably less than one per cent.

That severe and epidemic disease should find its way into the orphanages at all may seem strange to those who judge God's faithfulness by appearances, but many were the compensations for such trials. By them not only were the hearts of the children often turned to God, but the hearts of helpers in the Institution were made more sympathetic and tender, and the hearts of God's people at large were stirred up to practical and systematic help. God uses such seeming calamities as 'advertisements' of His work; many who would not have heard of the Institution, or on whom what they did hear would have made little impression, were led to take a deep interest in an orphanage where thousands of little ones were exposed to the ravages of some malignant and dangerous epidemic.

Looking back, in 1865, after thirty-one years, upon the work thus far done for the Lord, Mr. Müller gratefully records that, during the entire time, he had been enabled to hold fast the original principles on which the work was based on March 5, 1834. He had never once gone into debt; he had sought for the Institution no patron but the Living God; and he had kept to the line of demarcation between believers and unbelievers, in all his seeking for active helpers in the work.

His grand purpose, in all his labours, having been, from the beginning, the glory of God, in showing what could be done through prayer and faith, without any leaning upon man, his unequivocal testimony is: "Hitherto hath the Lord helped us." Though for about five years they had, almost daily, been in the constant trial of faith, they were as constantly proving His faithfulness. The work had rapidly grown, till it assumed gigantic proportions, but so did the help of God keep pace with all the needs and demands of its growth.

In January, 1866, Mr. Henry Craik, who had for thirty-six years been Mr. Müller's valued friend, and, since 1832, his coworker in Bristol, fell asleep after an illness of seven months. In Devonshire these two brethren had first known each other, and the acquaintance had subsequently ripened, through years of common labour and trial, into an affection seldom found among men. They were nearly of an age, both being a little past sixty when Mr. Craik died. The loss was too heavy to have been patiently and serenely borne, had not the survivor known and felt beneath him the Everlasting Arms. And even this bereavement, which in one aspect was an irreparable loss, was seen to be only another proof of God's love. The look ahead might be a dark one, the way desolate and even dangerous, but goodness and mercy were still following very close behind, and would in every new place of danger or difficulty be at hand to help over hard places and give comfort and cheer in the night season.

CHAPTER XVI

The Shadow of a Great Sorrow

"With clouds He covereth the light." No human life is without some experience of clouded skies and stormy days, and sometimes "the clouds return after the rain." It is a blessed experience to recognize the silver lining on the darkest storm cloud, and, better still, to be sure of the shining of God's light behind a sky that seems wholly and hopelessly overcast.

The year 1870 was made forever pathetically memorable by the decease of Mrs. Müller, who lived just long enough to see the last of the New Orphan Houses opened. From the outset of the work in November, 1835, for more than thirty-four years, this beloved, devoted wife had been also a sympathetic helper.

This wedded life had approached very near to the ideal of connubial bliss, by reason of mutual fitness, common faith in God and love for His work, and long association in prayer and service. In their case, the days of courtship were never passed; indeed the tender and delicate mutual attentions of those early days rather increased than decreased as the years went on; and the great maxim was both proven and illustrated, that the secret of winning love is the secret of keeping it. More than that, such affection grows and becomes more and more a fountain of mutual delight. Never had his beloved "Mary" been so precious to her husband as during the very year of her departure.

This marriage union was so happy that Mr. Müller could not withhold his loving witness that he never saw her at any time after she became his wife, without a new feeling of delight. And day by day they were wont to find at least a few moments of rest together, sitting after dinner, hand in hand, in loving intercourse of mind and heart, made the more complete by this touch of physical contact, and, whether in speech or silence, communing in the Lord. Their happiness in God and in each other was perennial, perpetual, growing as the years fled by.

Mr. Müller's solemn conviction was that all this wedded bliss was due to the fact that she was not only a devoted Christian, but that their one united object was to live only and wholly for God; that they had always abundance of work for God, in which they were heartily united; that this work was never allowed to interfere with the care of their own souls, or their seasons of private prayer and study of the Scriptures; and that they were wont daily, and often thrice a day, to secure a time of united prayer and praise when they brought before the Lord the matters which at the time called for thanksgiving and supplication.

Mrs. Müller had never been a very vigorous woman, and more than once had been brought nigh unto death. In October, 1859, after twenty-nine years of wedded life and love, she had been laid aside by rheumatism and had continued in great suffering for about nine months, quite helpless and unable to work; but it was felt to be a special mark of God's love and faithfulness that this very affliction was used by Him to reestablish her in health and strength, the compulsory rest made necessary for the greater part of a year being in Mr. Müller's judgment a means of prolonging her life and period of service for the ten years following. Thus a severe trial met by them both in faith had issued in much blessing both to soul and body.

SCRIPTURE TESTIMONY
There is no sting in death for the believer 1 Corinthians 15:54-57

The closing scenes of this beautiful life are almost too sacred to be unveiled to common eyes. For some few years before her departure, it was plain that her health and vitality were declining. With difficulty could she be prevailed on, however, to abate her activity, or, even when a distressing cough attacked her, to allow a physician to be called. Her husband carefully guarded and nursed her, and by careful attention to diet and rest, by avoidance of needless exposure, and by constant resort to prayer, she was kept alive through much weakness and sometimes much pain. But, on Saturday night, February 5th, she found that she had not the use of one of her limbs, and it was obvious that the end was nigh. Her own mind was clear and her own heart at peace. She herself remarked, "He will soon come." And a few minutes after four in the afternoon of the Lord's day, February 6, 1870, she sweetly passed from human toils and trials, to be forever with the Lord.

Under the weight of such a sorrow, most men would have sunk into depths of almost hopeless despair. But this man of God, sustained by a divine love, at once sought for occasions of thanksgiving; and, instead of repining over his loss, gratefully remembered and recorded the goodness of God in *taking* such a wife, releasing her saintly spirit from the bondage of weakness, sickness, and pain, rather than leaving her to a protracted suffering and the mute agony of helplessness; and, above all, introducing her to her heart's desire, the immediate presence of the Lord Jesus, and the higher service of a celestial sphere. Is not that grief akin to selfishness which dwells so much on our own deprivations as to be oblivious of the ecstatic gain of the departed saints who, withdrawn from us and absent from the body, are at home with the Lord?

It is only in those circumstances of extreme trial which prove to ordinary men a crushing weight, that implicit faith in the Father's unfailing wisdom and love proves its full power to sustain. Where self-will is truly lost in the will of God, the life that is hidden in Him is most radiantly exhibited in the darkest hour.

The death of this beloved wife afforded an illustration of this. Within a few hours after this withdrawal of her who had shared with him the planning and working of these long years of service, Mr. Müller went to the Monday-evening prayer meeting, then held in Salem Chapel, to mingle his prayers and praises as usual with those of his brethren. With a literally shining countenance, he rose and said: "Beloved brethren and sisters in Christ, I ask you to join with me in hearty praise and thanksgiving to my precious Lord for His loving kindness in having taken my darling, beloved wife out of the pain and suffering which she has endured, into His own presence; and as I rejoice in everything that is for her, happiness, so I now rejoice as I realize how far happier she is, in beholding her Lord whom she loved so well, than in any joy she has known or could know here. I ask you also to pray that the Lord will so enable me to have fellowship in her joy that my bereaved heart may be occupied with her blessedness instead of my unspeakable loss." These remarkable words are supplied by one who was himself present and on whose memory they made an indelible impression.

This occurrence had a marked effect upon all who were at that meeting. Mrs. Müller was known by all as a most valuable, lovely, and holy woman and wife. After nearly forty years of wedded life and love, she had left the earthly home for the heavenly. To her husband she had been a blessing beyond description, and to her daughter Lydia, at once a wise and tender mother and a sympathetic companion. The loss to them both could never be made up on earth. Yet in these circumstances this man of God had grace given to forget his own and his daughter's irreparable loss, and to praise God for the unspeakable gain to the departed wife and mother.

The body was laid to rest on February 11th, many thousands of sorrowing friends evincing the deepest sympathy. Twelve hundred orphans mingled in the funeral procession, and the whole staff of helpers so far as they could be spared from the houses. The bereaved husband strangely upheld by the arm of the Almighty Friend in whom he trusted, took upon himself the funeral service both at chapel and cemetery. He was taken seriously ill afterward, but, as soon as his returning strength allowed, he preached his wife's funeral sermon—another memorable occasion. It was the supernatural serenity of his peace in the presence of such a bereavement that led his attending physician to say to a friend, "I have never before seen so *unhuman* a man." Yes, *un*human indeed, though far from *in*human, lifted above the weakness of mere humanity by a power not of man.

House of Mr. Müller, Kingsdown, Bristol

That funeral sermon was a noble tribute to the goodness of the Lord even in the great affliction of his life. The text was:

> *"Thou art good and doest good."* (Psalm 119:68)

Its three divisions were: "The Lord was good and did good: first, in giving her to me; second in so long leaving her to me; and third, in taking her from me." It is happily preserved in Mr. Müller's journal, and must be read to be appreciated.[31]

This union, begun in prayer, was in prayer sanctified to the end. Mrs. Müller's chief excellence lay in her devoted piety. She wore that one ornament which is in the sight of God of great price—the meek and quiet spirit; the beauty of the Lord her God was upon her. She had sympathetically shared her husband's prayers and tears during all the long trial-time of faith and patience, and partaken of all the joys and rewards of the triumph hours. Mr. Müller's own witness to her leaves nothing more to be added, for it is the tribute of him who knew her longest and best. He writes:

"She was God's own gift, exquisitely suited to me even in natural temperament. Thousands of times I said to her, 'My darling, God Himself singled you out for me, as the most suitable wife I could possibly wish to have had.'"

As to culture, she had a basis of sensible practical education, surmounted and adorned by ladylike accomplishments which she had neither time nor inclination to indulge in her married life. Not only was she skilled in the languages and in such higher studies as astronomy, but in mathematics also; and this last qualification made her for thirty-four years an invaluable help to her husband, as month by month she examined all the account-books, and the hundreds of bills of the matrons of the orphan houses, and with the eye of an expert detected the least mistake.

All her training and natural fitness indicated a providential adaptation to her work, like "the round peg in the round hole." Her practical education in needle-work, and her knowledge of the material most serviceable for various household uses, made her competent to direct both in the purchase and manufacture of cloths and other fabrics for garments, bed-linen, etc. She moved about those orphan houses like an angel of Love, taking unselfish delight in such humble ministries as preparing neat, clean beds to rest the little ones, and covering them with warm blankets in cold weather. For the sake of Him who took little children in His arms, she became to these thousands of destitute orphans a nursing mother.

Shortly after her death, a letter was received from a believing orphan some seventeen years before sent out to service, asking, in behalf also of others formerly in the houses, permission to erect a stone over Mrs. Müller's grave as an expression

31 Narrative, III. 575-594

of love and grateful remembrance. Consent being given, hundreds of little offerings came in from orphans who during the twenty-five years previous had been under her motherly oversight—a beautiful tribute to her worth and a touching offering from those who had been to her as her larger family.

The dear daughter Lydia had, two years before Mrs. Müller's departure, found in one of her mother's pocketbooks a sacred memorandum in her own writing, which she brought to her bereaved father's notice two days after his wife had departed. It belongs among the precious relics of her history. It reads as follows:

"Should it please the Lord to remove M. M. [Mary Müller] by a sudden dismissal, let none of the beloved survivors consider that it is in the way of judgment, either to her or to them. She has so often, when enjoying conscious nearness to the Lord, felt how sweet it would be now to depart and to be *forever* with Jesus, that nothing but the shock it would be to her beloved husband and child, etc. has checked in her the longing desire that *thus* her happy spirit might take its flight. Precious Jesus! Thy will in this as in everything else, and not hers, be done!"

These words were to Mr. Müller her last legacy; and with the comfort they gave him, the loving sympathy of his precious Lydia who did all that a daughter could do to fill a mother's place, and with the remembrance of Him who hath said, 'I will never leave thee nor forsake thee,' he went on his lonely pilgrim way, rejoicing in the Lord, feeling nevertheless a wound in his heart, that seemed rather to deepen than to heal.

Sixteen months passed, when Mr. James Wright, who like Mr. Müller had been bereft of his companion, asked of him the hand of the beloved Lydia in marriage. The request took Mr. Müller wholly by surprise, but he felt that, to no man living, could he with more joyful confidence commit and intrust his choicest remaining earthly treasure; and, ever solicitous for others' happiness rather than his own, he encouraged his daughter to accept Mr. Wright's proffered love, when she naturally hesitated on her father's account. On November 16, 1871, they were married, and began a life of mutual prayer and sympathy which, like that of her father and mother, proved supremely and almost ideally happy, helpful, and useful.

While as yet this event was only in prospect, Mr. Müller felt his own lonely condition keenly, and much more in view of his daughter's expected departure to her husband's home. He felt the need of some one to share intimately his toils and prayers, and help him in the Lord's work, and the persuasion grew upon him that it was God's will that he should marry again. After much prayer, he determined to ask Miss Susannah Grace Sangar to become his wife, having known her for more than twenty-five years as a consistent disciple, and believing her to be well fitted to be his helper in the Lord. Accordingly, fourteen days after his daughter's marriage to Mr. Wright, he entered into similar relations with Miss Sangar, who for years after joined him in prayer, unselfish giving, and labours for souls.

The second Mrs. Müller was of one mind with her husband as to the stewardship of the Lord's property. He found her poor, for what she had once possessed she had lost; and had she been rich he would have regarded her wealth as an obstacle to marriage, unfitting her to be his companion in a self-denial based on scriptural principle. Riches or hoarded wealth would have been to both of them a snare, and so she also felt; so that, having still, before her marriage, a remnant of two hundred pounds, she at once put it at the Lord's disposal, thus joining her husband in a life of voluntary poverty; and although subsequent legacies were paid to her, she continued to the day of her death to be poor for the Lord's sake.

The question had often been asked Mr. Müller what would become of the work when he, the master workman, should be removed. Men find it hard to get their eyes off the instrument, and remember that there is only, strictly speaking, one AGENT, for an agent is *one who works,* and an instrument is what *the agent works with.* Though provision might be made, in a board of trustees, for carrying on the orphan work, where would be found the man to take the direction of it, a man whose spirit was so akin to that of the founder that he would trust in God and depend on Him just as Mr. Müller had done before him? Such were the inquiries of the somewhat doubtful or fearful observers of the great and many-branched work carried on under Mr. Müller's supervision.

To all such questions he had always one answer ready—his one uniform solution of all cares and perplexities: *the Living God.* He who had built the orphan houses could maintain them; He who had raised up one humble man to oversee the work in His name, could provide for a worthy successor, like Joshua who not only *followed* but *succeeded* Moses. Jehovah of hosts is not limited in resources.

Nevertheless much prayer was offered that the Lord would provide such a successor, and, in Mr. James Wright, the prayer was answered. He was not chosen, as Mr. Müller's son-in-law, for the choice was made before his marriage to Lydia Müller was even thought of by him. For more than thirty years, even from his boyhood, Mr. Wright had been well known to Mr. Müller, and his growth in the things of God had been watched by him. For thirteen years he had already been his "right hand" in all most important matters; and, for nearly all of that time, had been held up before God as his successor, in the prayers of Mr. and Mrs. Müller, both of whom felt divinely assured that God would fit him more and more to take the entire burden of responsibility.

When, in 1870, the wife fell asleep in Jesus, and Mr. Müller was himself ill, he opened his heart to Mr. Wright as to the succession. Humility led him to shrink from such a post, and his then wife feared it would prove too burdensome for him; but all objections were overborne when it was seen and felt to be God's call. It was twenty-one months after this, when, in November, 1871, Mr. Wright was married to Mr. Müller's only daughter and child, so that it is quite apparent that he had neither sought the position he now occupies, nor was he appointed to it because he was Mr. Müller's son-in-law, for, at that time, his first wife was living and in health. From May, 1872, therefore, Mr. Wright *shared* with his father-in-law the responsibilities of the Institution, and gave him great joy as a partner and successor in full sympathy with all the great principles on which his work had been based.

A little over three years after Mr. Müller's second marriage, in March, 1874, Mrs. Müller was taken ill, and became, two days later, feverish and restless, and after about two weeks was attacked with hemorrhage which brought her also very near to the gates of death. She rallied; but fever and delirium followed and obstinate sleeplessness, till, for a second time, she seemed at the point of death. Indeed so low was her vitality that, as late as April 17th, a most experienced London physician said that he had never known any patient to recover from such an illness; and thus a third time all human hope of restoration seemed gone. And yet, in answer to prayer, Mrs. Müller was raised up, and in the end of May, was taken to the seaside for change of air, and grew rapidly stronger until she was entirely restored. Thus the Lord spared her to be the companion of her husband in those years of missionary touring which enabled him to bear such worldwide witness. Out of the shadow of his griefs this beloved man of God ever came to find that divine refreshment which is as the "shadow of a great rock in a weary land."

CHAPTER XVII

The Period of World-Wide Witness

GOD'S REAL answers to prayer are often seeming denials. Beneath the outward request He hears the voice of the inward desire, and He responds to the mind of the Spirit rather than to the imperfect and perhaps mistaken words in which the yearning seeks expression. Moreover, His infinite wisdom sees that a larger blessing may be ours only by the withholding of the lesser good which we seek; and so all true prayer trusts Him to give His own answer, not in our way or time, or even to our own expressed desire, but rather to His own unutterable groaning within us which He can interpret better than we.

Monica, mother of Augustine, pleaded with God that her dissolute son might not go to Rome, that sink of iniquity; but he was permitted to go, and thus came into contact with Ambrose, bishop of Milan, through whom he was converted. God fulfilled the mother's *desire* while denying her *request.*

When George Müller, five times within the first eight years after conversion, had offered himself as a missionary, God had blocked his way; now, at sixty-five, He was about to permit him, in a sense he had never dreamed of, to be a missionary to the world. From the beginning of his ministry he had been more or less an itinerant, spending no little time in wanderings about in Britain and on the Continent; but now he was to go to the regions beyond and spend the major part of seventeen years in witnessing to the prayer-hearing God.

These extensive missionary tours occupied the evening of Mr. Müller's useful life, from 1875 to 1892. They reached, more or less, over Europe, America, Asia, Africa, and Australia; and would of themselves have sufficed for the work of an ordinary life.

They had a singular suggestion. While, in 1874, compelled by Mrs. Müller's health to seek a change of air, he was preaching in the Isle of Wight, and a beloved Christian brother for whom he had spoken, himself a man of much experience in preaching, told him how 'that day had been the happiest of his whole life'; and this remark, with others like it previously made, so impressed him that the Lord was about to use him to help on believers outside of Bristol, that he determined no longer to confine his labours in the Word and doctrine to any one place, but to go wherever a door might open for his testimony.

In weighing this question he was impressed with seven reasons or motives, which led to these tours:

1. To *preach the gospel* in its simplicity, and especially to show how salvation is based, not upon feelings or even upon faith, but upon the finished work of Christ; that justification is ours the moment we believe, and we are to accept and claim our place as accepted in the Beloved without regard to our inward states of feeling or emotion.
2. To *lead believers to know their saved state,* and to realize their standing in Christ, great numbers not only of disciples, but even preachers and pastors, being themselves destitute of any real peace and joy in the Lord, and hence unable to lead others into joy and peace.
3. To *bring believers back to the Scriptures,* to search the Word and find its hidden treasures; to test everything by this divine touchstone and hold fast only what will stand this test; to make it the daily subject of meditative and prayerful examination in order to translate it into daily obedience.
4. To *promote among all true believers, brotherly love;* to lead them to make less of those non-essentials in which disciples differ, and to make more of those great essential and foundation truths in which all true believers are united; to help all who love and trust one Lord to rise above narrow sectarian prejudices, and barriers to fellowship.
5. To *strengthen the faith of believers,* encouraging a simpler trust, and a more real and unwavering confidence in God, and particularly in the sure answers to believing prayer, based upon His definite promises.
6. To *promote separation from the world* and deadness to it, and so to increase heavenly-mindedness in children of God; at the same time warning against fanatical extremes and extravagances, such as sinless perfection while in the flesh.
7. And finally to *fix the hope of disciples on the blessed coming of our Lord Jesus;* and, in connection therewith, to instruct them as to the true character and object of the present dispensation, and the relation of the church to the world in this period of the out-gathering of the Bride of Christ.

These seven objects may be briefly epitomized thus: Mr. Müller's aim was to lead sinners to believe on the name of the Son of God, and so to *have eternal life;* to help those who have thus believed, to *know* that they have this life; to teach them so to *build up* themselves on their most holy faith, by diligent searching into the word of God, and praying in the Holy Ghost, as that this life shall be more and more a real possession and a conscious possession; to promote among all disciples the *unity of the Spirit* and the *charity* which is the bond of perfectness, and to help them to exhibit that life before the world; to incite them to cultivate an *unworldly and spiritual type of character* such as conforms to the life of God in them; to lead them to the *prayer of faith* which is both the expression and the expansion of the life of faith; and to direct their hope to the *final appearing of the Lord,* so that they should purify themselves even as He is pure, and occupy till He comes. Mr. Müller was thus giving himself to the double work of evangelization and edification, on a scale commensurate with his love for a dying world, as opportunity afforded doing good unto all men, and especially to them who are of the household of faith.

Of these long and busy missionary journeys, it is needful to give only the outline, or general survey. March 26, 1875, is an important date, for it marks the starting-point. He himself calls this "the beginning of his missionary tours."

From Bristol he went to Brighton, Lewes, and Sunderland—on the way to Sunderland preaching to a great audience in the Metropolitan Tabernacle, at Mr. Spurgeon's request—then to Newcastle-on-Tyne, and back to London, where he spoke at the Mildmay Park Conference, Talbot Road Tabernacle, and 'Edinburgh Castle.' This tour closed, June 5th, after seventy addresses in public, during about ten weeks.

Less than six weeks passed, when, on August 14th, the second tour began, in which case the special impulse that moved him was a desire to follow up the revival work of Mr. Moody and Mr. Sankey. Their short stay in each place made them unable to lead on new converts to higher attainments in knowledge and grace, and there seemed to be a call for some instruction fitted to confirm these new believers in the life of obedience. Mr. Müller accordingly followed these evangelists in England, Ireland, and Scotland, staying in each place from one week to six, and seeking to educate and edify those who had been led to Christ. Among the places visited on this errand in 1875, were London; then Kilmarnock, Saltwater, Dundee, Perth, Glasgow, Kirkentilloch in Scotland, and Dublin in Ireland; then, returning to England, he went to Leamington, Warwick, Kenilworth, Coventry, Rugby, etc. In some cases, notably at Mildmay Park, Dundee and Glasgow, Liverpool and Dublin, the audiences numbered from two thousand to six thousand, but everywhere rich blessing came from above. This second tour extended into the new year, 1876, and took in Liverpool, York, Kendal, Carlisle, Annan, Edinburgh, Arbroath, Montrose, Aberdeen, and other places; and when it closed in July, having lasted nearly eleven months, Mr. Müller had preached at least three hundred and six times, an average of about one sermon a day, exclusive of days spent in travel. So acceptable and profitable were these labours that there were over one hundred invitations urged upon him which he was unable to accept.

The third tour was on the Continent. It occupied most of the year closing May 26, 1877, and embraced Paris, various places in Switzerland, Prussia and Holland, Alsace, Wurtemberg, Baden, Hesse Darmstadt, etc. Altogether over three hundred addresses were given in about seventy cities and villages to all of which he had been invited by letter. When this tour closed more than sixty written invitations remained unaccepted, and Mr. Müller found that, through his work and his writings, he was as well known in the continental countries visited, as in England.

Turning now toward America, the fourth tour extended from August, 1877, to June of the next year. For many years invitations had been coming with growing frequency, from the United States and Canada; and of late their urgency led him to recognize in them the call of God, especially as he thought of the many thousands of Germans across the Atlantic, who as they heard him speak in their own native tongue would keep the more silence. (Acts 22:2)

Mr. and Mrs. Müller, landing at Quebec, thence went to the United States, where, during ten months, his labours stretched over a vast area, including the States of New York, New Jersey, Massachusetts, Pennsylvania, Maryland, District of Columbia, Virginia, South Carolina, Georgia, Florida, Alabama, Louisiana, and Missouri. Thus having swept round the Atlantic sea-border, he crossed to the Pacific coast, and returning visited Salt Lake City in Utah—the very centre and stronghold of Mormonism—Illinois, Ohio, etc. He spoke frequently to large congregations of Germans, and, in the Southern States, to the coloured population; but he regarded no opportunity for service afforded him on this tour as so inspiring as the repeated meetings with and for ministers, evangelists, pastors, and Christian workers; and, next to them in importance, his interviews with large bodies of students and professors in the universities, colleges, theological seminaries, and other higher schools of education. To cast the salt of the gospel into the very springs of social influence, the sources whence power flows, was to him a most sacred privilege. His singular catholicity, charity, and humility drew to him even those who differed with him, and all denominations of Christians united in giving him access to the people. During this tour he spoke three hundred times, and travelled nearly ten thousand miles; over one hundred invitations being declined, for simple lack of time and strength.

After a stay in Bristol of about two months, on September 5, 1878, he and his wife began the fifth of these missionary tours. In this case, it was on the Continent, where he ministered in English, German, and French; and in Spain and Italy, when these tongues were not available, his addresses were through an interpreter. Many open doors the Lord set before him, not only to the poorer and humbler classes, but to those in the middle and higher ranks. In the Riviera, he had access to many of the nobility and aristocracy, who from different countries sought health and rest in the equable climate of the Mediterranean, and at Mentone he and Mr. Spurgeon held sweet converse. In Spain Mr. Müller was greatly gladdened by seeing for himself the schools, entirely supported by the funds of the Scriptural Knowledge Institution, and by finding that, in hundreds of cases, even popish parents so greatly valued these schools that they continued to send their children, despite both the threats and persuasions of the Romish priests. He found, moreover, that the pupils frequently at their homes read to their parents the word of God and sang to them the gospel hymns learned at these schools, so that the influence exerted was not bounded by its apparent horizon, as diffused or refracted sunlight reaches with its illumining rays far beyond the visible track of the orb of day.

The work had to contend with governmental opposition. When a place was first opened at Madrid for gospel services, a sign was placed outside, announcing the fact. Official orders were issued that the sign should be painted over, so as to obliterate the inscription. The painter of the sign, unwilling both to undo his own work and to hinder the work of God, painted the sign over with water-colours, which would leave the original announcement half visible, and would soon be washed off by the rains; whereupon the government sent its own workman to daub the sign over with thick oil-colour.

Mr. Müller, ready to preach the gospel to those at Rome also, felt his spirit saddened and stirred within him, as he saw that city wholly given to idolatry—not pagan but papal idolatry—the Rome not of the Caesars, but of the popes. While at Naples he ascended Vesuvius. Those masses of lava, which seemed greater in bulk than the mountain itself, more impressed him with the power of God than anything else he had ever seen. As he looked upon that smoking cone, and thought of the liquid death it had vomited forth, he said within himself, "What cannot God do!" He had before felt somewhat of His Almightiness in love and grace, but he now saw its manifestation in judgment and wrath. His visit to the Vaudois valleys, where so many martyrs had suffered banishment and imprisonment, loss of goods and loss of life for Jesus' sake, moved him to the depths of his being and stimulated in him the martyr spirit.

When he arrived again in Bristol, June 18, 1879, he had been absent nine months and twelve days, and preached two hundred and eighty-six times and in forty-six towns and cities. After another ten weeks in Bristol, he and his wife sailed again for America, the last week of August, 1879, landing at New York the first week in September. This visit took in the States lying between the Atlantic Ocean and the valley of the Mississippi—New York and New Jersey, Ohio, Indiana, Michigan and Illinois, Wisconsin, Iowa, Minnesota—and, from London and Hamilton to Quebec, Canada also shared the blessing. This visit covered only two hundred and seventy-two days, but he preached three hundred times, and in over forty cities. Over one hundred and fifty written invitations still remained without response, and the number increased the longer his stay. Mr. Müller therefore assuredly gathered that the Lord called him to return to America, after another brief stay at Bristol, where he felt it needful to spend a season annually, to keep in close touch with the work at home and relieve Mr. and Mrs. Wright of their heavy responsibilities, for a time.

Accordingly on September 15, 1880, again turning from Bristol, these travellers embarked the next day on their seventh mission tour, landing, ten days later, at Quebec. Mr. Müller had a natural antipathy to the sea, in his earlier crossing to the Continent having suffered much from sea-sickness; but he had undertaken these long voyages, not for his own pleasure or profit, but wholly on God's errand; and he felt it to be a peculiar mark of the loving-kindness of the Lord that, while he was ready to endure any discomfort, or risk his life for His sake, he had not in his six crossings of the Atlantic suffered in the least, and on this particular voyage was wholly free from any indisposition.

From Quebec he went to Massachusetts, Connecticut, New York, New Jersey, and Pennsylvania. Among other places of special interest were Boston, Plymouth—the landing-place of the Pilgrims,—Wellesley and South Hadley colleges—the great schools for woman's higher education,—and the centres farther westward, where he had such wide access to Germans. This tour extended over a smaller area than before, and lasted but eight months; but the impression on the people was deep and permanent. He had spoken about two hundred and fifty times in all; and Mrs. Müller had availed herself of many opportunities of personal dealing with inquirers, and of distributing books and tracts among both believers and unbelievers. She had also written for her husband more than seven hundred letters,—this of itself being no light task, inasmuch as it reaches an average of about three a day. On May 30, 1881, they were again on British shores.

The eighth long preaching tour, from August 23, 1881, to May 30, 1882, was given to the Continent of Europe, where again Mr. Müller felt led by the low state of religious life in Switzerland and Germany.

This visit was extended to the Holy Land in a way strikingly providential. After speaking at Alexandria, Cairo, and Port Said, he went to Jaffa, and thence to Jerusalem, on November 28. With reverent feet he touched the soil once trodden by the feet of the Son of God, visiting, with pathetic interest, Gethsemane and Golgotha, and crossing the Mount of Olives to Bethany, thence to Bethlehem and back to Jaffa, and so to Haipha, Mt. Carmel, and Beirut, Smyrna, Ephesus, Constantinople, Athens, Brindisi, Rome, and Florence. Again were months crowded with services of all sorts whose fruit will appear only in the Day of the Lord Jesus, addresses being made in English, German, and French, or by translation into Arabic, Armenian, Turkish, and modern Greek. Sightseeing was always but incidental to the higher service of the Master. During this eighth tour, covering some eight months, Mr. Müller spoke hundreds of times, with all the former tokens of God's blessing on his seed-sowing.

The *ninth* tour, from August 8, 1882, to June 1, 1883, was occupied with labours in Germany, Austria, and Russia, including Bavaria, Hungary, Bohemia, Saxony, and Poland. His special joy it was to bear witness in Kroppenstadt, his birthplace, after an absence of about sixty-four years. At St. Petersburg, while the guest of Princess Lieven, at her mansion he met and ministered to many of high rank; he also began to hold meetings in the house of Colonel Paschkoff, who had suffered not only persecution but exile for the Lord's sake. While the Scriptures were being read one day in Buss, with seven poor Russians, a policeman summarily broke up the meeting and dispersed the little company. At Lodz in Poland, a letter was received, in behalf of almost the whole population begging him to remain longer; and so signs seemed to multiply, as he went forward, that he was in the path of duty and that God was with him.

On September 26, 1883, the *tenth* tour began, this time his face being turned toward the Orient. Nearly sixty years before he had desired to go to the East Indies as a missionary; now the Lord permitted him to carry out the desire in a new and strange way, and *India* was the twenty-third country visited in his tours. He travelled over 21,000 miles, and spoke over two hundred times, to missionaries and Christian workers, European residents, Eurasians, Hindus, Moslems, educated natives, native boys and girls in the orphanage at Colar, etc. Thus, in his seventy-ninth year, this servant of God was still in labours abundant, and in all his work conspicuously blessed of God.

After some months of preaching in England, Scotland, and Wales, on November 19, 1885, he and his wife set out on their fourth visit to the United States, and their *eleventh longer mission tour.* Crossing to the Pacific, they went to Sydney, New South Wales, and, after seven months in Australia, sailed for Java, and thence to China, arriving at Hong Kong, September 12th; Japan and the Straits of Malacca were also included in this visit to the Orient. The return to England was by way of Nice; and, after travelling nearly 38,000 miles, in good health Mr. and Mrs. Müller reached home on June 14, 1887, having been absent more than one year and seven months, during which Mr. Müller had preached whenever and wherever opportunity was afforded.

Less than two months later, on August 12, 1887, he sailed for South Australia, Tasmania, New Zealand, Ceylon, and India. This twelfth long tour closed in March, 1890, having covered thousands of miles. The intense heat at one time compelled Mr. Müller to leave Calcutta, and on the railway journey to Darjeeling his wife feared he would die. But he was mercifully spared.

It was on this tour and in the month of January, 1890, while at Jubbulpore, preaching with great help from the Lord, that a letter was put into Mr. Müller's hands, from a missionary at Agra, to whom Mr. Wright had sent a telegram, informing his father-in-law of his dear Lydia's death. For nearly thirty years she had laboured gratuitously at the orphan houses and it would he difficult to fill that vacancy; but for fourteen years she had been her husband's almost ideal companion, and for nearly fifty-eight years her father's unspeakable treasure—and here were two other voids which could never be filled. But Mr. Müller's heart, as also Mr. Wright's, was kept at rest by the strong confidence that, however mysterious God's ways, all His dealings belong to one harmonious spiritual mechanism in which every part is perfect and all things work together for good. (Romans 8:28)

This sudden bereavement led Mr. Müller to bring his mission tour in the East to a close and depart for Bristol, that he might both comfort Mr. Wright and relieve him of undue pressure of work.

After a lapse of two months, once more Mr. and Mrs. Müller left home for other extensive missionary journeys. They went to the Continent and were absent from July, 1890, to May, 1892. A twelvemonth was spent in Germany and Holland, Austria and Italy. This absence in fact included two tours, with no interval between them, and concluded the series of extensive journeys reaching through seventeen years.

SCRIPTURE TESTIMONY
Take the Gospel to the ends of the earth
Acts 1:8 · Acts 6:7 · Colossians 1:23

This man—from his seventieth to his eighty-seventh year—when most men are withdrawing from all activities, had travelled in forty-two countries and over two hundred thousand miles, a distance equivalent to nearly eight journeys round the globe! He estimated that during these seventeen years he had addressed over three million people; and from all that can be gathered from the records of these tours, we estimate that he must have spoken, outside of Bristol, between five thousand and six thousand times. What sort of teaching and testimony occupied these tours, those who have known the preacher and teacher need not be told. While at Berlin in 1891, he gave an address that serves as an example of the vital truths which he was wont to press on the attention of fellow disciples. We give a brief outline:

He first urged that believers should never, even under the greatest difficulties, be discouraged, and gave for his position sound scriptural reasons. Then he pointed out to them that the chief business of every day is first of all to seek to be truly at rest and happy in God. Then he showed how, from the word of God, all saved believers may know their true standing in Christ, and how in circumstances of particular perplexity they might ascertain the will of God. He then urged disciples to seek with intense earnestness to become acquainted with God Himself as revealed in the Holy Scriptures, and carefully to form and maintain godly habits of systematic Bible study and prayer, holy living and consecrated giving. He taught that God alone is the one all-satisfying portion of the soul, and that we must determine to possess and enjoy Him as such. He closed by emphasizing it as the one, single, all-absorbing, daily aim to glorify God in a complete surrender to His will and service.

In all these mission tours, again, the faithfulness of God conspicuously seen, in the bounteous supply of every need. Steamer fares and long railway journeys; hotel accommodations, ordinarily preferred to private hospitality, which seriously interfered with private habits of devotion, public work, and proper rest—such expenses demanded a heavy outlay; the new mode of life, now adopted for the Lord's sake, was at least three times as costly as the former frugal housekeeping; and yet, in answer to prayer and without any appeal to human help, the Lord furnished all that was required.

Accustomed to look, step by step, for such tokens of divine approval, as emboldened him to go forward, Mr. Müller records how, when one hundred pounds was sent to him for personal uses, this was recognized as a foretoken from his great Provider, "by which," he writes, "God meant to say to my own heart, 'I am pleased with thy work and service in going about on these long missionary tours. I will pay the expenses thereof, and I give thee here a specimen of what I am yet willing to do for thee.'"

Two other facts Mr. Müller specially records in connection with these tours: first, God's gracious guiding and guarding of the work at Bristol so that it suffered nothing from his absence; and secondly, the fact that these journeys had no connection with collecting of money for the work or even informing the public of it. No reference was made to the Institution at Bristol, except when urgently requested, and not always even then; nor were collections ever made for it. Statements found their way into the press that in America large sums were gathered, but their falsity is sufficiently shown by the fact that in his first tour in America, for example, the sum total of all such gifts was less than sixty pounds, not more than two thirds of the outlay of every day at the orphan houses.

These missionary tours were not always approved even by the friends and advisers of Mr. Müller. In 1882, while experiencing no little difficulty and trial, especially as to funds, there were not a few who felt a deep interest in the Institution on Ashley Down, who would have had God's servant discontinue his long absences, as to them it appeared that these were the main reason for the falling off in funds. He was always open to counsel, but he always reserved to himself an independent decision; and, on weighing the matter well, these were some of the reasons that led him to think that the work of God at home did not demand his personal presence:

1. He had observed year after year that, under the godly and efficient supervision of Mr. Wright and his large staff of helpers, every branch of the Scriptural Knowledge Institution had been found as healthy and fruitful during these absences as when Mr. Müller was in Bristol.
2. The Lord's approval of this work of wider witness had been in manner conclusive and in measure abundant, as in the ample supply of funds

for these tours, in the wide doors of access opened, and in the large fruit already evident in blessing to thousands of souls.

3. The strong impression upon his mind that this was the work which was to occupy the 'evening of his life,' grew in depth, and was confirmed by so many signs of God's leading that he could not doubt that he was led both of God's providence and Spirit.
4. Even while absent, he was never out of communication with the helpers at home. Generally he heard at least weekly from Mr. Wright, and any matters needing his counsel were thus submitted to him by letter; prayer to God was as effectual at a distance from Bristol as on the spot; and his periodical returns to that city for some weeks or months between these tours kept him in close touch with every department of the work.
5. The supreme consideration, however, was this: To suppose it necessary for Mr. Müller himself to be at home *in order that sufficient means should be supplied,* was a direct contradiction of the very principles upon which, and to maintain which, the whole work had been begun. *Real trust in God is above circumstances and appearances.* And this had been proven; for, during the third year after these tours began, the income for the various departments of the Scriptural Knowledge Institution was larger than ever during the preceding forty-four years of its existence; and therefore, notwithstanding the loving counsel of a few donors and friends who advised that Mr. Müller should stay at home, he kept to his purpose and his principles, partly to demonstrate that no man's presence is indispensable to the work of the Lord. "Them that honour Me I will honour." (1 Samuel 2:39) He regarded it the greatest honour of his life to bear this wide witness to God, and God correspondingly honoured His servant in bearing this testimony.

It was during the first and second of these American tours that the writer had the privilege of coming into personal contact with Mr. Müller. While I was at San Francisco, in 1878, he was to speak on Sabbath afternoon, May 12th, at Oakland, just across the bay, but conscientious objections to needless Sunday travel caused me voluntarily to lose what then seemed the only chance of seeing and hearing a man whose career had been watched by me for over twenty years, as he was to leave for the East a few days earlier than myself and was likely to be always a little in advance. On reaching Ogden, however, where the branch road from Salt Lake City joins the main line, Mr. and Mrs. Müller boarded my train and we travelled to Chicago together. I introduced myself, and held with him daily converse about divine things, and, while tarrying at Chicago, had numerous opportunities for hearing him speak there.

The results of this close and frequent contact were singularly blessed to me, and at my invitation he came to Detroit, Michigan, in his next tour, and spoke in the Fort Street Presbyterian Church, of which I was pastor, on Sundays, January 18 and 25, 1880, and on Monday and Friday evenings, in the interval.

In addition to these numerous and favourable opportunities thus providentially afforded for hearing and conversing with Mr. Müller, he kindly met me for several days in my study, for an hour at a time, for conference upon those deeper truths of the word of God and deeper experiences of the Christian life, upon which I was then very desirous of more light. For example, I desired to understand more clearly the Bible teaching about the Lord's coming. I had opposed with much persistency what is known as the premillennial view, and brought out my objections, to all of which he made one reply: "My beloved brother, I have heard all your arguments and objections against this view, but they have one fatal defect: *not one of them is based upon the word of God.* You will never get at the truth upon any matter of divine revelation unless you lay aside your prejudices and like a little child ask simply what is the testimony of Scripture."

With patience and wisdom he unravelled the tangled skein of my perplexity and difficulty, and helped me to settle upon biblical principles all matters of so-called expediency. As he left me, about to visit other cities, his words fixed themselves in my memory. I had expressed to him my growing conviction that the worship in the churches had lost its primitive simplicity; that the pew-rent system was pernicious; that fixed salaries for ministers of the gospel were unscriptural; that the church of God should be administered only by men full of the Holy Ghost, and that the duty of Christians to the non-church-going masses was grossly neglected, etc. He solemnly said to me: "My beloved brother, the Lord has given you much light upon these matters, and will hold you correspondingly responsible for its use. If you obey Him and walk in the light, you will have more; if not, the light will be withdrawn."

It is a singular lesson on the importance of an anointed tongue, that forty simple words, spoken over twenty years ago, have had a daily influence on the life of him to whom they were spoken. Amid subtle temptations to compromise the claims of duty and hush the voice of conscience, or of the Spirit of God, and to follow the traditions of men rather than the word of God, those words of that venerated servant of God have recurred to mind with ever fresh force. We risk the forfeiture of privileges which are not employed for God, and of obscuring convictions which are not carried into action. God's word to us is *"use or lose."* "To him that hath shall be given: from him that hath not shall be taken away even that which he seemeth to have." It is the hope and the prayer of him who writes this memoir that the reading of these pages may prove to be an interview with the man whose memorial they are, and that the witness borne by George Müller may be to many readers a source of untold and lifelong blessing.

It need not be said that to carry out conviction into action is a costly sacrifice. It may make necessary renunciations and separations which leave one to feel a strange sense both of deprivation and loneliness. But he who will fly as an eagle does into the higher levels where cloudless day abides, and live in the sunshine of God, must consent to live a comparatively lonely life. No bird is so solitary as the eagle. Eagles never fly in flocks: one, or at most two, and the two, mates, being ever seen at once. But the life that is lived unto God, however it forfeits human companionship, knows divine fellowship, and the child of God who like his Master undertakes to "do always the things that please Him," can like his Master say, "The Father hath not left me alone." "I am alone; yet not alone, for the Father is with me." Whosoever will promptly follow whatever light God gives, without regard to human opinion, custom, tradition, or approbation, will learn the deep meaning of these words: "Then shall we know, if we follow on to know the Lord."

CHAPTER XVIII

Faith and Patience in Serving

QUANTITY OF service is of far less importance than quality. To do well, rather than to do much, will be the motto of him whose main purpose is to please God. Our Lord bade His disciples tarry until endued with power from on high, because it is such enduement that gives to all witness and work the celestial savour and flavour of the Spirit.

Before we come to the closing scenes, we may well look back over the life-work of George Müller, which happily illustrates both quantity and quality of service. It may be doubted whether any other one man of this century accomplished as much for God and man, and yet all the abundant offerings which he brought to his Master were characterized by a heavenly fragrance.

The orphan work was but one branch of that tree—the Scriptural Knowledge Institution—which owed its existence to the fact that its founder devised large and liberal things for the Lord's cause. He sought to establish or at least to aid Christian schools wherever needful, to scatter Bibles and Testaments, Christian books and tracts; to aid missionaries who were witnessing to the truth and working on a scriptural basis in destitute parts; and though each of these objects might well have engrossed his mind, they were all combined in the many-sided work which his love for souls suggested.

An aggressive spirit is never content with what has been done, but is prompt to enter any new door that is providentially opened. When the Paris Exposition of 1867 offered such rare opportunities, both for preaching to the crowds passing through the French capital, and for circulating among them the Holy Scriptures, he gladly availed himself of the services of two brethren whom God had sent to labour there, one of whom spoke three, and the other, eight, modern languages; and through them were circulated, chiefly at the Exposition, and in thirteen different languages, nearly twelve thousand copies of the word of God, or portions of the same. It has been estimated that at this International Exhibition there were distributed in all over one and a quarter million Bibles, in sixteen tongues, which were gratefully accepted, even by Romish priests. Within six months those who thus entered God's open door scattered more copies of the Book of God than in ordinary circumstances would have been done by ten thousand colporteurs in twenty times that number of months, and thousands of souls are known to have found salvation by the simple reading of the New Testament. Of this glorious work, George Müller was permitted to be so largely a promoter.

At the Havre Exhibition of the following year, 1868, a similar work was done; and in like manner, when a providential door was unexpectedly opened into the Land of the Inquisition, Mr. Müller promptly took measures to promote the circulation of the Word in Spain. In the streets of Madrid the open Bible was seen for the first time, and copies were sold at the rate of two hundred and fifty in an hour, so that the supply was not equal to the demand. The same facts were substantially repeated when free Italy furnished a field for sowing the seed of the Kingdom. This wide-awake servant of God watched the signs of the times and, while others slept, followed the Lord's signals of advance.

One of the most fascinating features of the Narrative is found in the letters from his Bible distributors. It is interesting also to trace the story of the growth of the tract enterprise, until, in 1874, the circulation exceeded three and three-quarter millions, God in His faithfulness supplying abundant means.[32]

The good thus effected by the distributors of evangelical literature must not be overlooked in this survey of the many useful agencies employed or assisted by Mr. Müller. To him the world was a field to be sown with the seed of the Kingdom, and opportunities were eagerly embraced for widely disseminating the truth. Tracts were liberally used, given away in large quantities at open-air services, fairs, races and steeplechases, and among spectators at public executions, or among passengers on board ships and railway trains, and by the way. Sometimes, at a single gathering of the multitudes, fifteen thousand were distributed judiciously and prayerfully, and this branch of the work has, during all these years, continued with undiminished fruitfulness to yield its harvest of good.

SCRIPTURE TESTIMONY
God' work will not lack God's supply Philippians 4:19

All this was, from first to last, and of necessity, a work of faith. How far faith must have been kept in constant and vigorous exercise can be appreciated only by putting one's self in Mr. Müller's place. In the year 1874, for instance, about forty-four thousand pounds were needed, and he was compelled to count the cost and face the situation. Two thousand and one hundred hungry mouths were

32 Narrative, IV. 244.

daily to be fed, and as many bodies to be clad and cared for. One hundred and eighty-nine missionaries were needing assistance; one hundred schools, with about nine thousand pupils, to be supported; four million pages of tracts and tens of thousands of copies of the Scriptures to be yearly provided for distribution; and, beside all these ordinary expenses, inevitable crises or emergencies, always liable to arise in connection with the conduct of such extensive enterprises, would from time to time call for extraordinary outlay. The man who was at the head of the Scriptural Knowledge Institution had to look at this array of unavoidable expenses, and at the same time face the human possibility and probability of an empty treasury whence the last shilling had been drawn. Let him tell us how he met such a prospect:

> "God, our infinitely rich Treasurer, remains to us. It is this which gives me peace.... Invariably, with this probability before me, I have said to myself: 'God who has raised up this work through me; God who has led me generally year after year to enlarge it; God, who has supported this work now for more than forty years, will still help and will not suffer me to be confounded, because I rely upon Him. I commit the whole work to Him, and He will provide me with what I need, in future also, though I know not whence the means are to come.'"[33]

Thus he wrote in his journal, on July 28, 1874. Since then twenty-four years have passed, and to this day the work goes on, though he who then had the guidance of it sleeps in Jesus. Whoever has had any such dealings with God, on however small a scale, cannot even *think* of the Lord as failing to honour a faith so simple, genuine, and childlike a faith which leads a helpless believer thus to cast himself and all his cares upon God with utter abandonment of all anxiety. This man put God to proof, and proved to himself and to all who receive his testimony that it is blessed to wait only upon Him. The particular point which he had in view, in making these entries in his journal is the object also of embodying them in these pages, namely, to show that, while the annual expenses of this Institution were so exceedingly large and the income so apparently uncertain, the soul of this believer was, to use his own words, "THROUGHOUT, without the least wavering, stayed upon God, believing that He who had through him begun the Institution, enlarged it almost year after year, and upheld it for forty years in answer to prayer by faith, would do this still and not suffer this servant of His to be confounded."[34] Believing that God would still help, and supply the means, George Müller was willing, and THOROUGHLY in heart prepared, if necessary, to pass again through similar severe and prolonged seasons of trial as he had already endured.

33 Narrative, IV. 386, 387.
34 Narrative, IV. 389.

The Living God had kept him calm and restful, amid all the ups and downs of his long experience as the superintendent and director of this many-sided work, though the tests of faith had not been light or short of duration. For more than ten years at a time—as from August, 1838, to April, 1849, day by day, and for months together from meal to meal—it was necessary to look to God, almost without cessation, for daily supplies. When, later on, the Institution was twentyfold larger and the needs proportionately greater, for months at a time the Lord likewise constrained His servant to lean from hour to hour, in the same dependence, upon Him. All along through these periods of unceasing want, the Eternal God was his refuge and underneath were the Everlasting Arms. He reflected that God was aware of all this enlargement of the work and its needs; he comforted himself with the consoling thought that he was seeking his Master's glory; and that if in this way the greater glory would accrue to Him for the good of His people and of those who were still unbelievers, it was no concern of the servant; nay, more than this, it behooved the servant to be willing to go on in this path of trial, even unto the end of his course, if so it should please his Master, who guides His affairs with divine discretion.

The trials of faith did not cease even until the end. July 28, 1881, finds the following entry in Mr. Müller's journal:

> "The income has been for some time past only about a third part of the expenses. Consequently all we have for the support of the orphans is nearly gone; and for the first four objects of the Institution we have nothing at all in hand. The natural appearance now is that the work cannot be carried on. But I BELIEVE that the Lord will help, both with means for the orphans and also for other objects of the Institution, and that we shall not be confounded; also that the work shall not need to be given up. I am fully expecting help, and have written this to the glory of God, that it may be recorded hereafter for the encouragement of His children. The result will be seen. I expect that we shall not be confounded, though for some years we have not been so poor."

While faith thus leaned on God, prayer took more vigorous hold. Six, seven, eight times a day, he and his dear wife were praying for means, looking for answers, and firmly persuaded that their expectations would not be disappointed. Since that entry was made, seventeen more years have borne their witness that this trust was not put to shame. Not a branch of this tree of holy enterprise has been cut off by the sharp blade of a stern necessity.

Though faith had thus tenaciously held fast to the promises, the pressure was not at once relieved. When, a fortnight after these confident records of trust in

God had been spread on the pages of the journal, the balance for the orphans was less than it had been for twenty-five years, it would have seemed to human sight as though God had forgotten to be gracious. But, on August 22nd, over one thousand pounds came in for the support of the orphans and thus relief was afforded for a time.

Again, let us bear in mind how in the most unprecedented straits God alone was made the confidant, even the best friends of the Institution, alike the poor and the rich, being left in ignorance of the pressure of want. It would have been no sin to have made known the circumstances, or even to have made an appeal for aid to the many believers who would gladly have come to the relief of the work. But the *testimony to the Lord* was to be jealously guarded, and the main object of this work of faith would have been imperilled just so far as by any appeal to men this witness to God was weakened.

In this crisis, and in every other, faith triumphed, and so the testimony to a prayer-hearing God grew in volume and power as the years went on. It was while as yet this period of testing was not ended, and no permanent relief was yet supplied, that Mr. Müller, with his wife, left Bristol on August 23rd, for the Continent, on his eighth long preaching tour. Thus, at a time when, to the natural eye, his own presence would have seemed well-nigh indispensable, he calmly departed for other spheres of duty, leaving the work at home in the hands of Mr. Wright and his helpers. The tour had been already arranged for, under God's leading, and it was undertaken, with the supporting power of a deep conviction that God is as near to those who in prayer wait on Him in distant lands, as on Ashley Down, and needs not the personal presence of any man in any one place, or at any time, in order to carry on His work.

In an American city, a half-idiotic boy who was bearing a heavy burden asked a drayman, who was driving an empty cart, for a ride. Being permitted, he mounted the cart with his basket, but thinking he might so relieve the horse a little, while still himself riding, lifted his load and carried it. We laugh at the simplicity of the idiotic lad, and yet how often we are guilty of similar folly! We profess to cast ourselves and our cares upon the Lord, and then persist in bearing our own burdens, as if we felt that He would be unequal to the task of sustaining us and our loads. It is a most wholesome lesson for Christian workers to learn that all true work is primarily the Lord's, and only secondarily ours, and that therefore all 'carefulness' on our part is distrust of Him, implying a sinful self-conceit which overlooks the fact that He is the one Worker and all others are only His instruments.

As to our trials, difficulties, losses, and disappointments, we are prone to hesitate about committing them to the Lord, trustfully and calmly. We think we have done well if we take refuge in the Lord's promise to his reluctant disciple Peter, "What I do thou knowest not now, but thou shalt know hereafter," referring this 'hereafter' to the future state where we look for the solution of all problems. In Peter's case the hereafter appears to have come when the feet-washing was done and Christ explained its meaning; and it is very helpful to our faith to observe Mr. Müller's witness concerning all these trying and disappointing experiences of his life, that, without one exception, he had found already in this life that they worked together for his good; so that he had reason to praise God for them all. In the ninetieth psalm we read:

> "Make us glad according to the days wherein Thou hast afflicted us
> And the years wherein we have seen evil." (Psalm 90:15)

This is an inspired prayer, and such prayer is a prophecy. Not a few saints have found, this side of heaven, a divine gladness for every year and day of sadness, when their afflictions and adversities have been patiently borne.

Faith is the secret of both peace and steadfastness, amid all tendencies to discouragement and discontinuance in well-doing. James was led by the Spirit of God to write that the unstable and unbelieving man is like the "wave of the sea driven with the wind and tossed." There are two motions of the waves—one up and down, which we call undulation, the other to and fro, which we call fluctuation. How appropriately both are referred to—"tossed" up and down, "driven" to and fro! The double-minded man lacks steadiness in both respects: his faith has no uniformity of experience, for he is now at the crest of the wave and now in the trough of the sea; it has no uniformity of progress, for whatever he gains to-day he loses to-morrow.

Fluctuations in income and apparent prosperity did not take George Müller by surprise. He expected them, for if there were no crises and critical emergencies how could there be critical deliverances? His trust was in God, not in donors or human friends or worldly circumstances: and because he trusted in the Living God who says of Himself, "I am the Lord, I change not," amid all other changes, his feet were upon the one Rock of Ages that no earthquake shock can move from its eternal foundations.

Two facts Mr. Müller gratefully records at this period of his life: (Narrative, IV. 411, 418.)

First. "For above fifty years I have now walked, by His grace, in a path of complete reliance upon Him who is the faithful one, for everything I have needed; and yet I am increasingly convinced that it is by His help alone I am enabled to continue in this course; for, if left to myself, even after the precious enjoyment so long experienced of walking thus in fellowship with God, I should yet be tempted to abandon this path of entire dependence upon Him. To His praise, however, I am able to state that for more than half a century I have never had the least desire to do so."

SCRIPTURE TESTIMONY

Large groups of people converted at the same time

Acts 2:41 · Acts 4:4

Second. From May, 1880, to May 1881, a gracious work of the Spirit had visited the orphans on Ashley Down and in many of the schools. During the three months spent by Mr. Müller at home before sailing for America in September, 1880, he had been singularly drawn out in prayer for such a visitation of grace, and had often urged it on the prayers of his helpers. The Lord is faithful, and He cheered the heart of His servant in his absence by abundant answers to his intercessions. Before he had fairly entered on his work in America, news came from home of a blessed work of conversion already in progress, and which went on for nearly a year, until there was good ground for believing that in the five houses five hundred and twelve orphans had found God their Father in Christ, and nearly half as many more were in a hopeful state.

The Lord did not forget His promise, and He did keep the plant He had permitted His servant to set in His name in the soil on Ashley Down. Faith that was tried, triumphed. On June 7, 1884, a legacy of over eleven thousand pounds reached him, the *largest single gift* ever yet received, the largest donations which had preceded being respectively one thousand, two thousand, three thousand, five thousand, eight thousand one hundred, and nine thousand and ninety-one pounds.

This last amount, eleven thousand, had been due for over six years from an estate, but had been kept back by the delays of the Chancery Court. Prayer had been made day by day that the bequest might be set free for its uses, and now the full answer had come; and God had singularly timed the supply to the need, for there was at that time only forty-one pounds ten shillings in hand, not one half of the average daily expenses, and certain sanitary improvements were just about to be carried out which would require an outlay of over two thousand pounds.

As Mr. Müller closed the solemn and blessed records of 1884, he wrote:

"Thus ended the year 1884, during which we had been tried, greatly tried, in various ways, no doubt for the exercise of our faith, and to make us know God more fully; but during which we had also been helped and blessed, and greatly helped and blessed. Peacefully, then, we were able to enter upon the year 1885, fully assured that, as we had God *for* US and *with* US, *all, all* would be well." John Wesley had in the same spirit said a century before, "Best of all, God is with us."

Of late years the orphanage at Ashley Down has not had as many inmates as formerly, and some four or five hundred more might now be received. Mr. Müller felt constrained, for some years previous to his death, to make these vacancies known to the public, in hopes that some destitute orphans might find there a home. But it must be remembered that the provision for such children has been greatly enlarged since this orphan work was begun. In 1834 the total accommodation for all orphans, in England, reached thirty-six hundred, while the prisons contained nearly twice as many children under eight years of age. This state of things led to the rapid enlargement of the work until over two thousand were housed on Ashley Down alone; and this colossal enterprise stimulated others to open similar institutions until, fifty years after Mr. Müller began his work, at least one hundred thousand orphans were cared for in England alone. Thus God used Mr. Müller to give such an impetus to this form of philanthropy, that destitute children became the object of a widely organized charity both on the part of individuals and of societies, and orphanages now exist for various classes.

In all this manifold work which Mr. Müller did he was, to the last, self-oblivious. From the time when, in October, 1830, he had given up all stated salary, as pastor and minister of the gospel, he had never received any salary, stipend nor fixed income, of any sort, whether as a pastor or as a director of the Scriptural Knowledge Institution. Both principle and preference led him to wait only upon God for all personal needs, as also for all the wants of his work. Nevertheless God put into the hearts of His believing children in all parts of the world, not only to send gifts in aid of the various branches of the work which Mr. Müller superintended, but to forward to him money for his own uses, as well as clothes, food, and other temporal supplies. He never appropriated one penny which was not in some way indicated or designated as for his own personal needs, and subject to his personal judgment. No straits of individual or family want ever led him to use, even for a time, what was sent to him for other ends. Generally gifts intended for himself were wrapped up in paper with his name written thereon, or in other equally distinct ways designated as meant for him. Thus as early as 1874 his year's income reached upwards of twenty-one hundred pounds. Few nonconformist ministers, and not one in twenty of the clergy of the establishment, have any such income, which averages about six pounds for every day in the year—and all this came from the Lord, simply in answer to prayer, and without appeal of any sort to man or even the revelation of personal needs. If we add legacies paid at the end of the year 1873, Mr. Müller's entire income in about thirteen months exceeded thirty-one hundred pounds. Of this he gave, out and out to the needy, and to the work of God, the whole amount save about two hundred and fifty, expended on personal and family wants; and thus started the year 1875 as poor as he had begun forty-five years before; and if his personal expenses were scrutinized it would be found that even what he ate and drank and wore was with equal conscientiousness expended for the glory of God, so that in a true sense we may say he spent nothing on himself.

In another connection it has already been recorded that, when at Jubbulpore in 1890, Mr. Müller received tidings of his daughter's death. To any man of less faith that shock might have proved, at his advanced age, not only a stunning but a fatal blow. His only daughter and only child, Lydia, the devoted wife of James Wright, had been called home, in her fifty-eighth year, and after nearly thirty years of labour at the orphan houses. What this death meant to Mr. Müller, at the age of eighty-four, no one can know who has not witnessed the mutual devotion of that daughter and that father: and what that loss was to Mr. Wright, the pen alike fails to portray. If the daughter seemed to her father humanly indispensable, she was to her husband a sort of inseparable part of his being; and over such experiences as these it is the part of delicacy to draw the curtain of silence. But it should be recorded that no trait in Mrs. Wright was more pathetically attractive than her humility. Few disciples ever felt their own nothingness as she did, and it was this ornament of a meek and quiet spirit—the only ornament she wore—that made her seem so beautiful to all who knew her well enough for this 'hidden man of the heart' to be disclosed to their vision. Did not that ornament in the Lord's sight appear as of great price? Truly "the beauty of the Lord her God was upon her."

James Wright had lived with his beloved Lydia for more than eighteen years, in "unmarred and unbroken felicity." They had together shared in prayers and tears before God, bearing all life's burdens in common. Weak as she was physically, he always leaned upon her and found her a tower of spiritual strength in time of heavy responsibility. While, in her lowly-mindedness, she thought of herself as a 'little useless thing,' he found her both a capable and cheerful supervisor of many most important domestic arrangements where a competent woman's hand was needful: and, with rare tact and fidelity, she kept watch of the wants of the orphans as her dear mother had done before her. After her decease, her husband found among her personal effects a precious treasure—a verse written with her own hand:

> "I have seen the face of Jesus,
> Tell me not of aught beside;
> I have heard the voice of Jesus,
> All my soul is satisfied."

This invaluable little fragment, like that other writing found by this beloved daughter among her mother's effects, became to Mr. Wright what that had been to Mr. Müller, a sort of last legacy from his departed and beloved wife. Her desires were fulfilled; she had seen the face and heard the voice of Him who alone could satisfy her soul.

In the Fifty-third Report, which extends to May 26, 1892, it is stated that the expenses exceeded the income for the orphans by a total of over thirty-six hundred pounds, so that many dear fellow labourers, without the least complaint, were in arrears as to salaries. This was the second time only, in fifty-eight years, that the income thus fell short of the expenses. Ten years previous, the expenses had been in excess of the income by four hundred and eighty-eight pounds, but, within one month after the new financial year had begun, by the payment of legacies three times as much as the deficiency was paid in; and, adding donations, six times as much. And now the question arose whether God would not have Mr. Müller contract rather than expand the work.

He says: "The Lord's dealings with us during the last year indicate that it is His will we should contract our operations, and we are waiting upon Him for directions as to how and to what extent this should be done; for we have but one single object—the glory of God. When I founded this Institution, one of the principles stated was, 'that there would be no enlargement of the work by going into debt': and in like manner we cannot go on with *that which already exists* if we have not sufficient means coming in to meet the current expenses." Thus the godly man who loved to expand his service for God was humble enough to bow to the will of God if its contraction seemed needful.

Prayer was much increased, and faith did not fail under the trial, which continued for weeks and months, but was abundantly sustained by the promises of an unfailing Helper. This distress was relieved in March by the sale of ten acres of land, at one thousand pounds an acre, and at the close of the year there was in hand a balance of over twenty-three hundred pounds.

The exigency, however, continued more or less severe until again, in 1893-4, after several years of trial, the Lord once more bountifully supplied means. And Mr. Müller is careful to add that though the *appearance* during those years of trial was many times as if God had forgotten or forsaken them and would never care any more about the Institution, it was only in appearance, for he was as mindful of it as ever, and he records how by this discipline faith was still further strengthened, God was glorified in the patience and meekness whereby He enabled them to endure the testing, and tens of thousands of believers were blessed in afterward reading about these experience's of divine faithfulness.[35]

Five years after Mrs. Wright's death, Mr. Müller was left again a widower. His last great mission tour had come to an end in 1892, and in 1895, on the 13th of January, the beloved wife who in all these long journeys had been his constant companion and helper, passed to her rest, and once more left him peculiarly alone, since his devoted Lydia had been called up higher. Yet by the same grace of God which had always before sustained him he was now upheld, and not only kept in unbroken peace, but enabled to "kiss the Hand which administered the stroke."

At the funeral of his second wife, as at that of the first, he made the address, and the scene was unique in interest. Seldom does a man of ninety conduct such a service. The faith that sustained him in every other trial held him up in this. He lived in such habitual communion with the unseen world, and walked in such uninterrupted fellowship with the unseen God, that the exchange of worlds became too real for him to mourn for those who had made it, or to murmur at

35 Fifty-fifth Report, p. 32.

the infinite Love that numbers our days. It moved men more deeply than any spoken word of witness to see him manifestly borne up as on everlasting Arms.

SCRIPTURE TESTIMONY
God is able to bring good from any circumstances Romans 8:28

I remember Mr. Müller remarking that he waited eight years before he understood at all the purpose of God in removing his first wife, who seemed so indispensable to him and his work. His own journal explains more fully this remark. When it pleased God to take from him his second wife, after over twenty-three years of married life, again he rested on the promise that "All things work together for good to them that love God" and reflected on his past experiences of its truth. When he lost his first wife after over thirty-nine years of happy wedlock, while he bowed to the Father's will, how that sorrow and bereavement could work good had been wholly a matter of *faith,* for no compensating good was apparent to sight; yet he believed God's word and waited to see how it would be fulfilled. That loss seemed one that could not be made up. Only a little before, two orphan houses had been opened for nine hundred more orphans, so that there were total accommodations for over two thousand; she, who by nature, culture, gifts, and graces, was so wonderfully fitted to be her husband's helper, and who had with motherly love cared for these children, was suddenly removed from his side. Four years after Mr. Müller married his second wife, he saw it plainly to be God's will that he should spend life's evening-time in giving witness to the nations. These mission tours could not be otherwise than very trying to the physical powers of endurance, since they covered over two hundred thousand miles and obliged the travellers to spend a week at a time in a train, and sometimes from four to six weeks on board a vessel. Mrs. Müller, though never taking part in public, was severely taxed by all this travel, and always busy, writing letters, circulating books and tracts, and in various ways helping and relieving her husband. All at once, while in the midst of these fatiguing journeys and exposures to varying climates, it flashed upon Mr. Müller that his first wife, who had died in her seventy-third year, *could never have undertaken these tours,* and that the Lord had thus, in taking her, left him free to make these extensive journeys. She would have been over fourscore years old when these tours began, and, apart from age, could not have borne the exhaustion, because of her frail health; whereas the second Mrs. Müller, who, at the time, was not yet fifty-seven, was both by her age and strength fully equal to the strain thus put upon her.

CHAPTER XIX

At Evening-Time—Light

THE CLOSING scene of this beautiful and eventful life-history has an interest not altogether pathetic. Mr. Müller seems like an elevated mountain, on whose summit the evening sun shines in lingering splendour, and whose golden peak rises far above the ordinary level and belongs to heaven more than earth, in the clear, cloudless calm of God.

From May, 1892, when the last mission tour closed; he devoted himself mainly to the work of the Scriptural Knowledge Institution, and to preaching at Bethesda and elsewhere as God seemed to appoint. His health was marvelous, especially considering how, when yet a young man, frequent and serious illnesses and general debility had apparently disqualified him from all military duty, and to many prophesied early death or hopeless succumbing to disease. He had been in tropic heat and arctic cold, in gales and typhoons at sea, and on journeys by rail, sometimes as continuously long as a sea-voyage. He had borne the pest of fleas, mosquitoes, and even rats. He had endured changes of climate, diet, habits of life, and the strain of almost daily services, and come out of all unscathed. This man, whose health was never robust, had gone through labours that would try the mettle of an iron constitution; this man, who had many times been laid aside by illness and sometimes for months and who in 1837 had feared that a persistent head trouble might unhinge his mind, could say, in his ninety-second year: "I have been able, every day and all the day, to work, and that with ease, as seventy years since." When the writer was holding meetings in Bristol in 1896, on an anniversary very sacred to himself, he asked his beloved father Müller to speak at the closing meeting of the series, in the Y.M.C.A. Hall; and he did so, delivering a powerful address of forty-five minutes, on Prayer in connection with Missions, and giving his own life-story in part, with a vigour of voice and manner that seemed a denial of his advanced age.[36]

The marvelous preservation of such a man at such an age reminds one of Caleb, who at eighty-five could boast in God that he was as strong even for war as in the day that he was sent into the land as one of the spies; and Mr. Müller himself attributed this preservation to three causes: first, the exercising of himself to have always a conscience void of offence both toward God and toward men; secondly to the love he felt for the Scriptures, and the constant recuperative power they exercised upon his whole being; and third, to that happiness he felt in God and His work, which relieved him of all anxiety and needless wear and tear in his labours.

The great fundamental truth that this heroic man stamped on his generation was that the Living God is the same to-day and forever as yesterday and in all ages past, and that, with equal confidence with the most trustful souls of any age, we may believe His word, and to every promise add, like Abraham, our 'Amen'—IT SHALL BE SO![37] When, a few days after his death, Mr. E. H. Glenny, who is known to many as the beloved and self-sacrificing friend of the North African Mission, passed through Barcelona, he found written in an album over his signature the words: "Jesus Christ, the same yesterday and to-day and for ever." And, like the writer of the Epistle to the Hebrews, quoting from the 102nd Psalm, we may say of Jehovah, while all else changes and perishes:

> "Thou remainest";
> "Thou art the same."

Toward the close of life Mr. Müller, acting under medical advice, abated somewhat of his active labours, preaching commonly but once a Sunday. It was my privilege to hear him on the morning of the Lord's day, March 22, 1896. He spoke on the 77th Psalm; of course he found here his favourite theme—prayer; and, taking that as a fair specimen of his average preaching, he was certainly a remarkable expositor of Scripture even at ninety-one years of age. Later on the outline of this discourse will be found.

On Sunday morning, March 6, 1898, he spoke at Alma Road Chapel, and on the Monday evening following was at the prayer service at Bethesda, on both occasions in his usual health. On Wednesday evening following, he took his wonted place at the Orphan House prayer meeting and gave out the hymns:

---

36 Appendix K.
37 Genesis 15:6 (Hebrew)

"The countless multitude on high."

and

"We'll sing of the Shepherd that died."

When he bade his beloved son-in-law "good-night," there was no outward sign of declining strength. He seemed to the last the vigorous old man, and retired to rest as usual. It had been felt that one so advanced in years should have some night-attendant, especially as indications of heart-weakness had been noticed of late, and he had yielded to the pressure of love and consented to such an arrangement *after that night.* But the consent came too late. He was never more to need human attendance or attention. On Thursday morning, March 10th, at about seven o'clock, the usual cup of tea was taken to his room. To the knock at the door there was no response save an ominous silence. The attendant opened the door, only to find that the venerable patriarch lay dead, on the floor beside the bed. He had probably risen to take some nourishment—a glass of milk and a biscuit being always put within reach—and, while eating the biscuit, he had felt faint, and fallen, clutching at the table-cloth as he fell, for it was dragged off, with certain things that had lain on the table. His medical adviser, who was promptly summoned, gave as his opinion that he had died of heart-failure some hour or two before he had been found by his attendant.

Such a departure, even at such an age, produced a worldwide sensation. That man's moral and spiritual forces reached and touched the earth's ends. Not in Bristol, or in Britain alone, but across the mighty waters toward the sunrise and sunset was felt the responsive pulse-beat of a deep sympathy. Hearts bled all over the globe when it was announced, by telegraph wire and ocean cable, that George Müller was dead. It was said of a great Englishman that his influence could be measured only by "parallels of latitude"; of George Müller we may add, and by meridians of longitude. He belonged to the whole church and the whole world, in a unique sense; and the whole race of man sustained a loss when he died.

The funeral, which took place on the Monday following, was a popular tribute of affection, such as is seldom seen. Tens of thousands of people reverently stood along the route of the simple procession; men left their workshops and offices, women left their elegant homes or humble kitchens, all seeking to pay a last token of respect. Bristol had never before witnessed any such scene.

A brief service was held at Orphan House No. 3, where over a thousand children met, who had for a second time lost a 'father'; in front of the reading-desk in the great dining-room, a coffin of elm, studiously plain, and by request without floral offerings, contained all that was mortal of George Müller, and on a brass plate was a simple inscription, giving the date of his death, and his age.

Prayer Room, Orphan House No. 3

Mr. James Wright gave the address, reminding those who were gathered that, to all of us, even those who have lived nearest God, death comes while the Lord tarries; that it is blessed to die in the Lord; and that for believers in Christ there is a glorious resurrection waiting. The tears that ran down those young cheeks were more eloquent than any words, as a token of affection for the dead. The procession silently formed. Among those who followed the bier were four who had been occupants of that first orphan home in Wilson Street. The children's grief melted the hearts of spectators, and eyes unused to weeping were moistened that day. The various carriages bore the medical attendants, the relatives and connections of Mr. Müller, the elders and deacons of the churches with which he was associated, and his staff of helpers in the work on Ashley Down. Then followed forty or fifty other vehicles with deputations from various religious bodies, etc.

At Bethesda, every foot of space was crowded, and hundreds sought in vain for admission. The hymn was sung which Mr. Müller had given out at that last prayer meeting the night before his departure. Dr. Maclean of Bath offered prayer, mingled with praise for such a long life of service and witness, of prayer and faith, and Mr. Wright spoke from Hebrews 13:7, 8:

> "Remember them which have the rule over you,
> Who have spoken unto you the word of God:
> Whose faith follow,
> Considering the end of their conversation:
> Jesus Christ, the same yesterday and to-day and forever."

He spoke of those spiritual rulers and guides whom God sets over his people; and of the privilege of imitating their faith, calling attention to the two characteristics of his beloved father-in-law's faith: first, that it was based on that immovable Rock of Ages, God's written word; and secondly, that it translated the precepts and promises of that word into daily life.

Mr. Wright made very emphatic Mr. Müller's acceptance of the whole Scriptures, as divinely inspired. He had been wont to say to young believers, "Put your finger on the passage on which your faith rests," and had himself read the Bible from end to end nearly two hundred times. He fed on the Word and therefore was strong. He found the centre of that Word in the living Person it enshrines, and his one ground of confidence was His atoning work. Always in his own eyes weak, wretched, and vile, unworthy of the smallest blessing, he rested solely on the merit and mediation of His great High Priest.

George Müller *cultivated* faith. He used to say to his helpers in prayer and service, "Never let enter your minds a shadow of doubt as to the love of the Father's heart or the power of the Father's arm." And he projected his whole life forward, and looked at it in the light of the Judgment Day.

Mr. Wright's address made prominent one or two other most important lessons, as, for example, that the Spirit bids us imitate, not the idiosyncrasies or philanthropy of others, but *their faith.* And he took occasion to remind his hearers that philanthropy was not the foremost aim or leading feature of Mr. Müller's life, but above all else to magnify and glorify God, *"as still the living God who, now as well as thousands of years ago, hears the prayers of His children and helps those who trust Him."* He touchingly referred to the humility that led Mr. Müller to do the mightiest thing for God without self-consciousness, and showed that God can take up and use those who are willing to be only instruments.

Mr. Wright further remarked:

> "I have been asked again and again lately as to whether the orphan work would go on. It is going on. Since the commencement of the year we have received between forty and fifty fresh orphans, and this week expect to receive more. The other four objects of the Institution, according to the ability God gives us, are still being carried on. We believe that whatever God would do with regard to the future will be worthy of Him. We do not know much more, and do not want to. He knows what He will do. I cannot think, however, that the God who has so blessed the work for so long will leave our prayers as to the future unanswered."

SCRIPTURE TESTIMONY
God will exalt the humble Matthew 23:12 · James 4:10 · 1 Peter 5:5-6

Mr. Benjamin Perry then spoke briefly, characterizing Mr. Müller as the greatest personality Bristol had known as a citizen. He referred to his power as an expounder of Scripture, and to the fact that he brought to others for their comfort and support what had first been food to his own soul. He gave some personal reminiscences, referring, for instance, to his ability at an extreme old age still to work without hindrance either mental or physical, free from rheumatism, ache, or pain, and seldom suffering from exhaustion. He briefly described him as one who, in response to the infinite love of God, which called him from a life of sin to a life of salvation and service, wholly loved God above everybody and everything, so that his highest pleasure was to please and serve Him. As an illustration of his humility, he gave an incident. When of late a friend had said, "When God calls you home, it will be like a ship going into harbour, full sail."—"Oh no!" said Mr. Müller, "it is poor George Müller who needs daily to pray, 'Hold Thou me up in my goings, that my footsteps slip not.'" The close of such lives as those of Asa and Solomon were to Mr. Müller a perpetual warning, leading him to pray that he might never thus depart from the Lord in his old age.

After prayer by Mr. J. L. Stanley, Col. Molesworth gave out the hymn,

> "'Tis sweet to think of those at rest."

And after another prayer by Mr. Stanley Arnot, the body was borne to its resting-place in Arno's Vale Cemetery, and buried beside the bodies of Mr. Müller's first and second wives, some eighty carriages joining in the procession to the grave. Everything from first to last was as simple and unostentatious as he himself would have wished. At the graveside Col. Molesworth prayed, and Mr. George F. Bergin read from 1 Corinthians 15 and spoke a few words upon the tenth verse, which so magnifies the grace of God both in what we *are* and what we *do.*

Mr. E. K. Groves, nephew of Mr. Müller, announced as the closing hymn the second given out by him at that last prayer meeting at the orphanage.

> "We'll sing of the Shepherd that died."

Mr. E. T. Davies then offered prayer, and the body was left to its undisturbed repose, until the Lord shall come.

Other memorial services were held at the Y.M.C.A. Hall, and very naturally at Bethesda Chapel, which brought to a fitting close this series of loving tributes to the departed. On the Lord's day preceding the burial, in nearly all the city pulpits, more or less extended reference had been made to the life, the character, and the career of the beloved saint who had for so many years lived his irreproachable life in Bristol. Also the daily and weekly press teemed with obituary notices, and tributes to his piety, worth, and work.

It was touchingly remarked at his funeral that he first confessed to feeling weak and weary in his work that last night of his earthly sojourn; and it seemed specially tender of the Lord not to allow that sense of exhaustion to come upon him until just as He was about to send His chariot to bear him to His presence. Mr. Müller's last sermon at Bethesda Chapel, after a ministry of sixty-six years, had been from 2 Corinthians 5:1:

> "For we know that, if our earthly house of this tabernacle
> were dissolved, we have a building of God, a house
> not made with hands, eternal in the heavens."

It was as though he had some foretokens of his being about shortly to put off this his tabernacle. Evidently he was not taken by surprise. He had foreseen that his days were fast completing their number. Seven months before his departure, he had remarked to his medical attendant, in connection with the irregularity of his pulse: "It means *death.*"

Mr. Müller's Tombstone in Arno's Vale Cemetery

Many of the dear orphans—as when the first Mrs. Müller died—wrote, asking that they might contribute toward the erection of a monument to the memory of their beloved benefactor. Already one dear young servant had gathered, for the purpose, over twenty pounds. In conformity with the known wishes of his father-in-law that only the simplest headstone be placed over his remains, Mr. Wright thought necessary to check the inflow of such gifts, the sum in hand being quite sufficient.

Further urgent appeals were made both from British and American friends, for the erection of some statue or other large visible monument or memorial, and in these appeals the local newspapers united. At length private letters led Mr. Wright to communicate with the public press, as the best way at once to silence these appeals and express the ground of rejecting such proposals. He wrote as follows:

> "You ask me, as one long and closely associated with the late Mr. George Müller, to say what I think would be most in accordance with his own wishes as a fitting memorial of himself.
>
> "Will not the best way of replying to this question be to let him speak for himself?
>
> "1st. When he erected Orphan House No. 1, and the question came what is the building to be called, he deliberately avoided associating his own name with it, and named it 'The New Orphan House, Ashley Down.' N.B.—To the end of his life he *disliked* hearing or reading the words 'Müller's Orphanage.' In keeping with this, for years, in *every Annual Report,* when referring to the Orphanage he reiterated the statement, 'The New Orphan Houses on Ashley Down, Bristol, are not *my* Orphan Houses,... they are God's Orphan Houses.' (See, for example, the Report for 1897, p. 69.)
>
> "2nd. For years, in fact until he was nearly eighty years old, he steadily refused to allow any *portrait* of himself to be published; and only most reluctantly (for reasons which he gives with characteristic minuteness in the preface to 'Preaching Tours') did he at length give way on this point.
>
> "3rd. In the last published Report, at page 66, he states: 'The primary object I had in view in carrying on this work,' viz., 'that it might be seen that now, in the nineteenth century, *God is still the Living God, and that now, as well as thousands of years ago, He listens to the prayers of His children and helps those who trust in Him.*' From these words and ways of acting, is it not evident, that the only 'memorial' that George Müller cared about was that which consists in the effect of his example, Godward, upon his fellow men? Every soul converted to God (instrumentally) through his words or example constitutes a permanent memorial to him as the father in Christ of such an one. Every believer strengthened

in faith (instrumentally) through his words or example constitutes a similar memorial to his spiritual teacher.

"He knew that God had, already, in the riches of His grace, given him many such memorials; and he departed this life, as I well know, cherishing the most lively hope that he should greet *above* thousands more to whom it had pleased God to make him a channel of rich spiritual blessing.

"He used often to say to me, when he opened a letter in which the writer poured out a tale of sore pecuniary need, and besought his help to an extent twice or three or ten times exceeding the sum total of his (Mr. Müller's) earthly possessions at the moment, 'Ah! these dear people entirely miss the lesson I am *trying* to teach them, for they come to *me,* instead of going to *God.'* And if he could come back to us for an hour, and listen to an account of what his sincerely admiring, but mistaken, friends are proposing to do to *perpetuate* his memory, I can hear him, with a sigh, exclaiming, 'Ah! these *dear* friends are entirely missing the lesson that I tried for seventy years to teach them,' viz., 'That a *man* can receive nothing except it be *given* him *from above,'* and that, therefore, it is the Blessed *Giver,* and not the poor receiver, that is to be glorified.

"Yours faithfully,

"James Wright."

CHAPTER XX

The Summary of the Life-Work

DEATH SHUTS the door upon earthly service, whatever door it may open to other forms and spheres of activity. There are many intimations that service beyond the grave is both unceasing and untiring: the blessed dead "rest indeed from their *labours*"—toilsome and painful tasks—"but their works"—activities for God—"do follow them," where exertion is without exhaustion.

This is therefore a fit point for summing up the results of the work over which, from its beginning, one man had specially had charge. One sentence from Mr. Müller's pen marks the purpose which was the very pivot of his whole being: "I have joyfully dedicated my whole life to the object of exemplifying how much may be accomplished by prayer and faith." This prepared both for the development of the character of him who had such singleness of aim, and for the development of the work in which that aim found action. Mr. Müller's oldest friend, Robert C. Chapman of Barnstaple, beautifully says that "when a man's chief business is to serve and please the Lord, all his circumstances become his servants"; and we shall find this maxim true in Mr. Müller's life-work.

The Fifty-ninth Report, issued May 26, 1898, was the last up to the date of the publication of this volume, and the first after Mr. Müller's death. In this, Mr. Wright gives the brief but valuable summary not only of the whole work of the year preceding, but of the whole work from its beginning, and thus helps us to a comprehensive survey.

This report is doubly precious as it contains also the last contribution of Mr. Müller's own pen to the record of the Lord's dealings. It is probable that on the afternoon of March 9th he laid down his pen, for the last time, all unconscious that he was never again to take it up. He had made, in a twofold sense, his closing entry in life's solemn journal! In the evening of that day he took his customary part in the prayer service in the orphan house—then went to sleep for the last time on earth; there came a waking hour, when he was alone with God, and suddenly departed, leaving his body to its long sleep that knows no waking until the day of the Lord's coming, while his spirit returned unto God who gave it.

The afternoon of that day of death, and of 'birth' into the heavenly life—as the catacomb saints called it—found the helpers again assembled in the same prayer room to commit the work to him "who only hath immortality," and who, amid all changes of human administration, ever remains the divine Master Workman, never at a loss for His own chosen instruments.

Mr. Wright, in this report, shows himself God's chosen successor in the work, evidently like-minded with the departed director. The first paragraph, after the brief and touching reference to his father-in-law, serves to convey to all friends of this work the assurance that he to whom Mr. Müller left its conduct has also learned the one secret of all success in coworking with God. It sounds, as the significant *keynote* for the future, the same old keynote of the past, carrying on the melody and harmony, without change, into the new measures. It is the same oratorio, without alteration of theme, time, or even key: the leading performer is indeed no more, but another hand takes up his instrument and, trembling with emotion, continues the unfinished strain so that there is no interruption. Mr. Wright says:

> "It is written (Job 26:7): 'He hangeth the earth upon *nothing*'—that is, no *visible* support. And so we exult in the fact that 'the Scriptural Knowledge Institution for Home and Abroad' hangs, as it has ever hung, since its commencement, now more than sixty-four years ago, 'upon nothing,' that is, upon no VISIBLE support. It hangs upon no human patron, upon no endowment or funded property, but solely upon the good pleasure of the blessed God."

Blessed lesson to learn! that to hang upon the invisible God is not to hang "upon nothing," though it be upon nothing *visible.* The power and permanence of the invisible forces that hold up the earth after sixty centuries of human history are sufficiently shown by the fact that this great globe still swings securely in space and is whirled through its vast orbit, and that, without variation of a second, it still moves with divine exactness in its appointed path. We can therefore trust the same invisible God to sustain with His unseen power all the work which faith suspends upon His truth and love and unfailing word of promise, though to the natural eye all these may seem as nothing.

Mr. Wright records also a very striking answer to long-continued prayer, and a most impressive instance of the tender care of the Lord, in the *providing of an associate,* every way like-minded, and well fitted to share the responsibility falling upon his shoulders at the decease of his father-in-law.

SCRIPTURE TESTIMONY
God answers prayer
Luke 18:7 · John 15:7 · Acts 12:5 · James 5:15
God using an inner voice to communicate
Acts 10:19-20 · Acts 11:12

Feeling the burden too great for him, his one resource was to cast his burden on the Lord. He and Mr. Müller had asked of God such a companion in labour for three years before his departure, and Mr. Wright and his dear wife had, for twenty-five years before that—from the time when Mr. Müller's long missionary tours began to withdraw him from Bristol—besought of the Lord the same favour. But to none of them had any *name* been suggested, or, if so, it had never been mentioned.

After that day of death, Mr. Wright felt that a gracious Father would not long leave him to sustain this great burden alone, and about a fortnight later he felt assured that it was the will of God that he should ask Mr. George Frederic Bergin to join him in the work, who seemed to him a *"true yoke-fellow."* He had known him well for a quarter-century; he had worked by his side in the church; and though they were diverse in temperament, there had never been a break in unity or sympathy. Mr. Bergin was seventeen years his junior, and so likely to survive and succeed him; he was very fond of children, and had been much blessed in training his own in the nurture and admonition of the Lord, and hence was fitted to take charge of this larger family of orphans. Confident of being led of God, he put the matter before Mr. Bergin, delighted but not surprised to find that the same God had moved on his mind also, and in the same direction; for not only was he ready to respond to Mr. Wright's appeal, but he had been led of God to feel that he should, after a certain time, *go to Mr. Wright and offer himself.* The Spirit who guided Philip to the Eunuch and at the same time had made the Eunuch to inquire after guidance; who sent men from Cornelius and, while they were knocking at Simon's house, was bidding Peter go with them, still moves in a mysterious way, and simultaneously, on those whom He would bring together for cooperation in loving service. And thus Mr. Wright found the Living God the same Helper and Supplier of every need, after his beloved father-in-law had gone up higher; and felt constrained to feel that the God of Elijah was still at the crossing of the Jordan and could work the same wonders as before, supplying the need of the hour when the need came.

Mr. Müller's own gifts to the service of the Lord find in this posthumous report their first full record and recognition. Readers of the Annual Reports must have noticed an entry, recurring with strange frequency during all these thirty or forty years, and therefore suggesting a giver that must have reached a very ripe age: "from a servant of the Lord Jesus, who, constrained by the love of Christ, seeks to lay up treasure in heaven." If that entry be carefully followed throughout and there be added the personal gifts made by Mr. Müller to various benevolent objects, it will be found that the aggregate sum from this "servant" reaches, up to March 1, 1898, a total of *eighty-one thousand four hundred and ninety pounds eighteen shillings and eightpence.* Mr. Wright, now that this "servant of the Lord Jesus" is with his Master, who promised, "Where I am there shall also My servant be," feels free to make known that this donor was no other than *George Müller himself* who thus gave out of his own money—money given to him for his own use or left to him by legacies—the total sum of about sixty-four thousand five hundred pounds to the Scriptural Knowledge Institution, and, in other directions, seventeen thousand more.

This is a record of personal gifts to which we know no parallel. It reminds us of the career of John Wesley, whose simplicity and frugality of habits enabled him not only to limit his own expenditure to a very small sum, but whose Christian liberality and unselfishness prompted him to give all that he could thus save to purely benevolent objects. While he had but thirty pounds a year, he lived on twenty-eight and gave away forty shillings. Receiving twice as much the next year, he still kept his living expenses down to the twenty-eight pounds and had thirty-two to bestow on the needy; and when the third year his income rose to ninety pounds, he spent no more than before and gave away sixty-two. The fourth year brought one hundred and twenty, and he disbursed still but the same sum for his own needs, having ninety-two to spare. It is calculated that in the course of his life he thus gave away at least thirty thousand pounds, and four silver spoons comprised all the silver plate that he possessed when the collectors of taxes called upon him. Such economy on the one hand and such generosity on the other have seldom been known in human history. But George Müller's record will compare favourably with this or any other of modern days. His frugality, simplicity, and economy were equal to Wesley's, and his gifts aggregated eighty-one thousand pounds. Mr. Müller had received increasingly large sums from the Lord which he *invested* well and most profitably, so that for over sixty years he never lost a penny through a bad speculation! But his investments were not in lands or banks or railways, but in the *work of God.* He made friends out of the mammon of unrighteousness that when he failed received him into everlasting habitations. He continued, year after year, to make provision for himself, his beloved wife and daughter, by laying up treasure—in heaven. Such a man had certainly a right to exhort others to systematic beneficence. He gave—as not one in a million gives—not a tithe, not any fixed proportion of annual income, but *all that was left* after the simplest and most necessary supply of actual wants. While most Christians regard themselves as doing their duty if, after they have given a portion to the Lord, they spend all the rest on themselves, God led George Müller to reverse this rule and reserve only the most frugal sum

SCRIPTURE TESTIMONY
Store up treasure in heaven
Matthew 6:19-21

for personal needs, that the entire remainder might be given to him that needeth. The utter *revolution* implied in our habits of giving which would be necessary were such a rule adopted is but too obvious. Mr. Müller's own words are:

> "My aim never was, how much I could *obtain,*
> but rather how much I could give."

He kept continually before him *his stewardship* of God's property; and sought to make the most of the one brief life on earth, and to use for the best and largest good the property held by him in trust. The things of God were deep realities, and, projecting every action and decision and motive into the light of the judgment-seat of Christ, he asked himself how it would appear to him in the light of that tribunal. Thus he sought prayerfully and conscientiously so to live and labour, so to deny himself, and, by love, serve God and man, as that he should not be ashamed before Him at His coming. But not in a spirit of *fear* was this done; for if any man of his generation knew the perfect love that casts out fear, it was George Müller. He felt that God is love, and love is of God. He saw that love manifested in the greatest of gifts—His only-begotten Son at Calvary—he knew and believed the Love that God hath to us; he received it into his own heart; it became an abiding presence, manifested in obedience and benevolence, and, subduing him more and more, it became perfected so as to expel tormenting fear and impart a holy confidence and delight in God.

Among the texts which strongly impressed and moulded Mr. Müller's habits of giving was Luke 6:38:

> "Give and it shall be given unto you. Good measure, pressed down, shaken together and running over shall men give into your bosom."

SCRIPTURE TESTIMONY
Give and it shall be given unto you
Luke 6:38

He believed this promise and he verified it. His testimony is: "I had GIVEN, and God had caused to be GIVEN TO ME AGAIN, and bountifully."

Again he read: "It is more blessed to give than to receive."

He says that he BELIEVED what he found in the word of God, and by His grace sought to ACT ACCORDINGLY, and thus again records that he was blessed abundantly and his peace and joy in the Holy Ghost increased more and more.

It will not be a surprise, therefore, that, as has been already noted, Mr. Müller's *entire personal estate* at his death, as sworn to, when the will was admitted to probate, was only 169 pounds 9s. 4d., of which books, household furniture, etc., were reckoned at over one hundred pounds, the only *money* in his possession being a trifle over sixty pounds, and even this only awaiting disbursement as God's steward.

The will of Mr. Müller contains a pregnant clause which should not be forgotten in this memorial. It closes with a paragraph which is deeply significant as meant to be his posthumous word of testimony—"a last testament":

> "I cannot help admiring God's wondrous grace in bringing me to the knowledge of the Lord Jesus when I was an entirely careless and thoughtless young man, and that He has kept me in His fear and truth, allowing me the great honour, for so long a time, of serving Him."

In the comprehensive summary contained in this Fifty-ninth Report, remarkable growth is apparent during the sixty-four years since the outset of the work in 1834. During the year ending May 26, 1898, the number of day-schools was 7, and of pupils, 354; the number of children in attendance from the beginning, 81,501. The number of home Sunday-schools, 12, and of children in them, 1341; but from the beginning, 32,944. The number of Sunday-schools *aided* in England and Wales, 25. The amount expended in connection with home schools, 736 pounds 13s. 10d.; from the outset, 109,992 pounds 19s. 10d. The Bibles and parts thereof circulated, 15,411; from the beginning, 1,989,266. Money expended for this purpose the past year, 439 pounds; from the first, 41,090 pounds 13s. 3d. Missionary labourers aided, 115. Money expended, 2082 pounds 9s. 6d; from the outset, 261,859 pounds 7s. 4d. Circulation of books and tracts, 3,101,338. Money spent, 1001 pounds 3s.; and from the first, 47,188 pounds 11s. 10d. The number of orphans on Ashley Down, 1620; and from the first, 10,024. Money spent in orphan houses, last year, 22,523 pounds 13s. 1d.; and from the beginning, 988,829 pounds.

To carry out conviction into action is sometimes a costly sacrifice; but whatever Mr. Müller's fidelity to conviction cost in one way, he had stupendous results of his life-work to contemplate, even while he lived. Let any one look at the above figures and facts, and remember that here was one poor man who, dependent on the help of God only in answer to prayer, could look back over threescore years and see how he had built five large orphan houses and taken into his family over ten thousand orphans, expending, for their good, within twelve thousand pounds of a round million. He had given aid to day-schools and Sunday-schools, in this and other lands, where nearly one hundred and fifty thousand children have been taught, at a cost of over one hundred and ten thousand pounds more. He had circulated nearly two million Bibles and parts thereof at the cost of over forty thousand pounds; and over three million books and tracts, at a cost of nearly fifty thousand pounds more. And besides all this he had spent over two hundred and sixty thousand pounds to aid missionary labourers in various lands. The sum total of the money thus spent during sixty years has thus reached very nearly the astonishing aggregate of one and a half million of pounds sterling ($7,500,000).

SCRIPTURE TESTIMONY
The believer is to be persistent in prayer Luke 11:5-10

To summarize Mr. Müller's service we must understand his great secret. Such a life and such a work are the result of one habit more than all else,—daily and frequent communion with God. Unwearied in supplications and intercessions, we have seen how, in every new need and crisis, prayer was the one resort, the prayer of faith. He first satisfied himself that he was in the way of duty; then he fixed his mind upon the unchanging word of promise; then, in the boldness of a suppliant who comes to a throne of grace in the name of Jesus Christ and pleads the assurance of the immutable Promiser, he presented every petition. He was an unwearied intercessor. No delay discouraged him. This is seen particularly in the case of individuals for whose conversion or special guidance into the paths of full obedience he prayed. On his prayer list were the names of some for whom he had besought God, daily, by name, for one, two, three, four, six, ten years before the answer was given. The year just before his death, he told the writer of two parties for whose reconciliation to God he had prayed, day by day, *for over sixty years,* and who had not as yet to his knowledge turned unto God: and he significantly added, "I have not a doubt that I shall meet them both in heaven; for my Heavenly Father would not lay upon my heart a burden of prayer for them for over threescore years, if He had not concerning them purposes of mercy."

This is a sufficient example of his almost unparalleled perseverance and importunity in intercession. However long the delay, he held on, as with both hands clasping the very horns of the altar; and his childlike spirit reasoned simply but confidently, that the very fact of his own spirit being so long drawn out in prayer for one object, and of the Lord's enabling him so to continue patiently and believingly to wait on Him for the blessing, was a promise and prophecy of the answer; and so he waited on, so assured of the ultimate result that he praised God in advance, believing that he had practically received that for which he asked.

It is most helpful here to add that one of the parties for whom for so many years he unceasingly prayed has recently died in faith, having received the promises and embraced them and confessed Jesus as his Lord. Just before leaving Bristol with this completed manuscript of Mr. Müller's life, I met a lady, a niece of the man referred to, through whom I received a knowledge of these facts. He had, before his departure, given most unequivocal testimony to his faith and hope in the Saviour of sinners.

If George Müller could still speak to us, he would again repeat the warning so frequently found in his journal and reports, that his fellow disciples must not regard him as a *miracle-worker,* as though his experience were to be accounted so exceptional as to have little application in our ordinary spheres of life and service. With patient repetition he affirms that in all essentials such an experience is the privilege of all believers. God calls disciples to various forms of *work,* but all alike to the same *faith.* To say, therefore, "I am not called to build orphan houses, etc., and have no right to expect answers to my prayers as Mr. Müller did," is wrong and unbelieving. Every child of God, he maintained, is first to get into the sphere appointed of God, and therein to exercise full trust, and live by faith upon God's sure word of promise.

Throughout all these thousands of pages written by his pen, he teaches that every experience of God's faithfulness is both the reward of past faith and prayer, and the preparation of the servant of God for larger work and more efficient service and more convincing witness to his Lord.

No man can understand such a work who does not see in it the *supernatural* power of God. Without that the enigma defies solution; with that all the mystery is at least an open mystery. He himself felt from first to last that this supernatural factor was the key to the whole work, and without that it would have been even to himself a problem inexplicable. How pathetically we find him often comparing himself and his work for God to "the Burning Bush in the Wilderness" which, always aflame and always threatened with apparent destruction, was not consumed, so that not a few turned aside wondering to see this great sight. And why was it not burnt? Because Jehovah of hosts, who was in the Bush, dwelt in the man and in his work: or, as Wesley said with almost his last breath, "Best of all, God is with us."

This simile of the Burning Bush is the more apt when we consider the *rapid growth of the work.* At first so very small as to seem almost insignificant, and conducted in one small rented house, accommodating thirty orphans, then enlarged until other rented premises became necessary; then one, two, three, four, and even five immense structures being built, until three hundred, seven hundred, eleven hundred and fifty, and finally two thousand and fifty inmates could find shelter within them,—how seldom has the world seen such vast and, at the same time, rapid enlargement! Then look at the outlay! At first a trifling expenditure of perhaps five hundred pounds for the first year of the Scriptural Knowledge Institution, and of five hundred pounds for the first twelve month of the orphan work, and in the last year of Mr. Müller's life a grand total of over twenty-seven thousand five hundred, for all the purposes of the Institution.

The cost of the houses built on Ashley Down might have staggered a man of large capital, but this poor man only cried and the Lord helped him. The first house cost fifteen thousand pounds; the second, over twenty-one thousand; the third, over twenty-three thousand; and the fourth and fifth, from fifty thousand to sixty thousand more—so that the total cost reached about one hundred and fifteen thousand. Besides all this, there was a yearly expenditure which rose as high as twenty-five thousand for the orphans alone, irrespective of those occasional outlays made needful for emergencies, such as improved sanitary precautions, which in one case cost over two thousand pounds.

Here is a burning bush indeed, always in seeming danger of being consumed, yet still standing on Ashley Down, and still preserved because the same presence of Jehovah burns in it. Not a branch of this many-sided work has utterly perished, while the whole bush still challenges unbelievers to turn aside and see the great sight, and take off the shoes from their feet as on holy ground where God manifests Himself.

Any complete survey of this great life-work must include much that was wholly outside of the Scriptural Knowledge Institution; such as that service which Mr. Müller was permitted to render to the church of Christ and the world at large as a preacher, pastor, witness for truth, and author of books and tracts.

His preaching period covered the whole time from 1826 to 1898, the year of his departure, over seventy years; and from 1830, when he went to Teignmouth, his preaching continued, without interruption except from ill health, until his life closed, with an average through the whole period of probably three sermons a week, or over ten thousand for his lifetime. This is probably a low estimate, for during his missionary tours, which covered over two hundred thousand miles and were spread through' seventeen years, he spoke on an average about once a day notwithstanding already advanced age.

His church life was much blessed even in visible and tangible results. During the first two and a half years of work in Bristol, two hundred and twenty-seven members were added, about half of whom were new converts, and it is probable that, if the whole number brought to the knowledge of Christ by his preaching could now be ascertained, it would be found to aggregate full as many as the average of those years, and would thus reach into the thousands, exclusive of orphans converted on Ashley Down. Then when we take into account the vast numbers addressed and impressed by his addresses, given in all parts of the United Kingdom, on the Continent of Europe, and in America, Asia, and Australia, and the still vaster numbers who have read his Narrative, his books and tracts, or who have in various other ways felt the quickening power of his example and life, we shall get some conception—still, at best, inadequate—of the range and scope of the influence he wielded by his tongue and pen, his labours, and his life. Much of the best influence defies all tabulated statistics and evades all mathematical estimates; it is like the fragrance of the alabaster flask which fills all the house but escapes our grosser senses of sight, hearing, and touch. This part of George Müller's work we cannot summarize: it belongs to a realm where we cannot penetrate. But God sees, knows, and rewards it.

CHAPTER XXI

The Church Life and Growth

THROUGHOUT MR. Müller's journal we meet scattered and fragmentary suggestions as to the true conception of Christian teaching and practice, the nature and office of the Christian ministry, the principles which should prevail in church conduct, the mutual relations of believers, and the Spirit's relation to the Body of Christ, to pure worship, service, and testimony. These hints will be of more value if they are crystallized into unity so as to be seen in their connection with each other.

The founder of the orphan houses began and ended his public career as a preacher, and, for over sixty years, was so closely related to one body of believers that no review of his life can be complete without a somewhat extended reference to the church in Bristol of which he was one of the earliest leaders, and, of all who ministered to it, the longest in service.

His church-work in Bristol began with his advent to that city and ended only with his departure from it for the continuing city and the Father's House. The joint ministry of himself and Mr. Henry Craik has been traced already in the due order of events; but the development of church-life, under this apostolic ministry, furnishes instructive lessons which yield their full teaching only when gathered up and grouped together so as to secure unity, continuity, and completeness of impression.

When Mr. Müller and Mr. Craik began joint work in Bristol, foundations needed to be relaid. The church-life, as they found it, was not on a sufficiently scriptural basis, and they waited on God for wisdom to adjust it more completely to His word and will. This was the work of time, for it required the instruction of fellow believers so that they might be prepared to cooperate, by recognizing scriptural and spiritual teaching; it required also the creation of that bond of sympathy which inclines the flock to hear and heed the shepherd's voice, and follow a true pastoral leadership. At the outset of their ministry, these brethren carefully laid down some principles on which their ministry was to be based. On May 23, 1832, they frankly stated, at Gideon Chapel, certain terms on which alone they could take charge of the church: they must be regarded as simply God's servants to labour among them so long as, and in such way as might be His will, and under no bondage of fixed rules; they desired pew-rents to be done away with, and voluntary offerings substituted, etc.

There was already, however, a strong conviction that a new start was in some respects indispensable if the existing church-life was to be thoroughly modelled on a scriptural pattern. These brethren determined to stamp upon the church certain important features such as these: Apostolic simplicity of worship, evangelical teaching, evangelistic work, separation from the world, systematic giving, and dependence on prayer. They desired to give great prominence to the simple testimony of the Word, to support every department of the work by free-will offerings, to recognize the Holy Spirit as the one presiding and governing Power in all church assemblies, and to secure liberty for all believers in the exercise of spiritual gifts as distributed by that Spirit to all members of the Body of Christ for service. They believed it scriptural to break bread every Lord's day, and to baptize by immersion; and, although this latter has not for many years been a term of communion or of fellowship, believers have always been carefully taught that this is the duty of all disciples.

It has been already seen that in August, 1832, seven persons in all, including these two pastors, met at Bethesda Chapel to unite in fellowship, without any formal basis or bond except that of loyalty to the Word and Spirit of God. This step was taken in order to start anew, without the hindrance of customs already prevailing, which were felt to be unscriptural and yet were difficult to abolish without discordant feeling; and, from that date on, Bethesda Chapel has been the home of an assembly of believers who have sought steadfastly to hold fast the New Testament basis of church-life.

Such blessed results are largely due to these beloved colleagues in labour who never withheld their testimony, but were intrepidly courageous and conscientiously faithful in witnessing against whatever they deemed opposed to the Word. Love ruled, but was not confounded with laxity in matters of right and wrong; and, as they saw more clearly what was taught in the Word, they sought to be wholly obedient to the Lord's teaching and leading, and to mould and model every matter, however minute, in every department of duty, private or public, according to the expressed will of God.

In January, 1834, all teachers who were not believers were dismissed from the Sunday-school; and, in the Dorcas Society, only believing sisters were accepted to make clothes for the destitute. The reason was that it had been found unwise and unwholesome to mix up or yoke together believers and unbelievers.[38] Such association proved a barrier to spiritual converse and injurious to both classes, fostering in the unbelievers a false security, ensnaring them in a delusive hope that to help in Christian work might somehow atone for rejection of Jesus Christ as a Saviour, or secure favour from God and an open door into heaven. No doubt all this indiscriminate association of children of God with children of the world in a "mixed multitude" is unscriptural. Unregenerate persons are tempted to think there is some merit at least in mingling with worshippers and workers, and especially in giving to the support of the gospel and its institutions. The devil seeks to persuade such that it is acceptable to God to conform externally to religious rites, and forms, and take part in outward acts of service and sacrifice, and that He will deal leniently with them, despite their unbelief and disobedience. Mr. Müller and Mr. Craik felt keenly that this danger existed and that even in minor matters there must be a line of separation, for the sake of all involved.

When, in 1837, in connection with the congregation at Bethesda, the question was raised—commonly known as that of close communion—whether believers who had not been baptized as such should be received into fellowship, it was submitted likewise to the one test of clear scripture teaching. Some believers were conscientiously opposed to such reception, but the matter was finally and harmoniously settled by "receiving all who love our Lord Jesus into full communion, irrespective of baptism," and Mr. Müller, looking back forty-four years later upon this action, bears witness that the decision never became a source of dissension.[39]

In all other church matters, prayer and searching the Word, asking counsel of the Holy Oracles and wisdom from above, were the one resort, and the resolution of all difficulties. When, in the spring of 1838, sundry questions arose somewhat delicate and difficult to adjust, Mr. Müller and Mr. Craik quietly withdrew from Bristol for two weeks, to give themselves to prayer and meditation, seeking of God definite direction.

The matters then at issue concerned the scriptural conception, mode of selection and appointment, scope of authority and responsibility, of *the Eldership;* the proper mode of observance of the *Lord's Supper,* its frequency, proper subjects, etc. Nothing is ever settled finally until settled rightly, nor settled rightly until settled scripturally. A serious peril confronted the church—not of controversy only, but of separation and schism; and in such circumstances mere discussion often only fans the embers of strife and ends in hopeless alienation. These spiritually minded pastors followed the apostolic method, referring all matters to the Scriptures as the one rule of faith and practice, and to the Holy Spirit as the presiding Presence in the church of God; and they purposely retired into seclusion from the strife of tongues and of conflicting human opinion, that they might know the mind

38 2 Corinthians 6:14-18
39 Appendix L.

of the Lord and act accordingly. The results, as might be foreseen, were clear light from above for themselves, and a united judgment among the brethren; but more than this, God gave them wisdom so to act, combining the courage of conviction with the meekness and gentleness of Christ, as that all clouds were dispelled and peace restored.[40]

For about eight years, services had been held in both Gideon and Bethesda chapels; but on April 19, 1840, the last of the services conducted by Mr. Müller and Mr. Craik was held at Gideon,—Bethesda, from this time on, becoming the central place of assembly. The reasons for this step were somewhat as follows:

These joint pastors strongly felt, with some others, that not a few of the believers who assembled at Gideon Chapel were a hindrance to the clear, positive, and united testimony which should be given both to the church and world; and it was on this account that, after many meetings for prayer and conference, seeking to know God's mind, it was determined to relinquish Gideon as a place of worship. The questions involved affected the preservation of the purity and simplicity of apostolic worship, and so the conformity of church-life to the New Testament pattern. These well-yoked pastors were very jealous for the Lord God of hosts, that, among the saints to whom they ministered, nothing should find a lodgment which was not in entire accord with scriptural principles, precepts, and practices.

Perhaps it is well here to put on record, even at risk of repetition, the principles which Mr. Müller and his colleague were wont to enforce as guards or landmarks which should be set up and kept up, in order to exclude those innovations which always bring spiritual declension.

1. Believers should meet, simply as such, without reference to denominational lines, names, or distinctions, as a corrective and preventive of sectarianism.
2. They should steadfastly maintain the Holy Scriptures as the divine rule and standard of doctrine, deportment, and discipline.
3. They should encourage freedom for the exercise of whatever spiritual gifts the Lord might be pleased by His Spirit to bestow for general edification.
4. Assemblies on the Lord's day should be primarily for believers, for the breaking of bread, and for worship; unbelievers sitting promiscuously among saints would either hinder the appearance of meeting for such purposes, or compel a pause between other parts of the service and the Lord's Supper.
5. The pew-rent system should be abolished, as promoting the caste spirit, or at least the outward appearance of a false distinction between the

40 Appendix M.

poorer and richer classes, especially as pew-holders commonly look on their sittings as private property.

6. All money contributed for pastoral support, church work, and missionary enterprises at home and abroad should be by free-will offerings.

It was because some of these and other like scriptural principles were thought to be endangered or compromised by practices prevailing at Gideon Chapel before Mr. Müller and Mr. Craik took charge, that it seemed best on the whole to relinquish that chapel as a place of worship. As certain customs there obtaining had existed previously, it seemed to these godly-minded brethren that it would be likely to cause needless offence and become a root of bitterness should they require what they deemed unscriptural to be renounced; and it seemed the way of love to give up Gideon Chapel after these eight years of labour there, and to invite such as felt called on to separate from every sectarian system, and meet for worship where free exercise would be afforded for every spiritual gift, and where New Testament methods might be more fully followed, to assemble with other believers at Bethesda, where previous hindering conditions had not existed.

Mr. Müller remained very intimately connected with Bethesda and its various outgrowths, for many years, as the senior pastor, or elder,—though only *primus inter pares,* i.e., leader among equals. His opinions about the work of the ministry and the conduct of church-life, which did so much to shape the history of these churches, therefore form a necessary part of this sketch of the development of church-life.

It was laid upon his heart frequently to address his brethren in the ministry of the Word and the curacy of souls. Everywhere, throughout the world, he welcomed opportunities for interviews, whether with many or few, upon whom he could impress his own deep convictions as to the vital secrets of effective service in the pulpit and pastorate. Such meetings with brethren in the ministry numbered hundreds and perhaps thousands in the course of his long life, and as his testimony was essentially the same on all occasions, a single utterance may be taken as the type of all. During his American tours, he gave an hour's address which was reported and published, and the substance of which may therefore be given.

First of all he laid great stress upon the *need of conversion.* Until a man is both truly turned unto God and sure of this change in himself he is not fitted to convert others. The ministry is not a human profession, but a divine vocation. The true preacher is both a *herald* and a *witness,* and hence must back up his message by his personal testimony from experience.

But even conversion is not enough: there must be an *intimate knowledge of the Lord Jesus.* One must know the Lord as coming near to himself, and know the joy and strength found in hourly access. However it be done, and at any cost, the minister of Christ must reach this close relationship. It is an absolute necessity to peace and power.

Growth in happiness and love was next made very prominent. It is impossible to set limits to the experience of any believer who casts himself wholly on God, surrenders himself wholly to God, and cherishes deep love for His word and holy intimacy with Himself. The first business of every morning should be to secure happiness in God.

He who is to nourish others must carefully *feed his own soul.* Daily reading and study of the Scriptures, with much prayer, especially in the early morning hours, was strenuously urged. Quietness before God should be habitually cultivated, calming the mind and freeing it from preoccupation. Continuous reading of the Word, in course, will throw light upon the general teaching of the Word, and reveal God's thoughts in their variety and connection, and go far to correct erroneous views.

Holiness must be the supreme aim: prompt obedience to all known truth, a single eye in serving God, and zeal for His glory. Many a life has been more or less a failure because habits of heart well pleasing to God have been neglected. Nothing is more the crowning grace than the unconscious grace of *humility.* All praise of man robs God of His own honour. Let us therefore be humble and turn all eyes unto God.

The *message* must be gotten from God, if it is to be with power. "Ask God for it," said Mr. Müller, "and be not satisfied until the heart is at rest. When the text is obtained ask further guidance in meditating upon it, and keep in constant communion so as to get God's mind in the matter and His help in delivery. Then, after the work is done, pray much for blessing, as well as in advance." He then told some startling facts as to seed sown many years before, but even now yielding fruit in answer to prayer.

He laid also special emphasis upon *expounding the Scripture.* The word of God is the staple of all preaching; Christ and nothing else the centre of all true ministry of the Word. Whoever faithfully and constantly preaches Christ will find God's word not returning to him void. Preach simply. Luther's rule was to speak so that an ignorant maid-servant could understand; if she does, the learned professor certainly will; but it does not hold true that the simple understand all that the wise do.

Mr. Müller seldom addressed his brethren in the ministry without giving more or less counsel as to the conduct of church-life, giving plain witness against such hindrances as unconverted singers and choirs, secular methods of raising money, pew-rents and caste distinctions in the house of prayer, etc.; and urging such helps as inquirers' meetings, pastoral visits, and, above all else, believing prayer. He urged definite praying and importunate praying, and remarked that Satan will not mind how we labour in prayer for a few days, weeks, or even months, if he can at last discourage us so that we cease praying, as though it were of no use.

As to prayers for past seed-sowing, he told the writer of this memoir how in all supplication to God he looked not only forward but *backward.* He was wont to ask that the Lord would be pleased to bless seed long since sown and yet apparently unfruitful; and he said that, in answer to these prayers, he had up to that day evidence of God's loving remembrance of his work of faith and labour of love in years long gone by. He was permitted to know that messages delivered for God, tracts scattered, and other means of service had, after five, ten, twenty, and even sixty years, at last brought forth a harvest. Hence his urgency in advising fellow labourers to pray unceasingly that God would work mightily in the hearts of those who had once been under their care, bringing to their remembrance the truth which had been set before them.

The humility Mr. Müller enjoined he practised. He was ever only the *servant* of the Lord. Mr. Spurgeon, in one of his sermons, describes the startling effect on London Bridge when he saw one lamp after another lit up with flame, though in the darkness he could not see the lamplighter; and George Müller set many a light burning when he was himself content to be unseen, unnoticed, and unknown. He honestly sought not his own glory, but had the meek and quiet spirit so becoming a minister of Jesus Christ.

Mr. Henry Craik's death in 1866, after thirty-four years of co-labour in the Lord, left Mr. Müller comparatively alone with a double burden of responsibility, but his faith was equal to the crisis and his peace remained unbroken. A beloved brother, then visiting Bristol, after crowded services conducted by him at Bethesda, was about leaving the city; and he asked Mr. Müller, "What are you going to do, now that Mr. Craik is dead, to hold the people and prevent their scattering?" "My beloved brother," was the calm reply, "we shall do what we have always done, *look only to the Lord.*"

This God has been the perpetual helper. Mr. Müller almost totally withdrew from the work, during the seventeen years of his missionary tours, between 1875 and 1892, when he was in Bristol but a few weeks or months at a time, in the intervals between his long journeys and voyages. This left the assembly of believers still more dependent upon the great Shepherd and Bishop of souls. But Bethesda has never, in a sense, been limited to any one or two men, as the only acknowledged leaders; from the time when those seven believers gathered about the Lord's table in 1832, the New Testament conception of the equality of believers in privilege and duty has been maintained. The one supreme Leader is the Holy Ghost, and under Him those whom He calls and qualifies. One of the fundamental principles espoused by these brethren is that the Spirit of God controls in the assemblies of the saints; that He sets the members, every one of them, in the Body as it pleaseth Him, and divides unto them, severally as He will, gifts for service in the Body; that the only true ordination is His ordination, and that the manifestation of His gifts is the sufficient basis for the recognition of brethren as qualified for the exercise of an office or function, the possession of spiritual gifts being sufficient authority for their exercise. It is with the Body of Christ as with the human body: the eye is manifestly made for seeing and the ear for hearing, the hand and foot for handling and walking; and this adaptation both shows the design of God and their place in the organism. And so for more than threescore years the Holy Spirit has been safely trusted to supply and qualify all needed teachers, helpers, and leaders in the assembly. There has always been a considerable number of brethren and sisters fitted and disposed to take up the various departments of service to which they were obviously called of the Spirit, so that no one person has been indispensable. Various brethren have been able to give more or less time and strength to preaching, visiting, and ruling in the church; while scores of others, who, like Paul, Priscilla and Aquila, the tent-makers, have their various business callings and seek therein to "abide with God," are ready to aid as the Lord may guide in such other forms of service as may consist with their ordinary vocations. The prosperity of the congregation, its growth, conduct, and edification, have therefore been dependent only on God, who, as He has withdrawn one worker after another, has supplied others in their stead, and so continues to do.

To have any adequate conception of the fruits of such teaching and such living in church-life, it is needful to go at least into one of the Monday-night prayer meetings at Bethesda. It is primitive and apostolic in simplicity. No one presides but the unseen Spirit of God. A hymn is suggested by some brother, and then requests for prayer are read, usually with definite mention of the names of those by and for whom supplication is asked. Then prayer, scripture reading, singing, and exhortation follow, without any prearrangement as to subject, order in which or persons by whom, the exercises are participated in. The fullest liberty is encouraged to act under the Spirit's guidance; and the fact of such guidance is often strikingly apparent in the singular unity of prayer and song, scripture reading and remarks, as well as in the harmonious fellowship apparent. After more than half a century these Monday-night prayer services are still a hallowed centre of attraction, a rallying-point for supplication, and a radiating-point for service, and remain unchanged in the method of their conduct.

The original congregation has proved a tree whose seed is in itself after its kind. At the time of Mr. Müller's decease it was nearly sixty-six years since that memorable evening in 1832 when those seven believers met to form a church; and the original body of disciples meeting in Bethesda had increased to ten, six of which are now independent of the mother church, and four of which still remain in close affiliation and really constitute one church, though meeting in Bethesda, Alma Road, Stokes Croft, and Totterdown chapels. The names of the other churches which have been in a sense offshoots from Bethesda are as follows: Unity, Bishopston, Cumberland Hall, Charleton Hall, Nicholas Road, and Bedminster.

At the date of Mr. Müller's decease the total membership of the four affiliated congregations was upwards of twelve hundred.

In this brief compass no complete outline could be given of the church life and work so dear to him, and over which he so long watched and prayed. This church has been and is a missionary church. When on March 1, 1836, Mr. and Mrs. Groves, with ten helpers, left Bristol to carry on mission work in the East Indies, Mr. Müller felt deeply moved to pray that the body of disciples to whom he ministered might send out from their own members labourers for the wide world-field. That prayer was not forgotten before God, and has already been answered exceeding abundantly above all he then asked or thought. Since that time some sixty have gone forth to lands afar to labour in the gospel, and at the period of Mr. Müller's death there were at work, in various parts of the world, at least twenty, who are aided by the free-will offerings of their Bristol brethren.

When, in 1874, Mr. Müller closed the third volume of his Narrative, he recorded the interesting fact that, of the many nonconformist ministers of the gospel resident in Bristol when he took up work there more than forty-two years before, *not one remained*, all having been removed elsewhere or having died; and that, of all the Evangelical clergy of the establishment, only *one* survived. Yet he himself, with very rare hindrance through illness, was permitted to preach and labour with health and vigour both of mind and body; over a thousand believers were already under his pastoral oversight, meeting in three different chapels, and over three thousand had been admitted into fellowship.

It was the writer's privilege to hear Mr. Müller preach on the morning of March 22, 1896, in Bethesda Chapel. He was in his ninety-first year, but there was a freshness, vigour, and terseness in his preaching that gave no indication of failing powers; in fact, he had never seemed more fitted to express and impress the thoughts of God.

His theme was the seventy-seventh psalm, and it afforded him abundant scope for his favourite subject—prayer. He expounded the psalm verse by verse, clearly, sympathetically, effectively, and the outline of his treatment strongly engraved itself on my memory and is here reproduced.

"I cried unto God with my voice." Prayer seeks a voice—to utter itself in words: the effort to clothe our desires in language gives definiteness to our desires and keeps the attention on the objects of prayer.

"In the day of my trouble." The Psalmist was in trouble; some distress was upon him, perhaps physical as well as mental, and it was an unceasing burden night and day.

"My soul refused to be comforted." The words, "my sore ran in the night," may be rendered, "my hand reached out"—that is in prayer. But unbelief triumphed, and his soul refused all comfort—even the comfort of God's promises. His trouble overshadowed his faith and shut out the vision of God.

"I remembered, or thought of God, and was troubled." Even the thought of God, instead of bringing peace, brought distress; instead of silencing his complaint, it increased it, and his spirit was overwhelmed—the sure sign, again, of unbelief. If in trouble God's promises and the thought of God bring no relief, they will only become an additional burden.

"Thou holdest mine eyes waking." There was no sleep because there was no rest or peace. Care makes wakeful. Anxiety is the foe of repose. His spirit was unbelieving and therefore rebellious. He would not take God at His word.

"I have considered the days of old." Memory now is at work. He calls to remembrance former experiences of trouble and of deliverance. He had often sought God and been heard and helped, and why not now? As he made diligent search among the records of his experience and recollected all God's manifest and manifold interpositions, he began to ask whether God could be fickle and capricious, whether His mercy was exhausted and His promise withdrawn, whether He had forgotten His covenant of grace, and shut up His fountains of love.

Thus we follow the Psalmist through six stages of unbelief:

1. The thought of God is a burden instead of a blessing.
2. The complaining spirit increases toward God.
3. His spirit is agitated instead of soothed and calmed.
4. Sleep departs, and anxiety forbids repose of heart.
5. Trouble only deepens and God seems far off.
6. Memory recalls God's mercies, but only to awaken distrust.

At last we reach the *turning-point* in the psalm: he asks as he reviews former experiences, WHERE IS THE DIFFERENCE? IS THE CHANGE IN GOD OR IN ME? "Selah"—the pause marks this turning-point in the argument or experience.

"And I said, This is *my infirmity.*" In other words, "I HAVE BEEN A FOOL!" God is faithful. He never casts off. His children are always dear to Him. His grace is exhaustless and His promise unfailing. Instead of fixing his eyes on his trouble he now fixes his whole mind on God. He remembers His work, and meditates upon it; instead of rehearsing his own trials, he talks of His doings. He gets overwhelmed now, not with the greatness of his troubles, but the greatness of his Helper. He recalls His miracles of power and love, and remembers the mystery of His mighty deeds—His way in the sea, His strange dealings and leadings and their gracious results—and so faith once more triumphs.

What is the conclusion, the practical lesson?

Unbelief is folly. It charges God foolishly. Man's are the weakness and failure, but never God's. My faith may be lacking, but not His power. Memory and meditation, when rightly directed, correct unbelief. God has shown Himself great. He has always done wonders. He led even an unbelieving and murmuring people out of Egypt and for forty years through the wilderness, and His miracles of power and love were marvelous.

The psalm contains a *great lesson.* Affliction is inevitable. But our business is never to lose sight of the Father who will not leave His children. We are to roll all burdens on Him and wait patiently, and deliverance is sure. Behind the curtain He carries on His plan of love, never forgetting us, always caring for His own. His ways of dealing we cannot trace, for His footsteps are in the trackless sea, and unknown to us. But HE IS SURELY LEADING, and CONSTANTLY LOVING. Let us not be fools, but pray in faith to a faithful God.

This is the substance of that morning exposition, and is here given very inadequately, it is true, yet it serves not only to illustrate Mr. Müller's mode of expounding and applying the Word, but the exposition of this psalm is a sort of exponent also of his life. It reveals his habits of prayer, the conflicts with unbelief, and how out of temptations to distrust God he found deliverance; and thus is doubly valuable to us as an experimental commentary upon the life-history we are studying.

CHAPTER XXII

A Glance at the Gifts and the Givers

THERE IS One who still sits over against the Treasury, watching the gifts cast into it, and impartially weighing their worth, estimating the rich man's millions and the widow's mites, not by the amount given, but by the motives which impel and the measure of self-sacrifice accepted for the Lord's sake.

The ample supplies poured into Mr. Müller's hands came alike from those who had abundance of wealth and from those whose only abundance was that of deep poverty, but the rills as well as the rivers were from God. It is one of the charms of this life-story to observe the variety of persons and places, sums of money and forms of help, connected with the donations made to the Lord's work; and the exact adaptation between the need and the supply, both as to time and amount. Some instances of this have been given in the historic order; but to get a more complete view of the lessons which they suggest it is helpful to classify some of the striking and impressive examples, which are so abundant, and which afford such valuable hints as to the science and the art of giving.

Valuable lessons may be drawn from the beautiful spirit shown by givers and from the secret history of their gifts.

In some cases the facts were not known till long after, even by Mr. Müller himself; and when known, could not be disclosed to the public while the parties were yet alive. But when it became possible and proper to unveil these hidden things they were revealed for the glory of God and the good of others, and shine on the pages of this record like stars in the sky. Paul rejoiced in the free-will offerings of Philippian disciples, not because he desired a gift, but fruit that might abound to their account; not because their offerings ministered to his necessity, but because they became a sacrifice of a sweet smell acceptable, well pleasing to God. Such joy constantly filled Mr. Müller's heart. He was daily refreshed and reinvigorated by the many proofs that the gifts received had been first sanctified by prayer and self-denial. He lived and breathed amid the fragrance of sweet-savour offerings, permitted for more than threescore years to participate in the joy of the Lord Himself over the cheerful though often costly gifts of His people. By reason of identification with his Master, the servant caught the sweet scent of these sacrifices as their incense rose from His altars toward heaven. Even on earth the self-denials of his own life found compensation in thus acting in the Lord's behalf in receiving and disbursing these gifts; and, he says, "the Lord thus impressed on me from the beginning that the orphan houses and work were HIS, *not* MINE."

Many a flask of spikenard, very precious, broken upon the feet of the Saviour, for the sake of the orphans, or the feeding of starving souls with the Bread of Life, filled the house with the odour of the ointment, so that to dwell there was to breathe a hallowed atmosphere of devotion.

SCRIPTURE TESTIMONY
Giving all one has to live on, and trusting God for provision
Mark 12:41-44 · Luke 21:1-4

Among the first givers to the work was a poor needlewoman, who, to Mr. Müller's surprise, brought *one hundred pounds*. She earned by her work only an *average, per week*, of *three shillings and sixpence,* and was moreover weak in body. A small legacy of less than five hundred pounds from her grandmother's estate had come to her at her father's death by the conditions of her grandmother's will. But that father had died a drunkard and a bankrupt, and her brothers and sisters had settled with his creditors by paying them five shillings to the pound. To her conscience, this seemed robbing the creditors of three fourths of their claim, and, though they had no legal hold upon her, she privately paid them the other fifteen shillings to the pound, of the unpaid debts of her father. Moreover, when her unconverted brother and two sisters gave each fifty pounds to the widowed mother, she as a child of God felt that she should give double that amount. By this time her own share of the legacy was reduced to a small remainder, and it was out of this that she gave the one hundred pounds for the orphan work!

As Mr. Müller's settled principle was *never to grasp eagerly at any gift whatever the need or the amount of the gift,* before accepting this money he had a long conversation with this woman, seeking to prevent her from giving either from an unsanctified motive or in unhallowed haste, without counting the cost. He would in such a case dishonour his Master by accepting the gift, as though God were in need of our offerings. Careful scrutiny, however, revealed no motives not pure and Christlike; this woman had calmly and deliberately reached her decision. "The Lord Jesus," she said, "has given His last drop of blood for me, and should I not give Him this hundred pounds?" He who comes into contact with such givers in his work for God finds therein a means of grace.

This striking incident lends a pathetic interest to the beginnings of the orphan work, and still more as we further trace the story of this humble needlewoman. She had been a habitual giver, but so unobtrusively that, while she lived, not half a dozen people knew of either the legacy or of this donation. Afterward, however, it came to the light that in many cases she had quietly and most unostentatiously given food, clothing, and like comforts to the deserving poor. Her gifts were so disproportionate to her means that her little capital rapidly diminished. Mr. Müller was naturally very reluctant to accept what she brought, until he saw that the love of Christ constrained her. He could then do no less than to receive her offering, in his Master's name, while like the Master he exclaimed, "O woman, great is thy faith!"

Five features made her benevolence praiseworthy. First, all these deeds of charity were done in secret and without any show; and she therefore was kept humble, not puffed up with pride through human applause; her personal habits of dress and diet remained as simple after her legacy as before, and to the last she worked with her needle for her own support; and, finally, while her *earnings* were counted in shillings and pence, her *givings* were counted in sovereigns or five-pound notes, and in one case by the hundred pounds. Her money was entirely gone, years before she was called higher, but the faithful God never forgot His promise: "I will never leave thee nor forsake thee." Never left to want, even after bodily weakness forbade her longer to ply her needle, she asked no human being for help, but in whatever straits made her appeal to God, and was not only left to suffer no lack, but, in the midst of much bodily suffering, her mouth was filled with holy song.

Mr. Müller records the *first bequest* as from a dear lad who died in the faith. During his last illness, he had received a gift of some new silver coins; and he asked that this, his only treasure in money, might be sent for the orphans. With pathetic tenderness Mr. Müller adds that this precious little legacy of *six shillings sixpence halfpenny,* received September 15, 1837, was the first they ever had. Those who estimate all donations by money-worth can little understand how welcome such a bequest was; but to such a man this small donation, bequeathed by one of Christ's little ones, and representing all he possessed, was of inestimable worth.

In May, 1842, a gold watch and chain were accompanied by a brief note, the contents of which suggest the possibilities of service, open to us through the voluntary limitation of artificial or imaginary wants. The note reads thus: "A pilgrim does not want such a watch as this to make him happy; one of an inferior kind will do to show him how swiftly time flies, and how fast he is hastening on to that Canaan where time will be no more: so that it is for you to do with this what it seemeth good to you. It is the last relic of earthly vanity, and, while I am in the body, may I be kept from all idolatry!"

In March, 1884, a contribution reached Mr. Müller from one who had been enabled in a like spirit to increase the amount over all previous gifts by the sale of some jewelry which had been put away in accordance with 1 Peter 3:3. How much superfluous ornament, worn by disciples, might be blessedly sacrificed for the Lord's sake! The one ornament which is in His sight of great price would shine with far more lustre if it were the only one worn.

Another instance of turning all things to account was seen in the case of a giver who sent a box containing four old crown pieces which had a curious history. They were the wedding-day present of a bridegroom to his bride, who, reluctant to spend her husband's first gift, kept them until she passed them over, as heirlooms, to her four grand-children. They were thus at last put out to usury, after many years of gathering "rust" in hoarded idleness and uselessness. Little did bridegroom or bride foresee how these coins, after more than a hundred years, would come forth from their hiding-place to be put to the Lord's uses. Few people have ever calculated how much is lost to every good cause by the simple withdrawal of money from circulation. Those four crown pieces had they been carefully invested, so as to double in value, by compound interest, every ten years, would have increased to one thousand pounds during the years they had lain idle!

One gift was sent in, as an offering to the Lord, instead of being used to purchase an engagement-ring by two believers who desired their lives to be united by that highest bond, the mutual love of the Lord who spared not His own blood for them.

At another time, a box came containing a new satin jacket, newly bought, but sacrificed as a snare to pride. Its surrender marked an epoch, for henceforth the owner determined to spend in dress only what is needful, and not waste the Lord's money on costly apparel. Enlightened believers look on all things as inalienably God's, and, even in the voluntary diversion of money into sacred rather than selfish channels, still remember that they give to Him only what is His own! "The little child feels proud that he can drop the money into the box after the parent has supplied the means, and told him to do so; and so God's children are sometimes tempted to think that they are giving of their own, and to be proud over their gifts, forgetting the divine Father who both gives us all we have and bids us give all back to Him."

A gift of two thousand pounds on January 29,1872, was accompanied by a letter confessing that the possession of property had given the writer much trouble of mind, and it had been disposed of from a conviction that the Lord "saw it not good" for him to *hold so much* and therefore allowed its possession to be a curse rather than a blessing. Fondness for possessions always entails curse, and external riches thus become a source of internal poverty. It is doubtful whether any child of God ever yet hoarded wealth without losing in spiritual attainment and enjoyment. Greed is one of the lowest and most destructive of vices and turns a man into the likeness of the coin he worships, making him hard, cold, metallic, and unsympathetic, so that, as has been quaintly said, he drops into his coffin "with a chink."

God estimates what we *give* by what we *keep,* for it is possible to bestow large sums and yet reserve so much larger amounts that no self-denial is possible. Such giving to the Lord *costs us nothing.*

In 1853, a brother in the Lord took out of his pocket a roll of bank-notes, amounting to one hundred and ten pounds, and put it into Mr. Müller's hand, it being *more than one half of his entire worldly estate.* Such giving is an illustration of self-sacrifice on a large scale, and brings corresponding blessing.

The *motives* prompting gifts were often unusually suggestive. In October, 1857, a donation came from a Christian merchant who, having sustained a heavy pecuniary loss, *wished to sanctify his loss by a gift to the Lord's work.* Shortly after, another offering was handed in by a young man in thankful remembrance that twenty-five years before Mr. Müller had prayed over him, as a child, that God would convert him. Yet another gift, of thirty-five hundred pounds, came to him in 1858, with a letter stating that the giver had further purposed to give to the orphan work the chief preference in his will, but had now seen it to be far better to *act as his own executor* and give the whole amount while he lived. Immense advantage would accrue, both to givers and to the causes they purpose to promote, were this principle generally adopted! There is "many a slip betwixt the cup" of the legator and "the lip" of the legatee. Even a wrong wording of a will has often forfeited or defeated the intent of a legacy. Mr. Müller had to warn intending donors that nothing that was reckoned as real estate was available for legacies for charitable institutions, nor even money lent on real estate or in any other way derived therefrom. These conditions no longer exist, but they illustrate the ease with which a will may often be made void, and the design of a bequest be defeated.

Many donors were led to send thank-offerings for *avoided* or *averted calamities:* as, for example, for a sick horse, given up by the veterinary surgeon as lost, but which recovered in answer to prayer. Another donor, who broke his left arm, sends grateful acknowledgment to God that it was not the *right* arm, or some more vital part like the head or neck.

The offerings were doubly precious because of the unwearied faithfulness of God who manifestly prompted them, and who kept speaking to the hearts of thousands, leading them to give so abundantly and constantly that no want was unsupplied. In 1859, so great were the outlays of the work that if day by day, during the whole three hundred and sixty-five, fifty pounds had been received, the income would not have been more than enough. Yet in a surprising variety and number of ways, and from persons and places no less numerous and various, donations came in. Not one of twenty givers was personally known to Mr. Müller, and no one of all contributors had ever been asked for a gift, and yet, up to November, 1858, over *six hundred thousand pounds* had already been received, and in amounts varying from eighty-one hundred pounds down to a single farthing.

SCRIPTURE TESTIMONY
God answers prayer
Luke 18:7 · John 15:7 · Acts 12:5 · James 5:15

Unique circumstances connected with some donations made them remarkable. While resting at Ilfracombe, in September, 1865, a gentleman gave to Mr. Müller a sum of money, at the same time narrating the facts which led to the gift. He was a hard-working business man, wont to doubt the reality of spiritual things, and strongly questioned the truth of the narrative of answered prayers which he had read from Mr. Müller's pen. But, in view of the simple straightforward story, he could not rest in his doubts, and at last proposed to himself a test as to whether or not God was indeed with Mr. Müller, as he declared. He wished to buy a certain property if rated at a reasonable valuation; and he determined, if he should secure it at the low price which he set for himself, he would give to him one hundred pounds. He authorized a bid to be put in, in his behalf, but, curious to get the earliest information as to the success of his venture, he went himself to the place of sale, and was surprised to find the property actually knocked off to him at his own price. Astonished at what he regarded as a proof that God was really working with Mr. Müller and for him, he made up his mind to go in person and pay over the sum of money to him, and so make his acquaintance and see the man whose prayers God answered. Not finding him at Bristol, he had followed him to Ilfracombe.

Having heard his story, and having learned that he was from a certain locality, Mr. Müller remarked upon the frequent proofs of God's strange way of working on the minds of parties wholly unknown to him and leading them to send in gifts; and he added: "I had a letter from a lawyer in your very neighbourhood, shortly since, asking for the proper form for a bequest, as a client of his, not named, wished to leave one thousand pounds to the orphan work." It proved that the man with whom he was then talking was this nameless client, who, being convinced that his doubts were wrong, had decided to provide for this legacy.

In August, 1884, a Christian brother from the United States called to see Mr. Müller. He informed him how greatly he had been blessed of God through reading his published testimony to God's faithfulness; and that having, through his sister's death, come into the possession of some property, he had *come across the sea,* that he might see the orphan houses and know their founder, for himself, and hand over to him for the Lord's work the entire bequest of about seven hundred pounds.

Only seventeen days later, a letter accompanying a donation gave further joy to Mr. Müller's heart. It was from the husband of one of the orphans who, in her seventeenth year, had left the institution, and to whom Mr. Müller himself, on her departure, had given the first two volumes of the Reports. Her husband had read them with more spiritual profit than any volume except the Book of books, and had found his faith much strengthened. Being a lay preacher in the

Methodist Free Church, the blessed impulses thus imparted to himself were used of God to inspire a like self-surrender in the class under his care.

These are a few examples of the countless encouragements that led Mr. Müller, as he reviewed them, to praise God unceasingly.

A Christian physician enclosed ten pounds in a letter, telling how first he tried a religion of mere duty and failed; then, after a severe illness, learned a religion of love, apprehending the love of God to himself in Christ and so learning how to love others. In his days of darkness he had been a great lover of flowers and had put up several plant-houses; flower-culture was his hobby, and a fine collection of rare plants, his pride. He took down and sold one of these conservatories and sent the proceeds as "*the price of an idol,* cast down by God's power." Another giver enclosed a like amount from the sale of unnecessary books and pictures; and a poor man his half-crown, "the fruit of a little tree in his garden."

SCRIPTURE TESTIMONY
Divine punishment for deceiving the Holy Spirit Acts 5:1-11 *God leads believers in opposition to idolatry* Acts 17:16-17 · 1 Corinthians 8:4 · 1 John 5:21

A poor woman, who had devoted the progeny of a pet rabbit to the orphan work, when the young became fit for sale changed her mind and "kept back a part of the price"; *that part,* however, *two rabbits,* she found *dead* on the day when they were to be sold.

In July, 1877, ten pounds from an anonymous source were accompanied by a letter which conveys another instructive lesson. Years before, the writer had resolved before God to discontinue a doubtful habit, and send the cost of his indulgence to the Institution. The vow, made in time of trouble, was unpaid until God brought the sin to remembrance by a new trouble, and by a special message from the Word: "Grieve not the Spirit of God." The victory was then given over the habit, and, the practice having annually cost about twenty-six shillings, the full amount was sent to cover the period during which the solemn covenant had not been kept, with the promise of further gifts in redemption of the same promise to the Lord. This instance conveys more than one lesson. It reminds us of the costliness of much of our self-indulgence. Sir Michael Hicks-Beach, in submitting the Budget for 1897, remarked that what is annually wasted in the unsmoked remnants of cigars and cigarettes in Britain is estimated at a million and a quarter pounds—the equivalent of all that is annually spent on foreign missions by British Christians. And many forms of self-gratification, in no way contributing to either health or profit, would, if what they cost were dedicated to the Lord, make His treasuries overflow. Again, this incident reminds us of the many vows, made in time of trouble, which have no payment in time of relief. Many sorrows come back, like clouds that return after the rain, to remind of broken pledges and unfulfilled obligations, whereby we have grieved the Holy Spirit of God. "Pay that which thou hast vowed; for God hath no pleasure in fools." And again we are here taught how a sensitive and enlightened conscience will make restitution to God as well as to man; and that past unfaithfulness to a solemn covenant cannot be made good merely by keeping to its terms *for the future.* No honest man dishonours a past debt, or compromises with his integrity by simply beginning anew and paying as he goes. Reformation takes a retrospective glance and begins in restitution and reparation for all previous wrongs and unfaithfulness. It is one of the worst evils of our day that even disciples are so ready to bury the financial and moral debts of their past life in the grave of a too-easy oblivion.

One donor, formerly living in Tunbridge Wells, followed a principle of giving, the reverse of the worldly way. As his own family increased, instead of decreasing his gifts, he gave, for each child given to him of God, the average cost of maintaining one orphan, until, having seven children, he was supporting seven orphans.

An anonymous giver wrote:

> "It was my idea that when a man had sufficient for his own wants, he ought then to supply the wants of others, and consequently I never had sufficient. I now clearly see that God expects us to give of what we have and not of what we have not, and to leave the rest to Him. I therefore give in faith and love, knowing that if I first seek the kingdom of God and His righteousness, all other things will be added unto me."

SCRIPTURE TESTIMONY
Disciples must keep their word Matthew 5:37

Another sends five pounds in fulfillment of a secret promise that, if he succeeded in passing competitive examination for civil service, he would make a thank-offering. And he adds that Satan had repeatedly tried to persuade him that he could not afford it yet, and could send it better in a little while. Many others have heard the same subtle suggestion from the same master of wiles and father of lies. Postponement in giving is usually its practical abandonment, for the habit of procrastination grows with insensibly rapid development.

Habitual givers generally witnessed to the conscious blessedness of systematic giving. Many who began by giving a tenth, and perhaps in a legal spirit, felt constrained, by the growing joy of imparting, to increase, not the amount only, but the proportion, to a fifth, a fourth, a third, and even a half of their profits. Some wholly reversed the law of appropriation with which they began; for at first they gave a tithe to the Lord's uses, reserving nine tenths, whereas later on they appropriated nine tenths to the Lord's uses, and reserved for themselves only a tithe. Those who learn the deep meaning of our Lord's words, "It is more blessed to give than to receive," find such joy in holding all things at His disposal that even personal expenditures are subjected to the scrutiny of conscience and love, lest anything be wasted in extravagance or careless self-indulgence. Frances Ridley Havergal in her later years felt herself and all she possessed to be so fully and joyfully given up to God, that she never went into a shop to spend a shilling without asking herself whether it would be for God's glory.

Gifts were valued by Mr. Müller only so far as they were the Lord's money, procured by lawful means and given in the Lord's own way. To the last his course was therefore most conscientious in the caution with which he accepted offerings even in times of sorest extremity.

In October, 1842, he felt led to offer aid to a sister who seemed in great distress and destitution, offering to share with her, if need be, even his house and purse.

This offer drew out the acknowledgment that she had some five hundred pounds of her own; and her conversation revealed that this money was held as a provision against possible future want, and that she was leaning upon that instead of upon God. Mr. Müller said but little to her, but after her withdrawal he besought the Lord to make so real to her the exhaustless riches she possessed in Christ, and her own heavenly calling, that she might be constrained to lay down at His feet the whole sum which was thus a snare to her faith and an idol to her love. *Not a word spoken or written passed between him and her on the subject, nor did he even see her;* his express desire being that if any such step were to be taken by her, it might result from no human influence or persuasion, lest her subsequent regret might prove both a damage to herself and a dishonour to her Master.

For nearly four weeks, however, he poured out his heart to God for her deliverance from greed. Then she again sought an interview and told him how she had been day by day seeking to learn the will of God as to this hoarded sum, and had been led to a clear conviction that it should be laid entire upon His altar. Thus the goodly sum of five hundred pounds was within so easy reach, at a time of very great need, that a word from Mr. Müller would secure it. Instead of saying that word, he exhorted her to make no such disposition of the money at that time, but to count the cost; to do nothing rashly lest she should repent it, but wait at least a fortnight more before reaching a final decision. His correspondence with this sister may be found fully spread out in his journal,[41] and is a model of devout carefulness lest he should snatch at a gift that might be prompted by wrong motives or given with an unprepared heart. When finally given, unexpected hindrances arose affecting her actual possession and transfer, so that more than a third of a year elapsed before it was received; but meanwhile there was on his part neither impatience nor distrust, nor did he even communicate further with

41 Narrative, I. 487 *et seq.*

her. To the glory of God let it be added that she afterward bore cheerful witness that never for one moment did she regret giving the whole sum to His service, and thus transferring her trust from the money to the Master.

SCRIPTURE TESTIMONY
Giving all one has to live on, and trusting God for provision
Mark 12:41-44 · Luke 21:1-4

In August, 1853, a poor widow of sixty, who had sold the little house which constituted her whole property, put into an orphan-house box elsewhere, for Mr. Müller, the entire proceeds, ninety pounds. Those who conveyed it to Mr. Müller, knowing the circumstances, urged her to retain at least a part of this sum, and prevailed on her to keep five pounds and sent on the other eighty-five. Mr. Müller, learning the facts, and fearing lest the gift might result from a sudden impulse to be afterward regretted, offered to pay her travelling expenses that he might have an interview with her. He found her mind had been quite made up for ten years before the house was sold that such disposition should be made of the proceeds. But he was the more reluctant to accept the gift lest, as she had already been prevailed on to take back five pounds of the original donation, she might wish she had reserved more; and only after much urgency had failed to persuade her to reconsider the step would he accept it. Even then, however, lest he should be evil spoken of in the matter, he declined to receive any part of the gift for personal uses.

SCRIPTURE TESTIMONY
God's work will not lack God's supply
Philippians 4:19

In October, 1867, a small sum was sent in by one who had years before taken it from another, and who desired thus to *make restitution,* believing that the Christian believer from whom it was taken would approve of this method of restoring it. Mr. Müller promptly returned it, irrespective of amount, that restitution might be made directly to the party who had been robbed or wronged, claiming that such party should first receive it and then dispose of it as might seem fit. As it did not belong to him who took it, it was not his to give even in another's behalf.

During a season of great straits Mr. Müller received a sealed parcel containing money. He knew from whom it came, and that the donor was a woman not only involved in debt, but frequently asked by creditors for their lawful dues in vain. It was therefore clear that it was not *her* money, and therefore not hers to *give;* and without even opening the paper wrapper he returned it to the sender—and this at a time when there was *not in hand enough to meet the expenses of that very day.* In June, 1838, a stranger, who confessed to an act of fraud, wished through Mr. Müller to make restitution, with interest; and, instead of sending the money by post, Mr. Müller took pains to transmit it by bank orders, which thus enabled him, in case of need, to prove his fidelity in acting as a medium of transmission—an instance of the often-quoted maxim that it is the honest man who is most careful to provide things honest in the sight of all men.

Money sent as proceeds of a musical entertainment held for the benefit of the orphans in the south of Devon was politely returned, Mr. Müller had no doubt of the kind intention of those who set this scheme on foot, but he felt that money for the work of God *should not be obtained in this manner,* and he desired only money provided in God's way.

Friends who asked that they might know whether their gifts had come at a particularly opportune time were referred to the next Report for answer. To acknowledge that the help came very seasonably would be an indirect revelation of need, and might be construed into an indirect appeal for more aid—as help that was peculiarly timely would soon be exhausted. And so this man of God consistently avoided any such disclosure of an exigency, lest his chief object should be hindered, namely, "to show how blessed it is to deal with God alone, and to trust Him in the darkest moments." And though the need was continual, and one demand was no sooner met than another arose, he did not find this a trying life nor did he ever tire of it.

As early as May, 1846, a letter from a brother contained the following paragraph:

> "With regard to property, I do not see my way clearly. I trust it is all indeed at the disposal of the Lord; and, if you would let me know of any need of it in His service, any sum under two hundred pounds shall be at your disposal at about a week's notice."

The need at that time was great. How easy and natural to write back that the orphan work was then in want of help, and that, as Mr. Müller was just going away from Bristol for rest, it would be a special comfort if his correspondent would send on, say a hundred and ninety pounds or so! But to deal with the Lord alone in the whole matter seemed so indispensable, both for the strengthening of his own faith and for the effectiveness of his testimony to the church and the world, that at once this temptation was seen to be a snare, and he replied that only to the Lord could the need of any part of the work be confided.

Money to be laid up as a fund for his old age or possible seasons of illness or family emergencies was always declined. Such a donation of one hundred pounds was received October 12, 1856, with a note so considerate and Christian that the subtle temptation to lay up for himself treasures on earth would have triumphed but for a heart fixed immovably in the determination that there should be no dependence upon any such human provision. He had settled the matter beyond raising the question again, that he would live from day to day upon the Lord's bounty, and would make but *one investment,* namely, using whatever means God gave, to supply the necessities of the poor, depending on God richly to repay him in the hour of his own need, according to the promise:

> "He that hath pity upon the poor lendeth unto the Lord;
> And that which he hath given will He pay him again." (Proverbs 19:17)

God so owned, at once, this disposition on Mr. Müller's part that his courteous letter, declining the gift for himself, led the donor not only to ask him to use the hundred pounds for the orphan work, but to add to this sum a further gift of two hundred pounds more.

CHAPTER XXIII

God's Witness to the Work

THE ELEVENTH chapter of Hebrews—that "Westminster Abbey" where Old Testament saints have a memorial before God—gives a hint of a peculiar reward which faith enjoys, even in this life, as an earnest and foretaste of its final recompense.

By faith "the elders obtained a good report," that is, *they had witness borne to them* by God in return for witness borne to Him. All the marked examples of faith here recorded show this twofold testimony. Abel testified to his faith in God's Atoning Lamb, and God testified to his gifts. Enoch witnessed to the unseen God by his holy walk with Him, and He testified to Enoch, by his translation, and even before it, that he pleased God. Noah's faith bore witness to God's word, by building the ark and preaching righteousness, and God bore witness to him by bringing a flood upon a world of the ungodly and saving him and his family in the ark.

George Müller's life was one long witness to the prayer-hearing God; and, throughout, God bore him witness that his prayers were heard and his work accepted. The pages of his journal are full of striking examples of this witness—the earnest or foretaste of the fuller recompense of reward reserved for the Lord's coming.

Compensations for renunciations, and rewards for service, do not all wait for the judgment-seat of Christ, but, as some men's sins are open beforehand, going before to judgment, so the seed sown for God yields a harvest that is 'open beforehand' to joyful recognition. Divine love graciously and richly acknowledged these many years of self-forgetful devotion to Him and His needy ones, by large and unexpected tokens of blessing. Toils and trials, tears and prayers, were not in vain even this side of the Hereafter.

For illustrations of this we naturally turn first of all to the orphan work. Ten thousand motherless and fatherless children had found a home and tender parental care in the institution founded by George Müller, and were there fed, clad, and taught, before he was called up higher. His efforts to improve their state physically, morally, and spiritually were so manifestly owned of God that he felt his compensation to be both constant and abundant, and his journal, from time to time, glows with his fervent thanksgivings.

This orphan work would amply repay all its cost during two thirds of a century, should only its *temporal benefits* be reckoned. Experience proved that, with God's blessing, one half of the lives sacrificed among the children of poverty would be saved by better conditions of body—such as regularity and cleanliness of habits, good food, pure air, proper clothing, and wholesome exercise. At least two thirds, if not three fourths, of the parents whose offspring have found a shelter on Ashley Down had died of consumption and kindred diseases; and hence the children had been largely tainted with a like tendency. And yet, all through the history of this orphan work, there has been such care of proper sanitary conditions that there has been singular freedom from all sorts of ailments, and especially epidemic diseases; and when scarlet fever, measles, and such diseases have found entrance, the cases of sickness have been comparatively few and mild, and the usual percentage of deaths exceedingly small.

This is not the only department of training in which the recompense has been abundant. Ignorance is everywhere the usual handmaid of poverty, and there has been very careful effort to secure proper *mental* culture. With what success the education of these orphans has been looked after will sufficiently appear from the reports of the school inspector. From year to year these pupils have been examined in reading, writing, arithmetic, Scripture, dictation, geography, history, grammar, composition, and singing; and Mr. Horne reported in 1885 an average per cent of all marks as high as 91.1, and even this was surpassed the next year when it was 94, and, two years later, when it was 96.1.

But in the moral and spiritual welfare of these orphans, which has been primarily sought, the richest recompense has been enjoyed. The one main aim of Mr. Müller and his whole staff of helpers, from first to last, has been to save these children—to bring them up in the nurture and admonition of the Lord. The hindrances were many and formidable. If the hereditary taint of disease is to be dreaded, what of the awful legacy of sin and crime! Many of these little ones had no proper bringing up till they entered the orphan houses; and not a few had been trained indeed, but only in Satan's schools of drink and lust. And yet, notwithstanding all these drawbacks, Mr. Müller records, with devout thankfulness, that *"the Lord had constrained them,* on the whole, to behave exceedingly well, so much so as to attract the attention of observers." Better still, large numbers have, throughout the whole history of this work, given signs of a really regenerate state, and have afterwards maintained a consistent character and conduct, and in some cases have borne singular witness to the grace of God, both by their complete transformation and by their influence for good.

In August, 1858, an orphan girl, Martha Pinnell, who had been for over twelve years under Mr. Müller's care, and for more than five years ill with consumption, fell asleep in Jesus. Before her death, she had, for two and a half years, known the Lord, and the change in her character and conduct had been remarkable. From an exceedingly disobedient and troublesome child with a pernicious influence, she had become both very docile and humble and most influential for good. In her unregenerate days she had declared that, if she should ever be converted, she would be "a thorough Christian," and so it proved. Her happiness in God, her study of His word, her deep knowledge of the Lord Jesus, her earnest passion for souls, seemed almost incredible in one so young and so recently turned to God. And Mr. Müller has preserved in the pages of his Journal four of the precious letters written by her to other inmates of the orphan houses.[42]

SCRIPTURE TESTIMONY
Salvation transforms
2 Corinthians 5:16-17 · Galatians 6:15

At times, and frequently, extensive revivals have been known among them when scores and hundreds have found the Lord. The year ending May 26, 1858 was especially notable for the unprecedented greatness and rapidity of the work which the Spirit of God had wrought, in such conversions. Within a few days and without any special apparent cause except the very peaceful death of a Christian orphan, Caroline Bailey, more than fifty of the one hundred and forty girls in Orphan House No. 1 were under conviction of sin, and the work spread into the other departments, till about sixty were shortly exercising faith. In July, 1859, again, in a school of one hundred and twenty girls more than half were brought under deep spiritual concern; and, after a year had passed, shewed the grace of continuance in a new life. In January and February, 1860, another mighty wave of Holy Spirit power swept over the institution. It began among little girls, from six to nine years old, then extended to the older girls, and then to the boys, until, inside of ten days, above two hundred were inquiring and in many instances found immediate peace. The young converts at once asked to hold prayer meetings among themselves, and were permitted; and not only so, but many began to labour and pray for others, and, out of the seven hundred orphans then in charge, some two hundred and sixty were shortly regarded as either converted or in a most hopeful state.

Again, in 1872, on the first day of the week of prayer, the Holy Spirit so moved that, without any unusual occasion for deep seriousness, hundreds were, during

42 Narrative, III. 253-257.

that season, hopefully converted. Constant prayer for their souls made the orphan homes a hallowed place, and by August 1st, it was believed, after careful investigation, that seven hundred and twenty-nine might be safely counted as being disciples of Christ, the number of believing orphans being thus far in excess of any previous period. A series of such blessings have, down to this date, crowned the sincere endeavours of all who have charge of these children, to lead them to seek first the kingdom of God and His righteousness.

By far the majority of orphans sent out for service or apprenticeship, had for some time before known the Lord; and even of those who left the Institution unconverted, the after-history of many showed that the training there received had made impossible continuance in a life of sin.

Thus, precious harvests of this seed-sowing, gathered in subsequent years, have shown that God was not unrighteous to forget this work of faith, and labour of love, and patience of hope.

SCRIPTURE TESTIMONY

The Gospel is the power of God for salvation

Romans 1:16

God will provide for our daily needs

Matt 6:11

In April, 1874, a letter from a former inmate of the orphanage enclosed a thank offering for the excellent Bible-teaching there received which had borne fruit years after. So carefully had she been instructed in the way of salvation that, while yet herself unrenewed, she had been God's instrument of leading to Christ a fellow servant who had long been seeking peace, and so, became, like a sign-board on the road, the means of directing another to the true path, by simply telling her what she had been taught, though not then following the path herself.

Another orphan wrote, in 1876, that often, when tempted to indulge the sin of unbelief, the thought of that six years' sojourn in Ashley Down came across the mind like a gleam of sunshine. It was remembered how the clothes there worn, the food eaten, the bed slept on, and the very walls around, were the visible answers to believing prayer, and the recollection of all these things proved a potent prescription and remedy for the doubts and waverings of the child of God, a shield against the fiery darts of satanic suggestion.

During the thirty years between 1865 and 1895, two thousand five hundred and sixty-six orphans were known to have left the institution as believers, an average of eighty-five every year; and, at the close of this thirty years, nearly six hundred were yet in the homes on Ashley Down who had given credible evidence of a regenerate state.

Mr. Müller was permitted to know that not only had these orphans been blessed in health, educated in mind, converted to God, and made useful Christian citizens, but many of them had become fathers or mothers of Christian households. One representative instance may be cited. A man and a woman who had formerly been among these orphans became husband and wife, and they have had eight children, all earnest disciples, one of whom went as a foreign missionary to Africa.

From the first, God set His seal upon this religious training in the orphan houses. The *first two children* received into No. 1 both became true believers and zealous workers: one, a Congregational deacon, who, in a benighted neighbourhood, acted the part of a lay preacher; and the other, a laborious and successful clergyman in the Church of England, and both largely used of God in soul-winning. Could the full history be written of all who have gone forth from these orphan homes, what a volume of testimony would be furnished, since these are but a few scattered examples of the conspicuously useful service to which God has called those whose after-career can be traced!

In his long and extensive missionary tours, Mr. Müller was permitted to see, gather, and partake of many widely scattered fruits of his work on Ashley Down. When preaching in Brooklyn, N. Y., in September, 1877, he learned that in Philadelphia a legacy of a thousand pounds was waiting for him, the proceeds of a life-insurance, which the testator had willed to the work, and in city after city he had the joy of meeting scores of orphans brought up under his care.

He minutely records the remarkable usefulness of a Mr. Wilkinson, who, up to the age of fourteen and a half years, had been taught at the orphanage. Twenty years had elapsed since Mr. Müller had seen him, when, in 1878, he met him in Calvary Church, San Francisco, six thousand five hundred miles from Bristol. He found him holding fast his faith in the Lord Jesus, a happy and consistent Christian. He further heard most inspiring accounts of this man's singular service during the Civil War in America. Being on the gunboat Louisiana, he had there been the leading spirit and recognized head of a little Bethel church among his fellow seamen, who were by him led so to engage in the service of Christ as to exhibit a devotion that, without a trace of fanatical enthusiasm, was full of holy zeal and joy. Their whole conversation was of God. It further transpired that, months previous, when the cloud of impending battle overhung the ship's company, he and one of his comrades had met for prayer in the 'chain-locker'; and thus began a series of most remarkable meetings which, without one night's interruption, lasted for some twenty months. Wilkinson alone among the whole company had any previous knowledge of the word of God, and he became not only the leader of the movement, but the chief interpreter of the Scriptures as they met to read the Book of God and exchange views upon it. Nor was he satisfied to do thus much with his comrades daily, but at another stated hour he, with some chosen helpers, gathered the coloured sailors of the ship to teach them reading, writing, etc.

A member of the Christian Commission, Mr. J. E. Hammond, who gave these facts publicity, and who was intimately acquainted with Mr. Wilkinson and his work on shipboard, said that he seemed to be a direct "product of Mr.

Müller's faith, his calm confidence in God, the method in his whole manner of life, the persistence of purpose, and the quiet spiritual power," which so characterized the founder of the Bristol orphanage, being eminently reproduced in this young man who had been trained under his influence. When in a sail-loft ashore, he was compelled for two weeks to listen to the lewd and profane talk of two associates detailed with him for a certain work. For the most part he took refuge in silence; but his manner of conduct, and one sentence which dropped from his lips, brought both those rough and wicked sailors to the Saviour he loved, one of whom in three months read the word of God from Genesis to Revelation.

Mr. Müller went nowhere without meeting converted orphans or hearing of their work, even in the far-off corners of the earth. Sometimes in great cities ten or fifteen would be waiting at the close of an address to shake the hand of their "father," and tell him of their debt of gratitude and love. He found them in every conceivable sphere of service, many of them having households in which the principles taught in the orphan homes were dominant, and engaged in the learned professions as well as humbler walks of life.

God gave His servant also the sweet compensation of seeing great blessing attending the day-schools supported by the Scriptural Knowledge Institution.

The master of the school at Clayhidon, for instance, wrote of a poor lad, a pupil in the day-school, prostrate with rheumatic fever, in a wretched home and surrounded by bitter opposers of the truth. Wasted to a skeleton, and in deep anxiety about his own soul, he was pointed to Him who says, "Come unto Me,... and I will give you rest." While yet this conversation was going on, as though suddenly he had entered into a new world, this emaciated boy began to repeat texts such as "Suffer the little children to come unto me," and burst out singing:

> "Jesus loves me, this I know,
> For the Bible tells me so."

He seemed transported with ecstasy, and recited text after text and hymn after hymn, learned at that school. No marvel is it if that schoolmaster felt a joy, akin to the angels, in this one proof that his labour in the Lord was not in vain. Such examples might be indefinitely multiplied, but this handful of first-fruits of a harvest may indicate the character of the whole crop.

Letters were constantly received from missionary labourers in various parts of the world who were helped by the gifts of the Scriptural Knowledge Institution. The testimony from this source alone would fill a good-sized volume, and therefore its incorporation into this memoir would be impracticable. Those who would see what grand encouragement came to Mr. Müller from fields of labour where he was only represented by others, whom his gift's aided, should read the annual reports. A few examples may be given of the blessed results of such wide scattering of the seed of the kingdom, as specimens of thousands.

SCRIPTURE TESTIMONY
We must obey God rather than men
Acts 4:19-20 · Acts 5:29

Mr. Albert Fenn, who was labouring in Madrid, wrote of a civil guard who, because of his bold witness for Christ and renunciation of the Romish confessional, was sent from place to place and most cruelly treated, and threatened with banishment to a penal settlement. Again he writes of a convert from Borne who, for trying to establish a small meeting, was summoned before the governor.

"Who pays you for this?" "No one." "What do you gain by it?" "Nothing." "How do you live?" "I work with my hands in a mine." "Why do you hold meetings?" "Because God has blessed my soul, and I wish others to be blessed." "You? you were made a miserable day-labourer; I prohibit the meetings." "I yield to force," was the calm reply, "but as long as I have a mouth to speak I shall speak for Christ." How like those primitive disciples who boldly faced the rulers at Jerusalem, and, being forbidden to speak in Jesus' name, firmly answered: "We ought to obey God rather than men. Whether it be right in the sight of God to hearken unto you more than unto God judge ye: for we cannot but speak the things which we have seen and heard."

A missionary labourer writes from India, of three Brahman priests and scores of Santhals and Hindus, sitting down with four Europeans to keep the supper of the Lord—all fruits of his ministry. Within a twelvemonth, sixty-two men and women, including head men of villages, and four Brahman women, wives of priests and of head men, were baptized, representing twenty-three villages in which the gospel had been preached. At one time more than one hundred persons were awakened in one mission in Spain; and such harvests as these were not infrequent in various fields to which the founder of the orphan work had the joy of sending aid.

In 1885, a scholar of one of the schools at Carrara, Italy, was confronted by a priest. "In the Bible," said he, "you do not find the commandments of the church." "No, sir," said the child, "for it is not for the church of God to *command*, but to *obey.*" "Tell me, then," said the priest, "these commandments of God." "Yes, sir," replied the child; "I am the Lord thy God. Thou shalt have no other God before me. Neither shalt thou make any graven image." "Stop! stop!" cried the priest, "I do not understand it so." "But so," quietly replied the child, "it is written in God's word." This simple incident may illustrate both the character of the teaching given in the schools, and the character often developed in those who were taught.

Out of the many pages of Mr. Müller's journal, probably about one-fifth are occupied wholly with extracts from letters like these from missionaries, teachers, and helpers, which kept him informed of the progress of the Lord's work at home and in many lands where the labourers were by him enabled to continue their service. Bible-carriages, open-air services, Christian schools, tract distribution, and various other forms of holy labour for the benighted souls near and far, formed part of the many-branching tree of life that was planted on Ashley Down.

SCRIPTURE TESTIMONY
Believers are the aroma of Christ to those around them 2 Corinthians 2:14-16

Another of the main encouragements and rewards which Mr. Müller enjoyed in this life was the knowledge that his example had emboldened other believers to attempt like work for God, on like principles. This he himself regarded as the greatest blessing resulting from his life-work, that hundreds of thousands of children of God had been led in various parts of the world to trust in God in all simplicity; and when such trust found expression in similar service to orphans, it seemed the consummation of his hopes, for the work was thus proven to have its seed in itself after its kind, a self-propagating life, which doubly demonstrated it to be a tree of the Lord's own planting, that He might be glorified.

In December, 1876, Mr. Müller learned, for instance, that a Christian evangelist, simply through reading about the orphan work in Bristol, had it laid on his heart to care about orphans, and encouraged by Mr. Müller's example, solely in dependence on the Lord, had begun in 1863 with three orphans at Nimwegen in Holland, and had at that date, only fourteen years after, over four hundred and fifty in the institution. It pleased the Lord that he and Mrs. Müller should, with their own eyes, see this institution, and he says that in "almost numberless instances" the Lord permitted him to know of similar fruits of his work.

At his first visit to Tokyo, Japan, he gave an account of it, and as the result, Mr. Ishii, a native Christian Japanese, started an orphanage upon a similar basis of prayer, faith, and dependence upon the Living God, and at Mr. Müller's second visit to the Island Empire he found this orphan work prosperously in progress.

How generally fruitful the example thus furnished on Ashley Down has been in good to the church and the world will never be known on earth. A man living at Horfield, in sight of the orphan buildings, has said that, whenever he felt doubts of the Living God creeping into his mind, he used to get up and look through the night at the many windows lit up on Ashley Down, and they gleamed out through the darkness as stars in the sky.

It was the witness of Mr. Müller to a prayer-hearing God which encouraged Rev. J. Hudson Taylor, in 1863, thirty years after Mr. Müller's great step was taken, to venture wholly on the Lord, in founding the China Inland Mission. It has been said that to the example of A. H. Francké in Halle, or George Müller in Bristol, may be more or less directly traced every form of 'faith work,' prevalent since.

The Scriptural Knowledge Institution was made in all its departments a means of blessing. Already in the year ending May 26, 1860, a hundred servants of Christ had been more or less aided, and far more souls had been hopefully brought to God through their labours than during any year previous. About six hundred letters, received from them, had cheered Mr. Müller's heart during the twelve-month, and this source of joy overflowed during all his life. In countless cases children of God were lifted to a higher level of faith and life, and unconverted souls were turned to God through the witness borne to God by the institutions on Ashley Down. Mr. Müller has summed up this long history of blessing by two statements which are worth pondering.

First, that the Lord was pleased to give him far beyond all he at first expected to accomplish or receive.

And secondly, that he was fully persuaded that all he had seen and known would not equal the thousandth part of what he should see and know when the Lord should come, His reward with Him, to give every man according as his work shall be.

The *circulation of Mr. Müller's Narrative* was a most conspicuous means of untold good.

In November, 1856, Mr. James McQuilkin, a young Irishman, was converted, and early in the next year, read the first two volumes of that Narrative He said to himself: "Mr. Müller obtains all this simply by prayer; so may I be blessed by the same means," and he began to pray. First of all he received from the Lord, in answer, a spiritual companion, and then two more of like mind; and they four began stated seasons of prayer in a small schoolhouse near Kells, Antrim, Ireland, every Friday evening. On the first day of the new year, 1858, a farm-servant was remarkably brought to the Lord in answer to their prayers, and these *five* gave themselves anew to united supplication. Shortly a sixth young man was added to their number by conversion, and so the little company of praying souls slowly grew, only believers being admitted to these simple meetings for fellowship in reading of the Scriptures, prayer, and mutual exhortation.

About Christmas, that year, Mr. McQuilkin, with the two brethren who had first joined him—one of whom was Mr. Jeremiah Meneely, who is still at work for God—held a meeting by request at Ahoghill. Some believed and some mocked, while others thought these three converts presumptuous; but two weeks later another meeting was held, at which God's Spirit began to work most mightily and conversions now rapidly multiplied. Some converts bore the sacred coals and kindled the fire elsewhere, and so in many places revival flames began to burn; and in Ballymena, Belfast, and at other points the Spirit's gracious work was manifest.

Such was the starting-point, in fact, of one of the most widespread and memorable revivals ever known in our century, and which spread the next year in England, Wales, and Scotland. Thousands found Christ, and walked in newness of life; and the results are still manifest after more than forty years.

As early as 1868 it was found that one who had thankfully read this Narrative had issued a compendium of it in Swedish. We have seen how widely useful it has been in Germany; and in many other languages its substance at least has been made available to native readers.

SCRIPTURE TESTIMONY
God answers prayer
Luke 18:7 · John 15:7 · Acts 12:5 · James 5:15

Knowledge came to Mr. Müller of a boy of ten years who got hold of one of these Reports, and, although belonging to a family of unbelievers, began to pray: "God, teach me to pray like George Müller, and hear me as Thou dost hear George Müller." He further declared his wish to be a preacher, which his widowed mother very strongly opposed, objecting that the boy did not know enough to get into the grammar-school, which is the first step toward such a high calling. The lad, however, rejoined: "I will learn and pray, and God will help me through as He has done George Müller." And soon, to the surprise of everybody, the boy had successfully passed his examination and was received at the school.

SCRIPTURE TESTIMONY
God uses our testimonies to defeat the enemy
Revelation 12:11

A donor writes, September 20, 1879, that the reading of the Narrative totally changed his inner life to one of perfect trust and confidence in God. It led to the devoting of at least a tenth of his earnings to the Lord's purposes, and showed him how much more blessed it is to give than to receive; and it led him also to place a copy of that Narrative on the shelves of a Town Institute library where three thousand members and subscribers might have access to it.

Another donor suggests that it might be well if Prof. Huxley and his sympathisers, who had been proposing some new arbitrary "prayer-gauge" would, instead of treating prayer as so much waste of breath, try how long they could keep five orphan houses running, with over two thousand orphans, and without asking any one for help,—either "GOD OR MAN."

In September, 1882, another donor describes himself as "simply astounded at the blessed results of prayer and faith," and many others have found this brief narrative "the most wonderful and complete refutation of skepticism it had ever been their lot to meet with"—an array of facts constituting the most undeniable "evidences of Christianity." There are abundant instances of the power exerted by Mr. Müller's testimony, as when a woman who had been an infidel, writes him that he was "the first person by whose example she learned that there are some men who live by faith," and that for this reason she had willed to him all that she possessed.

Another reader found these Reports "more faith-strengthening and soul-refreshing than many a sermon," particularly so after just wading through the mire of a speech of a French infidel who boldly affirmed that of all of the millions of prayers uttered every day, not one is answered. We should like to have any candid skeptic confronted with Mr. Müller's unvarnished story of a life of faith, and see how he would on any principle of' compound probability' and 'accidental coincidences,' account for the tens of thousand's of answers to believing prayer! The fact is that one half of the infidelity in the world is dishonest, and the other half is ignorant of the daily proofs that God is, and is a Rewarder of them that diligently seek Him.

From almost the first publication of his Narrative, Mr. Müller had felt a conviction that it was thus to be greatly owned of God as a witness to His faithfulness; and, as early as 1842, it was laid on his heart to send a copy of his Annual Report gratuitously to every Christian minister of the land, which the Lord helped him to do, his aim being not to get money or even awaken interest in the work, but rather to stimulate faith and quicken prayer.[43]

Twenty-two years later, in 1868, it was already so apparent that the published accounts of the Lord's dealings was used so largely to sanctify and edify saints and even to convert sinners and convince infidels, that he records this as *the greatest of all the spiritual blessings* hitherto resulting from his work for God. Since then thirty years more have fled, and, during this whole period, letters from a thousand sources have borne increasing witness that the example he set has led others to fuller faith and firmer confidence in God's word, power, and love; to a deeper persuasion that, though Elijah has been taken up, God, the God of Elijah, is still working His wonders.

And so, in all departments of his work for God, the Lord to whom he witnessed bore witness to him in return, and anticipated his final reward in a recompense of present and overflowing joy. This was especially true in the long tours undertaken, when past threescore and ten, to sow in lands afar the seeds of the Kingdom! As the sower went forth to sow he found not fallow fields only, but harvest fields also, from which his arms were filled with sheaves. Thus, in a new sense the reaper overtook the ploughman, and the harvester, him that scattered the seed. In every city of the United Kingdom and in the "sixty-eight cities" where, up to 1877, he had preached on the continents of Europe and America, he had found converted orphans, and believers to whom abundant blessing had come through reading his reports. After this date, twenty-one years more yet remained crowded

43 The author of this memoir purposes to give a copy of it to every foreign missionary, and to workers in the home fields, so far as means are supplied in answer to prayer. His hope is that the witness of this life may thus have still wider influence in stimulating prayer and faith. The devout reader is asked to unite his supplications with those of many others who are asking that the Lord may be pleased to furnish the means whereby this purpose may be carried out. Already about one hundred pounds sterling have been given for this end, and part of it, small in amount but rich in self-denial, from the staff of helpers and the orphans on Ashley Down. A. T. P.

with experiences of good. Thus, before the Lord called George Müller higher, He had given him a foretaste of his reward, in the physical, intellectual and spiritual profit of the orphans; in the fruits of his wide seed-sowing in other lands as well as Britain; in the scattering of God's word and Christian literature; in the Christian education of thousands of children in the schools he aided; in the assistance afforded to hundreds of devoted missionaries; in the large blessing imparted by his published narrative, and in his personal privilege of bearing witness throughout the world to the gospel of grace.

CHAPTER XXIV

Last Looks, Backward and Forward

THE MOUNTAIN-CLIMBER, at the sunset hour, naturally takes a last lingering look backward at the prospect visible from the lofty height, before he begins his descent to the valley. And, before we close this volume, we as naturally cast one more glance backward over this singularly holy and useful life, that we may catch further inspiration from its beauty and learn some new lessons in holy living and unselfish serving.

George Müller was divinely fitted for, fitted into his work, as a mortise fits the tenon, or a ball of bone its socket in the joint. He had adaptations, both natural and gracious, to the life of service to which he was called, and these adaptations made possible a career of exceptional sanctity and service, because of his complete self-surrender to the will of God and his childlike faith in His word.

Three qualities or characteristics stand out very conspicuous in him: *truth, faith,* and *love.* Our Lord frequently taught His disciples that the childlike spirit is the soul of discipleship, and in the ideal child these three traits are central. Truth is one centre, about which revolve childlike frankness and sincerity, genuineness and simplicity. Faith is another, about which revolve confidence and trust, docility and humility. Love is another centre, around which gather unselfishness and generosity, gentleness and restfulness of spirit. In the typical or perfect child, therefore, all these beautiful qualities would coexist, and, in proportion as they are found in a disciple, is he worthy to be called *a child of God.*

In Mr. Müller these traits were all found and conjoined in a degree very seldom found in any one man, and this fact sufficiently accounts for his remarkable likeness to Christ and fruitfulness in serving God and man. No pen-portrait of him which fails to make these features very prominent can either be accurate in delineation or warm in colouring. It is difficult to overestimate their importance in their relation to what George Müller *was* and *did*.

Truth is the corner-stone of all excellence, for without it nothing else is true, genuine, or real. From the hour of his conversion his truthfulness was increasingly dominant and apparent. In fact, there was about him a scrupulous exactness which sometimes seemed unnecessary. One smiles at the mathematical precision with which he states facts, giving the years, days, and hours since he was brought to the knowledge of God, or since he began to pray for some given object; and the pounds, shillings, pence, halfpence, and even farthings that form the total sum expended for any given purpose. We see the same conscientious exactness in the repetitions of statements, whether of principles or of occurrences, which we meet in his journal, and in which oftentimes there is not even a change of a word. But all this has a significance. It *inspires absolute confidence* in the record of the Lord's dealings.

First, because it shows that the writer has disciplined himself to accuracy of statement. Many a falsehood is not an intentional lie, but an undesigned inaccuracy. Three of our human faculties powerfully affect our veracity: one is memory, another is imagination, and another is conscience. Memory takes note of facts, imagination colours facts with fancies, and conscience brings the moral sense to bear in sifting the real from the unreal. Where conscience is not sensitive and dominant, memory and imagination will become so confused that facts and fancies will fail to be separated. The imagination will be so allowed to invest events and experiences with either a halo of glory or a cloud of prejudice that the narrator will constantly tell, not what he clearly sees written in the book of his remembrance, but what he beholds painted upon the canvas of his own imagination. Accuracy will be, half unconsciously perhaps, sacrificed to his own imaginings; he will exaggerate or depreciate—as his own impulses lead him; and a man who would not deliberately lie may thus be habitually untrustworthy: you cannot tell, and often he cannot tell, what the exact truth would be, when all the unreality with which it has thus been invested is dissipated like the purple and golden clouds about a mountain, leaving the bare crag of naked rock to be seen, just as it is in itself.

George Müller felt the immense importance of exact statement. Hence he disciplined himself to accuracy. Conscience presided over his narrative, and demanded that everything else should be scrupulously sacrificed to veracity. But, more than this, God made him, in a sense, a *man without imagination*—comparatively free from the temptations of an enthusiastic temperament. He was a mathematician rather than a poet, an artisan rather than an artist, and he did not see things invested with a false halo. He was deliberate, not impulsive; calm and not excitable. He naturally weighed every word before he spoke, and scrutinized every statement before he gave it form with pen or tongue. And therefore the very qualities that, to some people, may make his narrative bare of charm, and even repulsively prosaic, add to its value as a plain, conscientious, unimaginative, unvarnished, and trustworthy statement of facts. Had any man of a more poetic mind written that journal, the reader would have found himself constantly and unconsciously making allowance for the writer's own enthusiasm, discounting the facts, because of the imaginative colouring. The narrative might have been more readable, but it would not have been so reliable; and, in this story of the Lord's dealings, nothing was so indispensable as exact truth. It would be comparatively worthless, were it not undeniable. The Lord fitted the man who lived that life of faith and prayer, and wrote that life-story, to inspire confidence, so that even skeptics and doubters felt that they were reading, not a novel or a poem, but a history.

Faith was the second of these central traits in George Müller, and it was purely the product of grace. We are told, in that first great lesson on faith in the Scripture, that (Genesis 15:6) Abram believed in Jehovah—literally, *Amened* Jehovah. The word "Amen" means not 'Let it be so,' but rather *'it shall be so.'* The Lord's word came to Abram, saying this 'shall not be,' but something else 'shall be'; and Abram simply said with all his heart, 'Amen'—'it shall be as God hath said.' And Paul seems to be imitating Abram's faith when, in the shipwreck off Malta, he said, "I believe God, that *it shall be* even as it was told me." That is faith in its simplest exercise and it was George Müller's faith. He found the word of the Lord in His blessed Book, a new word of promise for each new crisis of trial or need; he put his finger upon the very text and then looked up to God and said: "Thou hast spoken. I believe." Persuaded of God's unfailing truth, he rested on His word with unwavering faith, and consequently he was at peace.

Nothing is more noticeable, in the entire career of this man of God, reaching through sixty-five years, than the steadiness of his faith and the steadfastness it gave to his whole character. To have a word of God was enough. He built upon it, and, when floods came and beat against that house, how could it fall! He was never confounded nor obliged to flee. Even the earthquake may shake earth and heaven, but it leaves the true believer the inheritor of a kingdom which cannot be moved; for the object of all such shaking is to remove what can be shaken, that what cannot be shaken may remain.

If Mr. Müller had any great mission, it was not to found a world-wide institution of any sort, however useful in scattering Bibles and books and tracts, or housing and feeding thousands of orphans, or setting up Christian schools and aiding missionary workers. His main mission was to teach men that it is *safe to trust God's word,* to rest implicitly upon whatever He hath said, and obey explicitly whatever He has bidden; that prayer offered in faith, trusting His promise and the intercession of His dear Son, is never offered in vain; and that the life lived by faith is a walk with God, just outside the very gates of heaven.

Love, the third of that trinity of graces, was the other great secret and lesson of this life. And what is love? *Not* merely a complacent affection for what is lovable, which is often only a half-selfish taking of pleasure in the society and fellowship of those who love us. Love is the *principle of unselfishness:* love 'seeketh not her own'; it is the preference of another's pleasure and profit over our own, and hence is exercised toward the unthankful and unlovely, that it may lift them to a higher level. Such love is benevolence rather than complacence, and so it is "of God," for He loveth the unthankful and the evil: and he that loveth is born of God and knoweth God. Such love is obedience to a principle of unselfishness, and makes self-sacrifice habitual and even natural. While Satan's motto is 'spare thyself!' Christ's motto is to Deny thyself!' The sharpest rebuke ever administered by our Lord was that to Peter when he became a Satan by counselling his Master to adopt Satan's maxim.[44] We are bidden by Paul, *"Remember Jesus Christ,"*[45] and by Peter, *"Follow His steps."*[46] If we seek the inmost meaning of these two brief mottoes, we shall find that, about Jesus Christ's character, nothing was more conspicuous than the obedience of faith and self-surrender to God: and in His career, which we are bidden to follow, the renunciation of love, or self-sacrifice for man. The taunt was sublimely true: "He saved others, Himself He cannot save"; it was *because* he saved others that He could not save Himself. The seed must give up its own life for the sake of the crop; and he who will be life to others must, like his Lord, consent to die.

Here is the real meaning of that command, "Let him deny himself and take up his cross." Self-denial is not cutting off an indulgence here and there, but laying the axe at the root of the tree of self, of which all indulgences are only greater or smaller branches. Self-righteousness and self-trust, self-seeking and self-pleasing, self-will, self-defence, self-glory—these are a few of the myriad branches of that deeply rooted tree. And what if one or more of these be cut off, if such lopping off of some few branches only throws back into others the self-life to develop more vigorously in them?

And what is *cross*-bearing? We speak of our 'crosses'—but the word of God never uses that word in the plural, for there is but *one* cross—the cross on which the self-life is crucified, the cross of voluntary self-renunciation. How did Christ come to the cross? We read in Philippians the seven steps of his descent from heaven to Calvary. He had everything that even the Son of God could hold precious, even to the actual equal sharing of the glory of God. Yet for man's sake what did he do? He did not hold fast even His equality with God, He emptied Himself, took on Him the form of a servant, was made in the likeness of fallen humanity; even more than this, He humbled Himself even as a man, identifying Himself with our poverty and misery and sin; He accepted death for our sakes, and that, the death of shame

---

44 Matthew 16
45 2 Timothy 2 (Greek)
46 1 Peter 2:21

on the tree of curse. Every step was downward until He who had been worshipped by angels was reviled by thieves, and the crown of glory was displaced by the crown of thorns! That is what the cross meant to *Him.* And He says: "If any man will *come after Me,* let him deny himself, and *take up the cross* and follow Me." This cross is not *forced upon* us as are many of the little vexations and trials which we call 'our crosses'; it is *taken up* by us, in voluntary self-sacrifice for His sake. We choose self-abnegation, to lose our life in sacrifice that we may find it again in service. That is the self-oblivion of love. And Mr. Müller illustrated it. From the hour when he began to serve the Crucified One he entered more and more fully into the fellowship of His sufferings, seeking to be made conformable unto His death. He gave up fortune-seeking and fame-seeking; he cut loose from the world with its snares and joys; he separated himself from even its doubtful practices, he tested even churchly traditions and customs by the word of God, and step by step conformed to the pattern showed in that word. Every such step was a new self-denial, but it was following *Him.* He chose voluntary poverty that others might be rich, and voluntary loss that others might have gain. His life was one long endeavour to bless others, to be the channel for conveying God's truth and love and grace to them. Like Paul he rejoiced in such sufferings for others, because thus he filled up that which is behind of the afflictions of Christ in his flesh for His body's sake which is the church.[47] And unless Love's voluntary sacrifice be taken into account, George Müller's life will still remain an enigma. Loyalty to truth, the obedience of faith, the sacrifice of love—these form the threefold key that unlocks to us all the closed chambers of that life, and these will, in another sense, unlock any other life to the entrance of God, and present to Him an open door into all departments of one's being. George Müller had no monopoly of holy living and holy serving. He followed his Lord, both in self-surrender to the will of God and in self-sacrifice for the welfare of man, and herein lay his whole secret.

SCRIPTURE TESTIMONY

No longer I who live, but Christ who lives in me

Galatians 2:20

To one who asked him the secret of his service he said: "There was a day when I died, *utterly died;"* and, as he spoke, he bent lower and lower until he almost touched the floor—"died to George Müller, his opinions, preferences, tastes and will—died to the world, its approval or censure—died to the approval or blame even of my brethren and friends—and since then I have studied only to show myself approved unto God."

When George Müller trusted the blood for salvation, he took Abel's position; when he undertook a consecrated walk he took Enoch's; when he came into fellowship with God for his life-work he stood beside Noah; when he rested only

47 Colossians 1:24

on God's word, he was one with Abraham; and when he died to self and the world, he reached the self-surrender of Moses.

The godlike qualities of this great and good man made him none the less a man. His separation unto God implied no unnatural isolation from his fellow mortals. Like Terence, he could say: "I am a man, and nothing common to man is foreign to me." To be well known, Mr. Müller needed to be known in his daily, simple, home life. It was my privilege to meet him often, and in his own apartment at Orphan House No. 3. His room was of medium size, neatly but plainly furnished, with table and chairs, lounge and writing-desk, etc. His Bible almost always lay open, as a book to which he continually resorted.

His form was tall and slim, always neatly attired, and very erect, and his step firm and strong. His countenance, in repose, might have been thought stern, but for the smile which so habitually lit up his eyes and played over his features that it left its impress on the lines of his face. His manner was one of simple courtesy and unstudied dignity: no one would in his presence, have felt like vain trifling, and there was about him a certain indescribable air of authority and majesty that reminded one of a born prince; and yet there was mingled with all this a simplicity so childlike that even children felt themselves at home with him. In his speech, he never quite lost that peculiar foreign quality, known as accent, and he always spoke with slow and measured articulation, as though a double watch were set at the door of his lips. With him that unruly member, the tongue, was tamed by the Holy Spirit, and he had that mark of what James calls a 'perfect man, able also to bridle the whole body.'

Those who knew but little of him and saw him only in his serious moods might have thought him lacking in that peculiarly human quality, *humour.* But neither was he an ascetic nor devoid of that element of innocent appreciation of the ludicrous and that keen enjoyment of a good story which seem essential to a complete man. His habit was sobriety, but he relished a joke that was free of all taint of uncleanness and that had about it no sting for others. To those whom he best knew and loved he showed his true self, in his playful moods,—as when at Ilfracombe, climbing with his wife and others the heights that overlook the sea, he walked on a little in advance, seated himself till the rest came up with him, and then, when they were barely seated, rose and quietly said, "Well now, we have had a good rest, let us go on." This one instance may suffice to show that his sympathy with his divine Master did not lessen or hinder his complete fellow feeling with man. That must be a defective piety which puts a barrier between a saintly soul and whatsoever pertains to humanity. He who chose us out of the world sent us back into it, there to find our sphere of service; and in order to such service we must keep in close and vital touch with human beings as did our divine Lord Himself.

Service to God was with George Müller a passion. In the month of May, 1897, he was persuaded to take at Huntly a little rest from his constant daily work at the orphan houses. The evening that he arrived he said, What opportunity is there here for services for the Lord? When it was suggested to him that he had just come from continuous work, and that it was a time for rest, he replied that, being now free from his usual labours, he felt he must be occupied in some other way in serving the Lord, to glorify whom was his object in life. Meetings were accordingly arranged and he preached both at Huntly and at Teignmouth.

As we cast this last glance backward over this life of peculiar sanctity and service, one lesson seems written across it in unmistakable letters: PREVAILING PRAYER. If a consecrated human life is an *example* used by God to teach us the *philosophy* of holy living, then this man was meant to show us how *prayer, offered in simple faith, has power with God.*

SCRIPTURE TESTIMONY
The prayer of a person in right relationship with God is effective James 5:16-18

One paragraph of Scripture conspicuously presents the truth which George Müller's living epistle enforces and illustrates; it is found in James 5:16-18:

"The effectual fervent prayer of a righteous man availeth much," is the sentence which opens the paragraph. No translation has ever done it justice. Rotherham renders it: "Much avails a righteous man's supplication, working inwardly." The Revised Version translates, "avails much in its working." The difficulty of translating lies not in the *obscurity* but in the *fulness* of the meaning of the original. There is a Greek middle participle here (ἐνεργουμένη), which may indicate "either the *cause* or the *time* of the effectiveness of the prayer," and may mean, through its working, or while it is actively working. The idea is that such prayer has about it supernatural energy. Perhaps the best key to the meaning of these ten words is to interpret them in the light of the whole paragraph:

> "Elijah was a man subject to like passions as we are, and he prayed earnestly that it might not rain; and it rained not on the earth by the space of three years and six months. And he prayed again, and the heaven gave rain, and the earth brought forth her fruit."

Two things are here plainly put before us: first, that Elijah was but a man, of like nature with other men and subject to all human frailties and infirmities; and, secondly, that this man was such a power because he was a man of prayer: he prayed earnestly; literally "he prayed with prayer"; prayed habitually and importunately. No man can read Elijah's short history as given in the word of God, without seeing that he was a man like ourselves. Under the juniper-tree of doubt and despondency, he complained of his state and wished he might die. In the cave of a morbid despair, he had to be met and subdued by the vision of God and by the still, small voice. He was just like other men. It was not, therefore, because he was above human follies and frailties, but because he was subject to them, that he is held up to us as an encouraging example of power that prevails in prayer. He laid hold of the Almighty Arm because he was weak, and he kept hold because to lose hold was to let weakness prevail. Nevertheless, this man, by prayer alone, shut up heaven's floodgates for three years and a half, and then by the same key unlocked them. Yes, this man tested the meaning of those wonderful words: "concerning the work of My hands command ye Me." (Isaiah 45:11) God put the forces of nature for the time under the sway of this one man's prayer—one frail, feeble, foolish mortal locked and unlocked the springs of waters, because he held God's key.

George Müller was simply another Elijah. Like him, a man subject to all human infirmities, he had his fits of despondency and murmuring, of distrust and waywardness; but he prayed and kept praying. He denied that he was a miracle-worker, in any sense that implies elevation of character and endowment above other fellow disciples, as though he were a specially privileged saint; but in a sense he *was* a miracle-worker, if by that is meant that he wrought wonders impossible to the natural and carnal man. With God all things are possible, and so are they declared to be to him that believeth. God meant that George Müller, wherever his work was witnessed or his story is read, should be a standing rebuke, to the *practical impotence of the average disciple.* While men are asking whether prayer can accomplish similar wonders as of old, here is a man who answers the question by the indisputable logic of facts. *Powerlessness always means prayerlessness.* It is not necessary for us to be sinlessly perfect, or to be raised to a special dignity of privilege and endowment, in order to wield this wondrous weapon of power with God; but it *is* necessary that we be men and women of prayer—habitual, believing, importunate prayer.

George Müller considered nothing too small to be a subject of prayer, because nothing is too small to be the subject of God's care. If He numbers our hairs, and notes a sparrow's fall, and clothes the grass in the field, nothing about His children is beneath His tender thought. In every emergency, his one resort was to carry his want to his Father. When, in 1858, a legacy of five hundred pounds was, after fourteen months in chancery, still unpaid, the Lord was besought to cause this money soon to be placed in his hands; and he prayed that legacy out of the bonds of chancery as prayer, long before, brought Peter out of prison. The money was paid contrary to all human likelihood, and with interest at four per cent. When large gifts were proffered, prayer was offered for grace to know whether to accept or decline, that no money might be greedily grasped at for its own sake; and he prayed that, if it could not be accepted without submitting to conditions which were dishonouring to God, it might be declined so graciously, lovingly, humbly, and yet firmly, that the manner of its refusal and return might show that he was acting, not in his own behalf, but as a servant under the authority of a higher Master.

These are graver matters and might well be carried to God for guidance and help. But George Müller did not stop here. In the lesser affairs, even down to the least, he sought and received like aid. His oldest friend, Robert C. Chapman of Barnstaple, gave the writer the following simple incident:

In the early days of his love to Christ, visiting a friend, and seeing him mending a quill pen, he said: "Brother H——, do you pray to God when you mend your pen?" The answer was: "It would be well to do so, but I cannot say that I do pray when mending my pen." Brother Müller replied: "I always do, and so I mend my pen much better."

As we cast this last backward glance at this man of God, seven conspicuous qualities stand out in him, the combination of which made him what he was: Stainless uprightness, child-like simplicity, business-like precision, tenacity of purpose, boldness of faith, habitual prayer, and cheerful self-surrender. His *holy living* was a necessary condition of his *abundant serving,* as seems so beautifully hinted in the seventeenth verse of the ninetieth Psalm:

> "Let the *beauty of the Lord our God be upon us,*
> And *establish Thou the work of our hands upon us."*

How can the work of our hands be truly established by the blessing of our Lord, unless His beauty also is upon us—the beauty of His holiness transforming our lives and witnessing to His work in us?

So much for the backward look. We must not close without a forward look also. There are two remarkable sayings of our Lord which are complements to each other and should be put side by side:

> "If any man will come after Me, let him deny himself
> and take up his cross and follow Me."

> "If any man serve Me, let him follow Me; and where I am, there shall
> also my servant be. If any man serve Me, him will My Father honour."

One of these presents the cross, the other the crown; one the renunciation, the other the compensation. In both cases it is, "Let him follow Me"; but in the second of these passages the following of Christ *goes further than the cross of Calvary;* it reaches through the sepulchre to the Resurrection Life, the Forty Days' Holy Walk in the Spirit, the Ascension to the Heavenlies, the session at the Right Hand of God, the Reappearing at His Second Coming, and the fellowship of His final Reign in Glory. And two compensations are especially made prominent: first, the *Eternal Home with Christ;* and, second the *Exalted Honour from the Father.* We too often look only at the cross and the crucifixion, and so see our life in Christ only in its oneness with Him in suffering and serving; we need to look beyond and see our oneness with Him in recompense and reward, if we are to get a complete view of His promise and our prospect. Self-denial is not so much an *impoverishment* as a *postponement:* we make a sacrifice of a present good for the sake of a future and greater good. Even our Lord Himself was strengthened to endure the cross and despise the shame by the joy that was set before Him and the glory of His final victory. If there were seven steps downward in humiliation, there are seven upward in exaltation, until beneath His feet every knee shall bow in homage, and every tongue confess His universal Lordship. He that descended is the same also that ascended up far above all heavens, that He might fill all things.

George Müller counted all as loss that men count gain, but it was for the excellency of the knowledge of Jesus, his Lord. He suffered the loss of all things and counted them as dung, but it was that he might win Christ and be found in Him; that he might know Him, and not only the fellowship of His sufferings and conformity to His death, but the power of His resurrection, conformity to His life, and fellowship in His glory. He left all behind that the world values, but he reached forth and pressed forward toward the goal, for the prize of the high calling of God in Christ Jesus. "Let us, therefore, as many as be perfect, be thus minded."

When the Lord Jesus was upon earth, there was one disciple whom He loved, who also leaned on His breast, having the favoured place which only one could occupy. But now that He is in heaven, every disciple may be the loved one, and fill the favoured place, and lean on His bosom. There is no exclusive monopoly of privilege and blessing. He that follows closely and abides in Him knows the peculiar closeness of contact, the honour of intimacy, that are reserved for such as are called and chosen and faithful, and follow the Lamb whithersoever He goeth. God's self-denying servants are on their way to the final sevenfold perfection, at home with Him, and crowned with honour: "And there shall be no more curse; But the throne of God and of the Lamb shall be in it; And His servants shall serve Him; And they shall see His face; And His name shall be in their foreheads, And there shall be no night there, And they shall reign for ever and ever." Amen!

APPENDIX A

Scripture Texts that Moulded George Müller

CERTAIN MARKED Scripture precepts and promises had such a singular influence upon this man of God, and so often proved the guides to his course, that they illustrate Psalm 119:105:

> "Thy word is a lamp unto my feet,
> And a light unto my path."

Those texts which, at the parting of the way, became to him God's signboards, showing him the true direction, are here given, as nearly as may be in the order in which they became so helpful to him. The study of them will prove a kind of spiritual biography, outlining his career. Some texts, known to have been very conspicuous in their influence, we put in capitals. The italics are his own.

> "God so loved the world that He gave His only-begotten Son, that whosoever believeth in Him should not perish, but have everlasting life." (John 3:16)

> "Cursed be the man that trusteth in man and maketh flesh his arm." (Jeremiah 17:5)

> "O, fear the Lord, ye His saints; for there is no want to them that fear Him." (Psalm 34:9)

> "Owe no man anything, but to love one another." (Romans 8:8)

"Seek ye first the kingdom of God and His righteousness; and all these things shall be added unto you." (Matthew 6:33)

"The holy scriptures, which are able to make thee wise unto salvation." (2 Timothy 3:15)

"Ask, and it shall be given you; seek, and ye shall find; knock, and it shall be opened unto you: for every one that asketh receiveth; and he that seeketh findeth; and to him that knocketh it shall be opened." (Matthew 7:7, 8)

"Whatsoever ye shall ask in My name, that will I do, that the Father may be glorified in the Son: if ye shall ask anything in My name I will do it." (John 14:13, 14)

"Therefore I say unto you, Take no thought for your life, what ye shall eat, and what ye shall drink, nor yet for your body what ye shall put on.... Take, therefore, no thought for the morrow." (Matthew 6:25-34)

"If any man will do His will, he shall know of the doctrine." (John 7:17)

"If ye continue in My word, then are ye My disciples indeed; and ye shall know the truth, and the truth shall make you free." (John 8:31, 32)

"And the eunuch said, See, here is water: what doth hinder me to be baptized? And Philip said, If thou believest with all thine heart, thou mayest. And he answered and said, I believe that Jesus Christ is the Son of Gad. And they went down both into the water, both Philip and the eunuch, and he baptized him." (Acts 8:36-38)

"Know ye not that so many of us as were baptized into Jesus Christ were baptized into His death? Therefore we are buried with Him by baptism into death." (Romans 6:3, 4)

"Upon the first day of the week, when the disciples came together to break bread." (Acts 20:7)

"My brethren, have not the faith of our Lord Jesus Christ, the Lord of glory, with respect of persons. For if there come unto your assembly a man with a gold ring, in goodly apparel, and there come in also a man in vile raiment; and ye have respect unto him that weareth the gay clothing, and say unto him, Sit thou here in a good place; and say to the poor, Stand thou there, or sit here under my footstool, are ye not then partial in yourselves, and are become judges of evil thoughts?" (James 2:1-6)

"Having, then, gifts differing according to the grace that is given us." (Romans 7:6)

"All these worketh that one and the selfsame Spirit, dividing to every man severally as he will." (1 Corinthians 7:11)

"Not because I desire a gift, but I desire fruit that may abound to your account." (Philippians, 4:17)

"Take no thought for your life, what ye shall eat, or what ye shall drink; nor yet for your body what ye shall put on.".... "Behold the fowls of the air.... Consider the lilies of the field.... For your heavenly Father knoweth that ye have need of these things."
(Matthew 6:25-32)

"Lay not up for yourselves treasures upon earth." (Matthew 6:19)

"Sell that ye have and give alms." (Luke 12:33)

"A man can receive nothing except it be given him from heaven." (John 3:27)

"Simeon hath declared how God at the first did visit the Gentiles, to take out of them a people for His name."
(Acts 15:14. Compare Matthew 13:24-30, 36-43)

"This know also, that in the last days perilous times shall come.... Evil men and seducers shall wax worse and worse, deceiving and being deceived." (2 Timothy 3:1, 13)

"Come out from among them, and be ye separate, saith the Lord, and touch not the unclean thing." (2 Corinthians 6:14-18)

"Not by might, nor by power, but by My spirit, saith the Lord of hosts." (Zechariah 4:6)

"My grace is sufficient for thee." (2 Corinthians 12:9)

"Let every man abide in the same calling wherein he was called. Let every man, wherein he is called, therein abide with God." (1 Corinthians 7:20, 24)

"All scripture is given by inspiration of God, and is profitable for doctrine, for reproof, for correction, for instruction in righteousness." (2 Timothy 3:16)

"Open thy mouth wide, and I will fill it." (Psalm 81:10)

"Mine hour is not yet come." (John 2:4)

"He took a child, and set him in the midst of them; and when He had taken him in His arms, He said unto them, Whosoever shall receive one of such children in My name, receiveth Me; and whosoever shall receive Me, receiveth not Me, but Him that sent Me." (Mark 9:36, 37)

"If it be possible, as much as lieth in you, live peaceably with all men." (Romans 12:18)

"For they verily for a few days chastened us after their own pleasure; but He for our profit, that we might be partakers of His holiness. Now no chastening for the present seemeth to be joyous, but grievous; nevertheless, afterward it yieldeth the peaceable fruit of righteousness unto them which are exercised thereby." (Hebrews 12:10, 11)

"What things soever ye desire, when ye pray, believe that ye receive them, and ye shall have them." (Mark 11:24)

"He that believeth on Him shall not be confounded." (1 Peter 2:6)

"O Thou that hearest prayer, unto Thee shall all flesh come." (Psalm 65:2)

"Come and hear, all ye that fear God, and I will declare what He hath done for my soul." (Psalm 66:16)

"A Father of the fatherless." (Psalm 68:5)

"My son, despise not thou the chastening of the Lord; neither be weary of His correction." (Proverbs 3:11)

"Like as a father pitieth his children, so the Lord pitieth them that fear Him." (Psalm 103:13)

"Jesus Christ the same yesterday, and to-day, and for ever." (Heb. 13:8)

"To-morrow shall take thought for the things of itself."

"Sufficient unto the day is the evil thereof." (Matthew 6:34)

"Hitherto hath the Lord helped us." (1 Samuel 7:12)

"Oh taste and see that the Lord is good:"
"Blessed is the man that trusteth in Him!" (Psalm 34:8)

"All the fat is the Lord's." (Leviticus 3:16)

"I am poor and needy; yet the Lord thinketh upon me." (Psalm 40:17)

"Delight thyself also in the Lord, and He shall give thee the desires of thine heart." (Psalm 37:4)

"If I regard iniquity in my heart, the Lord will not hear me." (Psalm 66:18)

"Know that the Lord hath set apart him that is godly for Himself: The Lord will hear when I call unto Him." (Psalm 4:3)

"Jehovah jireh." (The Lord will provide.) (Genesis 22:14)

"He hath said, I will never leave thee, nor forsake thee; so that we may boldly say, The Lord is my helper." (Hebrews 13:5, 6)

"Be thou not one of them that strike hands, or of them that are sureties for debts." (Proverbs 22:26)

"He that hateth suretyship is sure." (Proverbs 11:15)

"I will very gladly spend and be spent for you; though the more abundantly I love you, the less I be loved." (2 Corinthians 12:15)

"Ye are all children of God by faith in Christ Jesus." (Galatians 3:26)

"Casting all your care upon Him for He careth for you." (1 Peter 5:7)

"Be careful for nothing, but in everything by prayer and supplication with thanksgiving let your requests be made known unto God." (Philippians 4:6)

"Said I not unto thee, that, if thou wouldest believe, thou shouldest see the glory of God?" (John 11:40)

"We know that all things work together for good to them that love God." (Romans 8:28)

"Shall not the judge of all the earth do right?" (Genesis 18:25)

"Of such (little children) is the kingdom of heaven." (Matthew 19:14)

"He that spared not His own Son, but delivered Him up for us all, how shall He not with Him also freely give us all things?" (Romans 8:32)

"Every good gift and every perfect gift is from above." (James 1:17)

"The young lions do lack and suffer hunger; but they that seek the Lord shall not want any good thing." (Psalm 34:10)

"There is that scattereth and yet increaseth; and there is that withholdeth more than is meet, but it tendeth to poverty. The liberal soul shall be made fat, and he that watereth shall be watered also himself." (Proverbs 11:24, 25)

"Give and it shall be given unto you: good measure, pressed down and shaken together, and running over, shall men give unto your bosom. For with the same measure that ye mete withal it shall be measured to you again." (Luke 6:38)

"The liberal deviseth liberal things; and by liberal things shall he stand." (Isaiah 32:8)

"For ye have the poor with you always, and whensoever ye will ye may do them good. (Mark 14:7)

"Let not then your good be evil spoken of." (Romans 14:16)

"Let your moderation (yieldingness) be known unto all men." (Philippians 4:5)

"My brethren, count it all joy when ye fall into divers temptations (*i.e.* trials); knowing this, that the trying of your faith worketh patience. But let patience have her perfect work, that ye may be perfect and entire, wanting nothing." (James 1:2-4)

"TRUST IN THE LORD WITH ALL THINE HEART; AND LEAN NOT UNTO THINE OWN UNDERSTANDING. IN ALL THY WAYS ACKNOWLEDGE HIM, AND HE SHALL DIRECT THY PATHS." (PROVERBS 3:5, 6)

"The integrity of the upright shall guide them; but the perverseness of transgressors shall destroy them." (Proverbs 11:3)

"Commit thy works unto the Lord and thy thoughts shall be established." (Proverbs 16:3)

"For I say through the grace given unto me, to every man that is among you, not to think of himself more highly than he ought to think; but to think soberly, according as God has dealt to every man the measure of faith." (Romans 12:3)

"Wait on the Lord; be of good courage, and he shall strengthen thine heart: Wait, I say, on the Lord." (Psalm 27:14)

"After he had patiently endured he obtained the promise." (Hebrews 6:15)

"Verily, verily, I say unto you, whatsoever ye shall ask the Father in My name, He will give it you." (John 16:23)

"He which soweth sparingly shall reap also sparingly; and he which soweth bountifully shall reap also bountifully." (2 Corinthians 9:6)

"Ye are bought with a price: therefore, glorify God in your body, and in your spirit, which are God's." (1 Corinthians 6:20)

"They that know Thy name will put their trust in Thee: for Thou, Lord, hast not forsaken them that trust Thee." (Psalm 9:10)

"Thou wilt keep him in perfect peace whose mind is stayed on Thee, because he trusteth in Thee. Trust ye in the Lord forever; for in the Lord Jehovah is everlasting strength." (Isaiah 26:3, 4)

"If there be first a willing mind it is accepted according to that a man hath and not according to that he hath not." (2 Corinthians 8:12)

"Be ye steadfast, unmovable, always abounding in the work of the Lord, forasmuch as ye know that your labour is not in vain in the Lord." (1 Corinthians 15:58)

"Let us not be weary in well doing, for *in due season* we shall reap if we faint not." (Galatians 6:9)

"Oh how great is Thy goodness, which Thou hast laid up for them that fear Thee; which Thou 'hast wrought for them that trust in Thee before the sons of men!" (Psalm 31:19)

"Thou art good and doest good." (Psalm 119:68)

"I KNOW, O LORD, THAT THY JUDGMENTS ARE RIGHT, AND THAT THOU IN FAITHFULNESS HAST AFFLICTED ME. (PSALM 119:75)

"My times are in Thy hand." (Psalm 31:15)

"The LORD God is a sun and shield: the LORD will give grace and glory: no good thing will He withhold from them that walk uprightly." (Psalm 84:11)

"Hold Thou me up and I shall be safe." (Psalm 119:117)

"Behold I come quickly, and My reward is with Me, to give every man according as his work shall be." (Revelation 22:12)

"It is more blessed to give than to receive." (Acts 20:35)

"Give us *this day* our *daily* bread." (Matthew 6:11)

"Able to do exceeding abundantly above all we ask or think." (Ephesians 3:20)

"Them that honour Me I will honour." (1 Samuel 2:30)

"That the trial of your faith, being much more precious than of gold that perisheth, though it be tried with fire, might be found unto praise and honour and glory at the appearing of Jesus Christ." (1 Peter 1:7)

APPENDIX B

Apprehension of Truth

Some points which God began to show Mr. Müller while at Teignmouth in 1829:

1. That the word of God alone is our standard of judgment in spiritual things; that it can be explained only by the Holy Spirit; and that in our day, as well as in former times, He is the teacher of His people. The office of the Holy Spirit I had not experimentally understood before that time. Indeed, of the office of each of the blessed persons, in what is commonly called the Trinity, I had no experimental apprehension. I had not before seen from the Scriptures that the Father chose us before the foundation of the world; that in Him that wonderful plan of our redemption originated, and that He also appointed all the means by which it was to be brought about. Further, that the Son, to save us, had fulfilled the law, to satisfy its demands, and with it also the holiness of God; that He had borne the punishment due to our sins, and had thus satisfied the justice of God. And further, that the Holy Spirit alone can teach us about our state by nature, show us the need of a Saviour, enable us to believe in Christ, explain to us the Scriptures, help us in preaching, etc. It was my beginning to understand this latter point in particular, which had a great effect on me; for the Lord enabled me to put it to the test of experience, by laying aside commentaries, and almost every other book, and simply reading the word of God and studying it. The result of this was, that the first evening that I shut myself into my room, to give myself to prayer and meditation over the Scriptures, I learned

more in a few hours than I had done during a period of several months previously. *But the particular difference was that I received real strength for my soul in doing so.* I now began to try by the test of the Scriptures the things which I had learned and seen, and found that only those principles which stood the test were really of value.

2. Before this period I had been much opposed to the doctrines of election, particular redemption, and final persevering grace: so much so that, a few days after my arrival at Teignmouth I called election a devilish doctrine. I did not believe that I had brought myself to the Lord, for that was too manifestly false; but yet I held, that I might have resisted finally. And further, I knew nothing about the choice of God's people, and did not believe that the child of God, when once made so; was safe for ever. In my fleshly mind I had repeatedly said, If once I could prove that I am a child of God for ever, I might go back into the world for a year or two, and then return to the Lord, and at last be saved. But now I was brought to examine these precious truths by the word of God. Being made willing to have no glory of my own in the conversion of sinners, but to consider myself merely as an instrument; and being made willing to receive what the Scriptures said; I went to the Word, reading the New Testament from the beginning, with a particular reference to these truths. To my great astonishment I found that the passages which speak decidedly for election and persevering grace were about four times as many as those which speak apparently against these truths; and even those few, shortly after, when I had examined and understood them, served to confirm me in the above doctrines. As to the effect which my belief in these doctrines had on me, I am constrained to state, for God's glory, that though I am still exceedingly weak, and by no means so dead to the lusts of the flesh, and the lust of the eyes, and the pride of life, as I might and as I ought to be, yet, by the grace of God, I have walked more closely with Him since that period. My life has not been so variable, and I may say that I have lived much more for God than before. And for this have I been strengthened by the Lord, in a great measure, through the instrumentality of these truths. For in the time of temptation, I have been repeatedly led to say: Should I thus sin? I should only bring misery into my soul for a time, and dishonour God; for, being a son of God for ever, I should have to be brought back again, though it might be in the way of severe chastisement. Thus, I say, the electing love of God in Christ (when I have been able to realize it) has often been, the means of *producing holiness, instead of leading me into sin.* It is only the notional apprehension of such truths, the want of having them in the heart, whilst they are in the head, which is dangerous.

3. Another truth, into which, in a measure, I was led, respected the Lord's coming. My views concerning this point, up to that time, had been completely vague and unscriptural. I had believed what others told me, without trying it by the Word. I thought that things were getting better and better, and that soon the whole world would be converted. But now I found in the Word that we have not the least Scriptural warrant to look for the conversion of the world before the return of our Lord. I found in the Scriptures that which will usher in the glory of the church, and uninterrupted joy to the saints, is the return of the Lord Jesus, and that, till then, things will be more or less in confusion. I found in the Word, that the return of Jesus, and not death, was the hope of the apostolic Christians; and that it became me, therefore, to look for His appearing. And this truth entered so into my heart that, though I went into Devonshire exceedingly weak, scarcely expecting that I should return again to London, yet I was immediately, on seeing this truth, brought off from looking for death, and was made to look for the return of the Lord. Having seen this truth, the Lord also graciously enabled me to apply it, in some measure at least, to my own heart, and to put the solemn question to myself—What may I do for the Lord, before He returns, as He may soon come?
4. In addition to these truths, it pleased the Lord to lead me to see a higher standard of devotedness than I had seen before. He led me, in a measure, to see what is my true glory in this world, even to be despised, and to be poor and mean with Christ. I saw then, in a measure, though I have seen it more fully since, that it ill becomes the servant to seek to be rich, and great, and honoured in that world where his Lord was poor, and mean, and despised.

APPENDIX C

Separation from the London Society for Promoting Christianity Among the Jews

It became a point of solemn consideration with me, whether I could remain connected with the Society in the usual way. My chief objections were these:

1. If I were sent out by the Society, it was more than probable, yea, almost needful, if I were to leave England, that I should labour on the Continent, as I was unfit to be sent to eastern countries on account of my health, which would probably have suffered, both on account of the climate, and of my having to learn other languages. Now, if I *did* go to the Continent, it was evident that without ordination I could not have any extensive field of usefulness, as unordained ministers are generally prevented from labouring freely there; but I could not conscientiously submit to be ordained by unconverted men, professing to have power to set me apart for the ministry, or to communicate something to me for this work which they do not possess themselves. Besides this, I had other objections to being connected with *any* state church or national religious establishment, which arose from the increased light which I had obtained through the reception of this truth, that *the word of God is our only standard, and the Holy Spirit our only teacher.* For as I now began to compare what I knew of the establishment in England and those on the Continent with this only true standard, the word of God, I found that all establishments, even because they are establishments, i.e., the world and the church mixed up together, not only contain in them the principles which necessarily must lead to departure from the word of God; but also, as long as they remain establishments, entirely preclude

the acting throughout according to the Holy Scriptures.—Then again, if I were to stay in England, the Society would not allow me to preach in any place indiscriminately, where the Lord might open a door for me; and to the ordination of English bishops I had still greater objections than to the ordination of a Prussian Consistory.

2. I further had a conscientious objection against being led and directed by *men* in my missionary labours. As a servant of Christ, it appeared to me I ought to be guided by the Spirit, and not by men, as to time and place; and this I would say, with all deference to others, who may be much more taught and much more spiritually minded than myself. A servant of Christ has but one Master.
3. I had love for the Jews, and I had been enabled to give proofs of it; yet I could not conscientiously say, as the committee would expect from me, that I would spend the greater part of my time only among them. For the scriptural plan seemed to me that, in coming to a place, I should seek out the Jews, and commence my labour particularly among them; but that, if they rejected the gospel, I should go to the nominal Christians.—The more I weighed these points, the more it appeared to me that I should be acting hypocritically, were I to suffer them to remain in my mind, without making them known to the committee.

APPENDIX D

The Scriptural Knowledge Institution for Home and Abroad

I. The Principles of the Institution.

1. We consider every believer bound, in one way or other, to help the cause of Christ, and we have scriptural warrant for expecting the Lord's blessing upon our work of faith and labour of love: and although, according to Matthew 13:24-43, 2 Timothy 3:1-13, and many other passages, the world will not be converted before the coming of our Lord Jesus, still, while He tarries, all scriptural means ought to be employed for the ingathering of the elect of God.
2. The Lord helping us, we do not mean to seek the patronage of the world; i.e., we never intend to ask *unconverted* persons of rank or wealth to countenance this Institution, because this, we consider, would be dishonourable to the Lord. In the name of our God we set up our banners, Psalm 20:5; He alone shall be our Patron, and if He helps us we shall prosper, and if He is not on our side, we shall not succeed.
3. We do not mean to *ask* unbelievers for money (2 Corinthians 6:14-18); though we do not feel ourselves warranted to refuse their contributions, if they, of their own accord should offer them. (Acts 28:2-10)
4. We reject altogether the help of unbelievers in managing or carrying on the affairs of the Institution. (2 Corinthians 6:14-18)
5. We intend never to enlarge the field of labour by contracting debts (Romans 13:8), and afterwards appealing to the Church of God for help, because this we consider to be opposed both to the letter and the spirit of the New Testament; but in secret prayer, God helping us, we shall

carry the wants of the Institution to the Lord, and act according to the means that God shall give.

6. We do not mean to reckon the success of the Institution by the amount of money given, or the number of Bibles distributed, etc., but by the Lord's blessing upon the work (Zechariah 4:6); and we expect this, in the proportion in which He shall help us to wait upon Him in prayer.
7. While we would avoid aiming after needless singularity, we desire to go on simply according to Scripture, without compromising the truth; at the same time thankfully receiving any instruction which experienced believers, after prayer, upon scriptural ground, may have to give us concerning the Institution.

II. The Objects of the Institution Are:

1. To *assist* day-schools, Sunday-schools, and adult-schools, in which instruction is given upon *scriptural principles,* and, as far as the Lord may give the means, and supply us with suitable teachers, and in other respects make our path plain, to establish schools of this kind.

   a. By day-schools upon scriptural principles, we understand day-schools in which the teachers are godly persons,—in which the way of salvation is scripturally pointed out,—and in which no instruction is given opposed to the principles of the gospel.
   b. Sunday-schools, in which all the teachers are believers, and in which the Holy Scriptures alone are the foundation of instruction, are such only as the Institution assists with the supply of Bibles, Testaments, etc.; for we consider it unscriptural that any persons who do not profess to know the Lord themselves should be allowed to give religious instruction.
   c. The Institution does not assist any adult-schools with the supply of Bibles, Testaments, spelling-books, etc., except the teachers are believers.

2. To circulate the Holy Scriptures.

   We sell Bibles and Testaments to poor persons at a reduced price. But while we, in general, think it better that the Scriptures should be *sold,* and not given altogether gratis, still, in cases of extreme poverty, we think it right to give, without payment, a cheap edition.

3. The third object of this Institution is to aid missionary efforts.

We desire to assist those missionaries whose proceedings appear to be most according to the Scriptures.

It is proposed to give such a portion of the amount of the donations to each of the fore-mentioned objects as the Lord may direct; but if none of the objects should claim a more particular assistance, to lay out an equal portion upon each; yet so that if any donor desires to give for one of the objects exclusively the money shall be appropriated accordingly.

APPENDIX E

Reasons Which Led Mr. Müller to Establish an Orphan House

I HAD CONSTANTLY cases brought before me which proved that one of the especial things which the children of God needed in our day was *to have their faith strengthened.* For instance: I might visit a brother who worked fourteen or even sixteen hours a day at his trade, the necessary result of which was that not only his body suffered, but his soul was lean, and he had no enjoyment in the things of God. Under such circumstances I might point out to him that he ought to work less, in order that his bodily health might not suffer, and that he might gather strength for his inner man by reading the word of God, by meditation over it, and by prayer. The reply, however, I generally found to be something like this: "But if I work less, I do not earn enough for the support of my family. Even now, whilst I work so much, I have scarcely enough. The wages are so low, that I must work hard in order to obtain what I need." There was no trust in God. No real belief in the truth of that word: "Seek ye first the kingdom of God, and His righteousness: and all these things shall be added unto you." I might reply something like this: "My dear brother, it is not your work which supports your family, but the Lord; and He who has fed you and your family when you could not work at all, on account of illness, would surely provide for you and yours if, for the sake of obtaining food for your inner man, you were to work only for so many hours a day as would allow you proper time for retirement. And is it not the case now, that you begin the work of the day after having had only a few hurried moments for prayer; and when you leave off your work in the evening, and mean then to read a little of the word of God, are you not too much worn out in body and mind to enjoy it, and do you not often fall asleep whilst reading the Scriptures, or whilst on your knees in prayer?" The brother would allow it was so; he would allow that my advice was good; but still I read in his countenance, even if he should not have actually said so, "How should I get on if I were to *carry out* your advice?" I longed, therefore, to have something to point the brother to, as a visible proof that our God and Father is the same faithful God as ever He was; as willing as ever to PROVE Himself to be the LIVING GOD, in our day as formerly, *to all who put their trust in Him.*—Again, sometimes I found children of God tried in mind by the prospect of old age, when they might be unable to work any longer, and therefore were harassed by the fear of having to go into the poor-house. If in such a case I pointed out to them how their Heavenly Father has always helped those who put their trust in Him, they might not, perhaps, always say that times have changed; but yet it was evident enough that God was not looked upon by them as the LIVING God. My spirit was ofttimes bowed down by this, and I longed to set something before the children of God whereby they might see that He does not forsake, even in our day, those who rely upon Him.—Another class of persons were brethren in business, who suffered in their souls, and brought guilt on their consciences, by carrying on their business almost in the same way as unconverted persons do. The competition in trade, the bad times, the over-peopled country, were given as reasons why, if the business were carried on simply according to the word of God it could not be expected to do well. Such a brother, perhaps, would express the wish that he might be differently situated; but very rarely did I see *that there was a stand made for God, that there was the holy determination to trust in the living God, and to depend on Him, in order that a good conscience might be maintained.* To this class likewise I desired to show, by a visible proof, that God is unchangeably the same.—Then there was another class of persons, individuals who were in professions in which they could not continue with a good conscience, or persons who were in an unscriptural position with reference to spiritual things; but both classes feared, on account of the consequences, to give up the profession in which they could not abide with God, or to leave their position, lest they should be thrown out of employment. My spirit longed to be instrumental in strengthening their faith by giving them not only instances from the word of God of His willingness and ability to help all those who rely upon Him, but *to show them by proofs* that He is the same in our day. I well knew *that the word of God ought to be enough,* and it was, by grace, enough to me; but still, I considered that I ought to lend a helping hand to my brethren, if by any means, by this visible proof to the unchangeable faithfulness of the Lord I might strengthen their hands in God; for I remembered what a great blessing my own soul had received through the Lord's dealings with His servant, A. H. Francké, who, in dependence upon the living God alone, established an immense orphan house, which I had seen many times with my own eyes. I, therefore, judged myself bound to be the servant of the Church of God, in the particular point on which I had obtained mercy: namely, *in being able to take God by His word and to rely upon it.* All these exercises of my soul, which resulted from the fact that so many believers, with whom I became acquainted, were harassed and distressed in mind, or brought guilt on their consciences, on account of not trusting in the Lord, were used by God to awaken in my heart the desire of setting before the church at large, and before the world, a proof that He has not in the least changed; and this seemed to me best done by the establishing of an orphan house. It needed to be something which could be seen, even by the natural eye. Now if I, a poor man, simply by prayer and faith, obtained, *without asking any individual,* the means for establishing and carrying on an orphan house, there would be something which, with the Lord's blessing, might be instrumental in strengthening the faith of the children of God, besides being a testimony to the consciences of the unconverted of the reality of the things of God. This, then, was the primary reason for establishing the orphan house. I certainly did from my heart desire to be used by God to benefit the bodies of poor children bereaved of both parents, and seek, in other respects, with the help of God, to do them good for this life;—I also particularly longed to be used by God in getting the dear orphans trained up in the fear of God;—but still, the first and primary object of the work was (and still is) that God might be magnified by the fact that the orphans under my care are provided with all they need only *by prayer and faith,* without any one being asked by me or my fellow labourers, whereby it may be seen that God is FAITHFUL STILL, and HEARS PRAYER STILL.

The three chief reasons for establishing an orphan house are: 1. That God may be glorified, should He be pleased to furnish me with the means, in its being seen that it is not a vain thing to trust in Him; and that thus the faith of His children may be strengthened. 2. The spiritual welfare of fatherless and motherless children. 3. Their temporal welfare.

That to which my mind has been particularly directed is to establish an orphan house in which destitute fatherless and motherless children may be provided with food and raiment, and scriptural education. Concerning this intended orphan house I would say:

1. It is intended to be in connection with the Scriptural Knowledge Institution for Home and Abroad, in so far as it respects the reports, accounts, superintendence, and the principles on which it is conducted, so that, in one sense, it may be considered as a new object of the Institution, yet with this difference, *that only those funds shall be applied to the orphan house which are expressly given for it.* If, therefore, any believer should prefer to support either those objects which have been hitherto assisted by the funds of this Institution, or the intended orphan house, it need only be mentioned, in order that the money may be applied accordingly.
2. It will only be established if the Lord should provide both the means for it and suitable persons to conduct it.

As to the means, I would make the following remarks: The reason for proposing to enlarge the field is not because we have of late particularly abounded in means; for we have been rather straitened. The many gracious answers, however, which the Lord had given us concerning this Institution led brother C——r and me to give ourselves to prayer, asking Him to supply us with the means to carry on the work, as we consider it unscriptural to contract debts. During five days, we prayed several times, both unitedly and separately. After that time, the Lord began to answer our prayers, so that, within a few days, about 50*l.* was given to us. I would further say that the very gracious and tender dealings of God with me, in having supplied, in answer to prayer, for the last five years, my own temporal wants without any certain income, so that money, provisions, and clothes have been sent to me at times when I was greatly straitened, and that not only in small but large quantities; and not merely from individuals living in the same place with me, but at a considerable distance; and that not merely from intimate friends, but from individuals whom I have never seen: all this, I say, has often led me to think, even as long as four years ago, that the Lord had not given me this simple reliance on Him merely for myself, but also for others. Often, when I saw poor neglected children running about the streets at Teignmouth, I said to myself: "May it not be the will of God that I should establish schools for these children, asking Him to give me the means?" However, it remained only a thought in my mind for two or three years. About two years and six months since I was particularly stirred up afresh to do something for destitute children, by seeing so many of them begging in the streets of Bristol, and coming to our door. It was not, then, left undone on account of want of trust in the Lord, but through an abundance of other things calling for all the time and strength of my brother Craik and myself; for the Lord had both given faith, and had also shown by the following instance, in addition to very many others, both what He can and what He will do. One morning, whilst sitting in my room, I thought about the distress of certain brethren, and said thus to myself: "Oh, that it might please the Lord to give me the means to help these poor brethren!" About an hour afterwards I had 60 pounds sent as a present for myself from a brother whom up to this day I have never seen, and who was then, and is still, residing several thousand miles from this. Should not such an experience, together with promises like that one in John 14:13, 14, encourage us to ask with all boldness, for ourselves and others, both temporal and spiritual blessings? The Lord, for I cannot but think it was He, again and again brought the thought about these poor children to my mind, till at last it ended in the establishment of "The Scriptural Knowledge Institution, for Home and Abroad"; since the establishment of which, I have had it in a similar way brought to my mind, first about fourteen months ago, and repeatedly since, but especially during these last weeks, to establish an orphan house. My frequent prayer of late has been, that if it be of God, He would let it come to pass; if not, that He would take from me all thoughts about it. The latter has not been the case, but I have been led more and more to think that the matter may be of Him. Now, if so, He can influence His people *in any part of the world* (for I do not look to Bristol, nor even to England, but to the living God, whose is the gold and the silver), to intrust me and brother C——r, whom the Lord has made willing to help me in this work with the means. Till we have *them,* we can do nothing in the way of renting a house, furnishing it, etc. Yet, when once as much as is needed for this has been sent us, as also proper persons to engage in the work, we do not think it needful to wait till we have the orphan house endowed, or a number of yearly subscribers for it; but we trust to be enabled by the Lord, who has taught us to ask for our *daily* bread, to look to Him for the supply of the *daily* wants of those children whom He may be pleased to put under our care. Any donations will be received at my house. Should any believers have tables, chairs, bedsteads, bedding, earthenware, or any kind of household furniture to spare, for the furnishing of the house; or remnants, or pieces of calico, linen, flannel, cloth, or any materials useful for wearing apparel; or clothes already worn, they will be thankfully received.

Respecting the persons who are needed for carrying on the work, a matter of no less importance than the procuring of funds, I would observe that we look for them to God Himself, as well as for the funds; and that all who may be engaged as masters, matrons, and assistants, according to the smallness or largeness of the Institution, must be known to us as true believers; and moreover, as far as we may be able to judge, must likewise be qualified for the work.

3. At present nothing can be said as to the time when the operations are likely to commence; nor whether the Institution will embrace children of both sexes, or be restricted either to boys or girls exclusively; nor of what age they will be received, and how long they may continue in it; for though we have thought about these things, yet we would rather be guided in these particulars by the amount of the means which the Lord may put into our hands, and by the number of the individuals whom He may provide for conducting the Institution. Should the Lord condescend to use us as instruments, a short printed statement will be issued as soon as something more definite can be said.
4. It has appeared well to us to receive only such destitute children as have been bereaved of both parents.

5. The children are intended, if girls, to be brought up for service; if boys, for a trade; and therefore they will be employed, according to their ability and bodily strength, in useful occupations, and thus help to maintain themselves; besides this, they are intended to receive a plain education; but the chief and the special end of the Institution will be to seek, with God's blessing, to bring them to the knowledge of Jesus Christ by instructing them in the Scriptures.

Further Account Respecting The Orphan House, Etc.

When, of late, the thoughts of establishing an orphan house, in dependence upon the Lord, revived in my mind, during the first two weeks I only prayed that if it were of the Lord He would bring it about; but if not, that He graciously would be pleased to take all thoughts about it out of my mind. My uncertainty about knowing the Lord's mind did not arise from questioning whether it would be pleasing in His sight that there should be an abode and scriptural education provided for destitute fatherless and motherless children; but whether it were His will that *I* should be the instrument of setting such an object on foot, as my hands were already more than filled. My comfort, however, was, that, if it were His will, He would provide not merely the means, but also suitable individuals to take care of the children, so that my part of the work would take only such a portion of my time as, considering the importance of the matter, I might give, notwithstanding my many other engagements. The whole of those two weeks I never asked the Lord for money or for persons to engage in the work. On December 5th, however, the subject of my prayer all at once became different. I was reading Psalm 81, and was particularly struck, more than at any time before, with verse 10: *"Open thy mouth wide and I will fill it."* I thought a few moments about these words, and then was led to apply them to the case of the orphan house. It struck me that I had never asked the Lord for anything concerning it, except to know His will respecting its being established or not; and I then fell on my knees, and opened my mouth wide, asking him for much. I asked in submission to His will, and without fixing a time when He should answer my petition. I prayed that He would give me a house, i.e., either as a loan, or that some one might be led to pay the rent for one, or that one might be given permanently for this object; further, I asked Him for 1000 pounds; and likewise for suitable individuals to take care of the children. Besides this, I have been since led to ask the Lord to put into the hearts of His people to send me articles of furniture for the house, and some clothes for the children. When I was asking the petition I was fully aware what I was doing, i.e., that I was asking for something which I had no natural prospect of obtaining from the brethren whom I know, but which was not too much for the Lord to grant.

APPENDIX F

Arguments in Prayer for the Orphan Work

The Arguments Which I Plead With God Are:

1. That I set about the work for the glory of God, i.e., that there might be a visible proof, by God supplying, *in answer to prayer only,* the necessities of the orphans, that He is the *living* God, and most willing, even in *our* day, to answer prayer: and that, therefore, He would be pleased to send supplies.
2. That God is the "Father of the fatherless," and that He, therefore, as their Father, would be pleased to provide. (Psalm 68:5)
3. That I have received the children in the name of Jesus, and that, therefore, He, in these children, has been received, and is fed, and is clothed; and that, therefore, He would be pleased to consider this. (Mark 9:36, 37)
4. That the faith of many of the children of God has been strengthened by this work hitherto, and that, if God were to withhold the means for the future, those who are weak in faith would be staggered; whilst, by a continuance of means, their faith might still further be strengthened.
5. That many enemies would laugh, were the Lord to withhold supplies, and say, did we not foretell that this enthusiasm would come to nothing?
6. That many of the children of God, who are uninstructed, or in a carnal state, would feel themselves justified to continue their alliance with the world in the work of God, and to go on as heretofore, in their unscriptural proceedings respecting similar institutions, so far as the obtaining of means is concerned, if He were not to help me.

7. That the Lord would remember that I am His child, and that He would graciously pity me, and remember that *I* cannot provide for these children, and that therefore He would not allow this burden to lie upon me long without sending help.
8. That He would remember likewise my fellow labourers in the work, who trust in Him, but who would be tried were He to withhold supplies.
9. That He would remember that I should have to dismiss the children from under our scriptural instruction to their former companions.
10. That He would show that those were mistaken who said that, *at the first,* supplies might be expected, while the thing was new, but not afterwards.
11. That I should not know were He to withhold means, what construction I should put upon all the many most remarkable answers to prayer which He has given me heretofore in connection with this work, and which most fully have shown to me that it is of God.

APPENDIX G

The Purchase of a Site, Etc.

SCRIPTURE TESTIMONY
God using circumstances and timing to communicate
Acts 11:11
God communicating in a dream
Matthew 1:20 · Matthew 27:19 · Acts 2:17

MR. BENJAMIN PERRY gives an account of the circumstances under which the land was purchased, prior to the erection of the orphan houses on Ashley Down, as he heard it from Mr. Müller's own mouth, showing how directly the Lord worked on the mind of the owner. Mr. Müller had been making inquiries respecting the purchase of land much nearer Bristol, the prices asked being not less than 1000 pounds per acre, when he heard that the land upon which the Orphan Houses Nos. 1 and 2 stand was for sale, the price being 200 pounds per acre. He therefore called at the house of the owner, and was informed that he was not at home, but that he could be seen at his place of business in the city. Mr. Müller went there, and was informed that he had left a few minutes before, and that he would find him at home. Most men would have gone off to the owner's house at once; but Mr. Müller stopped and reflected, "Peradventure the Lord, having allowed me to miss the owner twice in so short a time, has a purpose that I should not see him to-day; and lest I should be going before the Lord in the matter, I will wait till the morning." And accordingly he waited and went the next morning, when he found the owner at home; and on being ushered into his sitting-room, he said: "Ah, Mr. Müller, I know what you have come to see me about. You want to buy my land on Ashley Down. I had a dream last night, and I saw you come in to purchase the land, for which I have been asking 200 pounds per acre; but the Lord told me not to charge you more than 120 pounds per acre, and therefore if you are willing to buy at that price the matter is settled." And within ten minutes the contract was signed. "Thus," Mr. Müller pointed out, "by being careful to *follow* the Lord, instead of *going before* His leading, I was permitted to purchase the land for 80 pounds per acre less than I should have paid if I had gone to the owner the evening before."

APPENDIX H

God's Faithfulness in Providing

Mr. Perry writes: At one meeting at Huntly, by special request Mr. Müller gave illustrations of God's faithfulness in answer to prayer, connected with the orphan work, of which the following are examples:

SCRIPTURE TESTIMONY
God will provide for our daily needs Matthew 6:11 *God using an inner voice to communicate* Acts 10:19-20 · Acts 11:12

a. He stated that at various times, not only at the beginning of the work, but also in later years, God had seen fit to try his faith to the utmost, but only to prove to him the more definitely that He would never be other than his faithful covenant-keeping God. In illustration he referred to a time when, the children having had their last meal for the day, there was nothing left in money or kind for their breakfast the following morning. Mr. Müller went home, but nothing came in, and he retired for the night, committing the need to God to provide. Early the next morning he went for a walk, and while praying for the needed help he took a turn into a road which he was quite unconscious of, and after walking a short distance a friend met him, and said how glad he was to meet him, and asked him to accept 5 pounds for the orphans. He thanked him, and without saying a word to the donor about the time of need, he went at once to the orphan houses, praising God for this direct answer to prayer.

b. On another occasion, when there were no funds in hand to provide breakfast for the orphans, a gentleman called before the time for breakfast and left a donation that supplied all their present needs. When that year's report was issued, this proof of God's faithfulness in sending help just when needed was recorded, and a short time after the donor called and made himself known, saying that as his donation had been given at such a special time of need he felt he must state the circumstances under which he had given the money, which were as follows: He had occasion to go to his office in Bristol early that morning before breakfast, and on the way the thought occurred to him: "I will go to Mr. Müller's orphan house and give them a donation," and accordingly turned and walked about a quarter of a mile toward the orphanage, when he stopped, saying to himself, "How foolish of me to be neglecting the business I came out to attend to! I can give money to the orphans another time," and he turned round and walked back towards his office, but soon felt that he *must* return. He said to himself: "The orphans may be needing the money *now.* I may be leaving them in want when God had sent me to help them;" and so strong was this impression that he again turned round and walked back till he reached the orphanages, and thus handed in the money which provided them with breakfast. Mr. Mullets comment on this was: "Just like my gracious heavenly Father!" and then he urged his hearers to trust and prove what a faithful covenant-keeping God He is to those who put their trust in Him.

APPENDIX K

Further Recollections of Mr. Müller

Mr. Perry furnishes also the following reminiscences: As George Müller was engaged in free, homely conversation with his friends on a Sunday afternoon within about three weeks of his departure to be with the Lord, he referred to two visits he had made during the previous week to two old and beloved friends. He had fully appreciated that, though they were about ten years younger than himself, his power to walk, and specially his power to continue his service for his Lord, was far greater than theirs. So that he playfully said, with a bright smile: "I came away from both these beloved brethren feeling that I was quite young by comparison as to strength, though so much older," and then at once followed an ascription of praise to God for His goodness to him: "Oh, how very kind and good my heavenly Father has been to me! I have no aches or pains, no rheumatism, and now in my ninety-third year I can do a day's work at the orphan houses with as much ease and comfort to myself as ever."

One sentence aptly sets forth a striking feature in his Christian character, viz.:

> George Müller, nothing.
> In himself worse than nothing.
>
> The Lord Jesus, everything.
> By grace, in Christ, the son of the King.

And as such he lived; for all those who knew and loved this beloved and honoured servant of Christ best would testify that his habitual attitude towards the Lord was to treat Him as an ever-present, almighty, loving Friend, whose love was far greater to him than he could ever return, and who delighted in having his entire confidence about everything, and was not only ready at hand to listen to his prayers and praises about great and important matters, but nothing was too small to speak to Him about. So real was this that it was almost impossible to be enjoying the privilege of private, confidential intercourse with him without being conscious that at least to him the Lord was really present, One to whom he turned for counsel, in prayer, or in praise, as freely as most men would speak to a third person present; and again and again most marked answers to prayer have been received in response to petitions thus unitedly presented to the Lord altogether apart from his own special work.

APPENDIX L

Church Fellowship, Baptism, Etc.

When brother Craik and I began to labour in Bristol, and consequently some believers united with us in fellowship, assembling together at Bethesda, we began meeting together on the basis of the written Word only, without having any church rules whatever. From the commencement it was understood that, as the Lord should help us, we would try everything by the word of God, and introduce and hold fast that only which could be proved by Scripture. When we came to this determination on Aug. 13, 1832, it was indeed in weakness, but it was in uprightness of heart.—On account of this it was that, as we ourselves were not fully settled as to whether those only who had been baptized after they had believed, or whether all who believed in the Lord Jesus, irrespective of baptism, should be received into fellowship, nothing was determined about this point. We felt free to break bread and be in communion with those who were not baptized, and therefore could with a good conscience labour at Gideon, where the greater part of the saints, at least at first, were unbaptized; but, at the same time, we had a secret wish that none but believers who were baptized might be united with us at Bethesda. Our reason for this was that we had witnessed in Devonshire much painful disunion, resulting as we thought, from baptized and unbaptized believers being in fellowship. Without, then, making it a rule, that Bethesda Church was to be one of close communion, we nevertheless took care that those who applied for fellowship should be instructed about baptism. For many months there occurred no difficulty as none applied for communion but such as had either been already baptized, or wished to be, or who became convinced of the scriptural character of believers' baptism, after we had conversed with them; afterwards, however, three sisters applied for fellowship, none of whom had been baptized; nor were their views altered after we had conversed with them. As, nevertheless, brother Craik and I considered them true believers, and we ourselves were not fully convinced what was the mind of the Lord in such a case, we thought it right that these sisters should be received; yet so that it might be unanimously, as all our church acts *then* were done; but we knew *by that time* that there were several in fellowship with us who could not conscientiously receive unbaptized believers. We mentioned, therefore, the names of the three sisters to the church, stating that they did not see believers' baptism to be scriptural, and that, if any brother saw, on that account, a reason why they should not be received, he should let us know. The result was that several objected, and two or three meetings were held, at which we heard the objections of the brethren, and sought for ourselves to obtain acquaintance with the mind of God on the point. Whilst several days thus passed away before the matter was decided, one of those three sisters came and thanked us that we had not received her, before being baptized, for she now saw that it was only shame and the fear of man which had kept her back, and that the Lord had now made her willing to be baptized. By this circumstance those brethren who considered it scriptural that all ought to be baptized before being received into fellowship, were confirmed in their views; and as to brother Craik and me, it made us, at least, still more question whether those brethren might not be right; and we felt, therefore, that in such a state of mind we could not oppose them. The one sister, therefore, who wished to be baptized was received into fellowship, but the two others not. Our consciences were the less affected by this because all, though not baptized, might take the Lord's supper with us at Bethesda, though not be received into full fellowship; and because at Gideon, where there were baptized and unbaptized believers, they might even be received into full fellowship; for we had not then clearly seen that there is *no scriptural* distinction between being in fellowship with individuals and breaking bread with them. Thus matters stood for many months, i.e., believers were received to the breaking of bread even at Bethesda, though not baptized, but they were not received to all the privileges of fellowship.—In August of 1836 I had a conversation with brother K. C. on, the subject of receiving the unbaptized into communion, a subject about which, for years, my mind had been more or less exercised. This brother put the matter thus before me: either unbaptized believers come under the class of persons who walk disorderly, and, in that case, we ought to withdraw from them (2 Thessalonians 3:6); or they do not walk disorderly. If a believer be walking disorderly, we are not merely to withdraw from him at the Lord's table, but our behaviour towards him ought to be decidedly different from what it would be were he not walking disorderly, *on all occasions* when we may have intercourse with him, or come in any way into contact with him. Now this is evidently not the case in the conduct of baptized believers towards their unbaptized fellow believers. The Spirit does not suffer it to be so, but He witnesses that their not having been baptized does not necessarily imply that they are walking disorderly; and hence there may be the most precious communion between baptized and unbaptized believers. The Spirit does not suffer us to refuse fellowship with them in prayer, in reading or searching the Scriptures, in social and intimate intercourse, and in the Lord's work; and yet this ought to be the case, were they walking disorderly.—This passage, 2 Thessalonians 3:6, to which brother E. C. referred, was the means of showing me the mind of the Lord on the subject, which is, *that we ought to receive all whom Christ has received* (Romans 15:7), *irrespective of the measure of grace or knowledge which they have attained unto.*—Some time after this conversation, in May, 1837, an opportunity occurred, when we (for brother Craik had seen the same truth) were called upon to put into practice the light which the Lord had been pleased to give us. A sister, who neither *had been baptized,* nor considered herself under any obligation to be baptized, applied for fellowship. We conversed with her on this as on other subjects and proposed her for fellowship, though our conversation had not convinced her that she ought to be baptized. This led the church again to the consideration of the point. We gave our reasons, from Scripture, for considering it right to receive this unbaptized sister to all the privileges of the children of God; but a considerable number, one-third perhaps, expressed conscientious difficulty in receiving her. The example of the Apostles, in baptizing the first believers upon a profession of faith, was especially urged, which indeed would be an unsurmountable difficulty had not the truth been mingled with error for so long a time, so that it does not prove wilful disobedience if any one in our day should refuse to be baptized after believing. The Lord, however, gave us much help in pointing out the truth to the brethren, so that the number of those who considered that only baptized believers should be in communion decreased almost daily. At last, only fourteen brethren and sisters out of above 180 thought it right, this August 28, 1837, to separate from us, after we had had much intercourse with them. [I am glad to be able to add that, even of these fourteen, the greater part afterwards saw their error, and came back again to us, and that the receiving of all who love our Lord Jesus into full communion, irrespective of baptism, has never been the source of disunion among us, though more than fifty-seven years have passed away since.]

APPENDIX M

Church Conduct

I.—Questions respecting the Eldership.

(1) *How does it appear to be the mind of God that, in every church, there should be recognized Elders?*

Ans. From the following passages compared together: Matthew 24:45; Luke 12:42.

From these passages we learn that some are set by the Lord Himself in the office of rulers and teachers, and that this office (in spite of the fallen state of the church) should be in being, even down to the close of the present dispensation. Accordingly, we find from Acts 14:23, 20:17; Titus 1:5; and 1 Peter 5:1, that soon after the saints had been converted, and had associated together in a church character, Elders were appointed to take the rule over them and to fulfil the office of under-shepherds.

This must not be understood as implying that, when believers are associated in church fellowship, they ought to elect Elders according to their own will, whether the Lord may have qualified persons or not; but rather that such should wait upon God, that He Himself would be pleased to raise up such as may be qualified for teaching and ruling in His church.

(2) *How do such come into office?*

Ans. By the appointment of the Holy Ghost, Acts 20:28.

(3) *How may this appointment be made known to the individuals called to the office, and to those amongst whom they may be called to labour?*

Ans. By the secret call of the Spirit, 1 Timothy 3:1, confirmed by the possession of the requisite qualifications, 1 Timothy 3:2-7; Titus 1:6-9, and by the Lord's blessing resting upon their labours, 1 Corinthians 9:2.

In 1 Corinthians 9:2, Paul condescends to the weakness of some, who were in danger of being led away by those factious persons who questioned his authority. As an Apostle—appointed by the express word of the Lord—he needed not such outward confirmation. But if he used his success as an argument in confirmation of his call, how much more may ordinary servants of the Lord Jesus employ such an argument, seeing that the way in which they are called for the work is such as to require some outward confirmation!

(4) *Is it incumbent upon the saints to acknowledge such and to submit to them in the Lord?*

Ans. Yes. See 1 Corinthians 16:15, 16; 1 Thessalonians 5:12, 13; Hebrews 13:7, 17; and 1 Timothy 5:17.

In these passages obedience to pastoral authority is clearly enjoined.

II.—*Ought matters of discipline to be* FINALLY *settled by the Elders* IN PRIVATE, *or* IN THE PRESENCE OF THE CHURCH, AND AS THE ACT OF THE WHOLE BODY?

Ans. (1) Such matters are to be finally settled in the presence of the church. This appears from Matthew 28:17; 1 Corinthians 5:4, 5; 2 Corinthians 2:6-8; 1 Timothy 5:20.

(2) Such matters are to be finally settled *as the act of the whole body,* Matthew 28:17, 18. In this passage the act of exclusion is spoken of as the act of the whole body. 1 Corinthians 5:4, 5, 5:12, 13. In this passage Paul gives the direction, respecting the exercise of discipline, in such a way to render the whole body responsible: verse 7, "Purge out the old leaven that ye may be a new lump"; and verse 13, "Therefore put away from among yourselves that wicked person." From 2 Corinthians 2:6-8 we learn that the act of exclusion was not the act of the Elders only, but of the church: "Sufficient to such a man is this punishment [rather, public censure] *which was inflicted of many."* From verse 8 we learn that the act of restoration was to be a public act of the brethren: "Wherefore I beseech you that ye would confirm [rather, ratify by a public act] your love towards him."

As to the reception of brethren into fellowship, this is an act of simple obedience to the Lord, both on the part of the elders and the whole church. We are bound and privileged to receive all those who make a credible profession of faith in Christ, according to that Scripture, "Receive ye one another, as Christ also received us, to the glory of God." (Romans 15:7)

III.—*When should church acts (such as acts of reception, restoration, exclusion, etc.) be attended to?*

Ans. It cannot be expressly proved from Scripture whether such acts were attended to at the meeting for the breaking of bread, or at any other meeting; therefore this is a point on which, if different churches differ, mutual forbearance ought to be exercised. The way in which such matters have hitherto been managed amongst us has been by the church coming together on a week-evening. Before we came to Bristol we had been accustomed to this mode, and, finding nothing in Scripture against it, we continued the practice. But, after prayer and more careful consideration of this point, it has appeared well to us that such acts should be attended to on the Lord's days, when the saints meet together for the breaking of bread. We have been induced to make this alteration by the following reasons:

(1) *This latter mode prevents matters from being delayed.* There not being a sufficiency of matter for a meeting on purpose every week, it has sometimes happened that what would better have been stated to the church at once has been kept back from the body for some weeks. Now, it is important that what concerns the whole church should be made known as soon as possible to those who are in fellowship, that they may act accordingly. Delay, moreover, seems inconsistent with the pilgrim-character of the people of God.

(2) *More believers can be present on the Lord's days than can attend on week-evenings.* The importance of this reason will appear from considering how everything which concerns the church should be known to *as many as possible.* For how can the saints pray for those who may have to be excluded,—how can they sympathize in cases of peculiar trial,—and how can they rejoice and give thanks on account of those who may be received or restored, unless they are made acquainted with the facts connected with such cases?

(3) *A testimony is thus given that all who break bread are church members.* By attending to church acts in the meeting for breaking of bread, we show that we *make no difference* between receiving into fellowship at the Lord's Supper, and into church membership, but that the individual who is admitted to the Lord's table is therewith also received to all the privileges, trials, and responsibilities of church membership.

(4) There is a peculiar propriety in acts of reception, restoration, and exclusion being attended to when the saints meet together for the breaking of bread, as, in that ordinance especially, we show forth our fellowship with each other.

Objections answered.

(1) This alteration has the appearance of changeableness.

Reply. Such an objection would apply to any case in which increased light led to any improvement, and is, therefore, not to be regarded. It would be an evil thing if there were any change respecting the foundation truths of the Gospel; but the point in question is only a matter of church order.

(2) More time may thus be required than it would be well to give to such a purpose on the Lord's day.

Reply. As, according to this plan, church business will be attended to *every Lord's day,* it is more than probable that the meetings will be thereby prolonged for a few minutes only; but, should circumstance require it, a special meeting may still be appointed during the week, for all who break bread with us. This, however, would only be needful, provided the matters to be brought before the brethren were to require more time than could be given to them at the breaking of bread.[48]

N.B. (1) Should any persons be present who do not break bread with us, they may be requested to withdraw whenever such points require to be stated as it would not be well to speak of in the presence of unbelievers.

(2) As there are two places in which the saints meet for the breaking of bread, the matters connected with church acts must be brought out at each place.

IV.—Questions relative to the Lord's supper.

(1) *How frequently ought the breaking of bread to be attended to?*

Ans. Although we have no express command respecting the frequency of its observance, yet the example of the apostles and of the first disciples would lead us to observe this ordinance every Lord's day. (Acts 20:7)

(2) *What ought to be the character of the meeting at which the saints are assembled for the breaking of bread?*

Ans. As in this ordinance we show forth our common participation in all the benefits of our Lord's death, and our union to Him and to each other (1 Corinthians 10:16, 17), opportunity ought to be given for the exercise of the gifts of teaching or exhortation, and communion in prayer and praise. (Romans 12:4-8; Ephesians 4:11-16) The manifestation of our common participation in each other's gifts cannot be fully given at such meetings, if the whole meeting is, necessarily, conducted by one individual. This mode of meeting does not, however, take off from those who have the gifts of teaching or exhortation the responsibility of edifying the church as opportunity may be offered.

(3) *Is it desirable that the bread should be broken at the Lord's Supper by one of the elders, or should each individual of the body break it for himself?*

Ans. Neither way can be so decidedly proved from Scripture that we are warranted in objecting to the other as positively unscriptural, yet—

48 The practice, later on, gave place to a week-night meeting, on Tuesday, for transaction of such "church acts."—A. T. P.

(1) The letter of Scripture seems rather in favour of its being done by each brother and sister (1 Corinthians 10:16, 17): "The bread which *we break.*"

(2) Its being done by each of the disciples is more fitted to express that we all, by our sins, have broken the body of our Lord.

(3) By attending to the ordinance in this way, we manifest our freedom from the common error that the Lord's Supper must be administered by some particular individual, possessed of what is called a ministerial character, instead of being an act of social worship and obedience.

APPENDIX N

The Wise Sayings of George Müller

FEW WHO have not carefully read the Narrative of Mr. Müller and the subsequent Reports issued year by year, have any idea of the large amount of wisdom which there finds expression. We give here a few examples of the sagacious and spiritual counsels and utterances with which these pages abound.

THE BODY

Care Of The Body

I find it a difficult thing, whilst caring for the body, not to neglect the soul. It seems to me much easier to go on altogether regardless of the body, in the service of the Lord, than to take care of the body, in the time of sickness, and not to neglect the soul, especially in an affliction like my present one, when the head allows but little reading or thinking.—What a blessed prospect to be delivered from this wretched evil nature!

Habits Of Sleep

My own experience has been, almost invariably, that if I have not the *needful* sleep, my spiritual enjoyment and strength is greatly affected by it. I judge it of great moment that the believer, in travelling, should seek as much as possible to refrain from travelling by night, or from travelling in such a way as that he is deprived of the needful night's rest; for if he does not, he will be unable with renewed bodily and mental strength to give himself to prayer and meditation, and the reading of the Holy Scriptures, and he will surely feel the pernicious effects of this all the day long. There may occur cases when travelling by night cannot be avoided; but, if it can, *though we should seem to lose time by it, and though it should cost more money,* I would most affectionately and solemnly recommend the refraining from night-travelling; for, in addition to our drawing beyond measure upon our bodily strength, we must be losers spiritually. The next thing I would advise with reference to travelling is, with all one's might to seek morning by morning, before setting out, to take time for meditation and prayer, and reading the word of God; for although we are always exposed to temptation, yet we are so especially in travelling. Travelling is one of the devil's especial opportunities for tempting us. Think of that, dear fellow believers. Seek always to ascertain carefully the mind of God, before you begin anything; but do so in particular before you go on a journey, so that you may be quite sure that it is the will of God that you should undertake that journey, lest you should needlessly expose yourself to one of the special opportunities of the devil to ensnare you. So far from envying those who have a carriage and horses at their command, or an abundance of means, so that they are not hindered from travelling for want of means, let us who are not thus situated rather thank God that *in this particular* we are not exposed to the temptation of needing to be less careful in ascertaining the will of God before we set out on a journey.

CHILDREN

Conversion Of Children

As far as my experience goes, it appears to me that believers generally have expected far too little of present fruit upon their labours among children. There has been a hoping that the Lord some day or other would own the instruction which they give to children, and would answer at some time or other, though after many years only, the prayers which they offer up on their behalf. Now, while such passages as Proverbs 22:6, Ecclesiastes 11:1, Galatians 6:9, 1 Corinthians 15:58, give unto us assurance not merely respecting everything which we do for the Lord, in general, but also respecting bringing up children in the fear of the Lord, in particular, that our labour is not in vain in the Lord; yet we have to guard against abusing such passages, by thinking it a matter of little moment whether we see *present* fruit or not; but, on the contrary, we should give the Lord no rest till we see present fruit, and therefore, in persevering, yet submissive, prayer, we should make known our requests unto God. I add, as an encouragement to believers who labour among children, that during the last two years seventeen other young persons or children, from the age of eleven and a half to seventeen, have been received into fellowship among us, and that I am looking out now for many more to be converted, and that not merely of the orphans, but of the Sunday-school and day-school children.

Neglect Of Children

The power for good or evil that resides in a little child is great beyond all human calculation. A child rightly trained may be a world-wide blessing, with an influence reaching onward to eternal years. But a neglected or misdirected directed child may live to blight and blast mankind, and leave influences of evil which shall roll on in increasing volume till they plunge into the gulf of eternal perdition.

"A remarkable instance was related by Dr. Harris, of New York, at a recent meeting of the State Charities Aid Association. In a small village in a county on the upper Hudson, some seventy years ago, a young girl named 'Margaret' was sent adrift on the casual charity of the inhabitants. She became the mother of a long race of criminals and paupers, and her progeny has cursed the county ever since. The county records show *two hundred* of her descendants who have been criminals. In one single generation of her unhappy line there were twenty children; of these, three died in infancy, and seventeen survived to maturity. Of the seventeen, nine served in the State prison for high crimes an aggregate term of fifty years, while the others were frequent inmates of jails and penitentiaries and almshouses. Of the nine hundred descendants, through six generations, from this unhappy girl who was left on the village streets and abandoned in her childhood, a great number have been idiots, imbeciles, drunkards, lunatics, paupers, and prostitutes: but two hundred of the more vigorous are on record as criminals. This neglected little child has thus cost the county authorities, in the effects she has transmitted, *hundreds of thousands of dollars,* in the expense and care of criminals and paupers, besides the untold damage she has inflicted on property and public morals."

Training Of Children

Seek to cherish in your children early the habit of being interested about the work of God, and about cases of need and distress, and use them too at *suitable times,* and under *suitable circumstances,* as your almoners, and you will reap fruit from doing so.

CHRISTIAN LIFE

Beginning Of Life, Etc.

God alone can give spiritual life at the first, and keep it up in the soul afterwards.

Cross-Bearing

The Christian, like the bee, might suck honey out of every flower. I saw upon a snuffer-stand in bas-relief, "A heart, a cross under it, and roses under both." The meaning was obviously this, that the heart which bears the cross for a time meets with roses afterwards.

Keeping Promises

It has been often mentioned to me, in various places, that brethren in business do not sufficiently attend to the keeping of promises, and I cannot therefore but entreat all who love our Lord Jesus, and who are engaged in a trade or business, to seek for His sake not to make any promises, except they have every reason to believe they shall be able to fulfil them, and therefore carefully to weigh all the circumstances, before making any engagement, lest they should fail in its accomplishment. It is even in these little ordinary affairs of life that we may either bring much honour or dishonour to the Lord; and these are the things which every unbeliever can take notice of. Why should it be so often said, and sometimes with a measure of ground, or even much ground: "Believers are bad servants, bad tradesmen, bad masters"? Surely it ought not to be true that *we, who have power with God to obtain by prayer and faith all needful grace, wisdom, and skill,* should be bad servants, bad tradesmen, bad masters.

The Lot And The Lottery

It is altogether wrong that I, a child of God, should have anything to do with so worldly a system as that of the lottery. But it was also unscriptural to go to the lot at all for the sake of ascertaining the Lord's mind, and this I ground on the following reasons. We have neither a commandment of God for it, nor the example of our Lord, nor that of the apostles, *after the Holy Spirit had been given on the day of Pentecost.* 1. We have many exhortations in the word of God to seek to know His mind by prayer and searching the Holy Scriptures, but no passage which exhorts us to use the lot. 2. The example of the apostles (Acts 1) in using the lot, in the choice of an apostle in the room of Judas Iscariot, is the only passage which can be brought in favour of the lot from the New Testament (and to the Old we have not to go, under this dispensation, for the sake of ascertaining how we ought to live as disciples of Christ). Now concerning this circumstance we have to remember that the Spirit was not yet given (John 7:39; 14:16, 17; 16:7, 13), by whose teaching especially it is that we may know the mind of the Lord; and hence we find that, after the day of Pentecost, the lot was no more used, but the apostles gave themselves to prayer and fasting to ascertain how they ought to act.

New Tastes

What a difference grace makes! There were few people, perhaps, more passionately fond of travelling, and seeing fresh places, and new scenes, than myself; but now, since, by the grace of God, I have seen beauty in the Lord Jesus, I have lost my taste for these things.... What a different thing, also, to travel in the service of the Lord Jesus, from what it is to travel in the service of the flesh!

Obedience

Every instance of obedience, from right motives, strengthens us spiritually, whilst every act of disobedience weakens us spiritually.

Separation Unto God

May the Lord grant that the eyes of many of His children may be opened, so that they may seek, in all spiritual things, to be separated from unbelievers (2 Corinthians 6:14-18), and to do *God's work* according to *God's mind!*

Service To One's Generation

My business is, with all my might to serve my own generation; in doing so I shall best serve the next generation, should the Lord Jesus tarry.... The longer I live, the more I am enabled to realize that I have but one life to live on earth, and that this one life is but a *brief* life, for sowing, in comparison with *eternity,* for reaping.

Surety For Debt

How precious it is, even for this life, to act according to the word of God! This perfect revelation of His mind gives us directions for everything, even the most minute affairs of this life. It commands us, "Be thou not one of them that strike hands, or of them that are sureties for debts." (Proverbs 22:26.) The way in which Satan ensnares persons, to bring them into the net, and to bring trouble upon them by becoming sureties, is, that he seeks to represent the matter as if there were no danger connected with that particular case, and that one might be sure one should never be called upon to pay the money; but the Lord, the faithful Friend, tells us in His own word that the only way in such a matter "to be sure" is "to hate suretyship." (Proverbs 11:15) The following points seem to me of solemn moment for consideration, if I were called upon to become surety for another: 1. What obliges the person, who wishes me to become surety for him, to need a surety? Is it really a good cause in which I am called upon to become surety? I do not remember ever to have met with a case in which in a plain, and godly, and in all respects scriptural matter such a thing occurred. There was generally some sin or other connected with it. 2. If I become surety, notwithstanding what the Lord has said to me in His word, am I in such a position that no one will be injured by my being called upon to fulfil the engagements of the person for whom I am going to be surety? In most instances this alone ought to keep one from it. 3. If still I become surety, the amount of money for which I become responsible must be so in my power that I am able to produce it whenever it is called for, in order that the name of the Lord may not be dishonoured. 4. But if there be the possibility of having to fulfil the engagements of the person in whose stead I have to stand, is it the will of the Lord that I should spend my means in that way? Is it not rather His will that my means should be spent in another way? 5. How can I get over the plain word of the Lord, which is to the contrary, even if the first four points could be satisfactorily settled?

CHURCH LIFE

Assembly Of Believers

It has been my own happy lot, during the last thirty-seven years, to become acquainted with hundreds of individuals, who were not inferior to apostolic Christians.

That the disciples of Jesus should meet together on the first day of the week for the breaking of bread, and that that should be their principal meeting, and that those, whether one or several, who are truly gifted by the Holy Spirit for service, be it for exhortation, or teaching, or rule, etc., are responsible to the Lord for the exercise of their gifts—these are to me no matters of uncertainty, but points on which my soul, by grace, is established, through the revealed will of God.

Formalism

I have often remarked the injurious effects of doing things because others did them, or because it was the custom, or because they were persuaded into acts of *outward* self-denial, or giving up things whilst the heart did not go along with it, and whilst the *outward act* WAS NOT *the result of the inward powerful working of the Holy Ghost, and the happy entering into our fellowship with the Father and with the Son.*

Everything that is a mere form, a mere habit and custom in divine things, is to be dreaded exceedingly: *life, power, reality,* this is what we have to aim after. Things should not result from without, but from within. The sort of clothes I wear, the kind of house I live in, the quality of the furniture I use, all such like things should not result from other persons' doing so and so, or because it is customary among those brethren with whom I associate to live in such and such a simple, inexpensive self-denying way; but whatever be done in these things, in the way of giving up, or self-denial, or deadness to the world, should result from the joy we have in God, from the knowledge of our being the children of God, from the entering into the preciousness of our future inheritance, etc. Far better that for the time being we stand still, and do not take the steps which we see others take, than that it is merely the force of example that leads us to do a thing, and afterwards it be regretted. Not that I mean in the least by this to imply we should continue to live in luxury, self-indulgence, and the like, whilst others are in great need; but we should begin the thing in a right way, i.e., aim after the right state of heart; begin *inwardly* instead of *outwardly.* If otherwise, it will not last. We shall look back, or even get into a worse state than we were before. But oh, how different if joy in God leads us to any little act of self-denial! How gladly do we do it then! How great an honour then do we esteem it to be! How much does the heart then long to be able to do more for Him who has done so much for us! We are far then from looking down in proud self-complacency upon those who do not go as far as we do, but rather pray to the Lord that He would be pleased to help our dear brethren and sisters forward who may seem to us weak in any particular point; and we also are conscious to ourselves that if we have a little more light or strength with reference to one point, other brethren may have more light or grace in other respects.

Helping One Another

As to the importance of the children of God's opening their hearts to each other, especially when they are getting into a cold state, or are under the power of a certain sin, or are in especial difficulty; I know from my own experience how often the snare of the devil has been broken when under the power of sin; how often the heart has been comforted when nigh to be overwhelmed; how often advice, under great perplexity, has been obtained,—by opening my heart to a brother in whom I had confidence. We are children of the same family, and ought therefore to be helpers one of another.

Inquiry Meetings

1. Many persons, on account of timidity, would prefer coming at an appointed time to the vestry to converse with us, to calling on us in our own house. 2. The very fact of appointing a time for seeing people, to converse with them in private concerning the things of eternity, has brought some who, humanly speaking, never would have called on us under other circumstances; yea, it has brought even those who, though they thought they were concerned about the things of God, yet were completely ignorant; and thus we have had an opportunity of speaking to them. 3. These meetings have also been a great encouragement to ourselves in the work; for often, when we thought that such and such expositions of the Word had done no good at all, it was, through these meetings, found to be the reverse; and likewise, when our hands were hanging down, we have been afresh encouraged to go forward in the work of the Lord, and to continue sowing the

seed in hope, by seeing at these meetings fresh cases, in which the Lord had condescended to use us as instruments, particularly as in this way instances have sometimes occurred in which individuals have spoken to us about the benefit which they derived from our ministry, not only a few months before, but even as long as two, three, and four years before.

For the above reasons I would particularly recommend to other servants of Christ, especially to those who live in large towns, if they have not already introduced a similar plan, to consider whether it may not be well for them also to set apart such times for seeing inquirers. Those meetings, however, require much prayer, to be enabled to speak aright, to all those who come, according to their different need; and one is led continually to feel that one is not sufficient of one's self for these things, but that our sufficiency can be alone of God. These meetings also have been by far the most wearing-out part of all our work, though at the same time the most refreshing.

Pastoral Visitation

An *unvisited* church will sooner or later become an *unhealthy church.*

Pew-Rents

1. Pew-rents are, according to James 2:1-6, against the mind of the Lord, as, in general, the poor brother cannot have so good a seat as the rich. 2. A brother may gladly do something towards my support if left to his own time; but when the quarter is up, he has perhaps other expenses, and I do not know whether he pays his money grudgingly, and of necessity, or cheerfully; but God loveth a cheerful giver. *I knew it to be a fact* that sometimes it had not been convenient to individuals to pay the money, when it had been asked for by the brethren who collected it. 3. Though the Lord had been pleased to give me grace to be faithful, so that I had been enabled not to keep back the truth, when He had shown it to me; still I felt that the pew-rents were a snare to the servant of Christ. It was a temptation to me, at least for a few minutes, at the time when the Lord had stirred me up to pray and search the Word respecting the ordinance of baptism, because 30 pounds of my salary was at stake if I should be baptized.

State Churches

All establishments, even because they are establishment, i.e., the world and the church mixed up together, not only contain in them the principles which necessarily must lead to departure from the word of God; but also, as long as they remain establishments, entirely preclude the acting throughout according to the Holy Scriptures.

FAITH

Anxiety

Where Faith begins, anxiety ends;
Where anxiety begins, Faith ends.

Ponder these words of the Lord Jesus, "Only believe." As long as we are able to trust in God, holding fast in heart, that he is able and willing to help those who rest on the Lord Jesus for salvation, in all matters which are for His glory and their good, the heart remains calm and peaceful. It is only when we *practically* let go faith in His power or His love, that we lose our peace and become troubled. This very day I am in great trial in connection with the work in which I am engaged; yet my soul was calmed and quieted by the remembrance of God's power and love; and I said to myself this morning: "As David encouraged himself in Jehovah his God, when he returned to Ziklag, so will I encourage myself in God;" and the result was peace of soul.... It is the very time for *faith* to work, when *sight* ceases. The greater the difficulties, the easier for *faith.* As long as there remain certain natural prospects, faith does not get on even as easily (if I may say so), as when all natural prospects fail.

Dependence On God

Observe two things! We acted *for God* in delaying the public meetings and the publishing of the Report; but *God's way leads always into trial, so far as sight and sense are concerned. Nature* always will be tried *in God's ways.* The Lord was saying by this poverty, "I will now see whether you truly lean upon me, and whether you truly look to me." Of all the seasons that I had ever passed through since I had been living in this way, *up to that time,* I never knew any period in which my faith was tried so sharply, as during the four months from Dec. 12, 1841, to April 12, 1842. But observe further: We might even now have altered our minds with respect to the public meetings and publishing the Report; for *no one knew our determination, at this time,* concerning the point. Nay, on the contrary, we knew with what delight very many children of God were looking forward to receive further accounts. But the Lord kept us steadfast to the conclusion, at which we had arrived under His guidance.

Gift And Grace Of Faith

It pleased the Lord, I think, to give me in some cases something like the gift (not grace) of faith, so that unconditionally I could ask and look for an answer.

The difference between the *gift* and the *grace* of faith seems to me this. According to the *gift of faith* I am able to do a thing, or believe that a thing will come to pass, the not doing of which, or the not believing of which would not be sin; according to the *grace of faith* I am able to do a thing, or believe that a thing will come to pass, respecting which I have the word of God as the ground to rest upon, and, therefore, the not doing it, or the not believing it *would be sin.* For instance, *the gift of faith* would be needed, to believe that a sick person should be restored again, though *there is no human probability: for there is no promise to that effect; the grace of faith* is needed to believe that the Lord will give me the necessaries of life, if I first seek the kingdom of God and His righteousness: for *there is a promise to that effect.* (Matthew 6:33)

Self-Will

The natural mind is ever prone *to reason,* when we ought *to believe;* to be *at work,* when we ought to be *quiet;* to go our own way, when we ought steadily to walk on in God's ways, however trying to nature.

Trials Of Faith

The Lord gives faith, for the very purpose of trying it for the glory of His own name, and for the good of him who has it; and, by the very trial of our faith, we not only obtain blessing to our own souls, by becoming the better acquainted with God, if we hold fast our confidence in Him, but our faith is also, by the exercise, strengthened: and so it comes, that, if we walk with God in any measure of uprightness of heart, the trials of faith will be greater and greater.

It is for the church's benefit that we are put in these straits; and if, therefore, in the hour of need, we were to take goods on credit, the first and primary object of the work would be completely frustrated, and no heart would be further strengthened to trust in God, nor would there be any longer that manifestation of the special and particular providence of God, which has hitherto been so abundantly shown through this work, even in the eyes of unbelievers, whereby they have been led to see *that there is, after all, reality in the things of God,* and many, through these printed accounts, have been truly converted. For these reasons, then, we consider it our precious privilege, as heretofore, to continue to wait upon the Lord only, instead of taking goods on credit, or borrowing money from some kind friends, when we are in need. Nay, we purpose, as God shall give us grace, to look to Him only, though morning after morning we should have nothing in hand for the work—yea, though from meal to meal we should have to look to Him; being fully assured that He who is now (1845) in the tenth year feeding these many orphans, and who has never suffered them to want, and that He who is now (1845) in the twelfth year carrying on the other parts of the work, without any branch of it having had to be stopped for want of means, will do so for the future also. And here I do desire in the deep consciousness of my natural helplessness and dependence upon the Lord to confess that through the grace of God my soul has been in peace, though day after day we have had to wait for our daily provisions upon the Lord; yea, though even from meal to meal we have been required to do this.

GIVING

Asking Gifts, Etc.

It is not enough to obtain means for the work of God, but that these means should be obtained in God's way. To ask unbelievers for means is *not* God's way; to *press* even believers to give, is *not* God's way; but the *duty* and the *privilege* of being allowed to contribute to the work of God should be pointed out, and this should be followed up with earnest prayer, believing prayer, and will result in the desired end.

Claims Of God

It is true, the Gospel demands our *All;* but I fear that, in the general claim on *All,* we have shortened the claim on *everything.* We are not under law. True; but that is not to make our obedience less complete, or our giving less bountiful: rather, is it not, that after all claims of law are settled, the new nature finds its joy in doing more than the law requires? Let us abound in the work of the Lord more and more.

Giving In Adversity

At the end of the last century a very godly and liberal merchant in London was one day called on by a gentleman, to ask him for some money for a charitable object. The gentleman expected very little, having just heard that the merchant had sustained heavy loss from the wreck of some of his ships. Contrary, however, to expectation, he received about ten times as much as he had expected for his object. He was unable to refrain from expressing his surprise to the merchant, told him what he had heard, how he feared he should scarcely have received anything, and asked whether after all there was not a mistake about the shipwreck of the vessels. The merchant replied, It is quite true, I have sustained heavy loss, by these vessels being wrecked, but that is the very reason, why I give you so much; for I must make better use than ever of my stewardship, lest it should be entirely taken from me.

How have we to act if prosperity in our business, our trade, our profession, etc., should suddenly cease, notwithstanding our having given a considerable proportion of our means for the Lord's work? My reply is this: "In the day of adversity *consider.*" It is the will of God that we should ponder our ways; that we should see whether there is any particular reason, why God has allowed this to befall us. In doing so, we may find, that we have too much looked on our prosperity as a matter of course, and have not sufficiently owned and recognized *practically* the hand of God in our success. Or it may be, while the Lord has been pleased to prosper us, we have spent too much on ourselves, and may have thus, though unintentionally, *abused* the blessing of God. I do not mean by this remark to bring any children of God into bondage, so that, with a scrupulous conscience, they should look at every penny, which they spend on themselves; this is not the will of God concerning us; and yet, on the other hand, there is verily such a thing as propriety or impropriety in our dress, our furniture, our table, our house, our establishment, and in the yearly amount we spend on ourselves and family.

Giving And Hoarding

I have every reason to believe, that, had I begun to lay up, the Lord would have stopped the supplies, and thus, the ability of doing so was only *apparent.* Let no one profess to trust in God, and yet lay up for future wants, otherwise the Lord will first send him to the hoard he has amassed, before He can answer the prayer for more.

"There is that scattereth, and yet increaseth; and there is that withholdeth *more than is meet,* but it tendeth to poverty." (Proverbs 11:24) Notice here the word *"more than is meet;"* it is not said, withholdeth all; but "more than is meet" viz., while he gives, it is so little, in comparison with what it might be, and ought to be, that it tendeth to poverty.

Motives To Giving

Believers should seek more and more to enter into the grace and love of God, in giving His only-begotten Son, and into the grace and love of the Lord Jesus, in giving Himself in our room, in order that, constrained by love and gratitude, they may be increasingly led to surrender their bodily and mental strength, their time, gifts, talents, property, position in life, rank, and all they have and are to the Lord. By this I do not mean that they should give up their business, trade, or profession, and become preachers; nor do I mean that they should take all their money and give it to the first beggar who asks for it; but that they should hold all they have and are, for the Lord, not as owners, but as stewards, and be willing, *at His bidding,* to use for Him part or all they have. However short the believer may fall, nothing less than this should be his aim.

Stewardship

It is the Lord's order, that in whatever way He is pleased to make us His stewards, whether as to temporal or spiritual things, if we are indeed acting as *stewards* and not as *owners,* He will make us stewards over *more.*

Even in this life, and as to temporal things, the Lord is pleased to repay those who act for Him as stewards, and who contribute to His work or to the poor, as He may be pleased to prosper them? But how much greater is the *spiritual* blessing we receive, both in this life and in the world to come, if constrained by the love of Christ, we act as God's stewards, respecting that with which He is pleased to intrust us!

Systematic Giving

Only *fix even the smallest amount* you purpose to give of your income, and give this regularly; and as God is pleased to increase your light and grace, and is pleased to prosper you more, so give more. If you neglect an *habitual giving, a regular giving, a giving from principle and upon scriptural ground,* and leave it only to feeling and impulse, or particular arousing circumstances, you will certainly be a loser.

A merchant in the United States said in answer to inquiries relative to his mode of giving, "In consecrating my life anew to God, aware of the ensnaring influence of riches and the necessity of deciding on a plan of charity, before wealth should bias my judgment, I adopted the following system:

"I decided to balance my accounts as nearly as I could every month, reserving such portion of profits as might appear adequate to cover probable losses, and to lay aside, by entry on a benevolent account, one tenth of the remaining profits, great or small, as a fund for benevolent expenditure, supporting myself and family on the remaining nine tenths. I further determined that if at any time my net profits, that is profits from which clerk-hire and store expenses had been deducted, should exceed five hundred dollars in a month, I would give 12 per cent.; if over seven hundred dollars, 15 per cent.; if over nine hundred dollars, 17 per cent.; if over thirteen hundred dollars, 22 per cent.—thus increasing the proportion of the whole as God should prosper me, until at fifteen hundred dollars I should give 25 per cent, or 375 dollars a month. As capital was of the utmost importance to my success in business, I decided not to increase the foregoing scale until I had acquired a certain capital, after which I would give one quarter of all net profits, great or small, and, on the acquisition of another certain amount of capital, I decided to give half, and, on acquiring what I determined would be a full sufficiency of capital, then to give the whole of my net profits.

"It is now several years since I adopted this plan, and under it I have acquired a handsome capital, and have been prospered beyond my most sanguine expectations. Although constantly giving, I have never yet touched the bottom of my fund, and have repeatedly been surprised to find what large drafts it would bear. True, during some months, I have encountered a salutary trial of faith, when this rule has led me to lay by the tenth while the remainder proved inadequate to my support; but the tide has soon turned, and with gratitude I have recognized a heavenly hand more than making good all past deficiencies."

The following deeply interesting particulars are recorded in the memoir of Mr. Cobb, a Boston merchant. At the age of twenty-three, Mr. Cobb drew up and subscribed the following remarkable document:

SCRIPTURE TESTIMONY
Disciples must keep their word Matthew 5:37

> "By the grace of God I will never be worth more than 50,000 dollars,
>
> "By the grace of God I will give one fourth of the net profits of my business to charitable and religious uses.
>
> "If I am ever worth 20,000 dollars I will give one half of my net profits; and if ever I am worth 30,000 dollars, I will give three fourths; and the whole after 50,000 dollars. So help me God, or give to a more faithful steward, and set me aside."

"To this covenant," says his memoir "he adhered with conscientious fidelity. He distributed the profits of his business with an increasing ratio, from year to year, till he reached the point which he had fixed as a limit to his property, and then gave to the cause of God all the money which he earned. At one time, finding that his property had increased beyond 50,000 dollars, he at once devoted the surplus 7,500 dollars.

"On his death-bed he said, 'by the grace of God—*nothing else*—by the grace of God I have been enabled, under the influence of these resolutions to give away more than 40,000 dollars.' How good the Lord has been to me!"

Mr. Cobb was also an active, humble, and devoted Christian, seeking the prosperity of feeble churches; labouring to promote the benevolent institutions of the day; punctual in his attendance at prayer meetings, and anxious to aid the inquiring sinner; watchful for the eternal interests of those under his charge; mild and amiable in his deportment; and, in the general tenor of his life and character, an example of consistent piety.

His last sickness and death were peaceful, yea triumphant. "It is a glorious thing," said he, "to die. I have been active and busy in the world—I have enjoyed as much as any one—God has prospered me—I have everything to bind me here—I am happy in my family—I have property enough—but how small and mean does this world appear on a sick-bed! Nothing can equal my enjoyment in the near view

SCRIPTURE TESTIMONY
Jesus is worth more than worldly gain Philippians 3:7-10

of heaven. *My hope in Christ* is worth infinitely more than all other things. The blood of Christ—the blood of Christ—none but Christ! Oh! how thankful I feel that God has provided a way that I, sinful as I am, may look forward with joy to another world, through His dear Son."

GOD

Approval Of God

In the whole work we desire to stand with God, and not to depend upon the favourable or unfavourable judgment of the multitude.

Chastisements Of God

Our Heavenly Father never takes any earthly thing from His children except He means to give them something better instead.

The Lord, in His very love and faithfulness, will not, and cannot, let us go on in backsliding, but He will visit us with stripes, to bring us back to Himself!

The Lord never lays more on us, in the way of chastisement, than our state of heart makes needful; so that whilst He smites with the one hand, He supports with the other.

If, as believers in the Lord Jesus, we see that our Heavenly Father, on account of wrong steps, or a wrong state of heart, is dealing with us in the way of discipline or correction, we have to be grateful for it; for He is acting thus towards us according to that selfsame love, which led Him not to spare His only begotten Son, but to deliver Him up for us; and our gratitude to Him is to be expressed in words, and even by deeds. We have to guard against *practically* despising the chastening of the Lord, though we may not do so in word, and against *fainting* under chastisement: since all is intended for blessing to us.

Faithfulness Of God

Perhaps you have said in your heart: "How would it be, suppose the funds of the orphans were reduced to nothing, and those who are engaged in the work had nothing of their own to give, and a meal-time were to come, and you had no food for the children." Thus indeed it may be, for our hearts are desperately wicked. If ever we should be so left to ourselves, as that either we depend no more upon the living God, or that "we regard iniquity in our hearts," then such a state of things, we have reason to believe, would occur. But so long as we shall be enabled to trust in the living God, and so long as, though falling short in every way of what we might be, and ought to be, we are at least kept from living in sin, such a state of things cannot occur.

The Lord, to show His continued care over us, raises up new helpers. They that trust in the Lord shall never be confounded! Some who helped for a while may fall asleep in Jesus; others may grow cold in the service of the Lord; others may be as desirous as ever to help, but have no longer the means; others may have both a willing heart to help, and have also the means, but may see it the Lord's will to lay them out in another way;—and thus, from one cause or another, were we to lean upon man, we should surely be confounded; but, in leaning upon the living God alone, we are BEYOND *disappointment, and* BEYOND *being forsaken because of death,* or *want of means,* or *want of love,* or *because of the claims of other work.* How precious to have learned in any measure to stand with God alone in the world, and yet to be happy, and to know that surely no good thing shall be withheld from us whilst we walk uprightly!

Partnership With God

A brother, who is in about the same state in which he was eight years ago, has very little enjoyment, and makes no progress in the things of God. The reason is that, against his conscience, he remains in a calling, which is opposed to the profession of a believer. We are exhorted in Scripture to abide in our calling; but only if we can abide in it *"with God."* (1 Corinthians 7:24)

Power Of God

There is a worldly proverb, dear Christian reader, with which we are all familiar, it is this, "Where there is a will there is a way." If this is the proverb of those who know not God, how much more should believers in the Lord Jesus, who have power with God, say: "Where there is a will there is a way."

Trust In God

Only let it be trust *in God,* not in *man,* not in *circumstances,* not *in any of your own exertions,* but real trust in God, and you will be helped in your various necessities.... Not in circumstances, not in natural prospects, not in former donors, *but solely in God.* This is just that which brings the blessing. If we *say* we trust in Him, but in reality do not, then God, taking us at our word, lets us see that we do not really confide in Him; and hence failure arises. On the other hand, if our trust in the Lord is real, help will surely come, "According unto thy faith be it unto thee."

It is a source of deep sorrow to me, that, notwithstanding my having so many times before referred to this point, thereby to encourage believers in the Lord Jesus, to roll all their cares upon God, and to trust in Him at all times, it is yet, by so many, put down to mere natural causes, that I am helped; as if the Living God were no more the Living God, and as if in former ages answers to prayers might have been expected, but that in the nineteenth century they must not be looked for.

Will Of God

How important it is to ascertain the will of God, before we undertake anything, because we are then not only blessed in our own souls, but also the work of our hands will prosper.

Just in as many points as we are acting according to the mind of God, in so many are we blessed and made a blessing. Our manner of living is according to the mind of the Lord, for He delights in seeing His children thus come to Him (Matthew 6); and therefore, though I am weak and erring in many points, yet He blesses me in this particular.

First of all, to see well to it, that the work in which he desires to be engaged is *God's work;* secondly, that *he* is the person to be engaged in this work; thirdly, that *God's time* is come, when he should do this work; and then to be assured, that, if he seeks God's help in His own appointed way, He will not fail him. We have ever found it thus, and expect to find it thus, on the ground of the promises of God, to the end of our course.

1. Be slow to take new steps in the Lord's service, or in your business, or in your families. Weigh everything well; weigh all in the light of the Holy Scriptures, and in the fear of God. 2. Seek to have no will of your own, in order to ascertain the mind of God, regarding any steps you propose to take, so that you can honestly say, you are willing to do the will of God, if He will only please to instruct you. 3. But when you have found out what the will of God is, seek for His help, and seek it earnestly, perseveringly, patiently, believingly, and expectingly: and you will surely, in His own time and way, obtain it.

We have not to rush forward in self-will and say, I will do the work, and I will trust the Lord for means, this cannot be real trust, it is the counterfeit of faith, it is presumption; and though God, in great pity and mercy, may even help us finally out of debt; yet does this, on no account, prove that we were right in going forward before His time was come. We ought, rather, under such circumstances to say to ourselves: Am I indeed doing the *work of God?* And if so, *I* may not be the person to do it; or if I am the person, *His time* may not yet be come for me to go forward; it may be His good pleasure to exercise my faith and patience. I ought, therefore, quietly to wait His time; for when it is come, God will help. Acting on this principle brings blessing.

To ascertain the Lord's will we ought to use scriptural means. Prayer, the word of God, and His Spirit should be united together. We should go to the Lord repeatedly in prayer, and ask Him to teach us by His Spirit through His word. I say by His Spirit through His word. For if we should think that His Spirit led us to do so and so, because certain facts are so and so, and yet His word is opposed to the step which we are going to take, we should be deceiving ourselves.... No situation, no business will be given to me *by God,* in which I have not time enough to care about my soul. Therefore, however outward circumstances may appear, it can only be considered as permitted of God, to prove the genuineness of my love, faith, and obedience, but by no means as the leading of His providence to induce me to act contrary to His revealed will.

MARRIAGE

To enter upon the marriage union is one of the most deeply important events of life. It cannot be too prayerfully treated. Our happiness, our usefulness, our living for God or for ourselves after wards, are often most intimately connected with our choice. Therefore, in the most prayerful manner, this choice should be made. Neither beauty, nor age, nor money, nor mental powers, should be that which prompts the decision; but 1st, Much waiting upon God for guidance should be used; 2nd, A hearty purpose to be willing to be guided by Him should be aimed after; 3rd, True godliness without a shadow of doubt, should be the first and absolutely needful qualification, to a Christian, with regard to a companion for life. In addition to this, however, it ought to be, at the same time, calmly and patiently weighed, whether, in other respects, there is a suitableness. For instance, for an educated man to choose an entirely uneducated woman, is unwise; for however much on his part love might be willing to cover the defect, it will work very unhappily with regard to the children.

PRAYER

Answers To Prayer

SCRIPTURE TESTIMONY
The believer is to be persistent in prayer Luke 11:5-10

I myself have for twenty-nine years been waiting for an answer to prayer concerning a certain spiritual blessing. Day by day have I been enabled to continue in prayer for this blessing. At home and abroad, in this country and in foreign lands, in health and in sickness, however much occupied, I have been enabled, day by day, by God's help, to bring this matter before Him; and still I have not the full answer yet. Nevertheless, I look for it. I expect it confidently. The very fact that day after day, and year after year, for twenty-nine years, the Lord has enabled me to continue, patiently, believingly, to wait on Him for the blessing, still further encourages me to wait on; and so fully am I assured that

God hears me about this matter, that I have often been enabled to praise Him beforehand for the full answer, which I shall ultimately receive to my prayers on this subject. Thus, you see, dear reader, that while I have hundreds, yea, thousands of answers, year by year, I have also, like yourself and other believers, the trial of faith concerning certain matters.

Anxiety Avoided By Prayer

Though all believers in the Lord Jesus are not called upon to establish orphan houses, schools for poor children, etc., and trust in God for means; yet all believers, according to the will of God concerning them in Christ Jesus, may cast, and ought to cast, all their care upon Him who careth for them, and need not be anxiously concerned about anything, as is plainly to be seen from 1 Peter 5:7; Philippians 4:6; Matthew 6:25-34.

SCRIPTURE TESTIMONY
Don't be anxious, instead make requests known to God Philippians 4:6

My Lord is not limited; He can again supply; He knows that this present case has been sent to me; and thus, this way of living, so far from *leading to anxiety*, as it regards possible future want, is rather the means of *keeping from it*.... This way of living has often been the means of reviving the work of grace in my heart, when I have been getting cold; and it also has been the means of bringing me back again to the Lord, after I have been backsliding. For it will not do,—it is not possible, to live in sin, and at the same time, by communion with God, to draw down from heaven everything one needs for the life that now is.... Answer to prayer, obtained in this way, has been the means of quickening my soul, and filling me with much joy.

I met at a brother's house with several believers, when a sister said that she had often thought about the care and burden I must have on my mind, as it regards obtaining the necessary supplies for so many persons. As this may not be a solitary instance, I would state that, by the grace of God, this is no cause of anxiety to me. The children I have years ago cast upon the Lord. The whole work is His, and it becomes me to be *without carefulness*. In whatever points I am lacking, in this point I am able, by the grace of God, to roll the burden upon my heavenly Father. Though now (July 1845) for about seven years our funds have been so exhausted, that it has been comparatively a *rare* case that there have been means in hand to meet the necessities of the orphans for *three days* together; yet have I been only once tried in spirit, and that was on Sept. 18, 1838, when for the first time the Lord seemed not to regard our prayer. But when He did send help at that time, and I saw that it was only for the trial of our faith, and not because He had forsaken the work that we were brought so low, my soul was so strengthened and encouraged, that I have not only not been allowed to distrust the Lord since that time, but I have not even been cast down when in the deepest poverty. Nevertheless, in this respect also am I now, as much as ever, dependent on the Lord; and I earnestly beseech for myself and my fellow-labourers the prayers of all those, to whom the glory of God is dear. How great would be the dishonour to the name of God, if we, who have so publicly made our boast in Him, should so fall as to act in these very points as the world does! Help us, then, brethren, with your prayers, that we may trust in God to the end. We can expect nothing but that our faith will yet be tried, and it may be more than ever; and we shall fall, if the Lord does not uphold us.

Borrowing And Praying

As regards borrowing money, I have considered that there is no ground to go away from the door of the Lord to that of a believer, so long as He is willing to supply our need.

Communion With God In Prayer

How truly precious it is that every one who rests alone upon the Lord Jesus for salvation, has in the living God a father, to whom he may fully unbosom himself concerning the most minute affairs of his life, and concerning everything that lies upon his heart! Dear reader, do you know the living God? Is He, in Jesus, your Father? Be assured that Christianity is something more than forms and creeds and ceremonies: there is life, and power, and reality, in our holy faith. If you never yet have known this, then come and taste for yourself. I beseech you affectionately to meditate and pray over the following verses: John 3:16; Romans 10:9, 10; Acts 10:43; 1 John 5:1.

Conditions Of Prayer

Go for yourself, with all your temporal and spiritual wants, to the Lord. Bring also the necessities of your friends and relatives to the Lord. Only make the trial, and you will perceive how able and willing He is to help you. Should you, however, not at once obtain answers to your prayers, be not discouraged; but continue patiently, believingly, perseveringly to wait upon God: and as assuredly as that which you ask would be for your real good, and therefore for the honour of the Lord; and as assuredly as you ask it solely on the ground of the worthiness of our Lord Jesus, so assuredly you will at last obtain the blessing. I myself have had to wait upon God concerning certain matters for years, before I obtained answers to my prayers; but at last they came. At this very time, I have still to renew my requests daily before God, respecting a certain blessing for which I have besought

Him for eleven years and a half, and which I have as yet obtained only in part, but concerning which I have no doubt that the full blessing will be granted in the end.... The great point is that we ask only for that which it would be for the glory of God to give to us; for that, and that alone, can be for our real good. But it is not enough that the thing for which we ask God be for His honour and glory, but we must secondly ask it in the name of the Lord Jesus, viz., expect it only on the ground of His merits and worthiness. Thirdly, we should believe that God is able and willing to give us what we ask Him for. Fourthly, we should continue in prayer till the blessing is granted; without fixing to God a time when, or the circumstances under which, He should give the answer. Patience should be in exercise, in connection with our prayer. Fifthly, we should, at the same time, look out for and expect an answer till it comes. If we pray in this way, we shall not only have answers, thousands of answers to our prayers; but our own souls will be greatly refreshed and invigorated in connection with these answers.

If the obtaining of your requests were not for your real good, or were not tending to the honour of God, you might pray for a long time, without obtaining what you desire. The glory of God should be always before the children of God, in what they desire at His hands; and their own spiritual profit, being so intimately connected with the honour of God, should never be lost sight of, in their petitions. But now, suppose we are believers in the Lord Jesus, and make our requests unto God, depending alone on the Lord Jesus as the ground of having them granted; suppose, also, that, so far as we are able honestly and uprightly to judge, the obtaining of our requests would be for our real spiritual good and for the honour of God; we yet need, lastly, to *continue* in prayer, until the blessing is granted unto us. It is not enough to begin to pray, nor to pray aright; nor is it enough to continue *for a time* to pray; but we must patiently, believingly continue in prayer, until we obtain an answer; and further, we have not only to *continue* in prayer unto the end, but we have also *to believe* that God does hear us, and will answer our prayers. Most frequently we fail in not continuing in prayer until the blessing is obtained and *in not expecting* the blessing.

Faith, Prayer, And The Word Of God

Prayer and faith, the universal remedies against every want and every difficulty; and the nourishment of prayer and faith, God's holy word, helped me over all the difficulties.—I never remember, in all my Christian course, a period now (in March 1895) of sixty-nine years and four months, that I ever SINCERELY and PATIENTLY sought to know the will of God by *the teaching of the Holy Ghost,* through the instrumentality of the *word of God,* but I have been ALWAYS directed rightly. But if *honesty of heart* and *uprightness before God* were lacking, or if I did not *patiently* wait upon God for instruction, or if I preferred *the counsel of my fellow men* to the declarations of *the word of the living God,* I made great mistakes.

Secret Prayer

Let none expect to have the mastery over his inward corruption in any degree, without going in his weakness again and again to the Lord for strength. Nor will prayer with others, or conversing with the brethren, make up for secret prayer.

Snares Of Satan As To Prayer

It is a common temptation of Satan to make us give up the reading of the Word and prayer when our enjoyment is gone; as if it were of no use to read the Scriptures when we do not enjoy them, and as if it were of no use to pray when we have no spirit of prayer; whilst the truth is, in order to enjoy the Word, we ought to continue to read it, and the way to obtain a spirit of prayer is to continue praying; for the less we read the word of God, the less we desire to read it, and the less we pray, the less we desire to pray.

Work And Prayer

Often the work of the Lord itself may be a temptation to keep us from that communion with Him which is so essential to the benefit of our own souls.... Let none think that public prayer will make up for closet communion.

Here is the great secret of success. Work with all your might; but trust not in the least in your work. Pray with all your might for the blessing of God; but work, at the same time, with all diligence, with all patience, with all perseverance. Pray then, and work. Work and pray. And still again pray, and then work. And so on all the days of your life. The result will surely be, abundant blessing. Whether you *see* much fruit or little fruit, such kind of service will be blessed.... Speak also for the Lord, as if everything depended on your exertions; yet trust not the least in your exertions, but in the Lord, who alone can cause your efforts to be made effectual, to the benefit of your fellow men or fellow believers. Remember, also, that God delights to bestow blessing, but, generally, as the result of earnest, believing prayer.

PREACHING

It came immediately to my mind that such sort of preaching might do for illiterate country people, but that it would never do before a well-educated assembly in town. I thought, the truth ought to be preached at all hazards, but it ought to be given in a different form, suited to the hearers. Thus I remained unsettled in my mind as it regards the mode of preaching; and it is not surprising that I did not then see the truth concerning this matter, for I did not understand the work of the Spirit, and therefore saw not the powerlessness of human eloquence. Further, I did not keep in mind that if the most illiterate persons in the congregation can comprehend the discourse, the most educated will understand it too; but that the reverse does not hold true.

RESTITUTION

Restitution is the revealed will of God. If it is omitted, while we have it in our power to make it, guilt remains on the conscience, and spiritual progress is hindered. Even though it should be connected with difficulty, self-denial, and great loss, it is to be attended to. Should the persons who have been defrauded be dead, their heirs are to be found out, if this can be done, and restitution is to be made to them. But there may be cases when this cannot be done, and then *only* the money should be given to the Lord for His work or His poor. One word more. Sometimes the guilty person may not have grace enough, if the rightful owners are living, to make known to them the sin; under such circumstances, though not the best and most scriptural way, rather than have guilt remaining on the conscience, it is better to make restitution anonymously than not at all. About fifty years ago, I knew a man under concern about his soul, who had defrauded his master of two sacks of flour, and who was urged by me to confess this sin to his late employer, and to make restitution. He would not do it, however, and the result was that for twenty years he never obtained real peace of soul till the thing was done.

REWARDS

Christians do not practically remember that while we are saved by grace, altogether by grace, so that in the matter of salvation works are altogether excluded; yet that so far as the rewards of grace are concerned, in the world to come, there is an intimate connection between the life of the Christian here and the enjoyment and the glory in the day of Christ's appearing.

SIN AND SALVATION

Rumblings last our whole life. Jesus came not to save *painted* but *real* sinners; but He *has* saved us, and will surely make it manifest.

SPIRIT OF GOD

At Stuttgart, the dear brethren had been entirely uninstructed about the truths relating to the power and presence of the Holy Ghost in the church of God, and to our ministering one to another as fellow members in the body of Christ; and I had known enough of painful consequences when brethren began to meet professedly in dependence upon the Holy Spirit without knowing what was meant by it, and thus meetings had become opportunities *for unprofitable talking rather than for godly edifying*.... All these matters ought to be left to the ordering of the Holy Ghost, and that if it had been truly good for them, the Lord would have not only led me to speak *at that time,* but also on *the very subject* on which they desired that I should speak to them.

TRUTH—PROPORTION OF FAITH

Whatever parts of truth are made too much of, though they were even the most precious truths connected with our being risen in Christ, or our heavenly calling, or prophecy, sooner or later those who lay an *undue* stress upon *these parts* of truth, and thus make them too prominent, will be losers in their own souls, and, if they be teachers, they will injure those whom they teach.

UNIVERSALISM

In reference to universal salvation, I found that they had been led into this error because (1) They did not see the difference between the earthly calling of the Jews, and the heavenly calling of the believers in the Lord Jesus in the present dispensation, and therefore they said that, because the words "everlasting," etc., are applied to "the possession of the land of Canaan" and the "priesthood of Aaron," therefore, the punishment of the wicked cannot be without end, seeing that the possession of Canaan and the priesthood of Aaron are not without end. My endeavour, therefore, was to show the brethren the difference between the *earthly* calling of Israel and our *heavenly* one, and to prove from Scripture that, whenever the word "everlasting" is used with reference to things purely not of the earth, but beyond time, it denotes a period without end. (2) They had laid exceeding great stress upon a few passages where, in Luther's translation of the German Bible, the word hell occurs, and where it ought to have been translated either "hades" in some passages, or "grave" in others, and where they saw a *deliverance out of hell,* and a *being brought up out of hell,* instead of *"out of the grave."*

WORD OF GOD

The word of God is our only standard, and the Holy Spirit our only teacher.

Besides the Holy Scriptures, which should be always THE book, THE CHIEF book to us, not merely in theory, but also in practice, such like books seem to me the most useful for the growth of the inner man. Yet one has to be cautious in the choice, and to guard against reading too much.

WORK FOR GOD

When He orders something to be done for the glory of His name, He is both able and willing to find the needed individuals for the work and the means required. Thus, when the Tabernacle in the Wilderness was to be erected, He not only fitted men for the work, but He also touched the hearts of the Israelites to bring the necessary materials and gold, silver, and precious stones; and all these things were not only brought, but in such abundance that a proclamation had to be made in the camp, that no more articles should be brought, because there were more than enough. And again, when God for the praise of His name would have the Temple to be built by Solomon, He provided such an amount of gold, silver, precious stones, brass, iron, etc., for it, that all the palaces or temples which have been built since have been most insignificant in comparison.

SCRIPTURE TESTIMONY INDEX

The obvious need for a befitting biography on George Müller after his passing became a subject of prayer for his son-in-law and successor, James Wright. His prayer was answered when Arthur T. Pierson reached out to inform him that he had been led to write the memoir.

The wealthy and cultured Hermann Ball chose to abandon his worldly advantages and pursue missionary work in Poland amongst the Jews. Prior to this, George Müller had begun to drift away from God's calling, pursuing a young woman instead. Mr. Ball's bold decision helped George Müller return to his true calling.

George Müller's resolve to follow God's leading against his father's career advice, and the fallout of that decision, taught young Müller the hard but important lesson of becoming independent of man by depending fully on God for his material needs.

Young George Müller was working as an itinerant evangelist when the congregation at Teignmouth asked him to be their minister. Some in the congregation supported him while others were wary of his religious zeal. The cautious ones won out and, while Müller was offered the position, it was without pay. George Müller was undaunted, trusting God to supply all his needs, which He did.

From the very beginning of their marriage, Mr. and Mrs. Müller purposed to only have treasures in heaven. They sold what little they had and gave it to the poor, then lived—for the rest of their lives—a life of complete dependence upon God for their every need.

Mrs. Muller gave birth to a stillborn baby and was herself seriously ill for six weeks. Not only did this crisis give Mr. Müller a deeper gratefulness for his wife, but it taught them both a powerful lesson in trust, as God provided for their every need. They realized that no situation is an unforeseen emergency to Him. They need not—indeed must not, if they are to live a life of trust—save "for a rainy day."

No matter how pressing the need at hand, and no matter how temptingly large a gift may be, George Müller never accepted donations that were not freely given under clear divine leading.

On a trip to Bristol, God helped George Müller to see that a worker for God must first be a worker with God. He learned that nothing, not even the work of God must take the place of meditation and personal communion with Him.

While congregations preferred Mr. Craik's teaching of the Word to George Müller's, he did not become envious, but remained humble and content. In time God honored this humility and exalted Mr. Müller, who would go on to have a much wider and deeper witness for Christ not only in Bristol, but around the world.

Upon seeing the greater effectiveness of Mr. Craik's teachings over his own, Mr. Müller—after much introspection—committed himself to prayer and to studying so he too could become as skilled a workman in God's vineyard; one who need not be ashamed but one who could rightly divide God's Word.

to speak in the German state church, with which he differed greatly, he took the opportunity "for truth's sake" and "for love's sake." He was ready to be made all things to all men that by all means he might save some.

Matthew 25:31-46

In the spring of 1855, four siblings sick with consumption were admitted into the orphanage, in faith, even though it was a risk. A few weeks on, these children who could have died became healthy again, to the glory of God.

Luke 18:7 · John 15:7 · Acts 12:5 · James 5:15

In answer to Mr. Müller's specific prayer, not only was the weather—which had been freezing cold and windy—suddenly warm and friendly for the children when emergency repairs were needed on the boiler of one of the orphan houses, but the workers working to fix the problem volunteered to work overnight.

John 14:13-14 · Matthew 18:19 · John 16:23-24

Three instances of marked deliverance in answer to prayer from drought, from disease, and from storm damage, show that George Müller and his staff could truly ask anything of the faithful God.

Acts 2:41 · Acts 4:4

A seventeen-year-old orphan girl, well-known for her hardness of heart, was converted on her sick bed. Her sudden and complete transformation was such a powerful witness to the other orphans, that it led to the most extensive spiritual awakening up to that time, with hundreds of children being converted.

1 Corinthians 15:54-57

Rather than giving in to hopeless despair upon the death of his beloved wife, George Müller used the opportunity to offer heartfelt thanksgiving to God for the life she lived and for her being delivered unto her heart's desire, from earthly pain into the everlasting presence of her Savior.

Acts 1:8 · Acts 6:7 · Colossians 1:23

George Müller committed the latter years of his life to travelling the world with the good news of Christ. From age seventy to eighty-seven, he traveled to forty-two countries covering thousands of miles and reaching an estimated three million people with the gospel of Jesus Christ.

Walking Together Press is a non-profit publishing company devoted to supporting grassroots libraries in Africa through global book sales and through providing free library editions.

To read our story, to see our catalog, and to learn more about how you can help us in our mission, visit our website at:

https://walkingtogether.press